We the People

The Citizen and the Constitution

Center for Civic Education

5146 Douglas Fir Road ■ Calabasas, CA 91302-1467 ■ (818) 591-9321
Fax (818) 591-9330 ■ wethepeople@civiced.org ■ http://www.civiced.org

Directed by the
Center for Civic Education
and
Funded by the
U.S. Department of Education by act of Congress
Established 1987 under the
Commission on the Bicentennial of the United States Constitution

Cover photograph courtesy of Harlee Little, Washington, D.C.

Copyright © **Center for Civic Education** 1995

Eighth Printing 2001

The development of this text was originally funded and cosponsored by the Commission on the Bicentennial of the United States Constitution.

ISBN 0-89818-177-1

Acknowledgments

General Editor
Duane E. Smith

Contributing Writers
Herbert M. Atherton
J. Jackson Barlow
Charles N. Quigley
Duane E. Smith

Editors
Michael J. Conroy
Theresa M. Richard

Photo Research
Lisa Hartjens/Imagefinders

Editorial Assistants
David W. Hargrove
Esther G. Libman

Staff Associates
Charles F. Bahmueller
Margaret S. Branson
Michael Fischer
Jack N. Hoar
Joseph S. Jackson
Richard P. Longaker

**Principal Writer
Teacher's Guide**
Kenneth Rodriguez

Research Assistant
Andrea Kochan

Production Director
Pat Mathwig

Art Director and Illustrator
Richard Stein

Desktop Publishing
Valerie Milianni

Unit Resource Papers and Reviews
Jack Coogan, Consultant

Michelle Dye, Honors Research Associate, Dept. of Political
Science, University of Colorado

Howard Gillman, Assistant Professor, Dept. of Political
Science, University of Southern California

Calvin Jillson, Professor, Dept. of Political Science,
University of Colorado

Donald Nieman, Professor, Dept. of History,
Clemson University

Thomas Pangle, Professor, Dept. of
Political Science, University of Toronto

Melvin Urofsky, Professor, Dept. of
History, Virginia Commonwealth University

Tinsley Yarbrough, Professor, Dept. of
Political Science, East Carolina University

Outline Preparation
Howard Gillman, Assistant Professor
Dept. of Political Science,
University of Southern California

The Center wishes to acknowledge the invaluable support given to the development of the We the People... program by the Commission on the Bicentennial of the United States Constitution (1985–92) and by its chairman, the late Warren E. Burger, Chief Justice of the United States.

The Center is also grateful for the many helpful comments and suggestions that have been received from the following persons who reviewed the original manuscript. The Center has attempted to be responsive to all the many valuable suggestions for improvement in the text. The final product, however, is the responsibility of the Center and does not necessarily reflect the views of those who have contributed their thoughts and ideas.

Field Review and Critique

William Baker, Governor's Task
Force on Citizenship Education, Indiana

Alvin Bell, Teacher,
Findlay High School,
Findlay, Ohio

R. Freeman Butts, William F. Russell
Professor Emeritus in the Foundation
of Education, Teachers College,
Columbia University,
New York

John Calimano, Teacher,
East Brunswick High School,
East Brunswick, New Jersey

Jim Creighton, Teacher,
Alden Central High School,
Alden, New York

Carter Hart, Jr., Consultant,
New Hampshire Department
of Education,
Concord, New Hampshire

Martha de la Houssaye, Teacher,
Academy of the Sacred Heart,
New Orleans, Louisiana

Pat Hussein, Teacher,
Fremont High School,
Los Angeles, California

Leon Letwin, Professor,
School of Law,
University of California
at Los Angeles

Contents

Preface

Each year thousands of people visit our nation's capital, Washington, D.C. They come as individuals, in families, and in school groups. Most are American citizens. Some are citizens of other countries. Among the most popular attractions for these visitors is a massive stone building located on Pennsylvania and Constitution Avenues, about halfway between the White House at one end of Pennsylvania Avenue and the U.S. Capitol at the other end. This building is the National Archives.

The main entrance to the National Archives is on Constitution Avenue. The visitor climbs a broad flight of stairs, flanked by two statues representing "Heritage" and "Guardianship." She passes through a tall colonnade, and then through the entrance itself, guarded by the largest pair of bronze doors in the world, 49 feet high and one foot thick. Continuing on through a foyer, the visitor reaches the most important room in the Archives: the rotunda. Except on the most crowded days, the peacefulness of this room contrasts with the harsh daylight and traffic noise of the street outside. It is a place that commands silence and respect.

Along the wall opposite the rotunda's entrance is a set of bronze, marble, and glass cases. The contents are preserved in inert helium gas. Each evening, after the Archives closes its doors to the public, the contents of those cases are lowered by a hydraulic lift into a vault below. Every morning the contents are raised once again for public view.

The objects of all this care and attention are three documents. They are old. The parchment has been stained and frayed by the ages. The ink has faded. But the scars of time cannot diminish their importance. These three documents are our nation's charters: the Declaration of Independence, the Constitution of the United States of America, and the Bill of Rights.

Many places and place-names in our land have a special meaning to Americans: Plymouth Rock...Valley Forge...Independence Hall...Gettysburg...the Black Hills...Selma...Cape Canaveral. But if there is one place especially significant to all Americans, perhaps it would be here, in this room, in this building. For enshrined in those cases in the National Archives are not only three documents, but also the essence of what America is all about, of what it means to be an American.

What defines us as a nation is to be found in those three documents in the National Archives. We are not defined by religion, race, ethnicity, language, or national origin. We are defined by common commitments to the ideals contained in those documents. We are held together by our shared beliefs in such values as liberty, equality, and justice.

Our history, then, has been an **adventure in ideas.** This textbook will introduce you to that great adventure. The individuals who founded this country believed in the importance and the power of ideas to change people's lives.

You will learn about where the ideas about liberty, equality, and justice come from and what they meant to the nation's Founders and to the Framers of its Constitution. You will learn about those basic principles of government intended to protect each individual's right to the enjoyment of those ideas. You will learn about what it means to be a citizen in a country committed to them.

The American historian Richard Hofstader observed that America was the only nation which began in perfection and aspired to progress. The ideas on which America was founded may have been perfect, but we as a people have ever fallen short of perfection in realizing them. Our history of a little more than 200 years has been the story of a nation attempting to realize more perfectly the ideals on which it was founded. In a sense, it has been a never-ending pursuit of those ideals. Each generation, in its own way, has sought to live up to the promise of the nation's founding, to realize for the future the perfection of the past. It will eventually be your quest, too, as the rising generation of American citizens. You, too, will strive, in the words of Langston Hughes, to "let America be America again/The land that never has been yet."

An Introduction to the Study of the Constitution

There are six units in this book. The units will examine the

- historical and philosophical foundations of our country's ideas about constitutional government,
- creation of the Constitution,
- organizing of the national government,
- development of the Constitution,
- meaning of the various rights guaranteed in the Bill of Rights,
- expansion of rights during the last two hundred years, and finally,
- roles of citizens in American democracy.

Each unit consists of 6 to 9 lessons (40 lessons in all). Each lesson focuses on a particular question related to the theme of the unit. In each lesson you will find a series of other questions, each followed by an explanation. Each lesson also contains a list of key words or phrases which are important to the subject of the lesson and which you should know when you complete the lesson.

Most lessons also have one or more "Critical Thinking Exercises." These exercises give you an opportunity to analyze and discuss a particular problem or issue related to the subject of the lesson. These exercises are not only intended to increase your understanding of the material, but also to develop those skills which will prove useful to you as citizens.

The lessons conclude with several questions which will allow you to test your understanding and knowledge of the material covered in the lesson.

By the time you finish this course of study, you will be almost as well-informed as any of your fellow citizens about your country's system of government (and more informed than most). The next part of this introduction will give you an opportunity to test your current understanding of this subject. Don't worry about what you don't know. Appreciating what you have yet to learn will help you make the most of your reading and discussion of the lessons.

For the five Critical Thinking Exercises that follow, your class should be divided into groups. Each group should discuss the questions in one exercise.

A. What do you know about the Declaration of Independence?

The Declaration of Independence, drafted by Thomas Jefferson and adopted by the Continental Congress in July 1776, is our country's founding document. The words and ideas contained in that document will be referred to frequently throughout this text.

Critical Thinking Exercise A.
ANALYZING THE DECLARATION OF INDEPENDENCE

Let us see how much you already know about the meaning of this document. The Declaration of Independence appears in the Reference Section at the back of the book. Read very carefully the first two paragraphs, then try to answer the following questions:

1. What is the main purpose of the document? For whom is it written and what is it trying to explain?

2. What sort of action is the Declaration attempting to justify? Why do you think the Declaration regards this action as a very serious and unusual one?

3. What does the Declaration suggest is the relationship between a government and the people it governs? On what conditions is all legitimate government based? What justifies the ending of that relationship?

4. According to the Declaration, what is the primary purpose of government?

5. The Declaration speaks of "truths" which are "self-evident." What are these "truths"? Why are they called "truths"? What makes them "self-evident"?

B. What do you know about the Constitution?

If the Declaration of Independence is America's founding document, the Constitution is its charter of government. Drafted in 1787 and ratified by the American people the following year, it established the system of government with which the nation has lived for over 200 years.

Critical Thinking Exercise B.
ANALYZING THE PREAMBLE TO THE CONSTITUTION

The Constitution is also included in the Reference Section. Read carefully the Preamble to that document and then try to answer the following questions:

1. According to the Preamble, what is the purpose of the Constitution? Explain the meaning of each of its stated purposes.

2. By what authority is it "ordained and established"?

3. What is the connection between the stated goals of the Constitution and the purposes of government as outlined in the Declaration of Independence?

2. Review your answers to the other questions and make any changes or additions to them you think should be made.

C. What do you know about the Bill of Rights?

The first ten amendments to the Constitution are known as the Bill of Rights. This document was drafted and approved by Congress in 1789 and ratified by the people in 1791. The Bill of Rights contains some of the basic rights of individuals that the government is prohibited from violating. When the Framers wrote our Constitution and Bill of Rights, they were careful to include written protections of what they thought were many of the basic rights of a free people.

Test your current knowledge of the Bill of Rights by working through the following Critical Thinking Exercises.

Critical Thinking Exercise C.

Part I: EXAMINING YOUR KNOWLEDGE OF THE BILL OF RIGHTS

Develop your answers to the following questions based upon what you already know about the Bill of Rights. Do not refer to the Bill of Rights itself or any other reference material. Be prepared to discuss your answers with the class.

1. What is a "right"?

2. What rights are protected by the Bill of Rights?

3. From whom does the Bill of Rights protect you?

4. Does the Bill of Rights provide all the protections you need for your life, liberty, and property? Explain your answer.

Part II: REVISING YOUR ANSWERS TO PREVIOUS EXERCISE

The following exercise provides you an opportunity to reconsider some of your original ideas about the Bill of Rights. Read carefully the copy of the Bill of Rights in the Reference Section. Revise your answers in light of what you have learned. Follow these steps:

1. Find at least three rights in the Bill of Rights you did not list in response to Question 2. What appear to be the purposes of these rights?

D. What do you know about the rights and responsibilities of citizenship?

The primary purpose of this textbook is not to fill your head with a lot of facts about American history and government. Knowledge of these facts is important but only in so far as it deepens your understanding of the American constitutional system and its development.

Critical Thinking Exercise D.

ANALYZING THE PLEDGE OF ALLEGIANCE

For Americans, the most familiar expression of citizenship is taking the Pledge of Allegiance. The Pledge is something you have recited countless times and probably know by heart:

> *I pledge allegiance to the flag of the United States of America and to the republic for which it stands, one nation, under God, indivisible, with liberty and justice for all.*

The original draft of the Pledge of Allegiance was written by James B. Upham in 1888 and revised slightly four years later by Francis Bellamy, who included it in the 400th anniversary celebration of Columbus's first voyage to the New World. The phrase "under God" was added to the Pledge of Allegiance by act of Congress in 1954.

1. What is involved in pledging allegiance? What does allegiance mean? What does the taking of the pledge say about your relationship to government?

2. Why do we pledge allegiance to the American flag? Why not to the president of the United States, our members of Congress, or the justices of the Supreme Court?

3. Do we have the right to withhold our allegiance? What would be the consequences of doing that? If you were born here, when and how do you decide to be an American citizen? If you were not born an American citizen, how do you become one? How is a citizen different from someone else living in this country?

4. What is a "republic"? Does the Pledge define what that word means? How does a republic differ from a democracy?

E. Where can the most important protections of rights be found?

The existence of a written constitution or a bill of rights does not mean that citizens actually have the rights they contain. Nor does the existence of laws passed by our federal, state, and local governments guarantee that citizens will actually receive the rights the laws are supposed to protect.

Some people who have observed the common violations of individual rights in our own society and in others have argued that the most important protection of rights lies in the hearts and minds of ordinary citizens. The following exercise allows you to evaluate this argument.

Critical Thinking Exercise E.
ANALYZING JUDGE HAND'S STATEMENT

In 1941 a great American jurist, Learned Hand, delivered an address to the graduating class at Yale University; in 1944 he gave a speech in New York City, entitled "The Spirit of Liberty," restating his original remarks.

I often wonder whether we do not rest our hopes too much upon constitutions, upon laws and courts. These are false hopes; believe me, these are false hopes. Liberty lies in the hearts of men; when it dies there, no constitution, no law, no court can save it; no constitution, no law, no court can even do much to help it. While it lies there it needs no constitution, no law, no court to save it.

1. What are the major points in Judge Hand's argument?

2. What responsibilities of citizenship are implied by his position?

3. Do you agree with Judge Hand's position? Explain your answer.

4. In view of Judge Hand's statement about where liberty lies, do you think that constitutions and bills of rights are unnecessary? Explain your position.

Keep notes of your answers to the questions raised in the preceding exercises.

Compare them with what you learn in the lessons that follow.

Unit One: *What Are the Philosophical and Historical Foundations of the American Political System?*

Mayflower Compact (1620)	English Petition of Right (1628)	Massachusetts Body of Liberties (1641) The Law and Liberties (1648)					Glorious Revolution (1688)	English Bill of Rights (1689)	Declaration of Independence (1776) Virginia Declaration of Rights (1776) First Continental Congress (1774) The Stamp Act (1765)			
1610s	**1620s**	**1630s**	**1640s**	**1650s**	**1660s**	**1670s**	**1680s**	**1740s**	**1750s**	**1760s**	**1770s**
	Virginia House of Burgesses, colonies' first representative assembly (1619)	First colonial printing press (1639)			Bacon's Rebellion against the governor of Virginia (1676)		First newspaper published in the colonies (1690)	Britain defeats France in the Seven Years War (1763)			

Purpose of Unit

The people who led the American Revolution, which separated the American colonies from Great Britain, and who created the Constitution, which established the government we have today, were making a fresh beginning. They were also, however, the heirs to a philosophical and historical tradition as old as Western civilization itself.

The Founders were well-read. "I cannot live without books," Thomas Jefferson once told John Adams. Jefferson's library of 6,500 volumes now forms the core of the Library of Congress. Adams himself read 43 books when he was 81 years old! These Americans were familiar with the history, philosophy, and literature of the ancient world, as well as that of their own time. They also studied English history and law, from which their own constitutional traditions had derived. Religion had been an important part of the Founders' educational background. They knew the Bible and its teachings.

The knowledge these people possessed was not limited to what they read in books. In creating the new nation they drew upon their own experience. Many of the Constitution's Framers had fought in the Revolution and served in colonial government before America won its independence. They also had the experience of governing the newly independent states. They used both their knowledge and their experience when they wrote the Constitution. An understanding of what they had learned will help you understand why they wrote the Constitution as they did and why we have the kind of government we have today.

This unit provides an overview of some important philosophical ideas and historic events that influenced the writing of our Constitution and Bill of Rights. The first and second lessons in this unit introduce you to some basic ideas of the **natural rights philosophy** and theories of government. These ideas were of great importance in the development of our government. The remaining lessons in this unit examine in greater detail the historical background of these ideas. It is particularly important to understand the content of this unit because it provides a frame of reference or basis for understanding the other units. You will appreciate why our history as a people has been a great adventure in ideas and in trying to make these ideas a reality.

LESSON 1

What Would Life Be Like in a State of Nature?

Purpose of Lesson

This lesson introduces you to some basic ideas of the natural rights philosophy and theories of government that were of great importance in the development of our government.

These major ideas include the state of nature, the law of nature, natural rights, consent, and the social contract. You learn about these ideas as they were developed by the English philosopher John Locke (1632–1704).

When you finish this lesson, you should be able to describe how and why the natural rights philosophers used an imaginary state of nature to think about the basic problems of government. You should be able to explain some of the basic ideas of the natural rights philosophy.

Finally, you should be able to explain that the purpose of government based on the natural rights philosophy is to preserve our natural rights to life, liberty, and property.

This excerpt from the Declaration of Independence includes some of the most important philosophical ideas underlying our form of government. They are ideas that had been familiar to almost everyone in the American colonies long before the Revolutionary War.

These ideas had been preached in churches, written in pamphlets, and debated in public and private. They had been developed and refined by political philosophers such as the Englishman John Locke (1632–1704) and others. Locke was the most important influence on the thinking of the Founders at the time of the Revolution. Locke's political philosophy is often called the **natural rights philosophy**.

The natural rights philosophy is based on imagining what life would be like if there were no government. Locke and others called this imaginary situation a **state of nature**. By this, Locke did not necessarily mean people living in a wilderness. A state of nature is a condition in which there is no government. For example, even with the existence of the United Nations, international relations between countries today operate in a state of nature. There is no superior power that can act effectively as a government over these individual states.

Terms to Know

civil rights	natural rights
consent	political rights
human nature	social contract
law of nature	state of nature
legitimate	unalienable (inalienable)

What is the natural rights philosophy?

We hold these Truths to be self-evident, that all Men are created equal, that they are endowed by their Creator with certain unalienable Rights, that among these are Life, Liberty, and the Pursuit of Happiness—That to secure these Rights; Governments are instituted among Men, deriving their just Powers from the Consent of the Governed, that whenever any Form of Government becomes destructive of these Ends, it is the Right of the People to alter or to abolish it, and to institute new Government....
Declaration of Independence, 1776

Did the end of white rule in South Africa in 1993 result in a state of nature? Why?

Thinking about what life would be like if there were no government was very useful to philosophers such as Locke in answering questions like these:

- What is **human nature**? That is, what traits of personality and character, if any, do all human beings have in common? For example, are all people selfish or do they tend to care for the good of others?

- What should be the purpose of government?

- How do the people running a government get the right to govern?

- How should a government be organized?

- What kinds of government should be respected and supported?

- What kinds of government should be resisted and fought?

The natural rights philosophers' answers to these questions provided the foundation for many arguments the Founders made to explain and justify their decision to separate from Britain. They also used these ideas in writing state constitutions after the Revolutionary War and later in writing the Constitution of the United States and the Bill of Rights.

Critical Thinking Exercise
TAKING THE POSITION OF A POLITICAL PHILOSOPHER

To understand the natural rights philosophy, you should try to answer the questions it addresses. Some important questions are included in the following exercise. Your class should be divided into small discussion groups. The members of your group may not all agree on the answers. It is important to know that at various times in history, people have had very different views on these matters.

Imagine that all the students in your school were transported to a place with enough natural resources for you to live well, but where no one had lived before. When you arrive, you have no means of communicating with people in other parts of the world. With this imaginary situation in mind, answer the following questions. Discuss your answers, and then compare your answers with those of John Locke, in the next section.

1. Upon arrival would there be any government or laws to control how you lived, what rights or freedoms you exercised, or what property you had? Why?

2. Would anyone have the right to govern you? Would you have the right to govern anyone else? Why?

3. Would you have any rights? What would they be?

4. What might people who were stronger or smarter than others try to do? Why?

5. What might the weaker or less sophisticated people try to do? Why?

6. What might life be like for everyone?

John Locke (1632–1704)
In what ways did Locke's ideas influence the Founders?

How do your answers compare with those of John Locke?

Your answers may be similar to those developed by John Locke or they may differ. In this lesson we are focusing on understanding Locke's answers because they were widely shared by Americans living during the 1700s. They also played a very important role in the development of our government.

1. Locke believed that there were rules in a state of nature. He called these rules natural law or the **law of nature**. He said, "The state of nature has a law of nature to govern it which obliges every one.... No one ought to harm another in his life, health, liberty, or possessions...."

They were "the Laws of Nature and of Nature's God," as Thomas Jefferson called them in the Declaration of Independence. Jefferson believed they were laws made by a Supreme Being for the benefit of human beings.

According to Locke, how is personal property protected in a state of nature?

Locke believed that most people understood this law of nature through the use of their reason and followed it because their consciences obliged them to do so. Not all humans were reasonable or good, however. There might even be disagreement about what the "laws of nature" were. If there were no government, there would be no one with the right to interpret or enforce these laws.

According to Locke, there would be no government because a government cannot exist until it has been created. A **legitimate** government cannot exist until the people have given their **consent** to be ruled by it. Thomas Jefferson included this idea in the Declaration when he wrote that "Governments are instituted among men, deriving their just powers from the consent of the governed...."

2. No one would have the right to govern you, nor would you have the right to govern anyone else. According to Locke, the only way anyone gets the right to govern anyone else is if that person gives his or her consent. If the people to be governed have not consented to the creation of a government, there is no legitimate government.

3. Using his reason to determine what rights were provided for by the law of nature, Locke asked himself: "What are the things that all people always need and seek, no matter what they believe, no matter when or where they live?" His answer identified the following rights:

- **Life**. People want to survive and they want their lives to be as free as possible from threats to their security.

- **Liberty**. People want to be as free as possible from the domination of others, to be able to make their own decisions, and to live as they please.

- **Property**. People want the freedom to work and gain economic goods such as land, houses, tools, and money, which are necessary to survival.

These rights were called **natural rights** and you would have the right to defend them if other people threatened to take them away.

4. Locke believed that people are basically reasonable and sociable, but they are also self-interested. Since the only security people would have for the protection of their natural rights would be their own strength or cunning, people who were stronger or smarter would often try to take away the life, liberty, and property of the weak.

5. Weaker or less sophisticated people might try to protect themselves by joining together against the strong.

6. Since there would be no laws that everybody agreed upon, and no government to enforce them, everybody's rights would be very insecure.

Why did Locke believe it was necessary for people to create governments?

1. Give examples of problems that might arise when one individual's rights to life, liberty, and property conflict with those of other individuals. What considerations might be used to resolve these conflicts?

2. Should some rights be given more protection than other rights? Why? Give examples.

3. The natural rights philosophy claims that government is based on consent. How do we give our consent and how do we withdraw it?

4. Many people today believe that the rights to life, liberty, and property include the right to public education and health care. Would the founders have agreed? Do you agree? Why?

What is the significance of Locke's definition of the natural rights to life, liberty, and property?

References to "human rights," "political and economic rights," "student rights," "consumer rights," "parental rights," and other terms using the word appear in the news every day. "Rights" is a word you are already familiar with. We have become so accustomed to the word, we don't often think about what it means.

A **right** may be described as a claim to have or obtain something, or to act in a way that is justified on legal or moral grounds. For example, you might claim the right to practice your own religion and justify it by appealing to the First Amendment of the Constitution. This is not, of course, the only justification you could give.

In describing the concept of **natural rights**, philosophers like John Locke were making a bold, new departure from previous uses of the term rights. Before the time of Locke and the other natural rights philosophers, the concept of rights had been applied in a very limited and selective way. More often than not, rights were considered special privileges, enjoyed only by certain groups, classes, or nations of people. They were exclusive rights, not enjoyed by those outside the group.

The natural rights philosophers disagreed with this interpretation. They believed that people's opportunities should not be limited by the situation or group into which they were born. These philosophers regarded the individual, rather than the class or group, as the most important social unit. They saw society as a collection of individuals, all of whom shared the same right to pursue his or her own welfare.

Locke, for example, defined natural rights in terms of life, liberty, and property because he considered them to be the essence of humanity. They are what make us human beings and what define our purpose in life. They

are inclusive rights, belonging to every human being. These rights Locke also considered to be **unalienable**, the word that Jefferson used in the Declaration. This means they are so much a part of human nature that they cannot be taken away or given up. "The sacred rights of mankind," said another Founder, Alexander Hamilton, "are written, as with a sun beam in the whole volume of human nature, by the hand of the Divinity itself, and can never be erased or obscured by mortal power."

Governments and societies based on the natural rights philosophy guarantee specific rights to preserve our natural rights. Under the U.S. Constitution, for example, you possess **civil rights**, securing such things as freedom of conscience and privacy, and protecting you from unfair discrimination by government or others. You also possess certain **political rights**, like the right to vote or run for office, which give you control over your government. Such civil and political rights serve to protect natural rights to life, liberty, and property.

Why are political rights necessary to protect our natural rights?

What did Locke mean by the "social contract"?

In an ideal state of nature, the law of nature would prevail. No one would have the right to interfere with your life and your freedom to acquire and hold property. Locke, however, realized that because not all human beings were rational or good, there would always be people who would try to violate your rights. Since there would not be any government, you and others would have to defend your rights on your own. The result would be that in the state of nature, your rights and their enjoyment would be insecure. You would be in constant danger of losing them.

For Locke and the other natural rights philosophers, the great problem was to find a way to protect each person's natural rights so that all persons could enjoy them and live at peace with one another. Locke said that the best way to solve this problem in the state of nature is for each individual to agree with others to create and live under a government and give it the power to make and enforce laws. This kind of agreement is called the **social contract**.

As in all contracts, to get something, you must give up something. In the social contract everyone promises to give up the absolute right to do anything he or she has the right to do in a state of nature. In return, everyone receives the security that can be provided by a government. Each person consents to obey the limits placed upon him or her by the laws created by the government. Everyone gains the security of knowing that his or her rights to life, liberty, and property are protected.

Government, then, is the better alternative to an imperfect state of nature where some people will not obey the laws of nature. Government's purpose is to protect those natural rights that the individual cannot effectively secure in a state of nature.

What do *you* think?

1. If the purpose of government is to provide security for the rights to life, liberty, and property, under what circumstances, if any, should government be able to limit these rights?

2. What criteria should be used to determine when, if ever, government should be able to limit an individual's liberty to

   - believe as he or she wishes
   - practice his or her beliefs
   - use his or her property
   - associate with whomever he or she wishes

3. Imagine yourself living in a community where all order and authority have broken down. Violent lawlessness is widespread. Do you think **any** government is better than none? Explain your answer.

4. It has been said that since people are not equal in their intelligence and character, it is unjust for everyone to have the same rights. Do you agree? Be prepared to defend your answer.

Reviewing and Using the Lesson

1. Explain what is meant by each of the following ideas from the Declaration of Independence:

   - all men are created equal
   - people have certain rights that are unalienable
   - unalienable rights include rights to life, liberty, and the pursuit of happiness
   - governments are created to secure these rights
   - governments derive their just powers from the consent of the governed
   - people have the right to alter or abolish their government if it becomes destructive of the purposes for which it was created

2. What is meant by "the law of nature" or "natural law"? How did Locke try to establish or figure out what limitations it imposed on human conduct?

3. How did Locke use the idea of a "state of nature" to try to establish or figure out what the purpose of government should be?

4. What was Locke's view of human nature? How did it influence his ideas about what type of government is best?

5. What is meant by the term "social contract"? How is it connected to the idea that government derives its authority from the consent of the governed?

6. Do research to find out about the Mayflower Compact. Explain what it was, why it was created, and how it shows the connection between "social contracts" and the idea that government should be based on consent.

LESSON 2

How Does Government Secure Natural Rights?

Purpose of Lesson

This lesson introduces you to some basic ideas the Framers used in creating the kind of government they thought would best protect the natural rights of each individual and promote the good of all.

When you finish this lesson you should understand the difference between limited and unlimited government, the difference between written and unwritten constitutions, and how Americans have used the term constitutional government. You should be able to explain why a government with a constitution is not necessarily a constitutional government, and be able to identify alternative models of government that the Founders had to choose from.

Terms to Know

autocracy
canton
checks and balances
city-state
common good
constitution
constitutional government
delegate
delegated powers
democracy
dictatorship

equal protection
higher law
limited government
private domain
republic
separation of powers
totalitarianism
tyranny
unwritten constitution
written constitution

Critical Thinking Exercise

EXAMINING GOVERNMENT PROTECTION OF THE BASIC RIGHTS OF THE PEOPLE

Suppose you are not satisfied with living in a state of nature. You and others agree to enter into a social contract and a government to protect your natural rights. You must decide what kind of government you want and then establish it. Locke, Jefferson, and others knew that this is not an easy task. Throughout history governments have deprived people of their rights more often than they have protected them. Your problem is to design and establish the kind of government that will do what you want it to do, that is, protect your natural rights. This also means providing **equal protection** for the rights of everyone.

You and everyone else in your imaginary state of nature have agreed to live under a government. There are questions you must answer in deciding what kind of government to create. Your teacher will divide the class into small groups to discuss your answers. Then compare your answers with those of John Locke and explain why you agree or disagree with Locke.

1. What in your opinion is the main purpose of government?

2. How should government get the authority or right to make laws telling people what they can and cannot do?

3. What should the people have the right to do if their government does not serve the purposes for which it was created? Why should they have this right?

How do your answers compare with those of John Locke?

1. Locke and other natural rights philosophers said that the purpose of government is to protect natural rights. Thomas Jefferson agreed and in the Declaration of Independence argued that the protection of rights is the main purpose of government.

2. Another of Locke's ideas that Jefferson stated in the Declaration of Independence is that government gets its right to govern from the consent of the people. Its powers are delegated to it by the governed.

People give their consent in several ways. People can give **explicit** consent by

- agreeing to the contract that establishes the society whose members then establish the government and choose its officers

- joining a society that already is established

People give **implicit** consent, also called tacit consent, by accepting the laws and services of the government and nation of their birth.

3. Locke believed that since the people give the power to the government, they have the right to take it away if the government is not serving the purposes for which it was established. They can then create a new government. Locke argued and the Founders agreed that if a government fails to protect the people's rights, the people have a **right of revolution**.

Under what circumstances would Locke agree that people have the right to take up arms against an established government?

Who is to judge if a government has failed? Locke and the Founders said that the people have the right to make that decision. This position is in the following words from the Declaration of Independence: "Whenever any Form of Government becomes destructive of these Ends, it is the Right of the People to alter or abolish it, and to institute new Government…"

Revolution, however, is an extreme way in which to deal with bad government. Government should be designed or organized to limit its powers in order to protect individual rights and thus reduce the need for such extreme measures.

How do Americans express consent to their government?

The Americans who ratified our Constitution in 1787 gave explicit consent to their new government. So did the many immigrants who came to America to seek a better life. Those who are born here have implied their consent by remaining in this country and living under its laws.

Every native-born American, as he or she grows up, has the choice of seeking the citizenship of another country. By remaining in this country, accepting its laws, and enjoying its benefits, you imply your consent to be governed by your federal, state, and local governments. You also affirm your consent every time you take the Pledge of Allegiance, participate in an election, or engage in other civic actions.

What is constitutional government?

Limited governments have established and respected restraints on their powers, restraints such as laws and free and periodic elections. The opposite is **unlimited government**, in which those who govern are free to use their power as they choose, unrestrained by laws or elections. Tyranny, autocracy, dictatorship, and totalitarianism are other words to describe unlimited government.

What form of government was best suited to prevent the abuse of power in the newly independent states of America? From their reading of both history and the natural rights philosophers, the Founders believed that any government that served its proper ends would have to be a limited or constitutional government.

In a **constitutional government**, the powers of the person or group controlling the government are limited by a set of laws and customs called a **constitution.**

What is a constitution?

A constitution is a set of customs, traditions, rules, and laws that sets forth the basic way a government is organized and operated. Most constitutions are in writing, some are partly written and partly unwritten, and some are not written at all.

Notice that according to this definition of the word, every nation has a constitution. Good governments and bad governments may have constitutions. Some of the worst governments have constitutions that include lists of the basic rights of their citizens. The former Soviet Union had one of the longest and most elaborate constitutions in history, but in reality its citizens enjoyed few of the rights guaranteed by it.

Are all governments with written constitutions, constitutional governments? Why?

If you study the constitution of a government, you will be able to answer the following questions about the relationship between the government and its citizens:

- What are the purposes of government?

- How is the government organized?

- How is the government supposed to go about doing its business?

- Who is considered to be a citizen?

- Are the citizens supposed to have any power or control over their government? If so, how is it to be exercised?

- What rights and responsibilities, if any, are the citizens supposed to have?

It is very important to understand that having a constitution does not mean that a nation has a constitutional government. If a constitution provides for the unlimited exercise of political power—by one, few, or even many—such a constitution would not be the basis of a constitutional government. If a constitution provides that the government's power is to be limited, but it does not include ways to enforce those limitations, it is not the basis of a constitutional government. In a constitutional government the constitution is a form of **higher** or **fundamental law** that must be obeyed by everyone, including those in power.

How did the Founders characterize higher law?

According to the Founders, a constitution or higher law should have the following characteristics:

- It sets forth the basic rights of citizens to life, liberty, and property.

- It establishes the responsibility of the government to protect those rights.

- It establishes the principle of a **private domain**— which means that there are areas of citizens' lives that are no business of the government and in which the government cannot interfere.

- It establishes limitations on how those in government may use their powers with regard to
  - citizens' rights and responsibilities
  - the distribution of resources
  - the control of conflict

How does the principle of private domain protect you from government interference?

- It can only be changed with the widespread consent of the citizens, and according to established and well-known procedures. This distinguishes the higher law from the ordinary law that governments regularly create and enforce.

What do *you* think?

1. One of the purposes of the limitations imposed by constitutional government is to check the power of the majority. How can this be justified in a political system that is supposed to be democratic?

2. What are the major advantages, in your judgment, of limited government? What are the most serious disadvantages?

3. Are there advantages to unlimited government? If so, what are they?

How does a constitutional government protect natural rights?

Constitutional government assures the rights of its citizens in two ways:

- It establishes limits on the power of the government to prevent it from violating natural rights.

- It states that the government should be organized and its power distributed in such a way as to increase the possibility that those limitations will be effective.

The first is a purely **legal protection** of a citizen's freedom. The next is an **organizational protection**, having to do with the way in which government operates.

How can constitutional governments be organized to prevent the abuse of power?

In constitutional governments powers are usually distributed and shared among several branches of government. This distribution and sharing of power makes it less likely that any one branch can abuse or misuse its powers. It is also less likely that any group will gain so much power that it can ignore the limitations placed on it by the constitution.

To prevent our government from abusing its powers, the Framers provided for distribution and sharing of powers among three branches of the national government. Each branch has primary responsibility for certain functions, but each branch also shares these functions and powers with the other branches. For example,

- The Congress may pass laws, but the president may veto them.
- The president nominates certain government officials, but the Senate must approve them.
- The Congress may pass laws, but the Supreme Court may declare them unconstitutional.

It is this system of distributed and shared powers that provides the basis for **checks and balances**. Although each branch of the government has its own special powers, many of these powers are "checked" because they are shared with the other groups.

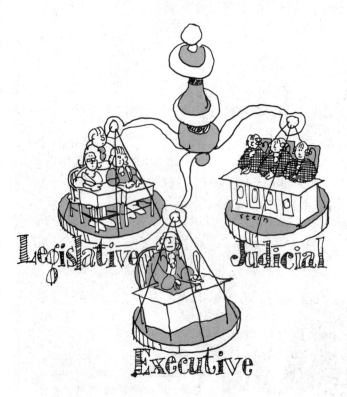

Does a system of checks and balances guarantee that power will not be abused?

The complicated ways in which constitutional governments are organized often mean that it takes them a long time to get things done. It may seem strange, but this "inefficiency" was seen by the Framers as an advantage. They thought that these difficulties would help to prevent the abuse of power and make it more likely that when a decision was finally made, it would be a good one.

Critical Thinking Exercise

EXAMINING WHY THE FOUNDERS FEARED THE ABUSE OF POWER BY GOVERNMENT

Given their knowledge of history and their experiences with the British government, it is not surprising that the Founders greatly feared the possible abuse of the powers of government. For example, read the following selections from some of their writings. Then discuss with the class your answers to the questions that follow.

> *Give all power to the many, they will oppress the few. Give all power to the few, they will oppress the many.*
>
> Alexander Hamilton, 1787

> *There are two passions which have a powerful influence on the affairs of men. These are ambition and avarice; the love of power and the love of money.*
>
> Benjamin Franklin, 1787

> *From the nature of man, we may be sure that those who have power in their hands...will always, when they can...increase it.*
>
> George Mason, 1787

1. Explain the view of human nature expressed in each of these quotations.

2. If you agreed with the views of human nature expressed in the quotations, what kind of safeguards to prevent the abuse of power would you include in your government?

3. Do you think the Founders' fear of government is as valid today as it was in the 1700s? Explain your answer.

What kinds of governments may be constitutional governments?

The Founders knew that constitutional government can take many forms. It is possible to have a constitutional government with one ruler, a group of rulers, or rule by the people as a whole, so long as those in power obey the limitations placed on them by the "higher law" of the constitution. Historically, constitutional governments have included monarchies, republics, democracies, and various combinations of these forms of government.

History has shown, however, that problems inevitably arise when a constitutional government is ruled by one person or a small group of people. If all power is given to a select few, it is difficult to ensure that they will obey the limitations placed on them by a constitution. The rulers in such nations would control the armed forces and law enforcement agencies. How could citizens force the rulers to obey their constitution?

Monarchy—rule by a king or queen—was by far the most common form of government in the eighteenth century. The Founders preferred a form of government more broadly representative of the interests of the whole nation.

What alternative models of government could the Founders choose from?

The most obvious alternative to monarchy was a **republic**, a model of government with which the Founders were familiar through their knowledge of ancient history. The Founders admired the republics of ancient Greece and Rome. They also had studied more recent examples of **republican governments**, such as the Italian **city-states** of the Renaissance and the **cantons** of Switzerland.

The Founders differed among themselves about exactly what a republican government was. In general it meant a form of government

- devoted to promoting the public good, the *res publicae*, which is Latin for "thing of the people"
- in which political authority was shared by all or most of the citizens rather than held by a hereditary monarch
- whose political authority was exercised through the community's chosen representatives in government

Today we view republican and democratic government as almost the same thing. The United States, we believe, is both a republic and a democracy. The Founders, however, drew a sharp distinction between the two forms of government.

Democracy had traditionally meant a form of government in which ultimate authority was based on the will of the majority.

How did the Founders' knowledge of ancient Rome shape their views about government?

This majority usually consisted of those classes in the community that had the greatest number of people—it came from the Greek *demos*, meaning people. These classes tended to be the poorer people.

In its purest form, democracy also meant a government in which members participated directly in their own governance instead of through representatives.

The Founders were familiar with democratic institutions. For generations, local government in many of the colonies tended to be democratic in nature. The New England "town meeting" is one example. Based on their reading of history and their own experience, however, the Founders were concerned about democracy as a model for state or national government. Their preference for the republican as opposed to the democratic model of government influenced the framing of the Constitution.

What do *you* think?

1. How would you organize a government so it would be fairly easy to remove and replace officials who were not doing a good job?

2. What might happen in a government where there was no agreed-on or peaceful means for removing officials? Give a recent example to support your answer.

3. How did the Founders describe the difference between republican and democratic forms of government? Why do you think the Framers of the Constitution favored the former rather than the latter?

Reviewing and Using the Lesson

1. How would you explain the difference between a limited government and an unlimited government? Do you think the difference is important? Why or why not?

2. In theory, the government of the United States gets its authority from the consent of the people. What evidence can you identify to show that people actually do consent to be governed by the United States government?

3. What is meant by the claim that the people have a "right of revolution"? What arguments can you make to support the claim that such a right does or does not exist?

4. What is a constitution? What is the difference between a constitution that establishes a constitutional government, and a constitution that does not?

5. Why did the Framers organize the government into separate branches with shared and divided powers? What are some examples of the ways in which governmental power is divided and shared? Why is this sometimes called a system of "checks and balances"?

6. Do research to find out about a country whose written constitution failed to protect the rights of the people. Why did the written constitution fail to establish a constitutional government in that country? What essential things were missing?

LESSON 3

What Did the Founders Learn about Republican Government from the Ancient World?

Purpose of Lesson

In this lesson you learn how the Founders were influenced by the ideas of classical republicanism: the importance of the Roman Republic and the moral ideal of civic virtue. You examine how these ideas shaped their thinking about what kind of government they wanted to create for the United States.

When you finish the lesson, you should understand not only the principles of classical republicanism but the difficulties the Founders encountered in attempting to apply those principles to the new American nation. You also should understand how classical republicanism differed from the natural rights philosophy in its account of human nature and individual rights. You should be able to explain how James Madison was able to adapt the ideas of classical republicanism, democracy, and civic virtue to American circumstances.

Terms to Know

civic virtue
classical republicanism
common good

established religion
factions
representative democracy

What ideas about government did the Founders find in classical republicanism?

Most of the public buildings and monuments in Washington, D.C., and state capitols across the nation are built in the "classical" style. This architectural tradition symbolizes our nation's indebtedness to the world of ancient Greece and Rome, especially to their ideas about government.

The Founders had studied the history of the classical periods of ancient Greece and Rome. The society that had the greatest influence on their ideas was that of the Roman Republic, which lasted for almost 500 years—509 B.C. to 27 B.C. Many philosophers and historians believed the Roman Republic had provided Roman citizens with the most liberty under government that the world had ever known. It also was believed widely that the Roman Republic promoted the **common**

good, that is, what was best for the entire society. The theory based on this form of society became known as **classical republicanism.**

How does the architectural style of some government buildings symbolize the influence of ancient Greece and Rome on the Founders?

Classical republicanism is a theory that the best kind of society is one that promotes the common good instead of the interests of only one class of citizens. In a classical republic, citizens and their government are supposed to work cooperatively to achieve the common good rather than their own personal or selfish interests. The Roman Republic was thought to be one of the best examples of this type of society. Americans in the eighteenth century shared the view that citizens should work to promote the common good. They also believed that the type of government and society most likely to promote the common good was only possible if the society and its citizens shared the following characteristics:

■ Civic virtue

■ Moral education

■ Small, uniform communities

Civic virtue. The classical republics demanded that their citizens have a high degree of civic virtue. A person with civic virtue was one who set aside personal interests to promote the common good. Today we might describe this as "public spiritedness."

President Jimmy Carter and wife Roslyn join
100 volunteers to construct low income housing.
Do all Americans have an obligation to practice civic virtue? Why?

Citizens were expected to participate fully in their government to promote the common good. They were not to be left free to devote themselves only to their personal interests. They were discouraged from spending much time doing such things as making money or caring for their families. They also were discouraged from traveling or reading and thinking about things that had nothing to do with their government. If citizens had the freedom to do such things, it was feared, they might stop being reliable and fully dedicated to the common good.

To make sure citizens participated in their government, the classical republics often drastically limited individual rights. There was little concern with protecting an individual's privacy, freedom of conscience or religion, or nonpolitical speech or expression.

Certain rights, however, were necessary for citizens to participate in governing themselves. These were political rights, such as the right to vote, to express ideas and opinions about government, and to serve in public office.

Moral education. People who believed in classical republicanism were convinced that civic virtue is not something that comes automatically to people. Citizens must be taught to be virtuous by moral education based on a civic religion consisting of gods, goddesses, and their rituals.

Classical republicans believed that young citizens must be raised in a manner that develops the right habits. They should learn to admire the people with civic virtue described in literature, poetry, and music. The Founders themselves admired such heroes of antiquity as the Roman patriot and orator Cato and the citizen soldier Cincinnatus. The Founders believed they were examples

of civic virtue whom Americans should emulate. His fellow Americans admired George Washington as a modern-day Cincinnatus because he sacrificed his private pursuits in order to lead the nation in war and peace. George Washington was often called "our Cincinnatus" because his fellow citizens believed he was an example of the civic virtue that all citizens should possess.

Is civic virtue as important in America today as it was in ancient Rome? Why? Why not?

According to classical republicans, children, as well as adults, should be encouraged—partly by the belief in a watchful god or gods—to practice virtues, such as generosity, courage, self-control, and fairness. They should learn the importance of taking part in political debate and military service. The whole community must closely supervise the upbringing of the next generation of citizens and be attentive to how individuals behave in their daily lives.

Small, uniform communities. Classical republicans believed that a republican government would only work in a small community. A small community is necessary if people are to know and care for each other and their common good. In addition, the people must be very much alike. A great degree of diversity should not be tolerated. They did not believe, for example, that people should be very different in their wealth, religious or moral beliefs, or ways of life.

Why did classical republicans believe that republican government could only work in small, uniform communities?

Classical republicans believed that if people differed greatly, they would divide into **factions** or interest groups, rather than work together for the common good. To prevent this, citizens should be encouraged, by education and example, to avoid the development of great differences in their ownership of property, religion, and way of life. To prevent diversity in religious beliefs and lifestyles, they believed the community should have one official, **established religion** and one set of family and moral standards to which all must conform.

Great inequalities of wealth led inevitably to corruption as well as to factions or interest groups. Individuals would be more concerned with their own interest rather than the interest of the community. Their fear of great economic inequality and the corrupting effect of luxury led the classical republicans to be wary of money-making and economic growth. Such economic growth, they thought, gave rise to the great economic inequality which was inconsistent with the goals of republicanism.

What do *you* think?

1. Identify someone living today who you think shows civic virtue. Explain the reason for your choice.

2. What did classical republicans think should be the goal of education? Do you agree? Why or why not?

3. What civic virtues are important for young people to have today and why?

4. What similarities and differences are there between your ideas about rights and those of the classical world?

Critical Thinking Exercise

UNDERSTANDING THE DIFFERENCES BETWEEN THE NATURAL RIGHTS PHILOSOPHY AND CLASSICAL REPUBLICANISM

You may work individually, with a study partner, or in small groups to develop responses to the following questions. Be prepared to share your answers with the class.

1. The classical republican idea of civic virtue conflicted with the Founders' belief in natural rights and their understanding of human nature as defined by John Locke. Create a chart, similar to the example below, that illustrates the differences between natural rights and classical republicanism. In completing your chart, you may need to review some of the ideas presented in Lesson 1.

Natural Rights Philosophy	Classical Republicanism
1. Stressed the rights of the individual to life, liberty, and property	1. Stressed promoting the common good above the rights of the individual
2.	2.
3.	3.

2. Suppose you were among the Founders chosen to participate in drafting a constitution. How might you reconcile these differences between natural rights and classical republicanism? Which ideas would you choose to emphasize? Why?

3. What problems might you encounter in transferring some of the ideas of classical republicanism to American society? How might you solve these problems?

How did the Founders think a government should be organized to promote the common good?

In addition to the example of the ancient Roman Republic, the Founders also learned about republican government from writers of their own time. One of the most important of these was the Baron de Montesquieu (1689–1755), a French writer who was widely admired by Americans.

Montesquieu advocated a system that **divided** and **balanced** the power of government among the classes. This, he believed, was the best way to ensure that the government would not be dominated by a single social class and would be able to enhance the common good.

He admired the Roman Republic as a representative government that combined elements of three basic types of government: monarchy, aristocracy, and democracy. Since all classes shared power, this type of government seemed best for serving the common good.

Even though Britain was a monarchy, Montesquieu admired the British constitution. He believed it embodied the idea of a **mixed government**, in which power was divided among different classes in British society.

What were some problems in transferring the ideas of classical republicanism to eighteenth-century America?

In some respects, the Founders were uncritical admirers of the ancient world, most especially the Roman Republic. They were inclined to exaggerate the degree to which these states represented the interests of the whole community rather than just the interests of the upper classes. They also overlooked the fact that the ancient republics depended on the institution of slavery. Their admiration for classical republicanism was based on a somewhat idealized version of antiquity.

The Founders were aware of the difficulty in transplanting ideals of classical republicanism to the newly independent American states. They differed concerning the degree to which these ideals could be adopted. The classical republicanism of the ancient world only flourished in small, uniform communities.

The following expectations of classical republicanism posed several problems for the founders of the new American nation:

- caring for each other and the common good in small communities
- believing that people must be very much alike
- supervising citizens to avoid the development of great differences among them in their ownership of property, religion, and way of life
- believing that great economic inequality is destructive of the common good
- having one official "established" religion and one set of family and moral standards which everyone would follow

How was a political ideal based on small, tightly knit communities to be applied to a new country as large as the young United States which represented people of different cultural backgrounds, economic conditions, and religious beliefs?

Baron de Montesquieu (1689–1755)
What important contribution did Montesquieu make to the Founders' ideas about government?

Were the Founders more representative of the ideas of the natural rights philosophy or classical republicanism? Why?

The classical republican idea of civic virtue conflicted with the Founders' belief in natural rights and with their understanding of human nature as defined by Locke and the other natural rights philosophers. The natural rights philosophy considered the rights of the individual to be primary in importance. The state existed to serve the interests of the individual, instead of the other way around. In classical republicanism, the rights of the community as a whole came first.

Americans of the founding era seemed more representative of human nature as described by the natural rights philosophers than the ideal expected by the civic virtue of the classical republicanism. They and their ancestors had come to the new land to take advantage of the opportunities it offered. Such restless, diverse, and ambitious people were ill-suited for the ideals of self-sacrifice and conformity of classical republicanism.

How did James Madison refine the ideas of classical republicanism?

James Madison was one of the most important Founders responsible for creating the U.S. Constitution. He has been called "the Father of the Constitution." He was very influential in translating the ideas of classical republicanism in such a way as to make them practical in the new American republic.

Madison defined the difference between democracies and republics in the following way:

- In a democracy, the people administer the government themselves. These "direct democracies" must be confined to small communities like the ancient city-states of Greece.

- In a republic, the people's representatives administer the government, allowing it to be extended over a much larger area.

Madison believed, therefore, that America could and should have a republican form of government. Laws would be made and administered by representatives elected by the people. Madison also accepted certain principles of democracy. He insisted that members of government should be elected by a large number of the people, rather than by a small number or a specially favored group. Such a form of government was a democracy in the sense that it derived its authority—its right to govern—from the people as a whole. Madison's new definition of a republican government, therefore, also could be defined as a **representative democracy**. In this way the two classical ideas of republic and democracy were adapted to the new form of government created by the Founders.

How did the Founders adapt the ideal of civic virtue to the American republic?

Like the other Founders, Madison understood the importance of informed and public-spirited citizens to this new government. He had to modify the classic definition of civic virtue to make it practical in the very different conditions of America. He accepted the natural rights philosophers' view of human nature—people were motivated primarily by self-interest. He believed that the pursuit of self-interest could in its own way further the common good. For example, a statesman's desire for fame and admiration from others would lead him to practice civic virtue. The common good could be served by each individual pursuing his or her economic self-interest. Each would contribute to the general prosperity.

James Madison (1751–1836)
*Why did James Madison favor a constitution
that limited the power of government?*

Madison also realized that as people pursue their own interests they sometimes act against the interests of others and against the common good. Any sound government had to make allowances for this. As Madison said, if all people were angels, there would be no need for government. He argued for a government that would encourage people to act as good republican citizens possessing the quality of civic virtue. At the same time, this government would guard against the consequences if they did not. This is why Madison favored a constitution that limited government by the following methods:

- **separation of powers**
- **a system of checks and balances**

The American adaptation of the principles of classical republicanism was, then, a sort of compromise. The Founders created a form of government they called **republican**, even though it was different from the models of republicanism in the ancient world.

They believed that it was important for citizens to possess civic virtue. Civic virtue could not always be relied upon, however. Therefore, the proper structure provided by a system of representation with separation of powers and checks and balances also was necessary to protect the common good.

What do *you* think?

1. Under a republican form of government, if elected officials hold views of the common good contrary to those of their constituents, what do you think the officials should do? Why?

2. Should a member of Congress vote against anti-smoking legislation intended to protect the health of the general population if it would hurt the economy of his or her state and put people out of work in that state?

3. To what extent do you think the common good in today's American society depends on the classical republican ideal of civic virtue and to what extent on the natural rights philosophy idea of each individual pursuing his or her own self-interest? Cite examples to support your case.

Reviewing and Using the Lesson

1. What is meant by "the common good"? Give an example of a rule or law that you think promotes the common good.

2. What is meant by the term "civic virtue"? Give an example of a situation in which someone is expected to show civic virtue.

3. What did classical republicans believe the purpose of government should be? What essential characteristics should a society and its citizens possess in order for a classical republican form of government to work? Why would these characteristics be important? How could these characteristics be established or maintained?

4. Why might small, uniform communities be more likely to foster civic virtue than large, diverse communities?

5. How would you describe the differences between the natural rights philosophy and classical republicanism?

6. How did James Madison adapt the ideals of classical republicanism to the large, diverse group of colonies that became the United States? How did he try to compensate or make up for the possible lack of civic virtue in the people?

7. What is the difference between a democracy and a republic? What aspects of the government of the United States suggest it is a democracy? What aspects suggest it is a republic?

8. Do research to find out more about the political philosophy of Baron de Montesquieu. What did he admire about mixed governments? What influence did his ideas have on the Founders?

LESSON 4

How Did Modern Ideas of Individual Rights Develop?

Purpose of Lesson

This lesson begins with a discussion of the Judeo-Christian tradition. You also examine the influence of the Renaissance, the Reformation, and the Enlightenment on the thinking of the Founders.

When you finish this lesson, you will be able to compare the difference between classical republican and Judeo-Christian ideas about the importance of the individual. You should understand how the Judeo-Christian tradition shaped people's outlook during the Middle Ages, providing one of the bases for modern constitutionalism. You also should be able to explain how the Renaissance, Reformation, rise of capitalism, rise of nationalism, and the Enlightenment led to the development of modern ideas about individual rights.

Terms to Know

Age of Enlightenment	papacy
capitalism	private morality
Christendom	Providence
hierarchical	public morality
Judeo-Christian	Reformation
Middle Ages	Renaissance
nation-state	secular government

How did the Judeo-Christian heritage contribute to the Founders' understanding of human rights?

The Founders were heirs to another legacy of antiquity, as important in its own way as that of the Greeks and Romans. They belonged to a religious tradition thousands of years old: Judeo-Christianity. Though of different faiths within this tradition, most of the Founders had grown up in a religious environment. From early childhood, they were familiar with the teachings of the Bible.

The **Judeo-Christian** tradition holds that the world was created and is governed by one God. Humanity occupies a special place in that creation. Each human being is created in God's image and each possesses an immortal soul. For many, the striving for salvation through obedience to God's divine law is of prime importance.

Some Founders were critical of organized religion and skeptical of certain religious doctrines. Most believed in a Supreme Being and in that Supreme Being's interest in humanity and affairs of the world. Above all, they were convinced of the importance of each person obeying the moral code that they believed was given by that Supreme Being.

As you know, the Declaration of Independence acknowledges the "Creator" who "endowed men with certain unalienable rights." The Founders often spoke of "**Providence**" to suggest their belief in God's interest and involvement in the affairs of the world. During the writing of the Constitution in the summer of 1787, Benjamin Franklin encouraged his fellow delegates by declaring his conviction that "God governs in the affairs of men."

Whatever their particular religious backgrounds, the Founders believed strongly in the importance of the moral principles of Judeo-Christianity to benefit the common good. Judeo-Christian morality was different from the Greek and Roman ideals of civic virtue. Instead of **public morality**, these principles emphasized **private morality** as expressed in biblical teachings such as the Ten Commandments and the Sermon on the Mount. To classical republican virtues—courage, moderation, and wisdom—Judeo-Christianity added other moral qualities, such as love and benevolence toward others.

To achieve what was best for society as a whole, the Founders thought that each person's moral principles and behavior should be based on both classical and Judeo-Christian virtues. They felt that the practice of religion would help people live according to such moral standards.

Their religious faith also strengthened the Founders' belief in the ideals of justice and liberty. The Bible stories of the struggle of the Hebrews against oppression and tyranny helped to inspire the American Revolution. These words from the Book of Leviticus are inscribed on the Liberty Bell in Philadelphia: "Proclaim liberty throughout all the land unto all the inhabitants thereof."

Finally, the teachings of Judeo-Christianity also helped to develop the Founders' appreciation of individual rights. Classical republicanism put the good of the state and community above that of the separate interests of the individuals who belonged to it.

How were a person's rights and responsibilities determined in the Middle Ages?

The Judeo-Christian view of the individual and his or her place in the world was different. Its teachings stressed the dignity and worth of each human being. It was believed that each person possessed an individual soul. Therefore, the individual assumed a new importance in people's thinking about society and government. Much in the Founders' commitment to liberty and individual rights sprang from their belief in the rightness of such ideals.

What were the concepts of the individual and society during the Middle Ages?

Christianity spread rapidly in the centuries following the death of Jesus and eventually became the predominant faith within the Roman Empire. The Roman Empire collapsed in the fifth century A.D., but Christianity survived to shape European society in the centuries that followed. This period, from the fifth century to the fourteenth, we call the **Middle Ages**—the period that lies between antiquity and modern times.

Medieval society was based on the ideas of unity, social harmony, and other-worldliness. The European people of the Middle Ages saw themselves united in a single society called **Christendom**. Their spiritual leader was the Pope in Rome. The Popes enjoyed great authority and respect throughout Europe. There were no nations at this time to compete for people's loyalty. Most people thought of themselves in terms of only two allegiances: to their own local community and to the great unity of Christendom with one "universal" or "catholic" church presiding over it.

Medieval ideas about society also reflected the harmony that was thought to exist between each individual and the whole of society. Society was sometimes compared to a body, in which some parts were more important than others but all parts were necessary for the good of the whole. The parts were dependent on each other.

- Society was divided into different classes and groups such as royalty, nobility, clergy, tradesmen, craftsmen, and peasants. Each class or group had certain rights and responsibilities.

- Society was **hierarchical**, that is, groups and classes were ranked from the most important at the top to the least important at the bottom. There was no equality between groups and classes.

- Each individual's role in society was defined by his or her role in one of these groups. A person had little chance of leaving the group into which he or she had been born.

Why did the Popes and the church attain such important status in the Middle Ages?

- Any rights and duties a person had were usually spoken of in terms of the group to which that person belonged. There was no concept of "natural" or "universal" rights belonging to all people. Rights were seen as privileges or "liberties" belonging to particular groups in society. Members of the group enjoyed its "rights." There were few individual rights.

Medieval society was also other-worldly in its interests and activities. Christianity taught that the primary purpose of this life was to achieve salvation after death in another spiritual eternal life. The most important institutions of the Middle Ages, including churches and monasteries, were devoted to this end. Whatever else people achieved in their lives was secondary.

Economic life in the Middle Ages was based on subsistence agriculture. Most people lived on small farms or manors, producing enough food for the inhabitants to live on. There were few towns or cities. Travel was limited. Most people spent their entire lives within a few miles of the place where they were born. The few economic markets were tightly regulated by the nobility.

How was people's understanding of rights shaped by the economic and social structure of the Middle Ages?

What do *you* think?

1. What is meant by the rights of groups as opposed to the rights of individuals?

2. What are the advantages and disadvantages of viewing rights as being possessed by individuals rather than groups?

3. Give some contemporary examples of claims for group rights. What arguments can you make for and against these claims?

4. Should certain individuals in our society be given special rights and privileges because they are members of a particular social group?

How did the Renaissance contribute to the development of individual rights?

During the medieval period, people did not strive to make "progress." That is, they did not believe that they could make things better for themselves and their children through hard work or individual initiative. Despite these attitudes, medieval cities did develop and prosper. Commerce began to flourish, cities grew, people started to travel more. **Nation-states** began to form. The invention of modern printing methods increased communication and knowledge.

The most important outcome of these changes was the **Renaissance**. The term Renaissance means "re-birth." It describes a rebirth or revival of intellectual life that began in Italy around the fourteenth century and spread throughout Europe. This new interest was inspired by the rediscovery of ancient Greek and Roman history, literature, and art, with a view of the world and humanity that was very different from that of medieval Christianity.

Instead of focusing only on other-worldly matters and the quest for salvation, people took a greater interest in the world around them. They directed their energy toward the possibilities of human achievement in this life rather than the life to come. They expanded their knowledge and began to develop new ideas about the world. Their art and architecture glorified the beauty of the human body; their literature and philosophy explored all aspects of human nature and human creativity.

During the Renaissance people began to accept the idea of progress and historical change. In many areas of life, greater importance was placed on the individual than on the class or group into which that individual had been born. People believed they could work to improve their positions in society. The new emphasis on individual opportunity led to an increased interest in the rights of individuals. This interest contributed to a reexamination of the individual's relationship to religious institutions and governments.

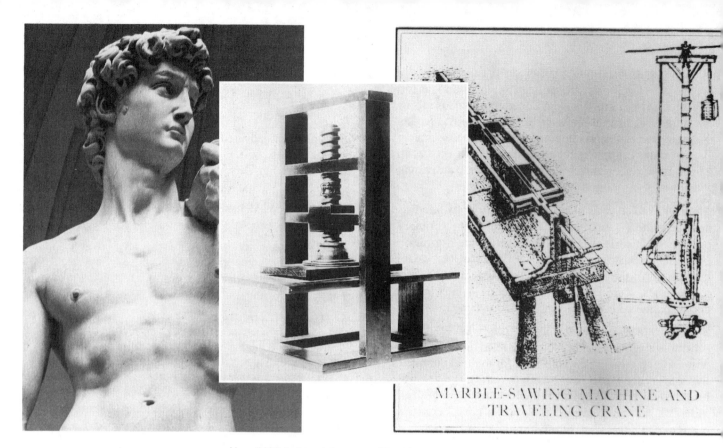

How did Michelangelo's statue of David and changes in technology reflect changes in thinking that occurred in the Renaissance?

MARBLE-SAWING MACHINE AND TRAVELING CRANE

How did the Protestant Reformation advance the cause of individual rights?

The Protestant Reformation was a powerful stimulus to modern individualism. The **Reformation** was a religious reform movement that began in the early sixteenth century in western Europe. It resulted in new ideas about religion, individual rights, and government. Like the Renaissance, the Reformation was a rebirth and rediscovery of certain things. Supporters of the Reformation believed they were returning to the original principles of Christianity.

Medieval society in western Europe had been dominated by the Church of Rome. Religious reformers, studying the Bible and other ancient religious texts, began to challenge the doctrines, traditions, and practices of the Church of Rome. They believed that the medieval church had become corrupt and had lost sight of the original truths of Christianity. Some critics attempted to reform the church from within, but many Protestant reformers, like Martin Luther and John Calvin, established their own churches with the help of **secular governments**.

The Reformation was aided by the invention of the printing press. Books that formerly were scarce now became more available. The Bible was the most important of these books. For centuries the Bible had been available only in Latin, which few people other than priests could read. Medieval Christians relied on the Church to interpret the word of God for them. During the Reformation, however, Bibles were printed in English, German, French, Italian, and Spanish. Individuals were encouraged to read the Bible in their native language to determine for themselves what it meant. Being able to read the Bible for oneself encouraged greater freedom of conscience.

Protestant religious doctrine emphasized the direct relationship between each individual believer and God. The result was to reduce the importance of the church and to increase the importance of the individual. All individuals were seen as equal in the eyes of God. Each person is to be respected and held accountable by God as an individual.

The spirit of free inquiry and individual conscience inspired by the Reformation contributed to the development of modern individualism. It also ultimately posed a threat to all established institutions and authority. Some religious reformers soon began to question the authority of the Protestant churches and the governments that supported them. In England, for example, reformers attacked the Church of England for not being Protestant enough. They were called Puritans because they wanted to "purify" the church. Some reformers sought to reform the established church. Others decided to separate from it. Many American colonies were originally settled by people seeking freedom to worship in their own way and new forms of government that would allow this.

What caused the rise of modern nation-states?

The modern nation-state's development was speeded by the forces of change created by the Renaissance and Reformation. There were no nations, as we understand that word today, during the Middle Ages. The power of kings and princes did not reach very far. Power was exercised locally by authorities who usually inherited their power. In theory, at least, all secular governments were subservient to the Church of Rome. They had little authority over church officials and institutions in their territories.

Toward the end of the Middle Ages many of these secular governments were expanding and consolidating their power into independent states. The Reformation helped this development by challenging the Church of Rome. Some states, like England, broke free from the Church of Rome and created their own national churches. Others remained loyal to the **papacy** but reduced the authority of the Church of Rome within their territory.

The rise of the modern nation-state was very important to the development of modern ideas about government and rights. People began to think of themselves as citizens of a particular state or country, with public rights and duties. Political thought began to focus on the question of what kind of government would be best for these states.

The modern nation-state also brought with it national legal systems and representative institutions of government.

What was the new economic system of capitalism?

Among the forces that helped to break up medieval society and pave the way for the Renaissance was the increase in commercial trade and its expansion over greater distances. Eventually, this growth produced a new economic system called **capitalism**. Capitalism is an economic system in which

- the means of producing and distributing goods are privately owned and operated for profit in competitive markets

- production and distribution are not controlled by the government

Under capitalism people gained more freedom to choose their occupations, start their own businesses, and own property. People had more control over their lives than had been possible in the Middle Ages.

People were able to pay more attention to their private interests than to the common good. They were encouraged to work to gain property and improve their positions in society. As a result, political and economic power shifted to a newly developed middle class of successful citizens.

How did the Renaissance, the Reformation, and the emergence of the modern nation-state make the rise of capitalism possible?

What do *you* think?

1. Why do you think Americans in the eighteenth century were so receptive to the new ideas that developed out of the Renaissance and Reformation?

2. With the development of capitalism, people began to view the individual differently than they had in antiquity or during the Middle Ages. What was this different view and why did it come about?

3. How were the rise of the nation-state and capitalism related to individualism? What effect did they have on the common good?

How did the Renaissance and Reformation contribute to the growth of individual rights?

The Renaissance and Reformation produced a greater emphasis on the importance of the individual than had existed in the Middle Ages or in classical Greece and Rome. The ideas and opinions of individuals were valued. As the Renaissance emphasized individual activity and creativity, the followers of the Protestant Reformation emphasized the relationship between the individual believer and God. The rise of nation-states stimulated new thought about government and rights. Capitalism translated this new spirit into economic opportunity. More individuals could compete on an equal footing and hope to improve their place in society.

Critical Thinking Exercise

UNDERSTANDING THE EFFECTS OF THE RENAISSANCE AND REFORMATION ON IDEAS ABOUT RIGHTS

Your teacher will ask you to work in small groups of four or five students to examine how the ideas of the Judeo-Christian tradition, the Middle Ages, the Renaissance, the Reformation, and the rise of the nation-state and capitalism supported the Founders' thinking about natural rights and classical republicanism.

1. Suppose that you lived in the American colonies during the eighteenth century. Like the Founders, you firmly believe in the ideas of the natural rights philosophers concerning individual rights and the purpose of government. You also believe in classical republican ideas of civic virtue and the common good. Examine what you have learned in this lesson about the Judeo-Christian tradition, the Middle Ages, the Renaissance, the Reformation, and the rise of the nation state and capitalism. Create a chart that illustrates which ideas prevalent during these historical periods influenced your thinking about the importance of the individual, individual rights, and the common good.

2. Were there any ideas prevalent during one of these periods which you, as a believer in natural rights and classical republicanism, do not agree with? What are these ideas? Why do you disagree with them?

3. Do you think the ideas about the importance of the individual, individual rights, and the common good that emerged during these historical periods have influenced your thinking about the nature and purpose of government? If so, explain how.

What do *you* think?

1. If the ideas about rights that prevailed during the Middle Ages were dominant today, how would they affect your life?

2. What conflicts arise in a society that emphasizes both the importance of individual rights and of the common good? What evidence, if any, do you see of such conflicts in your own experiences?

3. It has been said: "Each Protestant becomes his own Pope when he has a Bible in his hands." What does this mean? How did the religious revival of the Reformation contribute to modern ideas about individual rights? To constitutional government?

What was the Age of Enlightenment?

The natural rights philosophy was a product of what is sometimes called the **Age of Enlightenment**. The Enlightenment was an intellectual movement of the late seventeenth and eighteenth centuries that celebrated human reason and sought to realize its potential in all areas of human endeavor. The Age of Enlightenment is also called the Age of Reason.

How did increased interest in scientific study relate to the development of the natural rights philosophy?

The worldly interests inspired by the Renaissance stimulated natural science—the study of the natural world and the laws that govern it. This new interest also was encouraged by commercial expansion and voyages of discovery beyond Europe. These voyages brought new knowledge about the natural world and about other cultures.

One advocate of scientific discovery, the English philosopher Francis Bacon, believed in the power of human reason and observation not only to understand nature, but also to control it for humanity's own purposes. "The end of scientific study," he said, "is the enlarging of the bounds of human empire, to the effecting of all things possible." The discoveries of scientists like Copernicus, Galileo, and Newton seemed to confirm Bacon's faith.

Eventually this spirit of scientific discovery was applied to human nature and society as well. During the Enlightenment people began to apply the method of scientific thinking to the study of society and politics.

The American Founders belonged to the Age of Enlightenment. They believed in the powers of reason and observation to understand the workings of governmental and societal institutions. They thought these powers also would be a guide in ways to improve institutions. With such faith and self-confidence, the Framers of our Constitution thought they could create a new order of government during one summer's deliberations in Philadelphia.

Reviewing and Using the Lesson

1. How would you describe the difference between the classical republican idea of civic virtue and Judeo-Christian ideas of morality?

2. How did the Judeo-Christian heritage contribute to the Founders' understanding of human rights?

3. What features of society in the Middle Ages contributed to the view that rights belonged to groups, rather than to individuals?

4. How did the Renaissance contribute to modern ideas about rights? How did the Protestant Reformation contribute to modern ideas about rights? How did the rise of nation-states contribute? How did the economic system of capitalism contribute?

5. Why was the invention of the printing press important in promoting the spirit of individualism?

6. What was the "Age of Enlightenment" and why is it sometimes called the "Age of Reason"?

7. Working with a group of classmates, prepare and perform a skit that shows how ideas about rights during the Middle Ages were different from modern ideas about rights. Think about what the advantages and disadvantages of the view that prevailed during the Middle Ages might be, and find a way to present these advantages and disadvantages in your skit.

LESSON 5

What Were the British Origins of American Constitutionalism?

Purpose of Lesson

This lesson describes how some basic rights of Englishmen were established and why they were important to the American colonists. You examine English government in its early stages from the ninth through the thirteenth centuries, known as the feudal period. You also examine the initial development of the English constitution. Finally, you learn about the Magna Carta and its importance to the Founders.

When you finish this lesson you should be able to explain the importance to the Founders of the following ideas: the basic "rights of Englishmen," the Magna Carta, and the development of constitutional government in England.

Terms to Know

charter	manor and manorialism
contract	Parliament
custom	rights of Englishmen
common law	royal charter
due process of law	subject
feudalism	tenet
Magna Carta	vassal
monarch	

How did English government begin?

For several centuries after the fall of the Roman Empire, England was divided among a number of tribes, each ruled by its own leader or "king." These early kings were selected by councils of advisers because they were the strongest and most powerful members of their tribes. For many years these tribes were at war with each other. Eventually all the tribes of England became united under one king. Christianity increased the authority of kingship by teaching that kings were "anointed by God" and that all the people governed by the king were **subject** to his rule—which is why they were called "subjects."

England was too large for one person to rule because quick and efficient means of communication and travel did not exist. Most kings had to let people in local areas tend to their own affairs according to customs that had developed over the years.

What was feudalism?

A major change in the way England was ruled took place on October 14, 1066, when William the Conqueror, the leader of the Normans (from Normandy in France), invaded England and defeated King Harold at the Battle of Hastings. William introduced a new system of **feudalism** to control the conquered land.

How did feudalism change power relationships between people?

Feudalism is not easy to define because it varied greatly in different times and different places. Generally, feudalism was a form of political organization in which a lord gave land to other men in return for their personal allegiance and for military and other service. The men who received land from the lord were known as his **vassals**—they served their lord and were entitled to be protected by him.

How did feudalism change the way people were governed?

Feudalism is important to the development of constitutional government because of its ideas about **contracts**. Feudal government depended on a series of agreements or contracts between lords and vassals. Each contract included mutual rights and responsibilities. Thus, feudalism introduced the idea of government based on a contract—those in power pledged to respect the rights of the people who gave them allegiance.

The basis of this feudal system was land use. Parcels of land were divided into self-contained farms or **manors**. Peasants were legally required to remain on the land and in that sense were part of the property enjoyed by the owner or "lord" of the land. Even peasants, however, enjoyed certain customary rights on the manor. For this reason, the system of **manorialism** as well as feudalism helped to develop ideas about the fundamental rights of Englishmen.

What do we mean by the "rights of Englishmen"?

The **rights of Englishmen** had been established slowly over centuries of British history. They were certain basic rights that all subjects of the English **monarch**—king or queen—were believed to have. They were fundamental in the sense that they could not be changed or violated.

The Founders began their lives as loyal subjects of the British Crown, proud to enjoy the rights of Englishmen. This privilege, they believed, set them apart from the other peoples of the world.

Centuries of respect gave these rights a special status. They included

- the right to a trial by jury
- security in one's home from unlawful entry
- no taxation without consent

The historical sources of these rights are **custom** and **law**. They were confirmed by **royal charters** and became part of English **common law**. The common law consists of the accumulated legal opinions of judges explaining their decisions in specific court cases. These decisions provide guidelines or precedents for later judgments. The English common law provides the historical foundation of our American legal system.

What is the British constitution?

Unlike the U.S. Constitution, the British constitution did not exist before the creation of a government. The constitution of Great Britain is not a single written document. Instead it is made up of the common law, acts of Parliament, and political customs and traditions.

Three great historical documents are important in the development of the British constitution and the rights of the British people. These are the Magna Carta (1215), the Petition of Right (1628), and the English Bill of Rights (1689).

These documents were written during times of great conflict. Much of English history is the story of a bloody struggle for power between the most important groups in society. These groups were the royalty, nobility, and the clergy. By the thirteenth century, the struggle was mainly between royalty and the **Parliament**. Parliament was originally a council of nobles created to advise the monarch. It soon became the branch of government that represented the most powerful groups in the kingdom.

For hundreds of years, Parliament and the monarch struggled for power. During these conflicts, English subjects were jailed, tortured, and executed. Kings and queens defeated in battle were imprisoned and beheaded. Because of these conflicts, several important legal documents were written that limited the power of the monarch in order to protect the rights of other groups. These documents were important not only in English history, but they also had a great influence on the Founders. One of the most important of these documents is described below.

What was the Magna Carta and why is it important to us?

The first great landmark of British constitutionalism and one of the great **charters** of human liberty originated as a quarrel between a feudal lord and his vassals. One of William the Conqueror's successors, King John, tried to take back some rights and powers of his barons. This was the title of nobility given to principal vassals. The result was a war between the barons and their king, a war that the barons won.

With the support of the church and others, the barons, in June 1215, forced John to sign the **Magna Carta**—Great Charter—confirming certain traditional rights and, by implication, promising not to violate them again. Most of the rights in question were feudal privileges, enjoyed only by the feudal nobility.

The **tenets**—principles or doctrines—of the Magna Carta were very important in the later development of constitutional government:

Government should be based on the rule of law. The Magna Carta was perhaps the most important early example of a written statement of law limiting the power of a ruler. It expresses the idea of limited government by requiring the king to govern according to established rules of law. The Magna Carta, for example, states that no free man could be imprisoned or punished "except by the lawful judgment of his peers and by the law of the land." "Judgment of his peers" did not originally mean trial by jury as we understand it. This statement, however, did explain the principle of **due process of law**,

whereby no government could take action against those it governed except by settled and generally agreed on procedures and rules.

How did the Magna Carta reduce the power of the English monarch?

Certain basic rights may not be denied by government. In limiting the power of the king, the Magna Carta also expressed the idea that established rights of the governed could not be violated. Most of the rights guaranteed in the Magna Carta belonged only to the feudal nobility. The Magna Carta did, however, secure some rights for others in English society. The king, for example, promised to respect the "ancient liberties and free customs" of London and other towns.

Government should be based on an agreement or contract between the ruler and the people to be ruled. The agreement in the Magna Carta was between the king and a very limited number of his subjects. It did not include the majority of the English people. It did, however, express the feudal principle of drawing up an agreement between parties as a basis for legitimate government. Government by contract meant that if either side broke the agreement, that agreement would no longer be valid.

Later generations also would discover in the Magna Carta the seeds of other important constitutional principles. For example, the American colonists found in King John's promise not to levy certain feudal taxes without the consent of "our common counsel of the kingdom" the principle of no taxation without representation and consent.

Critical Thinking Exercise
ANALYZING AND EVALUATING SPECIFIC RIGHTS

People have fought and died to establish such rights as those described in this lesson. It is often difficult, however, to understand their importance from merely reading about them. By examining specific rights more closely and discussing your opinions about them, you may be able to gain a greater appreciation of their meaning and importance. Let's examine more closely some of the provisions of the Magna Carta.

Two parts of the Magna Carta, Articles 39 and 40, contain some of the most important principles of modern constitutionalism. Working in small groups, read and discuss these provisions. Then develop responses to the questions that follow. Be prepared to explain your answers to the class.

Article 39: *No freeman shall be taken or imprisoned or disseised [dispossessed] or banished or in any way destroyed, nor will We proceed against or prosecute him, except by the lawful judgment of his peers and by the law of the land*

Article 40: *To no one will we sell, to none will we refuse or delay,...justice.*

1. What rights are listed in Articles 39 and 40?

2. How do these rights limit the power of the king?

3. Why would the English nobles want to place such limits on the power of the king?

4. What values and interests are protected by these statements?

5. What events in the United States or other nations can you identify in which one or more of the above rights have been upheld or violated?

What do *you* think?

1. In what ways might the rights in Articles 39 and 40 be relevant to you today?

2. Do you think the declaration of these rights alone is enough to protect individuals from unfair and unreasonable treatment by their government? Why or why not?

Did the Magna Carta protect the rights of all Englishmen? Why?

3. At Runnymede in England, where King John signed the Magna Carta, there are three monuments. One is a tribute to U.S. President John Kennedy. Another is the Magna Carta memorial erected by the American Bar Association. In addition there is one honoring the British Commonwealth airmen who died in World War II. Why do you think the Magna Carta might be especially important to Americans?

Reviewing and Using the Lesson

1. What is meant by the "rights of Englishmen"? How were these rights established?

2. What is the common law? How does it develop?

3. What was feudalism and how did it contribute to the development of constitutional government?

4. What is the Magna Carta? How was it created? How did it contribute to the development of constitutional government?

5. What ideas in the U.S. Constitution or in your state constitution can you trace back to the Magna Carta?

LESSON 6

How Did Representative Government Begin in England?

Purpose of Lesson

This lesson describes the evolution of constitutional government in England after the Magna Carta. You examine some early documents that protected rights in England and the origins of England's representative governmental institutions. You learn how these ideas and institutions influenced American constitutionalism. You also learn about some important differences between British and American constitutionalism.

You also should be aware that we sometimes refer to England and other times to Britain. In 1707 Scotland agreed to join with England and Wales to create the United Kingdom of Great Britain. "Britain," therefore, is the name used for events occurring after that date.

When you finish this lesson, you should be able to explain how rights and representative government were established in British history and how this history influenced the Founders. You also will have a better understanding of the origins and importance of some of our most important constitutional rights today.

Terms to Know

balance of power	Parliament
burgess	Parliamentary supremacy
English Bill of Rights	Petition of Right
Glorious Revolution	realm
House of Lords	Revolution Settlement
House of Commons	writ of habeas corpus
jurist	

How did parliamentary government in England begin?

The Magna Carta brought the law to bear against a law-breaking king. It did not, however, solve the problem of how to make sure the king would continue to comply with the law. The Magna Carta gave King John's barons the right to go to war with him if he broke their agreement. Going to war, however, was not a satisfactory basis for assuring responsible government. A better way began to develop in the century following the Magna Carta.

In the feudal system English kings relied on councils to advise them in the task of governing. The councils came to be called **parliaments**, from the French word *parler*, to speak. At first these councils of advisers included only the leading nobles and clergy of the **realm**. Gradually, the number of members and the role of these councils expanded to more effectively represent the interests of the different groups in the realm.

In the fourteenth century these parliaments divided into two parts or houses: the **House of Lords**—representing the interests of the feudal nobility and major churchmen; the **House of Commons**—representing not the common people as we understand that term, but rather people who were not nobility but who still possessed wealth and stature in the kingdom. The Commons included knights, who represented the shires or counties of the kingdom, and **burgesses**, wealthy merchants and craftsmen, who represented the cities and towns of England.

How did the English Parliament come to represent the interests of more people?

Parliament developed as a representative institution of government because the kings of England found it an effective way to raise money from their subjects. They also found it an efficient way to make important laws. Henry VIII, for example, used the authority of Parliament to break away from the Church of Rome and to establish the Church of England. English subjects found Parliament to be an effective way to voice their grievances to their monarch and also to limit or check his or her power.

How did the struggles between the English kings and their subjects develop the British constitution?

Eventually, Parliament became so important to English government that it was capable of challenging the king's ability to act without its support. The struggle for ultimate power in England's government came to a head in the seventeenth century, when the Stuart kings and their Parliaments quarreled over a variety of issues, including money, religion, and foreign policy. At the heart of these struggles was a key constitutional issue:

- Did the king have the authority or prerogative to act independently of established law and parliamentary consent?

OR

- Must the king govern through Parliament and accept the ultimate supremacy of Parliamentary law?

On the outcome of this struggle, which included a bloody civil war, the execution of one king, Charles I, and the overthrow of another, James II, depended the future of British—and American—constitutional government.

What was the Petition of Right?

The constitutional struggles of seventeenth-century England included several important events. One of these events produced a constitutional document almost as important as the Magna Carta: the **Petition of Right** of 1628. Pressed for money, King Charles I sought to raise funds without the consent of Parliament. He also tried to force this money from his subjects through illegal pressures. For example, he required subjects to "quarter" or house soldiers in their homes.

In 1628 Parliament forced Charles to consent to the Petition of Right, which confirmed that taxes could only be raised with the consent of Parliament. It also guaranteed English subjects other rights, including a prohibition against requiring people to quarter soldiers in their homes. The Petition of Right thus strengthened the idea that English subjects enjoyed certain fundamental rights that no government could violate.

How did the Petition of Right of 1628 strengthen the principle of constitutional government?

What was the connection between the Petition of Right and the Magna Carta?

One parliamentary leader in favor of the Petition of Right was the famous **jurist** Sir Edward Coke, who was greatly admired by the Founders. Coke championed the rights of Englishmen. He believed that the Magna Carta was not only a victory for feudal privilege but also a confirmation of the fundamental rights belonging to all Englishmen, rights that had existed since time immemorial. The Petition of Right, he believed, was, like the Magna Carta, a confirmation of these ancient rights.

Why is habeas corpus such an important right?

Another important milestone in this constitutional struggle was the **Habeas Corpus Act** of 1678, in which Parliament gained from English monarchs the right of their subjects to a legal document called a **writ of habeas corpus.** The Latin phrase *habeas corpus* means to "have the body." A writ of habeas corpus orders the government to deliver a person it has arrested to a court of law and explain why that person has been arrested and held. If the government cannot produce evidence to show that the arrested person may have broken the law, the person must be set free.

The English subject's right to a writ of habeas corpus may have existed in English law even before the Magna Carta. Its guarantee was also one of the provisions of the Petition of Right. English monarchs, however, had for centuries ignored this guarantee by using unlawful arrest and prolonged imprisonment without trial as weapons against their subjects.

Critical Thinking Exercise

EVALUATING THE IMPORTANCE OF THE RIGHTS TO HABEAS CORPUS AND TRIAL BY JURY

The following exercise asks you to examine the rights of habeas corpus and trial by jury. Your class should be divided into two groups, one group will read selection 1 and the other selection 2. Then each group will answer the questions that accompany their selection. Discuss your reading with the entire class.

Group 1: Habeas corpus. The writ of habeas corpus has been called the "Great Writ of Liberty." One constitutional scholar called it "the greatest guarantee of human freedom ever devised by man." Let's examine why this right was thought to be so fundamental.

Suppose you were arrested and imprisoned by the Queen of England. Although you have the right to be tried by the law of the land, the queen's jailers keep you in prison. They refuse to bring you before a court to be charged with a crime and tried.

How could the right to a writ of habeas corpus protect you from such treatment? How could the jailers be forced to bring you into a court of law for a fair hearing?

Suppose you had a family member, a friend, or a lawyer who knew you had been arrested and were being kept in prison. That person could go to court and ask the judge to issue a writ of habeas corpus. This writ would be an order by the judge to your jailer to bring you, that is your "body," to court and present evidence that you have broken the law. If there is evidence, you would be held for trial. If there is no evidence, you would be set free.

Examining the Right

1. What limits does the right to a writ of habeas corpus place on the power of the monarch?

2. Why would the English Parliament want to place such limits on the power of the monarch?

3. What arguments can you make for this right today?

4. What examples of situations in the United States or other nations can you identify that uphold or violate this right?

5. Under what conditions, if any, do you think this right should be limited?

Why is the right to a writ of habeas corpus so important in protecting the rights of a person accused of crimes?

Group 2: Trial by jury. The right to a trial by a jury of one's peers is one of the oldest and most important of the fundamental rights of Englishmen. It has become an essential right in a free society.

Suppose you were arrested and imprisoned by the English king. A judge, appointed and paid by the king, has examined the evidence against you and decided you should be tried for breaking the law.

The English constitution guarantees you the right to be tried by a jury of your peers. This means that a group of people from your community will listen to the evidence the king's prosecutor has against you. They also will hear your side of the story. The jury has the authority to decide if you are guilty or innocent of breaking the law. Its verdict must be unanimous to find you guilty. Jurors also have the power to find you not guilty even if you have broken the law if they think the law in question is unfair.

Examining the Right

1. What limits does the right to a trial by jury place upon the power of the monarch?

2. Why would the English Parliament want to place such limits on the power of the monarch?

3. What relation does the right to a trial by jury have to the separation of powers and checks and balances?

4. What arguments can you make for this right?

5. Under what conditions if any, do you think this right should be limited?

What led to the English Bill of Rights of 1689?

The struggle between the monarch and Parliament came to a head in a bloodless revolution known as the **Glorious Revolution** of 1688. King James II was overthrown and forced to flee the country. The king's son-in-law, Prince William of Orange, and his followers had suspected James II of trying to make Roman Catholicism the established religion in England and of resorting to various illegal acts to accomplish this.

In the **Revolution Settlement** that followed the Glorious Revolution, Prince William and his wife, Mary, succeeded to the throne. A condition of their succession, however, was that they agree to a **Declaration of Rights**. The Declaration was then enacted into law by Parliament as the **English Bill of Rights**. It became the cornerstone of the Revolution Settlement and of England's constitution.

What protections did the English Bill of Rights include?

The English Bill of Rights was a practical and specific document rather than a statement of general constitutional principles. Its primary objective was to make sure that what James II had tried to do would never happen again. It limited the power of the monarch by placing the dominant power of government in Parliament and providing for the security of the Church of England against any attempts at counter-revolution by James or his descendants on behalf of Roman Catholicism.

The English Bill of Rights includes many ideas about rights and government that were later included in our Declaration of Independence, Constitution, and Bill of Rights. In addition to limiting the monarch's power to act without the consent of Parliament, it provides for such traditional rights of Englishmen as trial by jury, prohibition of cruel and unusual punishments, the right to petition the government, and the right to bear arms for personal defense—a right, however, granted only to Protestants.

The English Bill of Rights does not provide for freedom of religion. Nor does it guarantee freedom of the press or freedom of speech outside Parliament. An **Act of Toleration**, however, passed shortly after the Glorious Revolution, gave freedom of worship to Protestant dissenters. Though not included in the act, Roman Catholics were thereafter generally left alone to practice their faith. The government also expanded freedom of the press by repealing the act that allowed censorship of printed material.

How does the English Bill of Rights differ from the U.S. Bill of Rights?

The English Bill of Rights differs from the U.S. Bill of Rights in several important respects. The former was ratified by Parliament and could be changed by Parliament. The U.S. Bill of Rights was ratified by the people and could only be changed with their consent through the amending process of the Constitution.

The English Bill of Rights was intended primarily to limit the power of the monarch and increase the power of Parliament. The U.S. Bill of Rights was intended to prohibit the federal government from violating the individual rights of all people and to protect the rights of minorities.

The Glorious Revolution and the English Bill of Rights, however, express several important constitutional principles that influenced our Constitution and Bill of Rights. These were

- **Rule of law.** The English Bill of Rights restated the old idea that legitimate government must be according to the rule of law. Both government and the governed must obey the laws of the land.

- **Parliamentary supremacy.** The Glorious Revolution finally settled the question of supremacy in the English government. While retaining important executive powers, the monarch must govern through Parliament. Parliamentary law was the highest law in the land.

- **Government by contract and consent**. By over-throwing a monarch who broke the law and by declaring respect for the English Bill of Rights as a condition for his successors, the Glorious Revolution confirmed the idea that government is based on a contract between the rulers and those who are ruled.

What do *you* think?

1. In what ways did the British documents about rights reinforce the major ideas found in the Magna Carta? In what ways did they expand upon these ideas?

GLORIOUS REVOLUTION

BEFORE

AFTER

How did the Glorious Revolution of 1688 and the resulting English Bill of Rights change the balance of power between the monarch and Parliament?

2. How are the ideas in the Magna Carta, the Petition of Right, and the English Bill of Rights related to the natural rights philosophy?

3. Why might an understanding of British history have led the Founders to want to protect the right of religious freedom and dissent?

Why did Montesquieu admire the British constitution?

Many Europeans admired the British constitution in the eighteenth century. They were impressed by the degree of liberty enjoyed by British subjects and by the growing power and wealth of the British Empire. One admirer of the British constitution was the French philosopher Montesquieu, whose writings on classical republicanism we discussed in Lesson 3. His interpretation of the British constitution had a great influence on the Founders.

Montesquieu admired what he believed to be the "mixed" nature of the British constitution, which included the best of monarchy—the king or queen, aristocracy—the House of Lords, and democracy—the House of Commons. This constitution was, he believed, a modern example of the classical republican model of government. Montesquieu also saw in the British constitution the principle of separation of powers in government, whereby the executive, legislative, and judicial powers are independent of each other.

To some extent, however, Montesquieu misinterpreted how the British constitution worked. It was not as "mixed" in its composition as he believed. Both the House of Lords and House of Commons in the eighteenth century were predominantly aristocratic. Moreover, the three branches of government were not fully separated. The monarch through his or her ministers took an active

part in the affairs of Parliament. English judges also were considered part of the executive branch.

The British constitution as secured by the Glorious Revolution did, however, create a **balance of power** between the monarch and the two houses of Parliament. Judges were granted independence from both the monarch and Parliament to interpret the law fairly. This balance of power was a first step toward the idea of separation of powers and checks and balances in our Constitution.

Reviewing and Using the Lesson

1. How would you describe the evolution of parliamentary government in England?

2. Among the key events in the struggle for power between the Crown and Parliament were the Petition of Right of 1628, the Habeas Corpus Act of 1678, and the Glorious Revolution of 1688. Describe how each of these contributed to the development of constitutional government in England.

3. How does the English Bill of Rights differ from the U.S. Bill of Rights?

4. In recent years proposals have been made to limit or restrict the right to habeas corpus. Do research to find out about these proposals. What concerns are they intended to address? What arguments have been made for and against these proposals? Given what you have learned in this lesson about the importance of the writ of habeas corpus, what do you think of these proposals?

LESSON 7

What Basic Ideas about Rights and Constitutional Government Did Colonial Americans Have?

Purpose of Lesson

This lesson describes how the basic ideas of constitutional government were developed and used in the American colonies before they gained their independence from Britain. You learn about social and economic conditions that were special to America. These conditions sometimes required old ideas to be adapted or discarded. Sometimes the creation of entirely new solutions was necessary.

When you finish this lesson, you should understand the early development of America's own traditions of constitutional government. You should be able to explain how the differences between colonial America and Europe affected the Founders' political views. You also should have a better understanding of why the American colonists attached special importance to such constitutional principles as written guarantees of basic rights and representative government.

Terms to Know

constituents
covenant
established religion
Fundamental Orders of
  Connecticut
indentured servants
Laws and Liberties of
  Massachusetts

magistrate
Massachusetts Body of
  Liberties
Mayflower Compact
primogeniture
suffrage

How did the colonial settlement of America inspire new experiments in constitutional government?

Almost half of our history as a people—over 150 years—took place before we gained our independence in 1776. This history had a great influence on the Founders.

The many thousands of immigrants in the seventeenth and early eighteenth centuries came to America for various reasons. The most common were economic and religious. The English colonists brought with them English customs, laws, and ideas about good government. They were separated from England, however, by 3,000 miles of ocean. Consequently, the colonists soon discovered that they would have to improvise, adapt old ideas, and develop new ones if they were to survive.

In some respects, the settlement of America meant a return to a state of nature as later described by the natural rights philosophers. This new experience required new political solutions. One of our country's oldest and most famous charters, the **Mayflower Compact**, was a **covenant** or social contract, to which the Pilgrims agreed prior to landing in Plymouth, Massachusetts, in 1620. The Compact established a civil body authorized to make laws and appoint officers.

How does the Mayflower Compact reflect the principle of government by consent or social contract?

What was unique about the American experience?

The special conditions of an undeveloped land profoundly affected economic, social, and political life in colonial America. Land was cheap and readily available. People available to till this land or perform other jobs in colonial society were always in short supply.

Cheap land and the great demand for workers meant that most American colonists had far greater opportunities to get ahead and achieve prosperity than most people in Europe. While some became very wealthy, others failed, creating a class of American poor. But the great majority realized at least a moderate prosperity that was beyond their reach in Europe. Almost any white man with ambition could gain the fifty acres of land required as a qualification to vote in most colonies.

There was no nobility whose social and economic status was protected by law. In Great Britain laws prohibited the sale and distribution of property attached to a noble title; it had to be handed down to eldest sons—the right of **primogeniture**. Since economic and political power was based on this property, generations of noble families had a privileged status in English government and society.

It is true that those people who came from educated British families or those with great personal wealth had an advantage over those who arrived in the colonies almost penniless and unknown. But wealth and family name did not mean automatic success in a land without a rigid class system; and the lack of these advantages rarely held back for long those with ambition. The carpenter and brick mason, for example, enjoyed modest social status in England. The constant demand for new buildings in America, however, allowed such craftsmen to earn a living equal to many of their social "superiors." A well-born gentleman from Europe who considered hard work or manual labor beneath him might have a difficult time surviving in the colonies.

Thus, there was greater equality among Americans than among Europeans in their economic, social, and political life. While some upper class Americans might not have liked this situation, equality of opportunity and the chance to better one's position in life became fundamental ideals in the American experience. In this land of almost unlimited opportunity, one of a candlemaker's 17 children, Benjamin Franklin, could rise to become a great inventor, statesman, and diplomat. An English corset-maker's son, Thomas Paine, could become a famous writer on behalf of the American Revolution. Alexander Hamilton, the illegitimate son of poor parents, could become the first Secretary of the Treasury of the newly formed United States.

Critical Thinking Exercise
EXAMINING AN ORIGINAL DOCUMENT ABOUT COLONIAL LIFE

In the mid-eighteenth century a colonial farmer, Philip Taylor, wrote about his life on the border of what today is the state of Vermont. Read what he wrote and then be prepared to discuss your answers to the questions that follow.

> *We now have a comfortable dwelling and two acres of ground planted with potatoes, Indian corn, melon, etc. I have 2 hogs, 1 ewe and a lamb; cows in the spring were as high as 33 dollars, but no doubt I shall have 1 by fall.*
>
> *I am living in God's noble and free soil, neither am I slave to others...I have now been on American soil for two and a half years and I have not been compelled to pay for the privilege of living. Neither is my cap worn out from lifting it in the presence of gentlemen.*

1. What was it that Philip Taylor liked about life in America?

2. What rights did he enjoy? How are they related to the ideas of the natural rights philosophers? Do you enjoy these rights today?

How did life in the American colonies break down the social and economic barriers so common in Europe?

3. Given what you know of Philip Taylor's experiences, explain why he would be more or less likely to favor laws that

- guarantee each individual the right to be secure in his property
- limit an individual's right to buy and sell goods to anyone he or she chooses
- give people certain rights because they are wealthy or from a certain family background or group

What basic ideas of constitutional government did the colonial governments use?

The colonies were originally founded by charters or grants given to private groups or individuals. These charters and grants said little about what form of local government the colonies should have. As a result the colonies developed their own forms of government, and America became a fertile ground for constitution making. The colonies depended more on written constitutional arrangements than was the case in England, whose own unwritten constitution represented centuries of evolution.

In creating such limited government, the colonists tried to protect themselves not only from abuse of power by the English government in London, but also from abuses by colonial governments themselves. The first governments of many of the colonies lacked constitutional restraints that were later seen as essential. Some of the early colonial governments persecuted those who refused to conform to the **established religion**. Resistance to religious persecution in the colonies became an important stimulus to the advancement of constitutional ideas and institutions.

There are many stories of religious dissenters who were persecuted in these early years. Anne Hutchinson, a brilliant and talented woman, arrived in Massachusetts in 1634 with her husband and seven children. She gained great respect as a midwife, healer, and spiritual counselor. Before long she began preaching a theory of salvation that was contrary to the official Puritan beliefs. Not only was she a dissenter but as a woman she was particularly offensive to the male leaders of the community. Brought to trial, she was cast out of the colony as "a heathen and a leper."

Hutchinson fled Massachusetts to Rhode Island where religious dissenters were tolerated. It was the first colony to grant freedom of conscience to everyone. The Charter of 1663 provided that "noe person…shall bee any wise molested, punished, disquieted, or called in question, for any differences of opinione in matters of religion." Jews, Quakers, Catholics, and others not welcomed elsewhere found a haven in Rhode Island.

Why is it important to protect the right to dissent?

Others were inspired by constitutional values early on. The first colonial constitution was the **Fundamental Orders of Connecticut**, created in 1639 by three town settlements along the Connecticut River. Deriving its authority from all free men living in these towns, this constitution established a central legislative body for making laws. The other colonies would adopt constitutional arrangements of their own in the years that followed.

Some of these experiments were successful. Others failed or had to be revised many times before they became practical. The forms of colonial government varied somewhat from colony to colony. They all, however, shared certain basic constitutional principles. These principles generally reflected the influence of England but in some ways they differed. The ideas of British constitutionalism embodied in the governments of the British colonies follow.

Fundamental rights. The colonists were concerned foremost with protecting those fundamental rights they believed they had brought with them from England. At first these basic rights were seen as the ancient and fundamental rights of Englishmen. These basic rights were later described as the rights of all men. They were defined by the natural rights philosophers as the natural rights to life, liberty, and property.

Rule of law. In order to protect their fundamental rights, the colonists insisted on the creation of a government of laws, in which those responsible for making and enforcing the laws could not exercise arbitrary power as had been the case in some of the first colonial governments. The colonial constitutions also included the idea that the English law was higher law and was superior to any laws the colonial governments might make.

Separation of powers. To a greater extent than in the British government, colonial governments provided for a separation of powers among the three branches of government. In colonial governments the three branches tended to be more independent of each other. Separation of powers was evident in the following ways:

- **An executive branch. Governors** were responsible for carrying out and enforcing law. In most of the colonies by the time of the American Revolution, the governors were chosen either by the monarch or the proprietors. Only in Connecticut and Rhode Island were the governors elected by those men in the colonies who were allowed to vote.

- **A legislative branch.** All the colonies had **legislatures** that were responsible for making laws. All but Pennsylvania were similar to the Parliament in Britain with an "upper house" like the House of Lords and a "lower house" like the House of Commons. Members of the upper house were either appointed by the governor or elected by the most wealthy property owners of the colony. The lower house was elected by all the men in the colony who owned a certain amount of property. Pennsylvania was an exception; it had only one house. More independent of the executive branch than the British Parliament, the colonial legislatures would eventually become the strongest of the three branches of government.

- **A judicial branch.** This branch was made up of judges called **magistrates** who were usually appointed by the governor. Their responsibility was to handle conflicts over the laws and to preside at trials of those accused of breaking the law. They also were responsible for making sure the colonies were being governed in a way that was consistent with English law and tradition.

Checks and balances. Power was separated and in some cases shared among these branches, so that the use of power by one branch could be **checked** by that of another. That is, the power of one branch could be opposed and therefore limited by the power of another branch.

The powers of the **governors** were checked because they could not

- collect taxes without the consent of the legislature
- imprison people without a trial by a magistrate
- set their own salaries

The **legislatures'** powers were checked by

- reliance on the governor to enforce the laws that they passed

- the power of the judges to make sure they did not make laws that violated those of England
- the veto power held in some colonies by the governor

The powers of the **judges** were checked by

- their being appointed by the governor
- the governor or legislature having the power to remove them if their decisions seemed inappropriate
- their reliance on the governor to enforce their decisions
- the basic right of every Englishman to a trial by a jury of his peers from the community

How did early colonial governments reflect the ideas of English constitutionalism?

Representative government and the right to vote. One of the most important constitutional developments during the colonial period was the growth of representative institutions in government. Representative government began soon after the first colonies were established. The first representative assembly was held in Virginia as early as 1619. The right of colonists to elect representatives was seen as a way to

- reduce the possibility that members of government would violate the people's rights
- make sure that at least a part of the government could be counted on to respond to the needs and interests of the people, or at least of those people who had the right to vote. It also established firmly the principle that those governed could not be taxed without their consent or that of their representatives.

Why did colonial governments become more representative than Britain's?

Like their English counterparts, the American colonists believed that the security of life and liberty depended on the security of property. Thus, property had to be protected. This explains why in the colonies as well as England there was a property requirement for the enjoyment of political rights like voting. If one of the purposes of government was to protect property, it seemed reasonable to limit **suffrage**—the right to vote—to those who possessed at least a small amount of property.

Fifty acres was the usual requirement for voting in the colonies. Since land was easily acquired in America, the body of eligible voters was proportionally larger than in England and the colonial legislatures were accordingly more representative. The economic opportunities in America meant that a larger proportion of colonial society enjoyed political rights than was the case in England.

There were other important differences between elections to the colonial legislatures and those to Parliament. More colonial elections offered the voters a choice of candidates. The colonial legislators were elected more frequently than members of Parliament, who usually faced reelection only once in seven years.

Unlike their British counterparts, colonial legislators usually came from the districts they represented and were considered to be the agents of their **constituents'** interests. By the time of the Revolution, members of the British Parliament, on the other hand, were said to be representative of the interests of the nation as a whole. The colonists were considered part of the British nation. Therefore, the British argued, the colonies were represented in Parliament.

Why did more people in America enjoy the right to vote than in England?

What basic rights did most Americans enjoy?

The royal charter that established the Jamestown colony in Virginia in 1607 declared that

> [T]he persons that shall dwell within the colony shall have all Liberties as if they had been abiding and born within this our realm of England or any other of our said dominions.

Similar guarantees were included in the royal charters establishing Massachusetts, Maryland, and other colonies. Such guarantees echoed the ideals of the Magna Carta—that all Englishmen, wherever they went, enjoyed certain fundamental rights, which needed to be confirmed from time to time in official documents.

Why did the American colonists believe they enjoyed the same rights they had in England?

This tradition became a fundamental part of American constitutionalism and led eventually to the U.S. Bill of Rights. The first of the colonial charters of rights was the **Massachusetts Body of Liberties**, adopted in 1641. This charter secured the rule of law and protection of basic rights of persons living in that colony against any abuse of power by the colony's magistrates. In some respects this document was America's first bill of rights.

> No man shall be arrested, restrayned, banished nor anywayes punished...unless by vertue of some express laws of the country warranting the same.

The Body of Liberties guaranteed trial by jury, free elections, and the right of free men to own property. It also made it illegal for government to take property away without fair compensation. It prohibited forced self-incrimination as well as cruel and unusual punishment, rights that later were incorporated into the

U.S. Bill of Rights. Though it limited suffrage in Massachusetts, the Body of Liberties granted nonvoters certain political rights, including the right of petition, which was to become part of the First Amendment.

Similar chartered guarantees of basic rights were later passed in other colonies. In addition to such guarantees as freedom from illegal arrest, trial by jury, and no taxation without consent, Pennsylvania's first constitution provided for freedom of conscience. By the eighteenth century all of America's colonies had come to acknowledge this basic right, though in some colonies full enjoyment of political rights remained restricted to those belonging to the established religion in the colony.

Most of these charters guaranteed rights that were familiar to English law. Sometimes they went even further than English law. The Massachusetts Body of Liberties, for example, was followed seven years later by an even more comprehensive code of laws, called **The Laws and Liberties** (1648). This code abolished the laws of primogeniture. It also provided more humane treatment of convicted criminals and debtors and simplified the judicial process.

What do *you* think?

1. Did the colonists enjoy a greater degree of representation in their local governments than British citizens had in Parliament? Why or why not?

2. Why were voting rights limited to men of property in the colonies and England despite the belief in representative government?

3. In what ways did the colonists' experience with limited self-rule for over 150 years affect their ideas about government?

Did all Americans enjoy these rights?

Not all Americans, however, enjoyed the rights that had been secured in the colonial constitutions. In some colonies the right to vote or hold office remained restricted to male Protestants, in others it was restricted to those who belonged to the established state religion.

Women were denied political rights. Colonial laws limited their ability to own property and manage their own legal and personal affairs. Although laws varied in different colonies, women usually had the legal status of

underage children. When they married, they lost most of their legal identity to their husbands. According to English law,

> *The husband and wife, are one person…the very being or legal existence of the woman is suspended during the marriage.*

There were also in the colonies a large number of **indentured servants**, most of them white, who were little better than slaves while they completed their period of service.

The most glaring example of the violation of rights was the permanent enslavement of Africans, which had become well established in the American colonies by the eighteenth century. Slaves, who made up twenty per cent of the population at the time of the Revolution, were treated as property and thus denied their basic human rights. Much of the prosperity enjoyed by colonial Americans came from slave labor.

The contradiction between the colonists' demands for liberty and their continued tolerance of slavery was often noted by the British at the time of the American Revolution. As one English observer asked, "How is it that we hear the loudest yelps for liberty among the drivers of negroes?" The Reverend Samuel Hopkins criticized his fellow Americans for "making a vain parade of being advocates for the liberties of mankind, while…you at the same time are continuing this lawless, cruel, inhuman, and abominable practice of enslaving your fellow creatures."

Critical Thinking Exercise

EVALUATING THE INSTITUTION OF SLAVERY BY USING THE NATURAL RIGHTS PHILOSOPHY

Twenty percent (700,000) of the 3,500,000 people living in the colonies in 1776 were enslaved Africans. Slavery flourished in the plantation economy of the southern colonies, but existed elsewhere and was legally recognized throughout the colonies. New York City had a significant slave population, as did New England.

There was some opposition to slavery among the population of free citizens as well as among the slaves themselves. Some opponents sought its peaceful abolition; others were willing to use violent or illegal means.

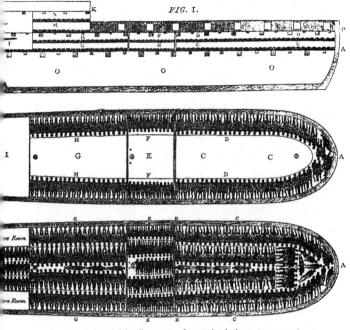

ESCRIPTION OF A SLAVE SHIP.

FIG. I.

How does this diagram of a typical slave transport vessel show the inhumanity of the slave trade?

1. How might the natural rights philosophy be used to oppose slavery in the colonies?

2. How might the supporters of slavery also have appealed to the natural rights philosophy to justify their cause?

3. Is slavery compatible with the natural rights philosophy? Explain.

How did the colonial experience prepare Americans for independence?

By the time Americans became independent, they had acquired more than 150 years of experience in self-government at the local level. Such self-government had become necessary because of the colonies' distance from the government in England. This long experience in self-government would become invaluable in building a new nation.

The colonists had adapted the governmental institutions and constitutional principles inherited from England to meet their own special needs. They had created colonial constitutions that embodied such important principles as the rule of law and a separation of powers between the executive, legislative, and judicial functions of government, thus limiting the power of government through checks and balances.

Perhaps most important to America's future were the legacies of strong representative government and written guarantees of basic rights. As they developed, colonial legislatures became more representative and independent

than the British Parliament. Colonial charters guaranteeing fundamental rights became treasured reminders of the colonists' constitutional inheritance. Together, these two traditions of representative government and written guarantees of rights would provide a basis for the American Revolution.

What do *you* think?

1. In what ways were eighteenth-century American and British societies similar or dissimilar in terms of the rights of individual liberty, equality of opportunity, and property?

2. What effect did colonial experiences have on the Founders' views about rights and government?

3. In what ways were liberty and opportunity for women and minorities restricted because of limited property rights in eighteenth-century America?

4. Do you think the same degree of social and economic opportunity exists for immigrants to America today? What has remained the same? What has changed?

Reviewing and Using the Lesson

1. What was the Mayflower Compact? Why was it drafted? How does it reflect the idea that government should be based on consent?

2. How would you describe the economic, social, and political conditions of life in colonial America? How were these conditions important in the development of American ideas about government?

3. What basic features of English constitutionalism were found in the governments of the colonies?

4. Why was the right to vote in the colonies limited to those who owned a certain amount of property? Why were colonial governments nevertheless more representative than the British government?

5. What examples can you identify of written guarantees of basic rights in colonial America? How were these written guarantees important in the development of Americans' ideas about government?

6. Do research to find out more about the controversies over slavery that existed in colonial America. What arguments were made to abolish it? What arguments were made to justify it? What actions were taken by people on each side of the issue to achieve their goals?

LESSON 8

Why Did the American Colonists Want to Free Themselves from Britain? What Basic Ideas about Government Did the Founders Put in the Declaration of Independence?

Purpose of Lesson

In this lesson you learn that the growth of the American colonies raised issues that were difficult to resolve peaceably. You consider the circumstances that produced the Declaration of Independence, as well as the major ideas about government and natural rights included in that document.

When you finish this lesson you should be able to describe British policies toward the colonies that the American colonists believed violated basic principles of constitutional government. You also should be able to explain the reasons why Americans resisted these policies and how this resistance led to the Declaration of Independence. Finally, you should be able to describe the arguments justifying the separation of the colonies from Great Britain that are found in the Declaration of Independence.

Terms to Know

Boston Tea Party
Boston Massacre
Declaration of
  Independence
First Continental
  Congress
Intolerable Acts
Minutemen

Quartering Act
Seven Years War
Sons of Liberty
sovereignty
Stamp Act Congress
Stamp Act
Tea Act
writs of assistance

What was Britain's new policy toward the colonies?

After 1763, several factors caused the British to exert more control over the American colonies than in the previous 150 years. Britain had incurred large debts in its great victory over the French in the **Seven Years War** of 1756–1763. In North America this war was known as the French and Indian War. The British government was under heavy pressure to reduce taxes at home. To the British ministers this meant the American colonists paying a fair share of the war debt.

Between the end of the war in 1763 and the Declaration of Independence in 1776, Britain tried to increase control of the colonies. To reduce tensions with the Native Americans, the British government passed a law forbidding the colonists from settling in the western territories. To raise revenue, the government increased control of trade and customs duties. The **Stamp Act** of 1765 introduced a new kind of tax on the colonists by imposing duties on stamps needed for official documents. To the British these measures seemed reasonable and moderate, but they had a common flaw. They lacked a fundamental principle of the natural rights philosophy—the consent of the governed.

Why were the colonists angered by the Stamp Act of 1765?

Why did the colonists resist British control?

Generations of colonists had grown used to very little interference from the British government in their affairs. The new policies meant a change in these conditions. Although some colonists accepted the new measures, many others resisted. New trade restrictions and taxes meant some colonists would lose money. Perhaps more important, the new regulations challenged their belief in representative government. Locke had said,

> ...the supreme power cannot take from any man any part of his property without his own consent..., that is, the consent of the majority, given it either by themselves or their representatives chosen by them.

The colonists believed that each man had a natural right to life, liberty, and property. Consequently, they thought that tax laws should only be passed in their own colonial legislatures, in which they were represented. "No taxation without representation" had become an established belief of settlers in the American colonies.

Colonists calling themselves the **Sons of Liberty** rioted against the Stamp Act. Representatives from the colonies met in the **Stamp Act Congress** to organize resistance—the first such gathering in American history. The British government's response created new grievances. For example, the **Quartering Act** of 1765 forced the colonists to shelter British soldiers in their homes. To the colonists this violated a basic guarantee of the Petition of Right.

What basic rights are violated when the government orders private citizens to "quarter" soldiers?

Writs of assistance gave government officials new powers to search and seize colonial property. Colonists charged with various crimes were transported to England for trials that were frequently delayed.

The **Boston Massacre** of 1770 helped convince many Americans that the British government was prepared to use military and arbitrary rule to force the colonists into obedience. The **Tea Act** of 1773 reasserted the right of Parliament to tax the colonists and led to the **Boston Tea Party.** The British government responded angrily with what were called the **Intolerable Acts**, closing Boston harbor to all trade. These measures attacked representative government in Massachusetts by giving more

power to the royal governor, limiting town meetings, weakening the court system, and authorizing a massive occupation of the colony by British troops.

Do you think Locke would have supported the colonists' actions in the Boston Tea Party? Why? Why not?

Critical Thinking Exercise

IDENTIFYING VIOLATIONS OF RIGHTS

Each of the following situations is based on the experiences of colonists in America. Each has at least one British violation of a right that Americans thought they should have. If you had been an American colonist at the time, what rights would you claim on the basis of such experiences?

1. Your name is Mary Strong. You have lived in Charlestown most of your life and have strong feelings about how Massachusetts is being governed. Whenever you speak your mind freely, you find yourself arrested and put in an iron device that fits over your head like a mask to prevent you from talking.

2. Your name is Elsbeth Merrill. While you were baking bread this afternoon and awaiting the return of your husband, an agent of the king arrived to inform you that you must shelter four British soldiers in your home.

3. Your name is Lemuel Adams and you have a warehouse full of goods near Boston Harbor. The king's magistrate gives British officials a writ of assistance that enables them to search all homes, stores, and warehouses by the harbor to look for evidence of smuggling.

4. Your name is James Otis. You represent colonists who have been imprisoned and are being denied their right to a trial by a jury from their own communities. You argue that to deny their traditional rights as British subjects is illegal because it violates the principles of the British constitution. The royal magistrate denies your request and sends the prisoners to England for trial.

5. Your name is William Bradford. You have been arrested and your printing press in Philadelphia destroyed for printing an article criticizing the deputy governor. In the article you said the governor was like "a large cocker spaniel about five foot five."

Should publishers be prohibited from printing criticisms of government leaders? Why? Why not?

How did the colonists organize to resist British control?

Committees of Correspondence were formed to publicize colonial opposition and coordinate resistance throughout the colonies. In the fall of 1774, twelve of the thirteen colonies sent representatives to a meeting in Philadelphia to decide on the best response to the actions of the British government. The meeting was the **First Continental Congress**. Its members agreed to impose their own ban on trade with Great Britain in an attempt to force the British government to change its policies toward the colonies. British officials, however, considered that decision an act of irresponsible defiance of authority and ordered the arrest of some leading colonists in Massachusetts.

By this time many of the more radical colonists, especially in New England, were beginning to prepare for war against Great Britain. They believed it was the right of the people to overthrow any government that no longer protected their rights. The colonists formed civilian militia of **Minutemen**, supposedly ready at a minute's notice to respond to the British attack that everyone expected.

On April 19, 1775, British troops tried to march to Concord, Massachusetts, where they had heard that the Minutemen had hidden arms and ammunition. The colonists were alerted by Paul Revere and William Dawes who rode through the countryside warning people that the British were about to attack. On that day, at the towns of Lexington and Concord, war broke out between the colonies and Great Britain—the "shot heard around the world" had been fired.

What ideas were used to justify the Revolutionary War?

What was the purpose of the Declaration of Independence?

With Americans fighting the British, Richard Henry Lee of Virginia introduced a resolution in the Continental Congress on June 7, 1776, that called for a declaration of independence.

The **Declaration of Independence** was drafted by Thomas Jefferson. The Declaration announced the final, momentous step in the colonies' resistance to the British government. It renounced that government's sovereignty over them.

Every state, no matter what its form of government or constitution, must have an authority beyond which there is no appeal. **Sovereignty** means that supreme authority in a state.

Why did colonial leaders believe a formal declaration of independence was needed?

Sovereignty in Britain rests in the British Parliament. Parliament can, as some have said, "do anything but make a man a woman." It could, if it wished, repeal the English Bill of Rights or the remaining guarantees of Magna Carta, or in other ways change Britain's unwritten constitution. Parliament would not likely use its sovereign power in such ways because of respect for the unwritten constitution by its members and by the British people as a whole.

Rebellion against the sovereignty of a government to which the colonists and generations of their forbears had sworn allegiance was a serious matter. Members of the Continental Congress believed it important to justify this action to other nations, to win both sympathy and active support.

What were the main ideas and arguments of the Declaration?

The Declaration of Independence is the best summary available of the colonists' ideas about government and their complaints about British rule. It does not make an appeal on behalf of the king's loyal subjects to the fundamental "rights of Englishmen." The Declaration renounces the monarchy itself and appeals to those natural rights common to all men and women everywhere. It identifies sovereignty with the people.

The complete text of the Declaration of Independence is in the Reference Section. These are its most important ideas and arguments:

1. The rights of the people are based on natural law, that is a higher law than laws made by men. Its existence is "self-evident." It is given by God and is "unalienable." Neither constitutions nor governments can violate this superior law. If a government violates the law and deprives the people of their rights, they have the right to change that government or abolish it and form a new government.

2. A compact or agreement existed between the colonists and the king. By the terms of this compact, the colonists consented to be governed by the king—deriving his "just powers from the consent of the Governed"—so long as he protected their rights to "life, liberty, and the pursuit of happiness."

3. "Whenever any form of government becomes destructive of those Ends" for which government is created, it is the right of the people to "alter or abolish it" and to create a new government that will serve those ends.

4. The king had violated the compact by repeatedly acting with Parliament to deprive the colonists of those rights he was supposed to protect. These violations and other abuses of power, the Declaration argued, suggest the creation of an "absolute Tyranny" over the colonies by a "Tyrant" who is "unfit to be the Ruler of a free People." He is accused of

   - seeking to destroy the authority of the colonial legislatures by dissolving some and refusing to approve the laws passed by others

   - obstructing the administration of justice by refusing to approve laws for support of the colonial judiciary and making judges dependent on his will alone

   - keeping standing armies among the people in time of peace without the approval of the colonial legislatures

   - quartering soldiers among the civilian population

   - imposing taxes without consent

   - depriving colonists of the right to trial by jury

   - attacking the colonial charters, abolishing laws, and changing fundamentally the constitutions of colonial governments.

5. The colonists therefore had the right to withdraw their consent to be governed by the king of Great Britain and to establish their own government as "Free and Independent States…absolved from all allegiance to the British Crown."

What problems did the newly independent states face?

What impact did the experience of the American Revolution have on American constitutionalism?

During the first years of independence, the grievances that had persuaded the American colonists to seek independence had an effect on how Americans shaped their state and national governments. The abuses of power by the British government made them distrustful of strong central government and strong executive power. The violation of such fundamental rights as

- freedom of speech and assembly
- trial by jury
- security from illegal search and seizure of property, and
- protection from military rule

convinced them to secure these rights by formal declarations in the new state constitutions and eventually in the U.S. Constitution.

What do *you* think?

1. The Declaration of Independence states that people have a right to abolish their government. Under what circumstances, if any, do you think such an action is justified? Would the Founders agree?

2. Would the Declaration of Independence justify a state leaving the union if a majority of its citizens wished to do so? Why or why not?

3. What was the intended audience for the Declaration of Independence? Does this focus explain the Declaration of Independence's appeal to "natural rights" instead of to "rights of Englishmen"?

Reviewing and Using the Lesson

1. How would you describe British policies toward the colonies before the 1750s? How did these policies change in the 1760s and 70s?

2. What were the colonists' objections to the new British policies? What rights did the colonists claim the policies violated?

3. How would you explain the term "sovereignty"? What was the conflict between Great Britain and the colonies over sovereignty? How was this conflict resolved?

4. What are the basic ideas and arguments set forth in the Declaration of Independence? Why was it written?

5. Imagine that you are a merchant, a farmer, a craftsman, or a royal official living in one of the American colonies in 1776. People all around are talking about fighting for independence from Great Britain; some are in favor and some are opposed. Write a speech, a letter to the editor, or a short skit expressing your views on this important issue. Be sure to explain the reasons for your position.

LESSON 9

What Basic Ideas about Government Did the State Constitutions Include? How Did the New States Protect Rights?

Purpose of Lesson

A review of the main ideas in the state constitutions will show you how the Founders designed their state governments to protect their rights and promote the common good. In this lesson you learn how the Massachusetts state constitution was uniquely designed to achieve these ends. You also learn about the bills or declarations of rights that these state constitutions included. These chartered guarantees of rights, for which Virginia's Declaration of Rights served as a model, had a great influence on the development of the U.S. Bill of Rights.

When you finish this lesson, you should be able to explain how the basic ideas about government and rights you have studied were included in state constitutions. You also should be able to explain how the experience of the states in developing their own constitutions and bills of rights influenced the framing of the U.S. Constitution and Bill of Rights.

Did the Revolution return the colonists to a state of nature? Why?

Terms to Know

absolute veto
legislative supremacy
Massachusetts state
   constitution
overriding a veto

popular sovereignty
state declarations of rights
Virginia Declaration of
   Rights

Why were the colonies returned to a "state of nature"?

In terms of the natural rights philosophy, the American Revolution returned the colonists to a state of nature. The old colonial governments under the authority of the British ceased to exist. New governments would have to be created. Soon after the Revolutionary War started in 1775, the 13 states began to develop their own written constitutions. Never before had so many new governments been created using the basic ideas of the natural rights philosophy, republicanism, and constitutional government.

What six basic ideas did the state constitutions include?

The experiments of the new American states in constitution-making provided the Framers with valuable experience that later greatly influenced their writing of the Constitution of the United States. The following basic ideas were included in these state constitutions:

- higher law and natural rights
- social contract
- popular sovereignty
- representation and the right to vote
- legislative supremacy
- checks and balances

Higher law and natural rights. Every state constitution was considered a **higher law** and was based on the idea that the purpose of government was to preserve and protect citizens' natural rights to life, liberty, and property.

Social contract. Each state constitution also made it clear that its government was formed as a result of a **social contract**—an agreement among its people to create a government to protect their natural rights.

Popular sovereignty. In all the new state constitutions sovereign authority existed in the people. The authority to govern was delegated to the government by the sovereign people.

Representation and the right to vote. One of the most significant characteristics about each state constitution was the importance it placed on **representation** of the people in their government. All the state constitutions created legislatures that were composed of elected representatives of the people. Most of these constitutions required annual elections to their legislatures.

Some state constitutions gave the right to vote for representatives to all white male taxpayers. In most states, this right was limited to people who owned a specified amount of property, as it had been when the states were colonies. Since property was relatively easy to acquire in America, about 70 percent of adult white males could vote.

In seven states, free African Americans and Native Americans could vote if they met the property requirements. In New Jersey, the vote was given to "all inhabitants…of full age, who were worth fifty pounds" and who met a twelve-month residency requirement. Under these rules, both women and free African Americans were able to vote until 1807, when the law in New Jersey was rewritten to exclude women. Twelve states specifically denied women the right to vote by inserting the word "male" in their constitutions.

Legislative supremacy. Legislative supremacy means a government in which most of the power is given to the legislature. Most state constitutions relied on a strong legislature and majority rule to protect the rights of citizens. This reliance continued a development that had begun in the colonial period when the legislatures had become strong.

All the state constitutions included some separation of powers. This reflected the former colonists' distrust of executive power which they believed had been abused under British rule.

The belief in legislative supremacy was based on the following:

- The **legislative branch** of government, composed of representatives who are elected by the voters and vulnerable to removal by the voters, is the most democratic branch of government. Therefore, in a government based on popular sovereignty it is considered the safest branch in which to place the most power and the most likely to protect the rights of citizens and promote their welfare.

- The **executive branch** should not be trusted with much power because it is not easily controlled by the people. You may remember that the colonists' greatest problems with the British government had been with its executive branch—the king's ministers and the royal governors in the colonies.

- The colonists also distrusted the **judicial branch**—the king's magistrates—who tried them for breaking British law.

The following examples of a preference for legislative supremacy can be found in the state constitutions:

- The constitutions of most of the new states provided for executive branches but made them dependent on the legislatures. Pennsylvania's new constitution eliminated the office of governor altogether and replaced it with a twelve-man council. In other states, legislatures were given the power to select the governor or to control his salary.

- Governors were allowed to stay in office for only one year. This limit was an attempt to make sure that the governor would not have time to gain much power while in office.

- Appointments made by a governor had to be approved by the legislature.

- Governors in most of the state constitutions were almost totally excluded from the process of law-making, which the legislatures kept to themselves. In all the states, the governor no longer had an **absolute veto** over legislation. He could still refuse to approve a proposed law in some states, but the legislatures in those states could **override** his veto by passing the proposed law again.

- State legislatures exercised influence over the judiciary through control of salaries and length of tenure.

Checks and balances. Although the powers in the state governments were **unbalanced** in favor of strong legislatures, there were some **checks** provided by their state constitutions. Most of these checks existed within the legislatures themselves. For example, in every state except Pennsylvania and Georgia, the legislature was divided into two houses, just as was the case in the British Parliament. Since most important decisions had to be made by both houses, each had a way to check the power of the other house. Unlike Parliament and the colonial governments, however, both houses of the new state legislatures were made up of representatives elected by the people. The voters could check the legislators' power by electing new representatives to both houses if they did not like the way the government worked.

Critical Thinking Exercise
EVALUATING LEGISLATIVE SUPREMACY

John Locke and the natural rights philosophers believed that in a representative government the legislative branch should be supreme because it was the branch closest to the people and it reflected most accurately the people's wishes. The legislative branch was, therefore, less likely to violate the people's rights.

Most of the state constitutions accepted this argument and heavily weighted the balance of power in favor of their legislatures.

1. What are the advantages and disadvantages of legislative supremacy?

2. Do you agree with Locke's argument presented above?

3. Does the legislative branch necessarily reflect the people's wishes?

4. How might the people's wishes pose a threat to basic rights?

5. Describe what a government might be like in which the executive or judicial branch was supreme.

How was the Massachusetts constitution different?

In 1780, Massachusetts became the last state to ratify a new constitution. Written principally by John Adams, the Massachusetts constitution was different from those of the other states. In addition to relying on popular representation as a means of preventing the abuse of power, it used a system of separation of powers and checks and balances. It gave government more effective checks on the powers of the state's legislature.

Since the Massachusetts constitution is more similar to the present Constitution of the United States than the other state constitutions, it is worth looking at in some detail. The following are some important characteristics of the Massachusetts constitution.

A strong executive branch. Under the Massachusetts constitution, the governor was elected by the people. The writers of this constitution believed that because the governor would be elected by the people, it would be safe to trust him with greater power so that he would be able to protect their rights and welfare.

To enable the governor to be more independent of the legislature and to allow him to check the legislature's use of power, the Massachusetts constitution contained the following provisions:

- The governor's salary was fixed and could not be changed by the legislature.

- The governor had the power to veto laws made by the legislature, and his veto could only be overridden by a two-thirds vote of the legislature.

- The governor could appoint officials to the executive branch and judges to the judicial branch.

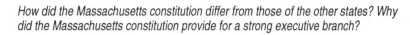

How did the Massachusetts constitution differ from those of the other states? Why did the Massachusetts constitution provide for a strong executive branch?

Representation of different groups in society. Several other parts of the Massachusetts constitution show how that government was organized more like the British model of government than were those of the other states. This state constitution separated powers among the different classes in society to prevent one group from dominating the others. The Massachusetts constitution divided the people of the state into groups based on their wealth since there was no royalty or nobility.

- Only people with a large amount of property could elect the governor.

- People with slightly less property could vote to elect members of the upper house of the state legislature.

- People with the minimum amount of property that qualified them to vote could vote for members of the lower house.

Thus, the Massachusetts state constitution expressed the classical republican ideal of mixed government. Consequently, it provided for more balance among the powers of the different branches of government. It did not make the legislature the most powerful branch as did the other state constitutions. This approach reveals different beliefs about the best ways to prevent the abuse of power by members of government.

The constitutions of the other states were based primarily on the idea that representation of the people in a strong state legislature was the best way to protect their rights. They reflected a basic trust in political power held directly by a majority of the people.

The Massachusetts constitution reflected a more skeptical view of human nature and of unchecked power held by any group in society. It was based on the idea that representation, separation of powers, and checks and balances were all essential for the protection of the rights of the people.

What do *you* think?

1. Which branch of government do you think is most responsive to the will of the people? Should that branch have more power than the other two branches? Why or why not?

2. In what ways was the Massachusetts constitution a forerunner of the U.S. Constitution?

What were the state declarations of rights?

None of the state constitutions, however, relied entirely on the form of their governments to protect individual liberties. Most of them began with a **declaration of rights**. By doing this, they indicated that the citizens to be governed by these new constitutions possessed certain basic rights that existed prior to government and that no constitution or government could take away.

Americans in the colonial era attached great importance to guarantees of basic rights. Although the lists of rights differed somewhat from state to state, they were all based on the idea that people have certain inherent rights that must be protected. It was only after safeguarding these rights at the very start that the authors of these constitutions believed it proper to form state governments.

Taken together, the rights protected in the state declarations included all the fundamental rights guaranteed today in our Bill of Rights. By looking at these declarations and how they were developed, we can learn a great deal about how we came to have the rights we enjoy today under both our state and federal constitutions.

What important ideas are in the Virginia Declaration of Rights?

On June 12, 1776, Virginia became the first state to adopt a declaration of rights, almost a month before the colonies declared their independence from Great Britain. The **Virginia Declaration of Rights** helped convince other colonies to vote for independence and influenced Thomas Jefferson's writing of the Declaration of Independence itself.

The Virginia Declaration was written primarily by George Mason (1725–1792), who later opposed the ratification of the U.S. Constitution because it did not include a bill of rights. In writing Virginia's own bill of rights, Mason relied heavily on the writings of John Locke. He also was influenced by the ideas of classical republicanism and by the American colonial experience.

The Virginia Declaration of Rights stated:

- That all power is derived from and kept by the people.

- That all men are by nature equally free and independent, and have certain inherent rights, of which, when they enter into a state of society, they cannot, by any compact, deprive or divest their posterity; namely, the enjoyment of life and liberty, with the means of acquiring and possessing property, and pursuing and obtaining happiness and safety.

- The government is, or ought to be, instituted for the common benefit, protection, and security of the people. If a government does not serve these purposes, the people have an unalienable right to alter or abolish it.

The Virginia Declaration also included many of the rights we enjoy today under both our state and federal bills of rights, such as the right to trial by jury, protection against forced self-incrimination and cruel and unusual punishments, freedom of the press, and the free exercise of religious beliefs. Concerning the right to religious freedom it stated:

> *That religion, or the duty we owe to our Creator, and the manner of discharging it, can be directed only by reason and conviction, not by force or violence; and therefore, all men are equally entitled to the free exercise of religion, according to the dictates of conscience.*

The Virginia Declaration ended with a statement based on the ideas of classical republicanism about civic virtue and religious values:

> *No free government, or the blessings of liberty, can be preserved to any people but by a firm adherence to justice, moderation, temperance, frugality, and virtue....it is the mutual duty of all to practice Christian forbearance, love, and charity, towards each other.*

The framers of the Virginia Declaration believed that listing rights and establishing a constitutional government were not enough to guarantee people their freedom. They argued that each individual must accept the responsibility to live according to certain moral principles and ideals.

It is important to note that the Virginia Declaration omitted some important rights found in other state declarations and later made part of the U.S. Constitution.

Critical Thinking Exercise

EXAMINING HISTORICAL DOCUMENTS

Work with a study partner to complete the following exercise.

1. Refer to the Virginia Declaration of Rights in the Reference Section to this text. Identify specific examples of the following basic ideas:

Natural rights	**Classical republicanism**
■ social contract	■ civic virtue
■ individual rights	■ common welfare
■ limited government	■ political rights

2. Which historical experiences of the colonists seemed to have the greatest influences on the authors of the state declarations?

3. Why do you think that, generally, state constitutions protected rights first and then created governments with limited powers?

George Mason (1725–1792)
What philosophical ideas and experiences influenced the Virginia Declaration of Rights?

What rights were protected by the other states?

Most states adopted declarations or bills of rights that resembled Virginia's. The few that did not have such declarations included guarantees of certain rights in the main body of their constitutions. Like Virginia's the other states' declarations began with statements about natural rights, popular sovereignty, and the purposes of government. Some declarations also included the idea that civic virtue and a commitment to certain moral and religious principles were essential to preserving freedom.

Other states' declarations varied in the rights they chose to include or leave out. Most included such **political guarantees** as

- the right to vote
- free and frequent elections
- freedom of speech and of the press
- the right to petition the government
- no taxation without representation

They all included important **procedural guarantees of due process** such as

- the rights to counsel and trial by jury
- protection from illegal search and seizure
- protection from forced self-incrimination, excessive bail and fines, and cruel and unusual punishment

Most of the state declarations, including Virginia's, expressed a fear of military tyranny by condemning professional standing armies in time of peace and the quartering of troops in civilian homes. Many endorsed the idea of "well regulated" civilian militia and the right to bear arms.

How did the state constitutions balance fear of military tyranny with recognition of a need for defense?

Vermont took its commitment to natural rights literally by becoming the first state to outlaw the institution of slavery.

In what ways were the state declarations different from the U.S. Bill of Rights?

The state declarations of rights would have a great influence on the later drafting and adoption of the U.S. Bill of Rights. Many states drew from their own declarations to propose the rights that should be included in the federal version. The principal writer of the U.S. Bill of Rights, James Madison of Virginia, was strongly influenced by his own state's Declaration of Rights.

The state declarations, however, differed from the U.S. Bill of Rights in many ways. They resemble more the Declaration of Independence. They were written as preambles to the state constitutions to establish the moral and philosophical foundations of the state governments. They describe the purpose of government and set forth the principles of the natural rights philosophy and classical republicanism.

The circumstances at the time prompted the authors to make these pronouncements. The state declarations were written while Americans were in the midst of fighting a revolution. The authors of these documents were principled, law-abiding citizens who wanted to explain to their fellow citizens and the rest of the world why the violation of their rights had forced them into armed rebellion.

The U.S. Bill of Rights, on the other hand, was written after independence had been won and the Constitution had created a new government for the nation. The principles of government were already established. The Framers of the Bill of Rights did not believe there was a need to list those principles again. What was needed was a list of specific rights that should be protected from this new and stronger national government. The Bill of Rights is such a list.

The Bill of Rights was to go much further than the state declarations in its guarantee of freedom of religion. Several states, as well as Virginia, provided for the free exercise of religion, but at the same time permitted state religious establishments. They allowed tax money in their states to be spent to support a particular religion or denomination. In most states there continued to be religious requirements for holding public office that excluded Roman Catholics and Jews. The Bill of Rights not only provides for freedom of religious practice, it also prohibits the federal government from passing any law for the establishment of a particular national religion. The Bill of Rights, therefore, protects **equality** as well as **freedom** of religion.

What do *you* think?

1. Why did Americans think that it was so important to have declarations of rights?

2. Do you think Americans place too much emphasis on individual rights? Explain your answer.

3. In your opinion what is the greatest challenge to individual rights today and what should be done about it?

Reviewing and Using the Lesson

1. What basic ideas about government were contained in the new state constitutions?

2. How would you explain the following terms?
   - higher law
   - popular sovereignty
   - legislative supremacy
   - checks and balances

3. What were the important differences between the Massachusetts constitution and the other state constitutions?

4. What important ideas did the Virginia Declaration of Rights contain? How was this document influential throughout the colonies?

5. Do research to find out how the original state constitutions dealt with the right to vote. What were the similarities among different states? What were the differences? What explanation can you give for these similarities and differences?

Unit Two: *How Did the Framers Create the Constitution?*

Northwest Ordinance (1787)
Philadelphia Convention (1787)
Constitution drafted (1787)

Articles of Confederation drafted (1776)

Articles of Confederation ratified (1781)

Treaty of Paris officially ends the Revolutionary War (1783)

Shays' Rebellion (1786)

| 1776 | 1777 | 1778 | 1779 | 1780 | 1781 | 1782 | 1783 | 1784 | 1785 | 1786 | 1787 |

Massachusetts adopts a state constitution, today the oldest written constitution in the world still in effect (1780)

British defeated at Yorktown (1781)

Commercial Treaty signed between Prussia and U.S. (1785)

First *Federalist* articles are published (1787)

Purpose of Unit

After declaring their independence from Great Britain, the colonists had to decide how they would govern themselves. The Articles of Confederation, which were the first attempt at establishing a government, were thought to be inadequate by leaders such as Madison, Washington, and Hamilton. Fifty-five men met in Philadelphia in 1787 and wrote and adopted the United States Constitution. These men became known as the Framers. The Constitution was not universally acclaimed, and its adoption and ratification gave rise to discussions of the most basic questions about political life and governmental institutions. In this unit, you learn why the Articles of Confederation were replaced by the Constitution. You learn the reasons the Framers created the United States government as they did. Different opinions held by Americans about the merits of the new Constitution also are presented.

LESSON 10

Why Did the Founders Want to Change the Articles of Confederation of 1781?

Purpose of Lesson

In this lesson you examine the national government formed by the Articles of Confederation. It was the first of two constitutions for a national government written between 1776 and 1787. In 1776, the Second Continental Congress voted to declare the colonies independent of the British government. The new states needed to cooperate to fight the war against the powerful British army and navy. One of the first tasks of the Congress was to organize a national government to fight the war.

The first government created by the Founders did not work well despite all their knowledge of political philosophy, history, and government. Knowing the shortcomings of that government is important in understanding that unless a government is organized properly, it may not work very well. It also helps in understanding why our government is organized as it is.

When you finish reading and discussing this lesson, you should be able to explain why the newly independent Americans created their first constitution, the Articles of Confederation, as they did. You also should be able to explain why some people thought the government under the Articles of Confederation was not strong enough.

How did independence create a need for a national government?

Terms to Know

Articles of Confederation
Second Continental
 Congress
factions
loyalists

majority rule
national government
Northwest Ordinance
Shays' Rebellion

How were the Articles of Confederation created?

In 1776, each of the newly independent states created its own government. In addition to these state governments, Americans also considered creating a **national government** to manage relationships among the states and to unite the states in their relations with the rest of the world.

A national government was necessary to control trade among the states, and between the states and foreign nations, and to manage conflicts among the states about such issues as borders.

Some leaders had seen the need for a national government for some time to deal with foreign relations and economic and commercial problems. Benjamin Franklin, who had proposed a colonial government in 1754, submitted a draft for articles of confederation to the **Second Continental Congress** in July 1775. Several other proposals were made that summer and fall, but the question of independence from Great Britain for the moment was more important than forming a national government.

On June 7, 1776, Richard Henry Lee introduced a set of resolutions to the Second Continental Congress—one was for independence, the other was to form a national government. From these resolutions came both the Declaration of Independence and the **Articles of Confederation**.

What problems were addressed in the Articles of Confederation?

Two major problems made it difficult for the Continental Congress and the states to accept the Articles of Confederation:

1. The fear of creating a national government that was too strong.

2. The fear that some states would have more power than others in a national government.

Problem 1. Fear of a strong national government. Once the war against Great Britain had started, each state was like a separate nation with its own constitution and government. To the people, their state was their "country" and all eligible voters could have a voice in government. They could elect members of their communities to represent their interests in their state legislatures. The government was close enough to most citizens so they could even participate in some of its activities.

The Founders agreed they needed a central government, but they were afraid of making one that was too strong. Americans believed that the British government had deprived people of their rights, including their right to be represented in government. They thought this was likely to happen with any central government that was both powerful and far away. Consequently, they were convinced that government should be close to the people so they could control it and make certain that it did not violate their rights. Finally, their study of history and political philosophy lead them to believe that republican government could only succeed in small communities where people shared common ideas and beliefs.

Solution: Create a weak national government. The Founders finally arrived at a solution to this problem—they created a weak national government. The government created by the Articles of Confederation was just a central legislature, the Confederation Congress. There were no executive or judicial branches. While Congress could establish courts for certain limited purposes, most legal disputes were handled in state courts. Moreover, Article II states,

> *Each state retains its sovereignty, freedoms, and independence, and every Power, jurisdiction, and right, which is not by this confederation expressly delegated to the United States, in Congress assembled.*

Why did the Founders create a weak national government?

The Articles of Confederation left most of the powers of government with the states; the national government had little power over the states and their citizens. For example:

- The Confederation Congress did not have any authority over any person in any state. Only the state governments had authority over their citizens.

- Congress did not have the power to collect taxes from the states or from the people directly. It could only request money from the state governments, which were supposed to raise the money from their citizens.

- Congress did not have the power to regulate trade among the various states.

New York State Currency
What problems might result from each state issuing its own currency?

Problem 2. Fear that some states would dominate others in the national government. The leaders in each state wanted to make sure that the new national government would be organized in a way that would not threaten their state's interests. As a result, the most important disagreement was about how states would vote in Congress. Would each state have one vote, or would states with greater population or wealth be given more votes than others? Decisions in the Congress would be made by majority vote. Some leaders were afraid that the majority would use its power for its own interest at the expense of those who were in the minority.

Solution: Give each state one vote. The solution to this problem was to give each state one vote in the Confederation Congress regardless of its population. The Articles also provided, however, that on important matters—for example whether to declare war—nine states would have to agree. This way the seven smaller states could not outvote the six larger states.

EXAMINING THE ADVANTAGES AND DISADVANTAGES OF THE ARTICLES OF CONFEDERATION

Work with a study partner, or in small groups, to complete the following exercise.

1. Read the following excerpts from the Articles of Confederation.

2. For each excerpt create a list of **advantages** to the states and/or to the national government resulting from the Article.

3. Create a second list of the **disadvantages** to the states and/or to the national government resulting from the Article.

4. When you finish, compare your lists and be prepared to share your ideas with the class.

Articles of Confederation

Article II. Each State retains it sovereignty, freedom and independence, and every power...which is not by the confederation expressly delegated to the United States, in Congress assembled.

Article V. No State shall be represented in Congress by less than two, nor more than seven members.... In determining questions in the United States, in Congress assembled, each State shall have one vote.

Article VIII. All charges of war, and all other expenses that shall be incurred for the common defense or general welfare...shall be defrayed out of a common treasury, which shall be supplied by the several States, in proportion to the value of all land within each State.... The taxes for paying that proportion shall be laid and levied by the authority and direction of the Legislatures of the several States....

Article IX. The United States in Congress assembled shall also be the last resort on appeal in all disputes and differences...between two or more States....

Article IX. The United States in Congress assembled shall also have the sole and exclusive right and power of regulating the alloy and value of coin struck by their own authority, or by that of the respective States....

Article XIII. ...nor shall any alteration at any time hereafter be made in any of [these articles]; unless such alteration be agreed to in a Congress of the United States, and be afterwards confirmed by the Legislatures of every state.

What were weaknesses in the Articles of Confederation?

On March 1, 1781, Maryland became the last state to ratify the Articles. Maryland had wanted western lands to be under the control of Congress, not of individual states. Not until New York, Connecticut, and Virginia surrendered their western claims did Maryland ratify the Articles.

You have seen how the people of the states attempted to deal with their fear of a strong national government—they created a national government that had very limited power. This reflected their belief that power that is not given is power that cannot be misused.

The limitations of the Articles of Confederation and the difficulties that arose under them led to the decision to develop our present Constitution. These limitations are described below.

1. No money and no power to get it. Congress had no power to tax. All it could do was request that state governments pay certain amounts to support the costs of the national government.

This system did not work. Congress had borrowed most of the money it needed to pay for the Revolutionary War from Americans and foreigners, but had no way to pay its debts. The state governments and many of the people living in the states were also deeply in debt after the war. Therefore, when Congress requested $10 million from the states to pay for the costs of fighting the war, the states paid only $1.5 million.

How was Congress's ability to govern hurt by not being able to collect taxes from the states?

2. No power over the state governments and their citizens. Congress did not have the power to make laws regulating the behavior of citizens or the states or to force state governments or their citizens to do anything. The citizens could be governed only by their own state governments. This meant that if members of a state government or citizens within a state disobeyed a resolution, recommendation, or request made by the national government, there was no way the national government could make them obey. The Articles clearly stated that each state kept its "sovereignty, freedom, and independence."

The national government's inability to make state governments and their citizens live up to treaties it had made led to a serious situation. Not all of the colonists had been in favor of the Revolutionary War; some had remained loyal to Great Britain. Thousands of these people, called **loyalists**, still lived in the United States. When the war was over, the national government signed a peace treaty with Great Britain called the Treaty of Paris. It was intended in part to protect loyalists' rights and ensure that they were treated fairly. Some of these loyalists owned property in the states and some had loaned money to other citizens.

Some state governments refused to respect this treaty. They often made it difficult for loyalists to collect the money owed to them by other citizens. In some cases the states had confiscated the loyalists' property during the war. The national government had no power to force the state governments to respect the property rights of the loyalists or to force individual citizens to pay back money owed to the loyalists. Thus, the national government was powerless to live up to its promise to the British government to protect the rights of these citizens.

3. Unenforceable trade agreements. Although Congress had the power to make agreements with foreign nations, it did not have the power to make state governments live up to these agreements. This raised another difficulty. Some citizens imported goods from other nations and then refused to pay for them. Not surprisingly, people in foreign countries became reluctant to trade with people in the United States. In addition, when Great Britain recognized how weak Congress was in controlling foreign trade, it closed the West Indies to American commerce. As a result, many Americans lost money because they were unable to sell their goods to people in other nations. Others were not able to buy goods from abroad.

4. Unfair competition among the states. Congress had no power to make laws regulating trade among the states. As a result, some states levied taxes on goods passing through them to other states. For example, both New York and Pennsylvania taxed goods going to New Jersey which was compared to "a keg tapped at both ends."

Such activities prevented efficient and productive trade across state lines. It also worsened the economy, which was still recovering from the devastation of the war.

5. Threats to citizens' right to property. Many people believed that one of the most serious problems in the United States during the 1780s was the failure of the state governments to protect their citizens' property rights. In most states the government was controlled by the legislative branch, composed of representatives elected by a majority of the people.

People with common interests formed **factions.** These factions sometimes formed majorities in the state legislatures. James Madison defined a faction as a group of people that seeks to promote its own interests above the interests of other individuals or groups. These groups were accused of making laws that benefited themselves at the expense of the minority and of the common good. For example, they passed laws that canceled debts and that confiscated the property of loyalists. They created paper money causing inflation that benefited debtors at the expense of their creditors.

People hurt by such laws argued that their property was not being protected by their state governments. They claimed that the state governments were being used by one class of people to deny the rights of others.

Some people argued that these problems were the result of too much democracy in the state governments. They claimed that representative government with **majority rule** did not adequately protect the natural rights of individual citizens or the common good. They argued that majority rule, when the majority pursued its own selfish interests at the expense of the rights of others, was just another form of tyranny, every bit as dangerous as that of an uncontrolled king.

What do *you* think?

1. The Articles of Confederation demonstrated a distrust of a strong national government. What were the historical and philosophical reasons for this distrust?

2. What were the positive and negative consequences of a weak national government?

3. Why do you think the smaller states were satisfied with government under the Articles of Confederation?

4. Many people today continue to distrust the federal government. In your opinion, is such distrust justified? Explain your position.

How did Shays' Rebellion sow the seeds of change?

Many people realized that the Articles of Confederation were weak, but it took a dramatic event to convince them of the need for a stronger national government. In 1786, a group of several hundred angry farmers in Massachusetts gathered under the leadership of Daniel Shays. Their intent was to attack the state government.

The farmers had serious economic problems. Those who could not pay their debts lost their homes and their farms. Some were sent to prison. Discontent arose among the people and mobs prevented the courts from selling the property of those who could not pay their debts.

Shays and his men needed weapons for their rebellion. They tried to capture the arsenal at Springfield, Massachusetts, where arms were kept for the state militia. Although Shays' men were defeated, their rebellion frightened many property owners who feared similar problems might arise in their states.

Why did Shays' Rebellion force people to examine the weaknesses of the national government?

The fears raised by such conflicts as **Shays' Rebellion,** combined with difficulties of raising revenues and regulating foreign trade, convinced a growing number of people to strengthen the national government. George Washington was one of these people. He wrote to James Madison saying, "We are either a united people or we are not. If the former, let us act as a nation. If we are not, let us no longer act a farce by pretending to it."

What were the achievements of the first national government?

Although the national government under the Articles of Confederation left much to be desired, it did accomplish a number of important things. The Revolutionary War was conducted under this government and, through the efforts of its diplomats, it secured recognition of American independence by European governments.

Molly Pitcher carried water to the troops during the Battle of Monmouth in 1778. When her husband fell from heat stroke, she took his place.

Perhaps the most lasting achievement of the Confederation government was the **Northwest Ordinance** of 1787, which defined the Northwest Territory and created a plan for its government. The ordinance provided for the transition from territory to statehood for what would become five states north of the Ohio River and east of the Mississippi. The ordinance saw to it that the states provided for education by setting aside land for that purpose, and also stated that slavery would be forever prohibited from those lands.

The Confederation Congress could make these regulations for the Northwest Territory because it had complete control over it. Yet Congress had not the slightest control over enforcing its own treaties in the 13 states. By 1787, many people had agreed that the power of Congress needed to be adjusted, because such a situation could not last. The first steps then were taken to create a stronger national government.

How did problems that arose in the Northwest Territory demonstrate the weaknesses of the new national government?

Reviewing and Using the Lesson

1. Why did the Articles of Confederation fail to provide for an executive and a judicial branch of government? How did the Articles of Confederation deal with fears that some states would dominate others in the national government?

2. What were some of the weaknesses of the Articles of Confederation? What were some of the achievements of the national government under the Articles of Confederation?

3. What was Shays' Rebellion? Why did it occur? What was its historical importance?

4. What is a "faction"? Why did some Founders consider factions to be a threat to natural rights?

5. Compare the government under the Articles of Confederation with one of the contemporary confederations of nations, e.g., the United Nations, the European Union, the Organization of American States, or the Organization of African States.

LESSON 11

Who Attended the Philadelphia Convention? What Did They Agree to Do?

Purpose of Lesson

The second U.S. Constitution was written at a convention held in Philadelphia in 1787. This lesson describes the idea of a constitutional convention, how the Philadelphia Convention came to be, some of the most important people who attended it, and some of the first steps they took to create our present Constitution.

When you complete this lesson, you should be able to describe the steps leading to the calling of the Philadelphia Convention and some of the leading Framers who attended it.

Terms to Know

Constitutional
   Convention
delegate

The Federalist
ratification
Virginia Plan

Alexander Hamilton (1757–1804)

What attempts were made to solve the problems of the Articles of Confederation?

Many political leaders, including Alexander Hamilton and James Madison, were dissatisfied with the government under the Articles of Confederation. They claimed the government was inadequate for meeting the problems of the United States.

A number of prominent leaders suggested holding a meeting of representatives of all the states. This idea of holding a special meeting or convention to discuss constitutional changes, instead of using the legislature, was an American invention. Most of the early state constitutions had been written by state legislatures. In 1780, Massachusetts became the first state to hold a constitutional convention. By 1786, Madison and other leaders decided that if a convention could be used successfully in a state, it was worth trying at the national level.

In 1786, a meeting to discuss commercial problems was held in Annapolis, Maryland. Only five states sent representatives. Disappointed at the low turnout, Hamilton, Madison, and others wrote a report asking Congress to call a meeting in Philadelphia to suggest ways to change the Articles of Confederation to strengthen the national government. Congress did so after a delay of several months. **Delegates** to the Philadelphia Convention were authorized only to propose amendments to the Articles, not to develop an entirely new constitution which is exactly what they did.

EVALUATING ALTERNATIVE POLITICAL STRATEGIES

Suppose you wanted to develop a plan to change the Constitution of the United States. Your class should be divided into two groups. Each group should adopt one of the positions. Be prepared to present and defend your assigned position.

Group 1. Position: The plan to change the Constitution should be developed by Congress and then submitted to state governments for approval.

Group 2. Position: The plan to change the Constitution should be developed at a special national convention of delegates from the states selected by their legislatures and then submitted to the people of their state for approval.

Who attended the Philadelphia Convention?

Fifty-five delegates attended the meeting that later became known as the **Philadelphia** or **Constitutional Convention**. This group of men are now often called the **Framers** of the Constitution. Most of the delegates were fairly young; the average age was 42. About three-fourths of them had served in Congress. Most were prominent in their states, and some had played important parts in the Revolution. Some were wealthy, but most were not. A French diplomat in America at the time said that the Framers "without being rich are all in easy circumstances."

Contemporary observers were impressed by the quality of the delegates to the Philadelphia Convention. Another French diplomat stationed in America observed that never before, "even in Europe," had there been "an assembly more respectable for talents, knowledge, disinterestedness, and patriotism." From Paris, Thomas Jefferson wrote to John Adams in London that the convention "is an assembly of demigods."

We should remember, however, that some of the Framers were men of modest abilities or questionable motives. Probably the most balanced view of the men at Philadelphia has been given by Max Farrand, a historian, who wrote: "Great men there were, it is true, but the convention as a whole was composed of men such as would be appointed to a similar gathering at the present time: professional men, business men, and gentlemen of leisure; patriotic statesmen and clever, scheming politicians; some trained by experience and study for the task before them; and others utterly unfit. It was essentially a representative body."

Most of the Framers' stories are worth telling in detail, but here we are limited to introducing you to those who were the most important. We also will mention some leaders who did not attend the convention but who played a part in the establishment of our constitutional government.

George Washington. George Washington was probably the most respected and honored man in the country. During the Revolutionary War, he had left Mount Vernon, his Virginia plantation, to lead the American army to victory over the British. When the war was over, Washington returned to private life. Although convinced of the necessity for a strong national government, he was not interested in holding public office.

Independence Hall where both the Declaration of Independence and the Constitution were signed.

At first Washington refused the invitation to attend the convention. He later agreed to be a delegate from Virginia, fearing that if he did not attend, people might think he had lost his faith in republican government. Washington was unanimously elected president of the convention, though he was not active in the debates. His presence and support of the Constitution, together with the widespread assumption that he would be the nation's first president, were essential to the Constitution's **ratification** by the states.

James Madison. Of all the Framers, James Madison probably had the greatest influence on the organization of the national government. Born in 1751, Madison was one of the youngest of the revolutionary leaders, but by 1787 his talents had long been recognized and admired. In 1776, at the age of 25, Madison had been elected to the Virginia convention, where he was named to a committee to frame the state constitution. There, he first displayed his lifelong commitment to freedom of religion. Madison was instrumental in persuading **George Mason**, author of the Virginia Bill of Rights, to change the clause that guaranteed "toleration" of religion to one that secured its "free exercise."

As a leader in Virginia politics and a member of the Confederation Congress, Madison was active in the 1780s in support of a stronger national government. His influence at the convention was great, in part because he brought with him a plan he had already developed for creating a new national government—the **Virginia Plan**. After much debate over alternatives, this plan was used as the basis for discussion on improving the government.

Had it not been for Madison, we probably would not know much about what happened during the convention. The Framers had decided to keep the discussions a secret, although delegates were free to take notes. Madison attended nearly every session and kept careful notes. Much of what we know today about what happened in the convention is based on his records.

After the convention, Madison collaborated with **Alexander Hamilton** and **John Jay** to write a defense of the new Constitution. This defense was a series of 85 articles written for newspapers in New York. In 1788, the articles were collected in a book called *The Federalist*. The articles urged citizens of New York to vote for delegates to the state ratifying convention who were favorable to the Constitution. *The Federalist* is probably the most important work written on the basic principles and ideas underlying our constitutional government.

What other important delegates attended?

In addition to Washington and Madison, the delegates included many other prominent men. **Benjamin Franklin** was 81 and in poor health, but because he was internationally respected, his mere presence lent an aura of wisdom to the convention. **Alexander Hamilton**, although one of the strongest supporters of a strong national government, was outvoted within his own state delegation and left in frustration before the convention was half over. He returned for a few days and he signed the completed document in September. Hamilton played a major role in the struggle over ratification, as a principal author of *The Federalist* and as the leader of pro-Constitution forces in New York. **James Wilson**, although not as well known as Madison or Hamilton, was also a major influence in shaping the theory of the Constitution. Later, Wilson would lead the Federalist forces in Pennsylvania, and in 1789 President Washington appointed him a justice of the Supreme Court.

George Washington
(1732–1799)

James Madison
(1751–1836)

James Wilson
(1742–1798)

Elbridge Gerry
(1744–1814)

Roger Sherman
(1721–1793)

Edmund Randolph
(1753–1813)

Besides Madison and Wilson, the delegate who spoke most frequently at the convention was **Gouverneur Morris** of Pennsylvania. **Edmund Randolph**, who as Governor of Virginia was officially the head of the Virginia delegation, introduced the Virginia Plan into the convention. Randolph, however, refused to sign the completed document. **Roger Sherman** of Connecticut was instrumental in forging the "Connecticut Compromise" on representation in Congress. **George Mason**, author of the Virginia Bill of Rights, believed that the national constitution also should contain explicit guarantees of fundamental rights. Like Randolph, he did not sign the Constitution. **Elbridge Gerry**, who also refused to sign the Constitution, later led the forces against ratification in Massachusetts. Later still, he served as vice president under President James Madison.

What important Founders did not attend the convention?

There also were some important political leaders who did not attend the Constitutional Convention.

Thomas Jefferson was in Paris as U.S. ambassador to France. **John Adams**, who was serving as U.S. ambassador to Great Britain, was recognized as a leading American political thinker. Adams had been a principal architect of the Massachusetts constitution of 1780. The first volume of his *Defence of the Constitutions of Government of the United States of America* had also appeared in early 1787.

Patrick Henry, the revolutionary leader, refused to attend the convention. He was against the development of a strong national government and was suspicious of what might happen at the convention. He supposedly said later that he had "smelt a rat."

Other leaders not present at Philadelphia included **John Hancock**, **Samuel Adams**, and **Richard Henry Lee**. Besides these prominent individuals, one state—Rhode Island—refused to be represented at the convention.

What do *you* think?

1. In what ways were the Framers representative of the American people in 1787? In what ways were they not?

   a. What criteria would you use to select a group of people to draft a constitution today?

   b. Explain any advantages and disadvantages that might result from using your criteria to select people to write a constitution compared with the group of Framers who actually wrote our Constitution.

   c. Are there any groups whose interests you feel do not need to be represented? Why or why not?

2. Would you agree with Thomas Jefferson's characterization of the Philadelphia Convention as an "assembly of demigods"? Explain your answer.

Why did the delegates to the Constitutional Convention decide to keep their deliberations secret?

What happened when the convention began?

By Friday, May 25, 1787, eleven days after the convention was scheduled to begin, delegations from a majority of the states were present in Philadelphia. George Washington was unanimously elected president of the convention, and a committee was appointed to draw up the rules for the meeting.

Once the rules were agreed on, the convention got to work. Almost immediately, the Framers decided to ignore their instructions from Congress to limit their work to amending the Articles of Confederation. Instead, they voted to work on the development of an entirely new constitution.

The Framers decided that what was said in the convention should be kept secret. There were two reasons for this.

- The Framers wanted to develop the best constitution they could. This required a free exchange of ideas. They were afraid that if their debates were made public, many of the delegates would not feel free to express their real opinions.

- The Framers thought the new constitution would have a greater chance of being accepted if people did not know about the arguments that went on while it was being created.

The Framers agreed that each state would have one vote at the convention, even though their delegations varied in size. They also agreed that a member could not be absent from the convention without permission if it would deprive a state of its vote. In addition, they adopted a rule making it possible to reconsider issues freely. This way no decision had to be made permanent until the entire plan was completed.

What do *you* think?

1. Were the members of the convention right to ignore their original instructions? Why?

2. Should the debates at the Constitutional Convention have been open to the public? Why?

Reviewing and Using the Lesson

1. Why did Congress call for a constitutional convention? What did Congress authorize the delegates to the Philadelphia Convention to do?

2. How would you describe the delegates to the Philadelphia Convention? What prominent political leaders attended?

3. Why did the delegates to the Philadelphia Convention decide to conduct their deliberations in secret?

4. In recent years there have been calls for a constitutional convention. If such a convention were to be held today, what should be the make-up of its members? List the characteristics desirable in members attending a contemporary constitutional convention.

LESSON 12

Why Did the Framers Use the Virginia Plan to Create the Constitution?

Purpose of Lesson

Both the Virginia and the New Jersey delegates to the Philadelphia Convention submitted plans to organize the new national government for the Framers' consideration. After considerable debate, the Virginia Plan was used as the basis for the new Constitution. Not all the recommendations in the plan were accepted. An understanding of both plans and the debates over them should increase your understanding of the Constitution and the continuing debates over how our government is organized.

When you finish this lesson, you should be able to explain the differences between the Virginia and the New Jersey Plans. You also should be able to explain why the Virginia Plan was used as the basis of our Constitution.

Terms to Know

equal representation
federal system
proportional
   representation

New Jersey Plan
Virginia Plan

What was the Virginia Plan?

Many delegates came to Philadelphia convinced that the defects of the Articles were so serious it would be better not to use them as a starting point. One of these was James Madison. Before the convention, he already had drafted a plan for a new national government, which came to be called the **Virginia Plan**. While they waited for the other state delegations to arrive, the Virginia delegates had agreed to put Madison's plan forward as a basis for the convention's discussions.

The most important thing to know about the Virginia Plan is that it proposed a strong national government. Under the Articles of Confederation, the national government could act only on the states, not on the people directly. For example, the national government could request money, but only the states had the authority to raise that money through taxes.

Under the Virginia Plan, the national government would have the power to make and enforce its own laws, and to collect its own taxes. Each citizen would be governed under the authority of two governments, the national government and a state government. Both governments would get their authority from the people. The existence of two governments, national and state, each given a certain amount of authority, is what we now call a **federal system**. In addition, the Virginia Plan recommended the following:

- Three branches—**legislative, executive, and judicial**—would compose the national government. The legislative branch would be more powerful than the other branches because, among other things, it would have the power to select people to serve in the executive and judicial branches.

- The national legislature, Congress, was to have two houses. A **House of Representatives** would be elected directly by the people of each state. A **Senate** would be elected by the members of the House of Representatives from lists of persons nominated by the legislature of each state.

- The number of representatives from each state in both the House and the Senate would be based on the size of its population or the amount of its contribution to the federal treasury. This system of **proportional representation** meant that states with larger populations would have more representatives in the legislature than states with smaller populations.

The Virginia Plan gave the legislative branch of the national government the following powers:

- to make all laws that individual states were not able to make, such as laws regulating trade between two or more states

- to strike down state laws that it considered to be in violation of the national constitution or the national interest

- to call forth the armed forces of the nation against a state, if necessary, to enforce the laws passed by Congress

- to elect people to serve in the executive and judicial branches of government

What do *you* think?

1. What are the advantages and disadvantages of having two houses of Congress? Explain what position you would take on this question.

2. Why do you suppose the Virginia Plan gave Congress the power to strike down laws made by state legislatures? What arguments could you make for or against giving Congress this power?

3. In what ways does the Virginia Plan correct what the Framers perceived to be weaknesses in the Articles of Confederation?

How did the Framers react to the Virginia Plan?

There was considerable debate among the Framers over the Virginia Plan. In the early weeks of the convention, as specific features of the plan were discussed, a major disagreement over representation became apparent.

■ The larger states wanted both houses of the national legislature to be based on proportional representation. They argued that a government that both acted on and represented the people should give equal voting power to equal numbers of people.

■ The smaller states wanted **equal representation**— equal voting power for each state. Their position was based on their fear that unless they had an equal voice, as they did under the Articles of Confederation, the larger states would dominate them.

By mid-June this disagreement had created a crisis for the convention. The delegates from the small states, led by **William Paterson** of New Jersey, asked for time to come up with an alternative to the Virginia Plan.

What was the New Jersey Plan?

On June 15, Paterson presented the small states' plan, which has become known as the **New Jersey Plan**. The small states did not wish to create a national government in which they had little power. They argued that the best and safest thing to do would be to keep the framework of the Articles of Confederation, as they had been asked to do. The following are some of the main parts of the plan.

1. **Legislative branch**. Congress would have only one house, as in the Confederation, and it would be given the following increased powers:

   ■ **Taxes**. The national government would be given the power to levy import duties and a stamp tax to raise money for its operations, together with the power to collect money from the states if they refused to pay.

   ■ **Trade**. Congress would be given the power to regulate trade among the states and with other nations.

   ■ **Control over the states**. The laws and treaties made by Congress would be considered the supreme law of the land. No state could make laws that were contrary to them.

Why were delegates from small states suspicious of the Virginia Plan?

2. **Executive branch**. This branch would be made up of several persons appointed by Congress. They would have the power to administer national laws, appoint other executive officials, and direct all military operations.

3. **Judicial branch**. A supreme court would be appointed by the officials of the executive branch. It would have the power to decide cases involving treaties, trade among the states or with other nations, and the collection of taxes.

Critical Thinking Exercise
DEVELOPING AND DEFENDING POSITIONS

The Virginia and New Jersey Plans each had certain benefits and costs. Understanding these is helpful in making intelligent decisions about which is the better plan. Work in small groups to identify and describe the benefits and costs of each plan and list them on a chart similar to the one below. Select the plan that your group thinks would make a better government. Be prepared to explain and defend the reasons for your decision.

Virginia Plan		New Jersey Plan	
Benefits	Costs	Benefits	Costs

Why was the Virginia Plan used?

The New Jersey Plan continued the system of government existing under the Articles of Confederation. In this system, the national government represented and acted upon the states rather than directly representing and acting upon the people. The New Jersey Plan did contain useful suggestions to solve some weaknesses of the Articles of Confederation. By the time the New Jersey Plan was presented, after two weeks of debate on the Virginia Plan, many delegates had become convinced that the national government needed new powers and a new organization for exercising those powers.

When the vote was taken on June 19, the New Jersey Plan was supported by the delegations from New Jersey and Delaware, by a majority of the New York delegation since Hamilton was always outvoted by his two colleagues, and by half the Maryland delegation. So, the Virginia Plan continued to be the basis for the convention's discussion.

A number of major issues had not been resolved, however. Among them were two potentially explosive ones.

■ How should the number of representatives from each state be determined? According to population? Many delegates still argued that each state should have an equal vote, no matter how large or small its population.

■ What powers should the national government have?

There were serious disagreements among the delegates. These disagreements were so intense that the convention nearly failed.

Reviewing and Using the Lesson

1. Why is it said the delegates to the Philadelphia Convention ignored their instructions?

2. What was the conflict between larger and smaller states over representation in Congress? Which states favored equal representation, and which favored proportional representation? What is the difference between equal and proportional representation?

3. What were the important differences between the Virginia Plan and the New Jersey Plan? Why did the Framers decide to work with the Virginia Plan?

4. Research the history of proportional representation in the United States and explain the changes in how United States senators are now selected.

LESSON 13

What Powers Were Granted to the Legislative Branch?

Purpose of Lesson

This lesson describes the basic organization of Congress. It explains why Congress was organized into two houses, why representation in the House of Representatives is based on population, and why each state selects two senators. The lesson also describes some powers of Congress as well as some limitations on its powers. It concludes with a discussion of the issues that caused disagreement between the southern and northern delegates.

When you complete this lesson, you should be able to explain how and why the present system of representation in Congress was adopted and the major powers of Congress. You should also be able to explain the major areas of contention between the northern and southern states and how they were settled.

Terms to Know

apportioned
bills of attainder
enumerated powers
equal [state]
  representation
ex post facto laws
fugitive slave clause
The Great (or Connecticut)
  Compromise

impeach
necessary and proper clause
proportional representation
separated powers
supremacy clause
treason

How should the legislative branch be organized?

After agreeing to use James Madison's Virginia Plan as the starting point for discussion of a new constitution, the Framers still faced two major decisions: they had to decide what powers to give the new government and how to organize the new government.

The Framers believed that the most important role would be held by the legislative branch. That is why Article I of the Constitution deals with the legislative branch. The first debates, therefore, were about the duties and powers that should be given to Congress and how it should be organized. The Framers encountered problems in developing Article I that are still being debated today.

What were the disagreements about representation?

Continuing the British and colonial practice of two-house legislatures, every state except Pennsylvania had a legislative branch with two houses. There also was a widespread belief that a two-house legislature would be less likely to violate the people's rights. Each house could serve as a check on the other.

The Virginia Plan's proposal to create a two-house Congress was not controversial. What was controversial in the plan was the principle of **proportional representation**. James Madison, James Wilson, Rufus King, and others who represented states with large populations, thought that the number of members in both houses should be based on the number of people they would represent. They argued that because the new government would operate directly on the people, it was only fair that a state with a larger number of people should have a greater voice, that is, more votes, in the national government.

The delegates from states with smaller populations were afraid that proportional representation would result in a national government dominated by the more populated states. They argued that each state should have the same number of representatives in Congress, **equal representation**. These delegates also were convinced that the people of their states would never approve the Constitution if it did not preserve equality among the states.

On July 2, the Framers voted on whether there should be equal representation in the upper house of Congress. The result was a tie, five states to five, with Georgia divided. Neither side seemed willing to compromise, and delegates began to fear that the convention would end in disagreement and failure.

Then a special committee, composed of one delegate from each state, was formed. This committee was responsible for developing a plan to save the situation. Some supporters of the Virginia Plan, including James Madison and James Wilson, were against giving this responsibility to a committee. Most of the Framers disagreed with them, however, and the committee went to work.

DEVELOPING AND DEFENDING PLANS FOR REPRESENTATION

Your class should be divided into committees of about five students each. Each committee should have some students who represent small states and some who represent large states. The task of each committee is as follows:

1. Develop a plan for how many representatives each state should be allowed to send to the Senate and to the House of Representatives. Your committee may decide, of course, that there is no need for a two-house Congress and that a single house will represent the people most effectively.

2. Select a spokesperson to present your committee's plan to the entire class. Then all members of the committee may help to defend its plan against criticisms by members of other committees.

3. Following the presentation of all the plans, each committee may revise its original plan if it wishes.

The entire class should then examine the plans made by all the committees and try to reach agreement on a plan.

Compare the plans of the committees and the final class plan with the plan of the Framers described in the next section.

What was the Great Compromise?

The result of the special committee's work is known as the **Connecticut Compromise** or the **Great Compromise**. The committee adopted a proposal previously suggested by Connecticut delegates Roger Sherman and Oliver Ellsworth. The Great Compromise contained the following ideas:

- The **House of Representatives** would be elected by the people on the basis of **proportional representation**.

- There would be **equal representation** of each state in the **Senate**. The legislature of each state would select two senators.

- The House of Representatives would be given the power to develop all bills for taxing and government spending. "Direct" taxes would be assigned and divided—**apportioned**—among the states by population. The Senate was limited to either accepting or rejecting these bills, but it could not change them. This provision was later changed to permit the Senate to amend tax bills developed in the House and to develop appropriation bills itself.

As in most compromises, each side gained a little and lost a little. The small states received the equal representation in the Senate that their delegates wanted

How did the Connecticut Compromise resolve differences in the Virginia and New Jersey Plans?

to protect their interests. Many delegates also believed that a constitution without equal representation of states in at least one house of Congress would not be approved by the smaller states. The large states gave up control of the Senate but kept their control of the House of Representatives. The House was also given important powers regarding taxation and government spending.

The result was that the more populous states would have more influence over laws to tax the people and over how the money would be spent. The larger states also would pay the larger share of any direct taxes imposed by Congress. The decisions of the House of Representatives, however, always would be subject to the check of the Senate, in which the small states had equal representation.

When the committee presented this compromise to the convention, it was bitterly fought by some members from the larger states, including Madison, Wilson, and Gouverneur Morris. They viewed the idea of state equality in the Senate as a step away from a national government, back toward the system under the Articles of Confederation. Delegates from the small states remained suspicious as well. Two delegates from New York, who had consistently voted with the smaller states, left the convention and did not return. The crisis was over when the compromise passed by one vote.

What do *you* think?

1. Are there good arguments today in support of continuing to divide Congress into two bodies, a Senate and a House of Representatives? If so, what are they?

2. What contemporary issues do you know about that involve conflict over the fairness of representation in Congress?

3. Why should senators be selected for six years and members of the House of Representatives for only two years? Do you think members of the House of Representatives would more effectively represent their constituents if they could serve longer terms?

What powers did the Constitution give to Congress?

The Framers intended the new government to be a government of **enumerated**—specifically listed—powers. They thought it was important to list the powers of each branch of government so that there would not be any confusion about what they could and could not do.

Most of the powers of Congress are listed in Article I, Section 8 of the Constitution. It includes such important matters as the power

- to lay and collect taxes
- to pay the debts and provide for the common defense and general welfare of the United States
- to regulate commerce with foreign nations, and among the several states
- to declare war
- to raise an army and navy
- to coin money

The Framers also intended the new system to be a government of **separated powers**, or, as political scientist Richard Neustadt has called it, "a government of separated institutions sharing powers."

Each branch of the government is given powers that enable it to check the use of power by the others. In Article I, Congress was given the power

- to **impeach** the president, other executive branch officials, or members of the federal judiciary and remove them from office.

Why did the Framers make it difficult to impeach government officials?

The executive and judicial branches also have checks, or controls, on Congress. The Framers specifically gave Congress the power to make all other laws that are "necessary and proper" for carrying out the enumerated powers. This is called the **necessary and proper clause**.

What power did the national government have over state governments and the people?

One reason the Framers agreed to meet in Philadelphia was their concern about some things that state governments were doing. They believed that some states were undermining Congress's efforts to conduct foreign relations, and they feared that, in others, individual rights might be threatened by the state governments. They also knew that the national government had no power to enforce its decisions. The Framers all agreed they had to create a national government with more power than the government had under the Articles of Confederation. They did not agree, however, about how much power the new national government should have over citizens and the state governments.

The Framers resolved their disagreements by establishing a **national government** with authority to act directly on the people in certain specific areas. The national government no longer would be dependent on the states for income or for law enforcement. The state governments, however, would keep many of the more important powers over people's daily lives. The states would keep their powers over education, family law, property regulations, and most aspects of everyday life. The people would not feel they had surrendered too much power to a distant government.

The Framers included a number of phrases in the Constitution that set forth the powers of the national government. They also included phrases that limited the power of both the national government and state governments. Some of the more important of these are listed below.

1. **Some powers of the national government**.

    ■ The **supremacy clause** says that the Constitution and all laws and treaties approved by Congress in exercising its enumerated powers are the supreme law of the land. It also says that judges in state courts must follow the Constitution, or federal laws and treaties, if there is a conflict with state law.

    ■ Article I, Section 8 gives Congress power to organize the militia of the states and to set a procedure for calling the militia into national service when needed.

    ■ Article IV, Section 3 gives Congress the power to create new states.

    ■ Article IV, Section 4 gives the national government the authority to guarantee to each state a **republican** form of government.

Why did the Framers believe it was necessary to maintain a national armed force?

    ■ Article IV, Section 4 also requires the national government to protect the states from invasion or domestic violence.

2. **Limits on power of the national government**. The Constitution includes several limitations on the power of the national government.

    ■ Article I, Section 9 prohibits the national government from

        a. banning the slave trade before 1808
        b. suspending the privilege of the **writ of habeas corpus** except in emergencies
        c. passing any **ex post facto laws**, laws that make an act a crime even though it was legal at the time it was committed
        d. passing any **bills of attainder**, laws that declare a person guilty of a crime and decrees a punishment without a judicial trial
        e. taxing anything exported from a state
        f. taking money from the treasury without an appropriation law
        g. granting titles of nobility

    ■ Article III defines the crime of **treason** and prohibits Congress from punishing the descendants of a person convicted of treason.

    ■ Article VI prohibits the national government from requiring public officials to hold any particular religious beliefs.

Why was it important to have only one monetary system for the nation?

3. Limits on powers of state governments

- Article I prohibits state governments from
    a. creating their own money
    b. passing laws that enable people to violate contracts, such as those between creditors and debtors
    c. making ex post facto laws or bills of attainder
    d. entering into treaties with foreign nations or declaring war
    e. granting titles of nobility

- Article IV prohibits states from
    a. unfairly discriminating against citizens of other states
    b. refusing to return fugitives from justice to the states from which they have fled

What issues separated the northern and southern states?

The Great Compromise had settled the disagreement between large and small states over how they would be represented in Congress. Many other issues still had to be resolved. Two of the most critical disagreements were those between the southern and northern states on the issues of slavery and regulation of commerce.

Slavery had been practiced for almost as long as there had been colonies in America. Many Framers were opposed to slavery, and some northern states had begun to take steps toward abolishing it. Still, in the south, slave labor was widely used in producing crops. Slaveholders considered their slaves to be personal property, and wanted to continue using them.

Delegates from the southern states told the convention that their states would not ratify a constitution that denied citizens the right to import and keep slaves. If the Constitution interfered with slavery, North Carolina, South Carolina, and Georgia made it clear that they

would not become part of the new nation. Some delegates from the New England states, whose shipping interests profited from the slave trade, were sympathetic to the southern position.

What compromises were made to persuade the southern states to sign the Constitution?

After considerable debate, the Framers agreed on a way to satisfy both northern and southern delegates. This agreement gave Congress the power to regulate commerce between the states, which the northern states wanted. The delegates defeated a southern attempt to require a two-thirds vote of both houses to pass laws regulating commerce. To satisfy the southern states, the Constitution provided that the national government would not interfere with the slave trade earlier than 1808.

The Framers also agreed that each slave would be counted as three-fifths of a person when determining how many representatives a state could send to the House of Representatives. Each slave also would be counted as three-fifths of a person when computing direct taxes. The **fugitive slave clause** of Article IV was another concession to the southern states. It provided that slaves who escaped to other states must be returned to their owners.

$100 REWARD
RANAWAY

From the undersigned, living on Curre River, about twelve miles above Donipha in Ripley County, Mo., on 2nd of March, 1860, **A NE GRO MAN,** about 30 years old, weighs ab 160 pounds; high forehead, with a scar on it; had on brown pants and c very much worn, and an old black wool hat; shoes size No. 11.

The above reward will be given to any person who may apprehend t said negro out of the State; and fifty dollars if apprehended in this State outside of Ripley county, or $25 if taken in Ripley county.
APOS TUCKER.

Why did the Framers give constitutional protection to slavery?

Critical Thinking Exercise
EXAMINING NORTHERN AND SOUTHERN POSITIONS ON SLAVERY

The words "slave" and "slavery" are never used in the Constitution. Although the delegates voted to give constitutional protection to slavery, many of them were not proud of having done so. They considered it to be a necessary evil, at best, and many hoped it would go away by itself, if left alone. As we now know, this protection of slavery almost destroyed the United States.

Work in small groups to develop positions on the following questions from both a northern and southern perspective. Then develop a position on the final question.

1. What arguments could have been made for or against the Framers' decision to include the value of property, including enslaved Africans, in calculating the number of representatives a state should have? Should property in the form of enslaved Africans have been treated differently from other forms of property?

2. Should the settling of fundamental issues, such as whether to allow slavery, have been left up to each state?

3. What problems, if any, arise from trying to make judgments about positions that were taken 200 years ago?

What do *you* think?

1. Why did northern delegates, some from states which had abolished slavery, vote for compromises which maintained the institution of slavery? Would you have done the same? Why or why not?

2. What disagreements might arise over the interpretation of the clause that says Congress has the power to make all laws necessary and proper for fulfilling its responsibilities as outlined in the Constitution. Why?

Reviewing and Using the Lesson

1. Why did the Framers appoint a special committee to deal with the issue of representation? How was the committee organized?

2. What was the Connecticut Compromise or Great Compromise? How did it resolve the conflict over representation?

3. What is meant by "enumerated powers"? Why did the Framers decide to specifically enumerate the powers granted to Congress?

4. What is the "necessary and proper clause"?

5. What is the "supremacy clause"?

6. How did the Framers deal with the issue of slavery? Why did they choose to take the approach they did?

7. Examine Article I, Section 8 of the Constitution. List any powers of Congress that are not included that you believe should be.

LESSON 14

What Powers Were Granted to the Executive and Judicial Branches?

Purpose of Lesson

This lesson explains why the Framers thought that the executive and judicial branches were needed in the new government and how they organized those branches. It also describes the difficulties the delegates had in deciding how best to control the power of the executive, and how and why they created an unusual way of selecting the president. In addition, it describes the responsibilities given to the judicial branch and considers some of the powers of both branches that were not directly given in the Constitution, such as the power of judicial review.

When you finish this lesson, you should be able to explain how the Constitution organizes the executive and judicial branches. This should include an explanation of the limits on the powers of the executive.

Terms to Know

appellate jurisdiction	impeach
balance of power	judicial review
electoral college	legislative power
electors	original jurisdiction
executive power	veto
executive departments	

Why did the Framers want to limit executive power?

The Articles of Confederation did not provide for an executive branch, but the Confederation Congress had found it necessary to create executive officials for specific purposes. The Framers wanted to give the executive branch of the new government enough power and independence to fulfill its responsibilities. They did not, however, want to give the executive any power or independence that could be abused. Americans and Englishmen believed that the king, through the use of bribes and special favors, had been able to control elections and exercise too much influence over Parliament. The British constitution permitted members of Parliament to hold other offices at the same time, and even today members of the executive branch, such as the prime minister, are also members of Parliament. In the eighteenth century, the Crown used its exclusive power to appoint people to office to reward friendly members of Parliament.

The Framers thought these actions upset the proper **balance of power** between the monarch and Parliament. It was the destruction of this balance that Americans referred to when they spoke of the corruption of Parliament by the Crown. They also believed that royal governors had tried to corrupt colonial legislatures in the same way.

This destruction of the proper balance of power among different branches of government, many Americans thought, led to tyranny. Consequently, it is not surprising that, after their experience with the king and his royal governors, the Americans provided for very weak executive branches in most of the state constitutions. This, however, created other difficulties. The weak executives were unable to check the powers of the state legislatures. These legislatures passed laws that, in the opinion of many, violated basic rights, such as the right to property.

The problem that faced the Framers, then, was how to create a system of government with balanced powers. They wanted to strengthen the executive branch without making it so strong that it could destroy the balance of power among the branches and thus endanger the rights of the people.

What basic questions did organizing the executive branch raise?

The Framers had to resolve a number of basic questions in organizing the executive branch. Each question concerned the best way to establish an executive branch strong enough to balance the power of the legislature, but not so powerful it would endanger democratic government.

Single or plural executive. Should there be more than one chief executive? The Framers agreed that there should be a single executive to avoid the possible problem of conflict between two or more leaders of equal power. Some delegates also argued that it would be easier for Congress to keep a watchful eye on a single executive. On the other hand, those who argued for a plural executive claimed that such an executive would be less likely to become tyrannical.

Term of office. How long should the chief executive remain in his position? The convention considered a seven-year term for the president, but many delegates thought seven years too long. The final decision was to set the term of office at four years.

Reelection. Should the executive be eligible for reelection? Under the original proposal for a seven-year term of office, the president would not have been eligible for reelection. When the term was reduced to four years. the Framers decided to allow the president to run again. The Constitution originally set no limit on the number of times a president could be reelected. The Twenty-second Amendment, passed in 1951, however, sets the limit at two terms.

What powers should be given to the president?

The most important question the Framers faced was what the powers of the executive branch would be. The **executive powers** include the responsibilities for

- carrying out and enforcing laws made by Congress
- nominating people for federal offices
- negotiating treaties with other nations
- conducting wars

In addition, the president is given the power

- to pardon people convicted of crimes
- to send and receive ambassadors to and from other countries

Although the Framers thought the executive branch should have enough power to fulfill its responsibilities, they also wanted to be sure it did not have too much power. They limited the powers of both the executive branch and the legislative branch by making them share many of their powers. This was intended to keep the powers balanced and to provide each branch with a way to check the use of power by the other branch. This sharing of powers was accomplished in the following ways:

- **Veto**. The president shares in the **legislative power** through the **veto**. Although the president can veto a bill passed by Congress, the bill can still become a law if two-thirds of both houses of Congress vote to override the veto.

- **Appointments**. The power to appoint executive branch officials and federal judges is shared with Congress. The president has the power to nominate persons to fill those positions, but the Senate has the right to approve or disapprove of the persons nominated. To prevent corruption of Congress, members of Congress are not allowed to hold another federal office.

The nation celebrates the swearing in of the first president, George Washington.

- **Treaties**. The power to make treaties also is shared. The president has the power to negotiate a treaty with another nation, but the treaty must be approved by a two-thirds vote of the Senate.

- **War**. Although the president is commander in chief, only Congress has the power to declare war. Congress also controls the money necessary to wage a war. Therefore, the power to declare and wage war also is shared.

Why did the Framers limit the power of the president to wage war?

Although it includes several important powers, Article II seems short and vague when compared with Article I. It speaks of "executive power" but does not define it. **Executive departments** are mentioned, but there are no provisions for creating them, deciding how many there should be, or how they should operate.

By comparison, Article I included a specific list of "legislative powers" granted by the Constitution. The veto power appears in Article I, Section 7, although the term is not used. Article II, Section 3 states that the president has the duty to suggest legislation. These are examples of the executive sharing the legislative power.

The Constitution also gives Congress the power to **impeach** the president, members of the executive branch, and federal judges. Only the House of Representatives can bring the charges. The Senate holds a trial to determine the official's guilt or innocence. If found guilty by two-thirds of the Senate, the official will be removed from office.

The Framers had some experience with elected executives in the states, yet they could not be sure exactly what the presidency of the United States should be like. Many decisions were left to Congress. The Framers also trusted George Washington, who was almost universally expected to become the first president. They thought that he could be counted on to fill in the Constitution's gaps and set wise examples that would be followed by later presidents.

Critical Thinking Exercise
IDENTIFYING THE POWERS OF THE PRESIDENT TO INFLUENCE LEGISLATION

The president has the power to veto bills passed by Congress and the power to recommend to Congress legislation that he considers "necessary and expedient." Answer the following questions. It may be helpful to consider some things that have changed since the Constitution was written.

1. In what other ways can a president have an influence on legislation being considered in Congress?

2. Does the party system give a president more influence in Congress when he is a member of the majority party?

3. Has the presence of television increased the power of the presidency and weakened that of Congress?

How should presidents be selected?

The main alternatives debated by the Framers were to have the president selected **indirectly** or **directly** by a majority vote of the people. Among the indirect methods they considered were selection by

- Congress
- state legislatures
- state governors
- a temporary group elected for that purpose

The Framers knew that the group with the power to select the president would have great power over the person who held the office. They were concerned that this power might be used to benefit some people at the expense of others. It might also make it difficult for the president to function properly.

If Congress were given the power to choose the president, then limiting the term of office to a single, long term would be a way to protect the president from being manipulated by Congress in order to get reelected. This is why the Framers also decided that Congress could neither increase nor decrease the president's salary once in office.

If a president were **not** chosen by Congress, then providing for a shorter term of office would make the president more accountable to the people. Reelection then would be the will of the people and the president could run for reelection many times.

The problem was given to a committee to develop a plan that a majority of the Framers would support. The committee's plan was a clever compromise. It did not give any existing group the power to select the president. The plan shows that the Framers did not trust any group —the people, the state legislatures, or Congress—to make the selection. In such a large country, the people could not be personally familiar with the candidates and their qualifications, in the Framers' judgment. The state legislatures and Congress, they thought, might use their power to upset the balance of power between the national and state governments, or between the executive and legislative branches.

Instead, the committee proposed what we now call the **electoral college**, which would have the responsibility of electing the president. The main parts of this plan are described below.

- The electoral college would be organized once every four years to select a president. After the election, the college would be dissolved.

- Each state would select members of the electoral college, called **electors**.

- Each state would have the same number of electors as it had senators and representatives in Congress. The method for choosing electors would be decided on by the state legislature.

- Each elector would vote for **two people**, one of whom had to be a resident of another state. This forced the elector to vote for at least one person who might not represent his particular state's interests.

- The person who received the highest number of votes, if it was a majority of the electors, would become president. The person who received the next largest number of votes would become vice president.

- If two people received a majority vote, or if no one received a majority vote, then the House of Representatives would select the president by a majority vote, with each state having only one vote. In case of a vice-presidential tie, the Senate would select the vice president.

The compromise was eventually approved by the Framers, but only after much debate and revision. Although quite complicated and unusual, it seemed to be the best solution to their problem. There was little doubt

in the Framers' minds that George Washington would easily be elected the first president. There was great doubt among the Framers, however, that anyone after Washington could ever get a majority vote in the electoral college. They believed that in almost all future elections the final selection of the president would be made by the House of Representatives.

How did the Framers' expectation that George Washington would be the first president affect their writing of Article II of the Constitution?

What do *you* think?

1. What arguments can you give to support the use of the electoral college to select the president? Explain why you agree or disagree with these arguments.

2. What qualifications do you think a person should have, beyond those already in the Constitution, in order to be president? Do you think these qualifications should be required by law? Why or why not?

3. Is it still reasonable to have one person serve as the head of the executive branch? Might it be more reasonable to have two people—one for domestic and one for foreign policy?

What questions did organizing the judicial branch raise?

A national government, with power to act directly on citizens, needed a system for deciding cases involving its laws. This function could be left to state courts, but then the federal laws might be enforced differently from state to state. The Framers realized that some kind of national courts would be needed, at least to resolve disputes involving federal laws.

A judicial branch also would complete the system of separation of powers. They had fewer problems agreeing on how to organize the judiciary than they had with the other two branches. Many of the Framers were lawyers, and so most of them already agreed about how courts should be organized and what responsibilities and powers they should be given. They also agreed that all criminal trials should be trials by jury. This was a very important check, in their minds, on the power of the government.

The Framers created the **Supreme Court** as the head of the federal judiciary, and gave Congress the power to create lower federal courts. They also reached several other important agreements:

■ Judges should be independent of politics so that they can use their best judgment to decide cases and not be influenced by political pressures.

■ The best way to make sure that judges would not be influenced by politics was to have them nominated by the president. The president's nomination would need to be ratified by the Senate. The Framers thought that appointing the judges by this method rather than electing them would remove them from the pressures of political influence. In addition, the judges would keep their positions "during good behavior." This meant that they could not be removed from their positions unless they were impeached and convicted of "treason, bribery, or other high crimes and misdemeanors."

There was also a good deal of agreement about the kinds of powers that the judicial branch should have. The judiciary was given the power to

■ decide conflicts between state governments

■ decide conflicts that involved the national government

And finally, they gave the Supreme Court the authority to handle two types of cases. These are

■ cases in which the Supreme Court has **original jurisdiction**. These are cases which the Constitution says are not to be tried first in a lower court, but which are to go directly to the Supreme Court. Such cases involve a state government, a dispute between state governments, and cases involving ambassadors.

■ cases which have first been heard in lower courts and which are appealed to the Supreme Court. These are cases over which the Supreme Court has **appellate jurisdiction**.

Why did the Framers think it was important to protect the independence of the judicial branch?

What do *you* think?

1. What are the advantages and disadvantages of having federal judges appointed, not elected, to serve "during good behavior"?

2. Should the composition of the Supreme Court be reflective of the political, economic, racial, ethnic, and gender diversity of our citizenry? Why or why not?

3. What role, if any, should public opinion play in the Supreme Court deciding a controversial case?

4. It has been argued that the Supreme Court is the least democratic branch of our federal government. What arguments can you give for and against this position?

Why was the question of judicial review left unanswered?

One important matter not decided by the Framers was whether the Supreme Court should be given the power of **judicial review** over the acts of the executive and legislative branches. To do so would give the judiciary the authority to declare acts of these branches of the national government unconstitutional. This would mean giving one branch the power to ensure that the other branches did not exceed the limitations placed on them by the Constitution. The power to declare that legislative acts had violated their state constitution already had been exercised by the courts in several states.

Some Framers simply assumed that the judiciary would have the power to rule on the constitutionality of laws made by Congress. Nothing specific was decided on this subject at the convention. This assumption, however, is one reason why the delegates rejected a proposal to let the Supreme Court and president act as a committee to review bills passed by Congress and decide if they should become law. The only reference in the Constitution to the general powers of the judiciary is at the beginning of Article III: The "judicial power of the United States, shall be vested in one supreme court...."

The power of the Supreme Court to declare acts of Congress unconstitutional was clearly established by the Supreme Court itself in 1803.

Reviewing and Using the Lesson

1. What issues did the Framers have to decide regarding the organization of the executive branch of government and how did they resolve these issues?

2. How did the Framers make sure the executive branch would have enough power to fulfill its responsibilities, but not so much power that it could dominate the other branches of government?

3. What is the electoral college and why did the Framers decide to create it?

4. What is the difference between "original jurisdiction" and "appellate jurisdiction"?

5. Why did the Framers provide that judges would be appointed by the president, rather than elected by the people? Why did the Framers provide that judges would keep their positions "during good behavior"?

6. What is meant by the term "judicial review"?

7. The electoral college still elects the president every four years, but it now functions very differently from the way the Framers intended. Do research to find out how the system has changed, and report your findings to the class.

LESSON 15

What Conflicting Opinions Did the Framers Have about the Completed Constitution?

Purpose of Lesson

This lesson describes some conflicting points of view of leading Framers about the Constitution. Most of the delegates argued for the adoption of the Constitution, although many had reservations about all or parts of it. The reservations of three were so serious that they refused to sign the document. The position of one of these Framers, George Mason, is explored in detail. You also will examine Benjamin Franklin's statement in defense of the Constitution.

When you have completed this lesson, you should be able to explain the positions of Franklin and Mason, and give arguments in support of and in opposition to these positions.

Critical Thinking Exercise

ANALYZING THE POSITIONS OF GERRY AND HAMILTON

The following remarks were made by two of the Framers on the last day of the convention. One of these Framers signed the Constitution; the other did not.

Work with a study partner or in small groups to analyze the statement. Then answer the questions and be prepared to present and defend your position. What do the following comments tell you about the differences of opinion among the Framers concerning the Constitution they had developed? What were some problems they thought might arise in getting it approved?

...every member [of the convention] should sign. A few characters of consequence, by opposing or even refusing to sign the Constitution, might do infinite mischief.... No man's ideas were more remote from the plan than [mine are] known to be; but is it possible to deliberate between anarchy... on one side, and the chance of good to be expected from the plan on the other?

Alexander Hamilton

...a Civil war may result from the present crisis.... In Massachusetts...there are two parties, one devoted to Democracy, the worst... of all political evils, the other as violent in the opposite extreme...for this and other reasons... the plan should have been proposed in a more mediating shape.

Elbridge Gerry

Howard Chandler Christy's "The Signing of the Constitution of the United States"

What did the Framers think when the Philadelphia Convention ended?

The Constitution has been described as "a bundle of compromises." As you have seen, such prominent features of the Constitution as the different plans for representation in the House and the Senate and the method of selecting the president were settled by compromise. Compromise, however, means that everyone gets less than they want. There were enough compromises in the completed Constitution that nearly every delegate could find something he did not like. During the four months the delegates had spent putting the Constitution together, there were some strong disagreements. Some had walked out of the convention. Three refused to sign the finished document.

Benjamin Franklin argued in support of the Constitution. George Mason argued against it. Mason was one of the three delegates remaining until the end of the convention who refused to sign the document.

How did Franklin defend the work of the convention?

On the last day of the convention, September 17, 1787, Benjamin Franklin prepared a speech intended to persuade all the delegates to sign the completed Constitution. The speech was read by James Wilson, because Franklin's age and illness made him too weak to deliver it himself.

I confess that there are several parts of this Constitution which I do not at present approve.... [But] the older I grow, the more apt I am to doubt my own judgment, and to pay more respect to the judgment of others.... In these sentiments...I agree with this Constitution with all its faults, if they are such; because I think a general Government necessary for us...[and] I doubt...whether any other Convention we can obtain, may be able to make a better Constitution. For when you assemble a number of men to have the advantage of their joint wisdom, you inevitably assemble with those men all their prejudices, their passions, their errors of opinion, their local interests, and their selfish views. From such an assembly can a perfect production be expected? It therefore astonishes me...to find this system approaching so near to perfection as it does.... Thus I consent...to this Constitution because I expect no better, and because I am not sure, that it is not the best.... If every one of us in returning to our Constituents were to report the objections he has had to it...we might prevent its being generally received, and thereby lose all the salutary effects and great advantages resulting naturally in our favor among foreign Nations as well as among ourselves, from a real or apparent unanimity.... On the whole...I cannot help expressing a wish that every member of the Convention who may still have objections to it, would with me on this occasion doubt a little of his own infallibility, and to make manifest our unanimity put his name to this instrument.

Why did George Mason object to the Constitution?

Less than a week before the convention ended, George Mason wrote a list of objections on his copy of the draft of the Constitution. The list was later printed as a pamphlet during the ratification debate. The following are some of his more important objections:

1. The Constitution does not contain a Bill of Rights.

2. Because members of the Senate are selected by state legislatures, it means that they are not representatives of the people or answerable to them. They have great powers, such as the right to approve the appointment of ambassadors and treaties recommended by the president. They also have the power to try the president and other members of the government in cases of impeachment. These powers place the senators in such close connection with the president that together they will destroy any balance in the government, and do whatever they please with the rights and liberties of the people.

3. The national courts have been given so much power that they can destroy the judicial branches of the state governments by overruling them. If this were to happen, and the only courts available were federal courts, most people would not be able to afford to have their cases heard in these courts, because they would need to travel a great distance. Rich people would have an advantage that would enable them to oppress and ruin the poor.

What changes in the Constitution would have satisfied George Mason's objections?

4. The Constitution does not provide for a council to serve as advisers to the president. Any safe and regular government has always included such a council. Such a council would take the place of the Senate in advising the president on appointments and treaties, and the head of the council would take the place of the vice president. Without it, the president will not get proper advice, and will usually be advised by flattering and obedient favorites; or he will become a tool of the Senate.

5. The president of the United States has the unlimited power to grant pardons for crimes, including treason. He may sometimes use this power to protect people whom he has secretly encouraged to commit crimes, and keep them from being punished. In this way he can prevent the discovery of his own guilt.

6. The Constitution says that all treaties are the supreme law of the land. Since they can be made by the president with the approval of the Senate, together they have an exclusive legislative power in this area. This means they can act without the approval of the House of Representatives, the only branch of the legislature that is directly answerable to the people.

7. The Constitution only requires a majority vote in Congress, instead of a two-thirds vote, to make all commercial and navigation laws. The economic interests of the five southern states, however, are totally different from those of the eight northern states, which will have a majority in both houses of Congress. Requiring only a majority vote means that Congress may make laws favoring the merchants of

the northern and eastern states, at the expense of the agricultural interests of the southern states. This could ruin the southern states' economies.

8. Because the Constitution gives Congress the power to make any laws it thinks are "necessary and proper" to carry out its responsibilities, there is no adequate limitation on its powers. Congress could grant monopolies in trade and commerce, create new crimes, inflict severe or unusual punishments, and extend its powers as far as it wants. As a result, the powers of the state legislatures and the liberties of the people could be taken from them.

Mason also had made other criticisms of the Constitution during the convention. Some were accepted by the Convention; others were incorporated in the Bill of Rights, which was added in 1791.

How did Franklin describe the significance of the convention?

The final entry that James Madison made in his notes on the convention describes the scene as the delegates were signing the document they hoped would become the Constitution of the United States.

Whilst the last members were signing it, Doctor Franklin looking toward the President's Chair, at the back of which a rising sun happened to be painted, observed to a few members near him that Painters had found it difficult to distinguish in their art a rising from a setting sun. I have, said he, often in the course of the

Session...looked at that [sun] behind the President without being able to tell whether it was rising or setting: But now at length I have the happiness to know that it is a rising and not a setting Sun.

During convention sessions, why might Franklin have had trouble telling if the "sun behind the president" was "rising or setting"?

What do *you* think?

1. Describe Benjamin Franklin's attitude toward the Constitution. What reasons did he give for his view?

2. Select one of Mason's objections; identify and describe an event in American history or a contemporary event that provides evidence in support of his objection.

3. Select one of George Mason's objections and explain what remedies our constitutional government provides for the problem he identified. Then take and defend a position on whether the remedy is adequate.

Reviewing and Using the Lesson

1. Why is the Constitution sometimes described as "a bundle of compromises"?

2. What was Benjamin Franklin's opinion of the Constitution crafted by the Framers?

3. Why did George Mason refuse to sign the Constitution?

LESSON 16

What Was the Anti-Federalists' Position in the Debate about Ratification?

Purpose of Lesson

The people who opposed ratification of the Constitution, which created a federal government, were called Anti-Federalists. To understand their point of view, we will focus on the writings of Mercy Otis Warren, the author of many plays and political pamphlets. The Anti-Federalists' position was based mainly on the ideas that had been discussed for more than 2,000 years about the kind of society that was necessary for a republic. You also learn about the Bill of Rights, one of the most important contributions to our Constitution.

When you complete this lesson you should understand the contributions of Anti-Federalists and be able to explain their arguments.

Terms to Know

agrarian community
Anti-Federalists
diverse community

How did the Anti-Federalists view the importance of representative government and civic virtue?

Most Americans were very suspicious of government, but the **Anti-Federalists** were especially mistrustful of government in general and strong national government in particular. This mistrust was the basis of their opposition to the Constitution. They feared it had created a government the people could not control.

In general, the Anti-Federalists were older Americans who had grown up believing in the basic ideas of republicanism. These included the idea that in a republic, the greatest power should be placed in a legislature composed of representatives elected by the people of the community. It had always been thought that this kind of representative government would only work in a small community of citizens with similar interests and beliefs, because in such a community it would be easier for people to agree on what was in their common interest.

In addition, it was widely believed that people living in small **agrarian communities** would be more likely to possess the **civic virtue** required of republican citizens. Living closely together they would be more willing to set aside their own interests when necessary and work for the common good.

The Anti-Federalists understood that the Federalists were proposing a government that was the opposite of this type of republican government. It was large and powerful, it included numerous **diverse communities**, and its capital would be far away from most of the people it represented. The Anti-Federalists believed such a system would inevitably pose a threat to the rights of the people.

Many distinguished Americans were Anti-Federalists. Leaders included George Mason and Elbridge Gerry. Both had attended the Philadelphia Convention but had refused to sign the Constitution. Richard Henry Lee was a leading revolutionary and signer of the Declaration of Independence, but fought against the ratification of the Constitution. Patrick Henry had always opposed the idea of a strong national government; he became a leading Anti-Federalist. Mercy Otis Warren, a playwright, also opposed ratification. She, like the others, wrote pamphlets explaining why she did not support the Constitution. Other prominent Anti-Federalists included Luther Martin, Robert Yeates, and George Clinton.

Many arguments were made both for and against the Constitution. Most of them had to do with three basic questions:

- Would the new Constitution maintain a republican form of government?

- Would the federal government have too much power?

- Was a bill of rights needed in the Constitution?

What were the arguments of Anti-Federalists?

Mercy Otis Warren was a playwright as well as an Anti-Federalist writer. She is noteworthy because of her unusual ability to enter the man's world of early American politics. Her main criticisms of the Constitution are a good example of the Anti-Federalist position. The Anti-Federalists argued that the Constitution had the following flaws:

- It should have been developed in meetings whose proceedings were open to the public.

- It would undermine a republican form of government.

- It gave too much power to the national government at the expense of the powers of the state governments.

- It gave too much power to the executive branch of the national government at the expense of the other branches.

- It gave Congress too much power because of the "necessary and proper clause."

- It did not adequately separate the powers of the executive and legislative branches.

- It allowed the national government to keep an army during peacetime.

- It did not include a bill of rights.

Why did the Anti-Federalists fear a strong national government

Warren and the other Anti-Federalists feared that, because of these flaws in the Constitution, the new national government would be a threat to their natural rights. They also thought that the Constitution had been developed by an elite and privileged group to create a national government for the purpose of serving its own selfish interests. Warren and most of the Anti-Federalists thought that the only safe government was one that was

- local and closely linked with the will of the people
- controlled by the people, by such means as
  - yearly elections
  - replacing people in key positions often

What do *you* think?

1. How did the arguments of the Anti-Federalists reflect their point of view regarding natural rights, republicanism, and constitutionalism?

2. Why did the Anti-Federalists believe that the Constitution would not be able to maintain a system of republican government?

3. Did the Anti-Federalists have less faith in human nature than did the Federalists? Explain your answer.

Should there be a bill of rights?

The lack of a bill of rights proved to be the strongest and most powerful weapon of the Anti-Federalists in their struggle to defeat the Constitution. The most frequent arguments they used were the following:

- The way the government is organized does not adequately protect rights. Only the House of Representatives is chosen directly by the people. The federal government is too far removed from average citizens to care about their concerns. The federal government's power could be used to violate citizens' rights.

Mercy Otis Warren
(1728–1814)

Patrick Henry
(1736–1799)

Why did the Anti-Federalists demand a bill of rights?

- The federal government's powers are so general and vague that they can be used to give the government almost unlimited power. It can make all laws that are "necessary and proper" to promote the "general welfare." The Constitution allows the federal government to act directly on citizens. Therefore, its powers over citizens are almost unlimited.

- There is nothing in the Constitution to stop the federal government from violating all the rights that are not mentioned in it. Some rights are included and some are not. There is no mention, for example, of freedom of religion, speech, press, or assembly. Since they are omitted from the Constitution, the government is free to violate them.

- A bill of rights would quiet the fears of many people that a strong central government could violate their rights. After all, Americans recently fought a revolutionary war to secure their fundamental rights. They do not want a constitution that places those rights in jeopardy.

- A bill of rights is necessary to remind the people of the principles of our political system. As one Anti-Federalist put it, there is a necessity of "constantly keeping in view…the particular principles on which our freedom must always depend."

How did the demand for a bill of rights unite the Anti-Federalists?

The Anti-Federalists often disagreed with each other about why they opposed the Constitution, and they were not a well-organized group. They were united, however, in their opposition to the new federal government described in the Constitution. They soon realized that the best way to defeat the Constitution was to use the issue of a bill of rights.

There was a widespread fear of a strong and powerful federal government combined with the belief that a bill of rights was necessary to protect people from government. If people needed to be protected from their relatively weak state governments, they certainly needed protection from the vastly more powerful federal government. In addition, it was easier for the Anti-Federalists to dramatize the lack of a bill of rights than the issues of taxes or the powers of the state governments.

The lack of a bill of rights became the focus of the Anti-Federalist campaign. It was a highly emotional issue for the men and women who had just fought a revolution to secure their rights. In several states, the question of a bill of rights was used effectively to organize opposition to the ratification of the Constitution.

What do you think are the most compelling arguments for and against ratification of the Constitution?

Many Anti-Federalist leaders, like George Mason, hoped to defeat the Constitution so that a second constitutional convention would be held. There, the Anti-Federalists hoped, they would have more influence in creating a new government.

What do *you* think?

1. What criticism of the Constitution by the Anti-Federalists seems to you the most valid? Why?

2. Would you have voted to ratify the Constitution as it was written in 1787? Why?

3. The original Constitution did not secure equal rights for women. Would you have opposed the Constitution for this reason? Why?

4. Which fears of the Anti-Federalists are expressed today? In your opinion are those fears justified? Why?

Reviewing and Using the Lesson

1. What objections and concerns did Anti-Federalists have with regard to the Constitution drafted at the Philadelphia Convention?

2. What arguments did the Anti-Federalists make with regard to the need for a bill of rights?

3. How did the Anti-Federalists use the ideas of classical republicanism to support their position?

4. Conduct research on Mercy Otis Warren, George Mason, and other prominent Anti-Federalists and report your findings to the class.

LESSON 17

What Was the Federalists' Position in the Debate about Ratification?

Purpose of Lesson

The people who supported ratification of the Constitution, which created a federal government, were called Federalists. It is important to understand the difference of opinion between the Federalists and the Anti-Federalists. This lesson describes the strategy and the arguments the Federalists used to get the Constitution ratified. These include the concepts of the social contract and consent. You learn that in the larger states, such as New York and Virginia, the debates about ratification were very close and, to get some Anti-Federalist support, the Federalists agreed that when the first Congress was held it would draft a bill of rights to be added to the Constitution.

When you complete this lesson you should be able to explain why the Federalists wanted the Constitution to be ratified in state conventions, the arguments that were used to justify this procedure, and the arguments made by the Federalists in support of the Constitution.

Terms to Know

Federalists
ratifying conventions
The Federalist

Why did the Federalists ask voters to approve the Constitution?

The **Federalists** knew that many members of Congress and the state governments were against the new Constitution, largely because it reduced their powers. So the Federalists decided **not** to ask the Congress or state governments to approve the Constitution, even though they were expected to do so.

James Madison developed the plan presented by the Federalists. The plan was to go directly to the voters to get them to approve the Constitution. The Constitution would be presented to special **ratifying conventions** to be held in each state. The delegates would be elected by popular vote of the people for the sole purpose of approving the Constitution. Madison's plan was consistent with the idea in the Preamble to the Constitution that says, "We the People…do ordain and establish this Constitution.… "

The Federalists' plan was another example of the social contract idea. The people who were to be governed by the new national government were asked to consent to its creation and obey its decisions. You may recognize this as the method for establishing a government set forth in the natural rights philosophy of John Locke and in the Declaration of Independence. In Jefferson's words, just governments "derive their…powers from the consent of the governed." Some people had argued, for example, that the Articles of Confederation were not valid or legitimate because they had never been presented to the people for their consent.

The Framers at the convention approved this plan for ratifying the Constitution. They included a provision that would put it into effect after being ratified by just nine of the thirteen state conventions.

Once they had agreed on their strategy, the Federalists encouraged their associates in the states to organize the state conventions and elect delegates to them as quickly as possible. They knew the Anti-Federalists had not had enough time to organize their opposition.

The Federalists had worked on the Constitution for almost four months. They knew the arguments for and against it and had gathered support. They thought that if the conventions acted quickly, the Anti-Federalists would have little time to organize their opposition to the Constitution's ratification.

What methods were used in the struggle for ratification?

Despite the advantages of the Federalists' position, the Anti-Federalists were able to put up a strong fight. The debates in the states over ratification lasted ten months. It was an intense and sometimes bitter political struggle. One of the most difficult fights for ratification was in New York. To help the Federalist cause, three men—Alexander Hamilton, James Madison, and John Jay—wrote a series of essays published in three New York newspapers. They also were used in the Virginia ratification debates and are an important source of information about the conflict over the convention. The articles were not intended to present all sides. Their purpose was to convince people to support the ratification of the Constitution. These essays are now called *The Federalist*. They are considered to be the most important work written in defense of the new Constitution.

In defending the new Constitution, the writers of *The Federalist* were very skilled at using basic ideas about government that most Americans understood and accepted. They presented the Constitution as a well-organized, agreed-on plan for national government. The conflicts and compromises that had taken place during its development were not stressed in an attempt to present the Constitution as favorably as possible.

How did the Federalists respond to Anti-Federalists

The Anti-Federalists had some traditional arguments about what made a good government on their side as well. The Federalists were better organized, however. The Federalists' arguments in support of the Constitution claimed that it provided a solution for the problem of creating a republican government in a large and diverse nation. They were able to convince a significant number of people to support their position by the following three arguments:

1. The civic virtue of the people cannot be relied on alone to protect basic rights.

2. The way the government is organized will protect basic rights.

3. The representation of different interests in the government will protect basic rights.

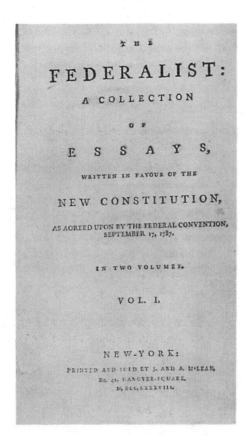

What role did The Federalist *play in ratification of the Constitution?*

The civic virtue of the people could no longer be relied on as the sole support of a government that would protect the people's rights and promote their welfare. Throughout history, the Federalists argued, the greatest dangers in republics to the common good and the natural rights of citizens had been from the selfish pursuit of their interests by groups of citizens who ignored the common good. Therefore, for almost 2,000 years, political philosophers had insisted that republican government was only safe if the citizens possessed civic virtue. By civic virtue they meant that citizens had to be willing to set aside their interests if it was necessary to do so for the common good.

Recent experiences with their state governments had led a number of people to doubt that they could rely on the virtue of citizens to promote the common good and protect the rights of individuals. Many of the state legislatures had passed laws that helped people in debt at the expense of those to whom they owed money. These laws were seen by many as an infringement on property rights that were, after all, one of the basic natural rights for which the Revolution had been fought in the first place.

If the proper working of a republican form of government could not rely on the virtue of its citizens, what could it rely on? How could a government be organized so it would not be dominated by self-interested individuals or factions at the expense of others?

The way in which the Constitution organized the government, including the separation of powers and checks and balances, was the best way to promote the goals of republicanism. A major idea in *The Federalist* is that the national government set forth in the Constitution did not have to rely solely on the civic virtue of the people to protect citizens' rights and promote their welfare. The writers believed that it was unrealistic to expect people in a large and diverse nation, living hundreds of miles apart, to be willing to give up their own interests for the benefit of others.

The Federalists argued that the rights and welfare of all would be protected by the complicated system of **representation, separation of powers**, and **checks and balances** provided by the Constitution. They also believed that the method of electing senators and presidents would increase the possibility that they would have the qualities required of good governing officials.

The Federalists took the position that the Constitution's strength was that it provided for different branches of government that would represent the different interests of the people. They also claimed that this complicated system would make it impossible for any individual or faction—or even a majority—to take complete control of the government to serve its own interests at the expense of the common good or the rights of individuals.

The large size of the nation, they argued, would make it particularly difficult for any one faction to attain a majority. Since so many interests and factions would be represented in the national government, it would be less likely that any one of them would dominate.

Some would argue that the system was so complicated that it would be difficult to get anything done, especially if one or more interested and powerful groups objected to something that was being planned. Madison, in *The Federalist*, clearly did not see this as a disadvantage. One of his criticisms of the state legislatures had been that they passed too many laws in the first place. Most of the Framers believed that the best way to prevent a bad law from being passed was to prevent a law from being passed at all.

The representation of different interests in the government would protect basic rights. The branches of the national government, the power each had distributed to it by the Constitution, and the interests each was supposed to represent are as follows:

- **Legislative branch.** The **House of Representatives** would protect the people's **local interests**, since representatives would be chosen from small congressional districts. The **Senate** would protect the people's **state interests**, since it would be elected by state legislatures.

- **Executive branch.** The **president** would protect the people's **national interests**, since he would be elected by a method that required electors to select him from among leaders who had achieved national prominence.

- **Judicial branch.** The **Supreme Court** would protect the people's **fundamental interests**, since it was independent of political manipulation and therefore responsible only to the Constitution.

What do *you* think?

1. How did the arguments of the Federalists reflect their point of view regarding natural rights, republicanism, and constitutionalism?

2. Why did the Federalists think they could not rely just on civic virtue to make the new nation work properly? Do you agree?

3. What effects did the size and population of the new nation have on the positions of the Federalists?

Alexander Hamilton (1757–1804)

Did the national government have too much power?

The Federalists admitted that the new national government had much more power than the old national government. It had more control over the states, but it was a government limited to enumerated powers. The federal system and checks and balances ensured that those limits would not be violated. As a result, they claimed, the increased powers given to the government under the Constitution could only be used to protect, not violate, the rights of the people. Critics feared that giving so much power to a national government might be a serious threat to their rights and welfare.

Should there be a bill of rights?

The Federalists used a number of arguments to counter those demanding a bill of rights. The most important of these arguments follow:

- The complexity of the government and the diversity of the nation protect rights. A large republic makes it nearly impossible for a "majority faction" to have its way.

- The Constitution does protect a number of specific rights. These include right to habeas corpus, prohibition of ex post facto laws and bills of attainder, protection against violations of contracts, guarantee in criminal cases of trial by jury in the state where the crime was committed, and protection against accusations of treason by its careful definition.

- A bill of rights is unnecessary in a nation with popular sovereignty. Previous bills of rights, such as the English Bill of Rights, protected people from a powerful monarch over whom they had no control. Under the Constitution, the people have the power to remove elected officials from office. The protections of such bills of rights are therefore unnecessary under the Constitution.

- The Constitution does not give the federal government the power to deprive people of their rights. It gives government only limited powers to do specific things—enumerated powers. There is no need to list rights that the government has no power to violate.

- Declarations of rights are ineffective and dangerous. Most state constitutions are prefaced with bills of rights, but these bills did not stop state governments from violating citizens' rights. No state had a comprehensive list of rights, that is, a bill that listed all the rights that were protected. Apparently as a result, some state governments felt free to violate important rights unlisted in their bills. Since it is impossible to list all rights, it is better to have no list at all. Government officials might feel free to violate unlisted rights.

Despite these arguments, the Federalists found it necessary to agree to the Anti-Federalists' demands for a bill of rights.

Why did the Federalists give in to the demand for a bill of rights?

The Federalists worked hard to overcome the objections of the Anti-Federalists. By June of 1788, nine states had voted to ratify the Constitution. New Hampshire was the ninth and last state needed to make the Constitution the highest law of the land. The important states, New York and Virginia, had not yet approved the Constitution. The debates were very close in these states because of the fear of creating such a large and powerful national government.

Finally, a compromise was reached. To get some Anti-Federalists to support the Constitution, the Federalists agreed that when the first Congress was held, it would draft a bill of rights to be added to the Constitution. The bill was to list the rights of citizens that were not to be violated by the federal government. The Federalists insisted that the bill of rights include a statement saying that the list of rights should not be interpreted to mean that they were the only rights the people had.

The Federalists' agreement to sponsor a bill of rights reduced much of the Anti-Federalists' support. It deprived the Anti-Federalists of their most powerful weapon. In some states, Massachusetts for example, the agreement was enough to win a close ratification vote, 187 to 168. Then, at last, New York and Virginia also voted for ratification. The Anti-Federalists had lost their battle to reject or revise the Constitution but they had won an agreement to add a bill of rights.

The Federalists deserve the credit for writing the Constitution, which created our present form of government. The debate resulting from the Anti-Federalists' objections to the Constitution resulted in the addition of the Bill of Rights. The Bill of Rights has proved to be vitally important to the protection of basic rights of the American people and an inspiration to many beyond America's shores.

What do *you* think?

1. Explain the Federalists' argument that the Constitution did not need a bill of rights. Do you agree with their position? Why or why not?

2. Why do you think the Framers protected certain rights in the body of the Constitution and not others?

3. What do you think were the most important reasons put forth by the Federalists to support the Constitution in 1787? What do you think were the least important reasons?

Reviewing and Using the Lesson

1. Why did the Federalists propose that the Constitution be approved by ratifying conventions in each state, rather than by Congress or by the state legislatures?

2. What tactics did the Federalists employ to win the struggle for ratification of the Constitution?

3. What is *The Federalist*? How and why was it written?

4. What arguments did the Federalists make to support the ratification of the Constitution?

5. What arguments did the Federalists make to resist the demand for a bill of rights? Why did they eventually give in to this demand?

6. Prepare a report for the class in which you explain why Rhode Island took so long to join the Union under the Constitution.

Unit Three: *How Did the Values and Principles Embodied in the Constitution Shape American Institutions and Practices?*

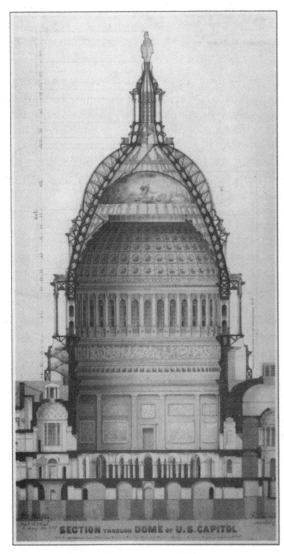

SECTION THROUGH DOME OF U.S. CAPITOL

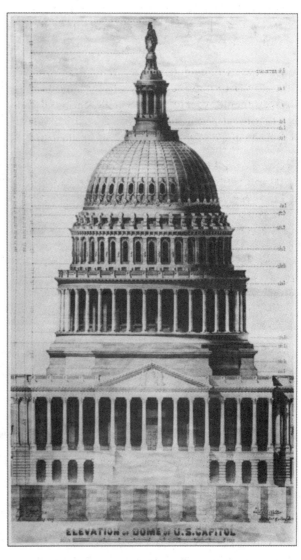

ELEVATION OF DOME OF U.S. CAPITOL

First Congress (1789)	First Bank of the United States (1791)		Second Bank of the United States (1819)		
Judiciary Act of 1789		Alien and Sedition Acts (1798)			
George Washington inaugurated (1789)	Bill of Rights ratified (1791)	*Marbury v. Madison* (1803)	*McCulloch v. Maryland* (1819)	*Gibbons v. Ogden* (1824)	*Barron v. Baltimore* (1833)
1780s	**1790s**	**1800s**	**1810s**	**1820s**	**1830s**
America's first English language Bible printed (1782)	Washington lays cornerstone for the U.S. Capitol (1793)	Washington, D.C. becomes permanent national capital (1800)	Connecticut bans property qualifications for voting (1818)	The Monroe Doctrine (1823)	The Anti-Masonic party holds the first national nominating convention for president and vice president (1831)

Purpose of Unit

The Constitution was a plan for creating and operating the new government. It described the organization of the national government, its powers, and the limits on it. It is important to understand that the Framers had purposely written the Constitution as a general framework for the government. They left out many details they knew would have to be added in the future.

In this unit you learn how the government was organized under the Constitution. You also learn how the Bill of Rights came to be added to the Constitution. In addition, we highlight some unexpected developments that have had a significant influence on the way our nation is governed today.

LESSON 18

How Was the Constitution Used to Organize the New Government?

Purpose of Lesson

This lesson explains the steps taken by the First Congress to name a president and vice president, to provide funding for the new government, to draft a bill of rights, and to organize the executive and judicial branches.

When you complete this lesson, you should be able to explain how the Constitution provides an outline of the federal government's organization and that details are added by the government itself. You also should be able to explain how the First Congress used the Constitution to name a president and vice president and to raise revenue to fund the new government. You should be able to describe how Congress organized the executive branch and how it has expanded. In addition, you should be able to describe how the federal court system was established in the Judiciary Act of 1789. Finally, you should be able to explain how the Bill of Rights was added to the Constitution.

Why was it so important for the First Congress to succeed?

Terms to Know

bureaucracy	Judiciary Act of 1789
federal district court	president's cabinet

What were the tasks of the First Congress?

The newly elected senators and representatives of the First Congress met in New York in April 1789 to begin their work. Five of their tasks were

- naming the new president and vice president
- providing money for the government
- organizing the executive branch of government
- organizing the judicial branch of government
- drafting a bill of rights

How did Congress accomplish these tasks within constitutional guidelines?

1. Naming the new president and vice president. Article II of the Constitution deals with the executive branch of the federal government. Section 1 of that

article sets forth the way the president and vice president are selected. Electors are appointed by state legislators; these electors vote for the candidates. Once the ballots are collected, the president of the Senate is to supervise the counting of the ballots. In 1789 the votes showed, as expected, that George Washington had been elected president. John Adams, with the second highest number of votes, became vice president.

2. Providing money for the government. The First Congress was faced with a serious problem—the federal government had no income. Finding a source of income was a matter of high priority. In addition to deciding what taxes to collect, besides those on imports, Congress had to design a method for collecting them. Many members of the First Congress thought that raising revenue would be one of their most important accomplishments. They were reluctant to put off discussing the issue, and believed it should be addressed even before something as important as a bill of rights.

3. Organizing the executive branch. The Constitution gives Congress the power to organize the executive branch. When the First Congress met, its members were concerned about controlling the executive branch and preventing the president from gaining too much power. This concern was made clear in the debate over how the president should be addressed. It was first proposed that he be referred to or introduced as "His Highness, the President of the United States of America." They decided that this would not be proper because the nation was a republic, not a monarchy. Instead, Congress agreed on the simpler, more democratic title of "The President of the United States."

The First Congress created three departments to carry on the business of the executive branch. The persons in charge of these departments were to be appointed by the president and called "secretaries." These officials were very important under President Washington since he used the secretaries as his advisers. It was not until President Jackson's time, in the 1830s, that they became known as the **president's cabinet**. The first departments and their secretaries were

- **State Department** – Thomas Jefferson was the first secretary of state. This department was responsible for dealing with other nations, as well as for many domestic matters, such as registering patents and copyrights.

- **War Department** – Henry Knox was the first secretary of war. This department was responsible for handling the nation's defense.

- **Treasury Department** – Alexander Hamilton was the first secretary of the treasury. This department was responsible for taking care of the financial affairs of the federal government.

In addition to these three, Edmund Randolph was selected to be the attorney general. It was his responsibility to handle all Supreme Court cases involving the federal government, and to give legal advice to the president and other members of the executive branch.

Today the organization of the executive branch of the federal government is far more complex than it was during the early years of the nation. When Thomas Jefferson was president, 1801–1809, there were 2,210 people working in the branch and its 3 departments. By the mid-1990s, more than 3 million people were working in the 14 departments and numerous other federal agencies of the executive branch.

The Constitution does not mention a federal **bureaucracy**— the nonelective employees and organizations that implement government policy. The Founders probably did not expect the executive branch to grow so large or to have so many responsibilities. Still, the framework for government set up in the Constitution has been able to deal with these developments. To get a better understanding of the organization of the executive branch today, see the simplified organizational chart. below.

The Executive Branch

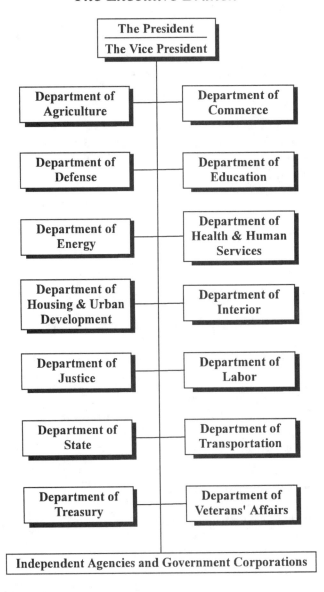

The President
The Vice President

Department of Agriculture	Department of Commerce
Department of Defense	Department of Education
Department of Energy	Department of Health & Human Services
Department of Housing & Urban Development	Department of Interior
Department of Justice	Department of Labor
Department of State	Department of Transportation
Department of Treasury	Department of Veterans' Affairs

Independent Agencies and Government Corporations

President Washington and his secretaries
What factors were considered in organizing the executive branch?

Why has the executive branch grown so much larger than originally envisioned by the Framers?

4. Organizing the judicial branch. Article III of the Constitution says that the "the judicial power of the United States, shall be vested in one supreme court, and in such inferior courts as the Congress may from time to time…establish." The Framers wrote only this very general guideline and gave the First Congress the task of organizing a system of federal courts.

Congress complied by passing a law known as the **Judiciary Act of 1789**. It established two kinds of federal courts below the Supreme Court.

- Congress established a **federal district court** in each state. These federal courts were responsible for the first hearing or trial of many cases involving the Constitution, federal laws, and disputes between citizens of different states.

- Congress also established a system of **circuit courts**, in which serious crimes could be tried. These courts would also hear appeals from the district courts and review their cases for errors of law. Until 1891, when the Circuit Courts of Appeals were established, a circuit court was composed of a district judge and a justice of the Supreme Court.

In addition to the system of federal courts established by the Constitution and Congress to rule on federal cases, each state had its own courts established by its legislature to rule on cases of state law. This system of federal and state courts is organized today in much the same way it was in 1789.

Today the United States Supreme Court plays an important role in our federal government. In the beginning, however, the Supreme Court's role was much less significant. One of the first justices, John Rutledge, did not attend a single session of the Supreme Court during the first two years. The first chief justice, John Jay, spent little time on the job; he spent a year in England on a diplomatic mission and ran for governor of New York twice. Oliver Ellsworth, the next chief justice, resigned his position in 1800. No one considered the Supreme Court an important part of the federal government.

5. Drafting a bill of rights. As you know, during the struggle to get the states to ratify the Constitution, the document had been criticized for not having a bill of rights. To answer this objection, the Federalists agreed to the addition of a bill of rights as soon as the new government was established.

In his inaugural address on April 30, 1789, George Washington urged Congress to respond to the widespread demand to add a bill of rights to the Constitution. When the First Congress met, James Madison wanted to fulfill the promise made by the Federalists during the ratification debates. Madison was aware that many people were still very suspicious of the new government. They would be watching closely to see if the Federalists would keep their promises.

The United States Court System

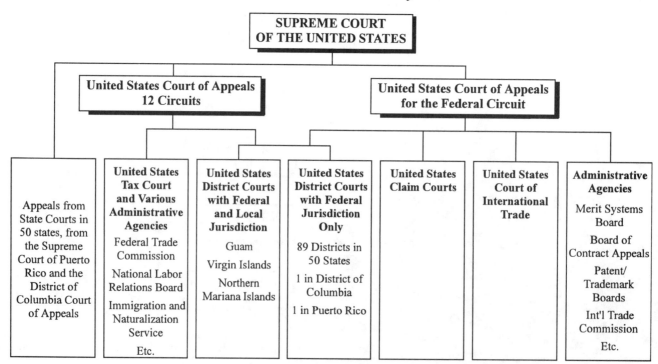

Why has the U.S. court system grown so much more complex than originally outlined by the Framers?

Madison began his task by sorting through the more than 200 amendments recommended by states during the ratification debates. Most fell into two groups:

- They placed additional limitations on the powers of the federal government.

- They protected individual rights.

When he introduced a bill of rights, Madison was careful not to include any proposals that would limit the power of the federal government and increase that of the states. This led some Anti-Federalists, such as Patrick Henry, to reject Madison's bill. Others, George Mason for example, approved of the amendments. Madison's draft did include many of the suggestions from the states that protected individual rights such as freedom of religion, speech, press, and assembly, and the rights of petition and trial by jury. Introduction of the Bill of Rights convinced enough Anti-Federalists to support the government so that the movement for a second constitutional convention quickly died. Now the new government could get on to other important tasks.

Reviewing and Using the Lesson

1. What were some of the important tasks the First Congress had to address in 1789?

2. What departments did Congress create to do the work of the executive branch of the national government? What responsibilities did each of these departments have?

3. How would you define the term "bureaucracy"? How has the federal government's bureaucracy changed since Jefferson was president?

4. How did the Judiciary Act of 1789 organize the system of federal courts?

5. Some 200 suggested amendments to the Constitution were proposed in the state ratifying conventions. In general, what did these proposed amendments do? In drafting the Bill of Rights, what group of proposed amendments did Madison exclude? How did Anti-Federalists react to Madison's proposal?

6. Conduct research on how cases on appeal reach the U.S. Supreme Court and the procedures the Court applies in reaching its decisions.

LESSON 19

What Rights Did the Constitution Protect?
How Was the Bill of Rights Added to the Constitution?

Purpose of Lesson

The Federalists argued that separation of powers, checks and balances, the federal system, and the size and diversity of the nation provided the best protection for the rights of individuals. In particular, they pointed to provisions in the new Constitution that prohibited both the federal and state governments from violating important rights.

In this lesson you examine the rights the Framers included in the Constitution and discuss their importance. In addition, you learn of the struggle to add a bill of rights to the Constitution, reactions to the Bill of Rights, and the reasons it provided only limited protection of rights.

After completing this lesson, you should be able to list the rights the Framers included in the Constitution. You should be able to describe these rights, explain why they were chosen, and explain their importance. You also should be able to explain the conflict over adding a bill of rights to the Constitution, the result of the conflict, and why the Bill of Rights had such a limited effect on the lives of Americans at the time.

Terms to Know

bills of attainder	impeachment
enumeration	Ninth Amendment
ex post facto laws	provision
Fourteenth Amendment	religious tests
habeas corpus	

What rights were specifically protected in the Constitution?

The Framers included a number of **provisions** in the Constitution to protect specific rights. These provisions protected rights of individual citizens and persons holding public office in the federal government. Each provision was designed to prevent the type of abuse the Framers had seen in British history, their own colonial and state governments, or the national government under the Articles of Confederation.

These rights are divided into three groups to make it easier to understand their functions and importance. The Constitution provides protection of

- political independence and other rights of public officials
- individual rights against violation by state governments
- individual rights against violation by the federal government

Protection of the political independence and other rights of public officials.

- Freedom of speech for members of Congress is protected—they cannot be arrested for anything they say on the floor of Congress.

Daniel Webster addressing Congress
Should members of Congress have immunity for statements made in Congress?

- They cannot be be arrested for minor crimes they commit while Congress is in session.

- Congress also is prohibited from imposing a **religious test** on people who hold federal office. This means that people cannot be required to express certain religious beliefs as a qualification for holding office.

- If members of the executive or judicial branches are accused of misconduct in office, the **impeachment** clauses protect their right to a fair hearing.

Protection of individual rights against violation by state governments.

■ One of these provisions says that no state can pass any law "impairing the obligation of contracts." This means, among other things, that a state legislature cannot pass a law releasing people from the responsibility to pay their debts.

Why did the Framers believe it was necessary to protect the obligation of contracts?

■ In another provision, the Constitution protected the property rights of citizens who held slaves. Enslaved Africans were considered the personal property of the slaveholder. This provision required state governments to return any slave who had fled from another state, a provision later overturned by the Thirteenth Amendment.

■ The Constitution also prohibits both federal and state governments from passing **ex post facto laws** and **bills of attainder**. An ex post facto law makes an act a crime, even though it was not a crime when it was done. A bill of attainder is a punishment ordered by a legislature, rather than a court.

Protection of individual rights against violation by the federal government.

■ Two of these rights are **habeas corpus** and **trial by jury** in criminal cases.

■ The Constitution also offers protection from the accusation of **treason** by defining this crime very specifically and narrowly. This definition cannot be modified by Congress; it can only be changed by a constitutional amendment.

Critical Thinking Exercise
EXAMINING THE IMPORTANCE OF RIGHTS GUARANTEED IN THE CONSTITUTION

Work in small groups to complete this activity. Each group should be assigned one of the following readings concerning rights guaranteed in the Constitution. Discuss your answers to the questions. Then select a spokesperson to present your group's opinions to the rest of the class.

Group 1. "No bill of attainder...shall be passed." Article I, Section 9, Clause 3 and Section 10, Clause 1.

A bill of attainder is a law passed by a legislature that calls for the arrest and punishment of a named person or group without a trial in a court of law. Bills of attainder were first used in England in 1459. They give the government the power to imprison people, take their property, and even order their execution without a trial. Because bills of attainder allow the government to ignore the court system and due process of law, they are a dangerous instrument of tyranny.

A bill of attainder has been introduced against you. If it passes the Virginia legislature, you will be ordered to surrender to the government or you will be arrested. The bill passes, but you refuse to surrender. You and all your property are seized.

1. Would you give your government the right to pass bills of attainder? Why or why not?

2. Why might a legislature want the power to pass bills of attainder? Against whom might they be used?

3. What limitations on government would be gained by prohibiting bills of attainder?

4. What relationship, if any, does prohibiting bills of attainder have to the separation of powers and checks and balances?

5. What other rights, if any, would you want included to protect yourself further against this type of government activity?

Group 2. "No...ex post facto law shall be passed." Article I, Section 9, Clause 3 and Section 10, Clause 1.

An ex post facto law declares an act a crime after the act has already taken place. It punishes people for acts that, when they did them, were not against the law. This prohibition would forbid the government from passing laws that

■ make something a crime that was not a crime when it was done

■ make a crime greater or more serious after the act was committed

- make the punishment for a crime more severe after the crime was committed
- change the rules of a trial after an act was done to make it easier to convict a person

You agree with Alexander Hamilton's criticisms that ex post facto laws have been "in all ages" one of "the favorite and most formidable instruments of tyranny." You know they have been used by political leaders to prevent people from opposing them, or to imprison their opponents.

1. What arguments can you make for prohibiting ex post facto laws?

2. Why might a legislature want the power to pass ex post facto laws? Against whom might they be used?

3. What limitations on government would be achieved by prohibiting ex post facto laws?

4. What relationship, if any, does prohibiting ex post facto laws have to the separation of powers and checks and balances?

5. What other rights, if any, would you want included to protect yourself further against this type of government activity?

Group 3. "Treason against the United States, shall consist only in levying war against them, or in adhering to their enemies, giving them aid and comfort. No person shall be convicted of treason unless on the testimony of two witnesses to the same overt act, or on confession in open court." Article III, Section 3, Clause 1.

You have been accused of treason by the new government of the United States. You want to see that people with different political views are not persecuted under the new Constitution. You want treason to be defined very narrowly in the new Constitution to protect people who may be merely disagreeing with the government. You think treason should refer only to citizens who are fighting against the United States or giving aid and comfort to its enemies. Finally, you want the Constitution to set very strict standards for proving that a person has committed treason.

1. In what way could a loose definition of treason lead to a denial of rights?

2. How would the power of government be limited by defining treason very narrowly and requiring you to be tried in a court?

3. What arguments can you make for including the protections you have discussed in the Constitution?

4. What other rights, if any, would you want included to protect yourself further against unfair accusations of treason?

Group 4. "[N]o religious test shall ever be required as a qualification to any office or public trust under the United States." Article VI, Section 3.

You believe that immigrating to a new nation which boasts of its religious tolerance and freedom was worth the price of uprooting your family and leaving your friends. However, you think it is unfair that several of the new state constitutions prohibit people of certain religions from holding public office.

You hope that a provision will be included in the Constitution to enable all qualified people to run for office in the new nation. You believe there should be no religious test to hold political office.

1. Why might a government wish to require a religious test for public office?

2. How might requiring a religious test for public office be related to the ideas of classical republicanism? To the natural rights philosophy?

3. Would you give your government the right to require you to belong to a particular religion or to take a religious test before you could hold a public office? Why or why not?

4. What other rights, if any, would you want included to protect yourself further from discrimination because of your religion?

What amendments to the Constitution did Madison propose?

When the First Congress met, on June 8, 1789, James Madison introduced his amendments on the floor of the House of Representatives. In his speech, he tried to assure the Federalists that his amendments would not radically change the Constitution they had supported. He also tried to convince the Anti-Federalists that his amendments would protect individual liberties.

Madison suggested that an introductory statement be added to the Constitution. This introduction would contain the basic ideas about government stated in the Declaration of Independence:

- The purpose of government is to protect the rights of the people.

- The people are the ultimate source of its authority.

Why were members of the House of Representatives not interested in Madison's speeches in support of a bill of rights?

Such statements frequently appeared at the beginning of state constitutions to reaffirm the principle of popular sovereignty.

Madison was convinced that the greatest danger to individual rights came from groups who might use the government to serve their own interests at the expense of others. He thought that state governments were more easily used by factions than the national government. Consequently, he feared that state governments were a greater threat to individual rights than the federal government. He proposed what he considered "the most valuable amendment in the whole list." This proposed amendment stated

> *No state shall violate the equal rights of conscience, or the freedom of the press, or the trial by jury in criminal cases.*

Madison also included in his proposal an amendment to deal with the criticism that a list of rights would endanger those rights not listed. When adopted it became the **Ninth Amendment**. The Ninth Amendment clearly states that the Bill of Rights is only a partial list of the people's rights. It says

> *The enumeration in the Constitution of certain rights shall not be construed to deny or disparage others retained by the people.*

This means that the specific **enumeration**—listing—of people's rights should not be interpreted to deny or lessen the importance of other rights held by the people.

Finally, Madison argued that the amendments he had drafted should be included in the Constitution itself. He did not think they should be added as a separate list at the end of the Constitution.

How did Congress respond to Madison's proposals?

Although Madison's speech was eloquent, members of the House of Representatives appeared completely unmoved by his suggestions. Every speaker who followed him either opposed a bill of rights or argued that the House had far more important business. Six weeks later Madison again asked the House to vote on his amendments, but the House sent them to a committee instead of debating them.

Finally, in August, the House agreed to consider Madison's amendments. The House made some changes and sent Madison's draft to the Senate. At the insistence of Roger Sherman, the amendments were to be added at the end of the Constitution rather than placed in the body of the document as Madison had suggested. Sherman argued that it was too early to begin rewriting the Constitution itself. If amendments were listed separately, it would be clear which parts were original, and which ones had been added later. He also feared that if they were added to the body of the Constitution, the entire document would need to be ratified again.

Since Senate debate was not open to the public, little is known about what happened there. We do know that the Senate made significant changes in the House version.

The senators also eliminated the amendment that would have prohibited state governments from violating the right to freedom of conscience, speech, press, and trial by jury in criminal cases.

With ratification by Virginia, the ninth state to give its approval, the Bill of Rights became a part of the Constitution on December 15, 1791.

What do *you* think?

1. Where did Madison think the greatest danger to individual rights came from? Why did he think this? What evidence is there to support or refute his position?

2. How might our constitutional history have been different if Madison's proposed amendment safe-guarding the rights of conscience, press, and trial by jury from violation by the states had been adopted?

3. What do you think was the best argument for and against a federal bill of rights?

4. Does the Bill of Rights seem more or less important now than when it was adopted and ratified?

What did people think of the Bill of Rights in 1791?

The reaction of most Americans to the Bill of Rights was lukewarm at best. Its passage had little effect on the average person. The Supreme Court ruled in 1833, that the Bill of Rights applied only to the federal government. As a result, it was not until adoption of the **Fourteenth Amendment** in 1868—and its vigorous application by the nation's courts in the twentieth century—that citizens would be protected from violations of these rights by their state governments.

The Anti-Federalists, who had based much of their opposition to the Constitution on the lack of a bill of rights, were unhappy with its passage. They thought it spoiled their chances to rewrite the Constitution. They said the amendments were "good for nothing." "I believe," said Senator William Grayson of Virginia, "as many others do, they will do more harm than good."

At the same time, many Federalists were angry with Madison for pushing the Bill of Rights through Congress. At best, they considered it of little importance. Even Madison, tired of all the disagreement and dissent, had come to think of the whole experience as a "nauseous project."

Critical Thinking Exercise

DEVELOPING AND DEFENDING POSITIONS ON THE SECOND AMENDMENT

A well regulated Militia, being necessary to the security of a free State, the right of the people to keep and bear Arms, shall not be infringed.
Second Amendment

One basic belief of classical republicanism was that a standing professional army was the enemy of freedom. Only a citizen militia, in which each member of the community had the duty to serve, could provide security without threatening the liberties of the people.

This fear of standing armies and the belief in a citizen militia was supported by political philosophers as well as by historical experience. For example, when the American colonists began to oppose British policies, Parliament passed a law banning the shipment of arms to the colonies. The first colonial armed rebellion was a patriot raid on the British Fort William and Mary. It was there that arms and ammunition were seized and secretly distributed throughout the colonies—arms that were later used to fire the "shot heard 'round the world" at Lexington and Concord.

Weapons seizure in New York, 1991
Why is the question of a person's right to bear arms more controversial today than when the Constitution was written?

James Madison argued during the ratification debates that one reason Americans need not fear the power of the new federal government was that the citizens had "the advantage of being armed, which you possess over the people of almost every other nation.... In the several Kingdoms of Europe...the governments are afraid to trust the people with arms." The Anti-Federalists strongly supported the right of citizens to bear arms. Patrick Henry declared, "The great principle is that every man be armed. Everyone who is able may have a gun." Richard Henry Lee argued that "to preserve liberty, it is essential that the whole body of people always possess arms, and be taught alike, especially when young, how to use them."

It was with this understanding that the Second Amendment was written. It was passed on a voice vote, without objection, and was approved by the Senate. It was ratified by the people with little debate.

Work in small groups to develop positions on the following questions. Then be prepared to present and defend your positions.

1. Do you think the Second Amendment is as important today as it was in the eighteenth century? Explain your answer.

2. What argument would you make for the right of the citizens to bear arms today? How might that argument differ from the arguments Americans made in the 1790s?

3. What limitations, if any, do you think should be placed on the right to bear arms? How would you justify those limits?

Were the Framers aware of other threats to rights?

Some people argue that the Framers were not sufficiently aware of important threats to rights from sources other than government. They did not foresee threats arising from economic power, for example, or religious and racial prejudice. Therefore, some people argue, the Framers did not understand that the power of government can be used to protect the rights of some individuals against threats from other individuals, groups, or organizations.

In the twentieth century, the Bill of Rights has become something it never was in the eighteenth century. It is, perhaps, the most important single document protecting individual rights. The struggle to extend its protections to all Americans has taken more than 200 years, however, and the struggle continues.

Reviewing and Using the Lesson

1. What rights did the Framers include in the body of the Constitution? Why did they choose to protect these rights? Why are these rights important?

2. How would you explain the meaning of the Ninth Amendment?

3. Why was Madison concerned about the possible violation of individual rights by state governments? What amendment did he propose to address this concern?

4. Why did the Bill of Rights have little effect on the average person when it was first adopted?

5. What are some threats to individual rights that the Bill of Rights does not address? What can be done to guard against these threats?

6. Imagine that you are a member of the First Congress writing a newsletter to mail to your constituents. In your newsletter write a report on the accomplishments of the First Congress.

LESSON 20

What Caused the Rise of Political Parties?

Purpose of Lesson

Soon after the government was established, there was an unforeseen development to which the Framers were very much opposed. This was the formation of political parties. This lesson describes how they came to be formed. The lesson also describes the importance of political parties to our present system of government.

When you complete the lesson, you should be able to explain why the Framers were opposed to the idea of political parties. You should also be able to explain the conflicting points of view that led to the development of political parties, the reasons for the demise of the Federalist party, and the role that political parties play in American politics today.

Terms to Know

Alien and Sedition Acts
faction
Federalist Party
general welfare clause

necessary and proper clause
political parties
Republican Party
revolution of 1800

What did Madison say about factions?

James Madison argued in *The Federalist* that one of the Constitution's major advantages was that it organized the government in such a way that "factions" would be controlled. He defined a **faction** as a group of citizens, either a majority or a minority, that pursues its own interests at the expense of the common good. Many Framers agreed that factions were dangerous to republican government for this very reason.

George Caleb Bingham's "The County Election"
What has been the role of political parties in elections?

Madison argued that people would always join with others of similar interests and opinions to advocate policies favorable to themselves. There would be, however, many interests and opinions in a large commercial society. This diversity, he said, would keep any one interest group or faction from gaining control of the government. He argued that the influence of factions would be limited by the complicated system of government planned by the Constitution.

The size and diversity of the nation, as well as the complexity of the government, would limit the ability of any single faction to form a majority. That way, no single group could control the government solely for its own interests. Instead, the different groups would have to work together through bargaining and compromise to create coalitions that would promote the interests of a majority as well as protect minority interests.

In spite of Madison's intent and these safeguards, factions in the form of **political parties** did develop and are now an accepted part of the American political system.

What conflicting ideas led to the development of political parties?

When George Washington was president, he sought advice from people whose opinions he most valued. He appointed two such persons as his secretaries, Secretary of State Thomas Jefferson and Secretary of the Treasury Alexander Hamilton. Each had very different ideas about what the government's policies should be, and the two were often in conflict.

In time, after Washington began to accept Hamilton's opinions in foreign as well as domestic affairs, Jefferson resigned from his position. During this period, Hamilton and his followers became known as **Federalists.** Jefferson and his followers became known as **Republicans**. Jefferson's Republicans eventually became today's Democratic Party, not the Republican Party. The differences of opinion between the Federalists and the Republicans played a large part in the development of political parties in the United States.

The basic disagreement between Hamilton and Jefferson concerned the way the powers of the new federal government were to be used.

- Hamilton and the Federalists argued that the Constitution had created a government designed to take on national problems. As long as a problem was national, they said, the federal government could and should deal with it, whether or not it was specifically mentioned in the Constitution.

- Jefferson and the Republicans argued that the Constitution's description of the powers of the federal government was so vague that, using the Federalists' approach, the government would be able to do whatever it wanted. Republicans believed that if the government were free to define its own powers, the liberty of the people would be threatened. They argued that the government should be strictly limited to its enumerated powers.

Why was Jefferson concerned about the interpretation of the Constitution?

No part of the Constitution did more to raise the fears of Jefferson and his followers than Article I, Section 8, which sets forth the powers of Congress. Although it does seem to limit Congress by clearly listing a number of its responsibilities and powers, it also contains two clauses which are very general. These are the **general welfare** and the **necessary and proper clauses**. These clauses state that Congress shall have the following powers:

Why is there no mention of political parties in the Constitution?

- to lay and collect taxes…to pay the debts and provide for the common defence and **general welfare** of the United States
- to make all laws which shall be **necessary and proper** for carrying into execution the foregoing powers, [the powers given to Congress under Section 8]

The Federalists thought that the Constitution gave the federal government certain broad responsibilities and its powers should be equal to those responsibilities. This "energetic" use of the federal government's power was exactly what Jefferson and some Republicans feared.

The Federalists believed that since the people had delegated these powers to the federal government, the people could reduce or eliminate the powers by amending the Constitution, if they chose. The enumeration of powers in the Constitution clearly gave the federal and state governments independent spheres of responsibility and this was a sufficient limitation on the powers of both.

Critical Thinking Exercise
IDENTIFYING JEFFERSON'S CONCERN

Suppose you gave your student government the power to make whatever rules for your school they thought were "necessary and proper" for your "general welfare."

1. Who would be in the position to decide what was "necessary and proper"?

2. Who would decide what the "general welfare" was?

3. What limitations would there be on their powers?

What conflicts arose between the Federalists and the Republicans?

The differences in political philosophy between Hamilton and Jefferson led them to disagree greatly on a number of specific issues regarding how the new government should be run. One of the issues on which they took opposing sides was the establishment of the Bank of the United States.

As secretary of the treasury, Hamilton wanted to demonstrate the power of the federal government and strengthen the new nation's weak economy. To achieve these goals he made a number of recommendations to the Congress. One was that it pass a law establishing the Bank of the United States. Congress passed the law and, thus, aroused much controversy.

Hamilton said that the creation of the Bank was a "necessary and proper" method of carrying out the responsibilities given to Congress by the Constitution, such as collecting taxes and regulating trade.

Jefferson replied that the "necessary and proper" clause should be interpreted as if it read "absolutely and indispensably necessary." Clearly, this interpretation would have severely limited the power of Congress. Certainly, the creation of the Bank would not have passed this restrictive test. Jefferson understood this, and this was exactly what he intended.

President Washington accepted Hamilton's position. He signed the legislation establishing the Bank of the United States. Thus, a large step was taken toward increasing the power of the federal government.

Why did the Federalists and Republicans take opposing views on the war between Great Britain and France?

In 1793, war broke out between France and Great Britain. The Federalists and Republicans disagreed on what the United States should do.

Federalists wanted the United States to help the British since Americans had more trade with the British than with the French. They also opposed the radicalism of the French Revolution of 1789.

The Republicans wanted the United States to help the French, who had helped the Americans fight the British during the Revolutionary War. They also supported the revolution against the French monarchy.

President Washington tried to prevent people from dividing into opposing camps over this issue. He declared that the United States was neutral and would not take sides in the war. When he left office after his second term, he warned the country against entering into permanent alliances with foreign governments. He also warned the American people to avoid what he called the "spirit of party."

By the time Washington retired, however, party conflict was becoming a fixture in American politics. Washington's great personal prestige had shielded him from attacks. No one could take the place of Washington though, and his successors have all been subject to attacks from the opposition.

What were the Alien and Sedition Acts?

In the election of 1796, John Adams, a Federalist, became president. But Thomas Jefferson, a Republican, was elected vice president. This increased the conflict between the Federalists and the Republicans.

Jefferson and his followers criticized the way Adams and the Federalist majority in Congress were running the government. Adams and the Federalists were able to get laws passed called the **Alien and Sedition Acts**. These laws gave the president the power to force foreigners to

Why did the Federalists try to silence criticism of the government in the press?

leave the country if he considered them dangerous. They also made it a crime for editors, writers, or speakers to attack the government.

Jefferson and the other Republicans were outraged at the laws and at their enforcement by Federalist judges. They knew the laws were intended to keep them from criticizing the government. They hoped that federal judges would declare the acts unconstitutional. But several Republican newspaper editors and a member of Congress were fined and put in jail for writing and speaking against the government.

Finally, Madison joined with Jefferson to write the "Kentucky and Virginia Resolutions." They claimed that the states had a right to decide if the federal government had exceeded its powers. These resolutions claimed the state legislatures had the power to declare laws made by Congress, such as the Alien and Sedition Acts, null and void. The resolutions were not accepted by the other states. If they had been, they would have given the states a large amount of power over the federal government.

What was the "revolution of 1800"?

The presidential election of 1800 was the first to feature candidates for president and vice president who were openly supported by political parties. Federalists supported John Adams for president. Republicans supported Thomas Jefferson. Although the candidates themselves did not campaign, the election created bitter party disagreements. The Alien and Sedition Acts were often cited by Republicans as proof that Federalists were not fit to govern.

The election of 1800 was of great importance to the new government. Both the Federalists and the Republicans accused each other of wishing to destroy the Constitution, yet they both accepted the results of the election. On March 4, 1801, the Federalists turned over control of the federal government to the Republicans. For the first time in modern history, control of a government was given to new leaders as the result of a "democratic revolution" rather than by hereditary succession or violent overthrow. Jefferson later called it the **"revolution of 1800"** and said that it was more important than the Revolution of 1776!

The Federalists tended to be suspicious of democracy. The mood of the country, however, was becoming increasingly democratic. In the face of this growing spirit of equality, Federalists could not compete with Republicans, who represented the beliefs and opinions of the common people. After the War of 1812, the Federalist Party was no longer significant in American politics.

What part do political parties play in today's political system?

Political parties are now an accepted part of the American political system. Many people argue that as the nation became more democratic, political parties were inevitable. Political parties serve several important purposes:

- They provide people with a way to organize support for candidates for public office.
- They are a means of persuading more people to vote.
- By joining a political party, people indicate their support for the policies of that party.
- Political parties serve as an outlet for popular passions and provide forums for deliberating about public policies.
- In times of rapid political change, parties can provide a way of making sure that people demand a change of government, not a change of constitutions.

George Bush, Ross Perot, and Bill Clinton in a 1992 presidential debate

Have political parties advanced or inhibited representative democracy?

What do *you* think?

1. What were the Federalists' objections to political parties? What relevance, if any, do these objections have today?

2. What are the functions of political parties today? In what ways, if any, do they serve the common good?

3. Is it possible to have a democracy without political parties? Explain your position.

4. What are the advantages and disadvantages of being a member of a political party? How can you be sure the political party of your choice reflects your interests?

Reviewing and Using the Lesson

1. What is a "faction"? What factors did Madison rely on to prevent factions from gaining control of the national government?

2. What basic difference of opinion originally caused the rise of political parties in the United States?

3. What are the "general welfare" and "necessary and proper" clauses of the Constitution? Why were Jefferson and other Founders concerned about these clauses?

4. What were the Alien and Sedition Acts? How did Jefferson and Madison respond to these laws?

5. Why did Jefferson refer to the presidential election of 1800 as the "revolution of 1800"? What was significant about this election?

6. Research the development and evolution of political parties from the Civil War to the present.

LESSON 21

What Is Judicial Review? Why Is It Controversial?

Purpose of Lesson

Throughout our history, there have been strong differences of opinion about whether the judicial branch should have the power of judicial review and how that power should be used. The controversy raises basic questions about representative government and majority rule on the one hand, and constitutional government, its constitutional powers, and the protection of basic rights and of minorities on the other.

This lesson defines the practice of judicial review and explains how the Supreme Court gained this power. It also helps you understand the continuing controversies resulting from the Supreme Court having the power of judicial review.

When you finish this lesson, you should be able to explain different positions regarding judicial review and its role in a constitutional democracy. You also should be able to describe the issues raised in the Supreme Court case *Marbury v. Madison* (1803) and how Chief Justice Marshall claimed the power of judicial review for the Supreme Court.

How does judicial review strengthen the judicial branch of government?

Terms to Know

commission	original jurisdiction
judicial review	precedents
legal remedy	Privy Council
Marbury v. Madison (1803)	unconstitutional
	writ of mandamus
null and void	

What is judicial review?

Judicial review is the power of the judicial branch of a government to decide if acts of the legislative or executive branches violate their constitution. If a court reaches the decision that the action of the other branch violates the constitution, it then declares the action to be **null and void**. That means that the law or act is not to be obeyed or enforced. In the United States, the federal judiciary, headed by the United States Supreme Court, now has this power, even though it is not specifically mentioned in the Constitution. State courts have this power over the other branches of state governments.

Should the Supreme Court have the power to declare acts of the president and Congress unconstitutional?

One new idea about government that developed in this nation was the idea that the judicial branch should have the power to interpret the Constitution and decide what it means. The Supreme Court can decide that a law passed by Congress or a state legislature violates the Constitution and therefore is not to be obeyed or enforced.

The Founders were familiar with the idea that a part of government could be given the power to decide whether activities of other parts of government violated the "higher law" of a nation. Under British rule, the **Privy Council**, a group that advised the monarch, had the power to veto laws passed by colonial legislatures if they violated British laws. After the American Revolution, some state courts had declared laws made by their own legislatures **unconstitutional**.

If you read the Constitution, you will not find any mention of the power of judicial review. As you will see, however, soon after the beginning of the new government, the Constitution was interpreted to give the Supreme Court this power.

How did the Supreme Court establish its power of judicial review?

The question of whether the Supreme Court should have the power of judicial review over the legislative and executive branches of the federal government was discussed during the Philadelphia Convention and ratification debates. Although nothing in the Constitution clearly gives the Court this power, many historians believe that most of the Framers assumed that the federal courts would have this power. Alexander Hamilton, for example, made this assumption in *The Federalist #78*.

> [T]he courts were designed to be an intermediate body between the people and the legislature, in order, among other things, to keep the latter within the limits assigned to their authority.... [W]hen the will of the legislature, declared in its statutes, stands in opposition to that of the people, declared in the Constitution, the judges ought to be governed by the latter rather than the former.

One of the arguments in favor of a bill of rights made by James Madison in 1789 was that it would give the judiciary a "check" on congressional violations of rights. This argument also had been made by Thomas Jefferson when he wrote to Madison encouraging him to support a bill of rights.

The first use of the power of judicial review, however, did not have to do with fundamental rights but with taxes. In 1794, Congress put a federal tax on carriages. The Supreme Court agreed to hear a case challenging the tax as unconstitutional. The Court decided that the tax was constitutional. Since the Court upheld the law, the case was not controversial. When the Court first decided that an act of Congress was **not** constitutional, the idea of judicial review became very controversial. The case was *Marbury v. Madison*, decided in 1803.

Critical Thinking Exercise

EVALUATING, TAKING, AND DEFENDING A POSITION ON THE POWER OF JUDICIAL REVIEW

Suppose you could step back in time to decide whether the Supreme Court should be given the power of judicial review. Your class should be divided into small groups to consider the two positions described below. Be prepared to take and defend a position in favor of one of the alternatives.

Position 1. Give the Supreme Court the power to declare laws passed by Congress unconstitutional.

Result. A particular law passed by a majority of representatives in Congress, elected by citizens to represent their views and interests, should not be obeyed or enforced.

Position 2. Deny the Supreme Court the power to declare laws passed by Congress unconstitutional.

Result. All laws passed by a majority of representatives in Congress must be obeyed and enforced.

To develop and defend your decision, consider the following questions:

1. In what way does your choice conflict with the principles of representative government and majority rule?

2. Is your choice more democratic? If so, how?

3. Explain how your choice might subject basic rights to the whims of temporary emotions and current popularity.

4. Would your choice result in the majority tyrannizing the minority? If so, how?

5. If you do not approve of the practice of judicial review, what alternative would you propose for settling disagreements over the meaning of the Constitution? Defend your choice.

What events led to the Supreme Court case *Marbury v. Madison*?

In the election of 1800, Republican candidate Thomas Jefferson defeated the incumbent Federalist president, John Adams. Although the election was decided on February 17, Jefferson did not take office until March 4, 1801. Until then, John Adams and the Federalists were still in power. The Federalists passed a new judiciary act creating a number of new federal courts. Adams appointed Federalists to these courts. Some were not appointed until March 2 and 3, 1801. He also appointed his secretary of state, John Marshall, to be the chief justice of the United States.

When Thomas Jefferson became president, the **commissions**, which officially gave several of these Federalists their new jobs as judges, had not been delivered to them. They were supposed to have been delivered by the outgoing secretary of state, John Marshall. Jefferson did not want more Federalists serving as judges, so he forbade the new secretary of state, James Madison, to deliver the commissions.

One commission not delivered was that of William Marbury. He had been appointed by President Adams to serve as a justice of the peace for the District of Columbia. Marbury tried to find a way to get what he believed was rightfully his. He discovered that the Judiciary Act of 1789 gave the Supreme Court the power to issue a **writ of mandamus**. A writ of mandamus is a court order that forces an officer of the government to do something that the officer is supposed to do. In this case, Marbury argued that it was Madison's duty to give him the commission. He asked the Supreme Court to issue a writ of mandamus ordering Madison to deliver it.

This put Chief Justice Marshall in a difficult position. He was worried about what might happen if the Supreme Court ordered Madison to deliver Marbury's document and President Jefferson ordered him not to, as he had threatened. Courts must rely on the executive branch for enforcement of laws. If Jefferson were to refuse to obey the order of the Supreme Court, it would make the Court appear weak and powerless. If the Supreme Court did not order the president to deliver the document, however, the Court would look weak.

Chief Justice John Marshall (1755–1835)

What were the major issues in *Marbury v. Madison*?

Chief Justice Marshall was faced with a difficult problem. He solved the problem in a very unusual and ingenious way. In arriving at his solution, Marshall asked three key questions:

1. Does Marbury have a right to the appointment?

2. If Marbury has a right to the appointment and his right has been violated, do the laws of the country give him a way to set things right?

3. If the laws of the country give Marbury a way to deal with this problem, is that a writ of mandamus from the Supreme Court?

What was Marshall's decision?

Marshall answered "yes" to the first two questions and "no" to the third.

1. **Does Marbury have a right to the appointment?**

Marshall reasoned that the appointment had been signed by the president and sealed by the secretary of state; therefore, Marbury had the right to hold the office for five years as provided by law.

2. **Do the laws of the country give Marbury a way to have things set right?**

Marshall reasoned that the secretary of state is an officer of the government directed by the Constitution and laws made by Congress to perform certain duties, such as delivering commissions. When the secretary of state refused to do so, he broke the law and violated Marbury's rights. Marshall also determined that Marbury should have a **legal remedy**, that is, a way to set things right through the courts.

3. **Is asking the Supreme Court for a writ of mandamus the right legal remedy?**

On this point, Marshall said "no." He argued that the part of the Judiciary Act that gave Marbury the right to ask the Supreme Court to issue a writ of mandamus was unconstitutional. The Constitution clearly limits the Supreme Court's **original jurisdiction**, that is, the cases it can hear without their first being heard by a lower court, to "cases affecting ambassadors, other public ministers and consuls, and those in which a state shall be a party." Marbury was not an ambassador, minister, consul, or a state, so the Supreme Court did not have the power to hear his case unless it was first heard in a lower court and then appealed to the Supreme Court.

Marshall reasoned that the part of the Judiciary Act that gave Marbury the right to have his case heard before the Supreme Court changed the Constitution. Since Congress did not have the authority to change the Constitution, that part of the Judiciary Act was unconstitutional.

Chief Justice Marshall did not order Secretary Madison to deliver the documents. Thus, the Court avoided the almost certain embarrassment of having the president, Thomas Jefferson, refuse to obey the Court's order. In the process, Marshall established a much more important power for the Supreme Court. By declaring a part of the Judiciary Act unconstitutional, the Supreme Court gained the power of judicial review simply by exercising it.

What was the significance of the Supreme Court's decision in *Marbury v. Madison*?

Although a direct confrontation over the Marbury appointment was avoided, Jefferson was opposed to the idea of judicial review. He argued that each branch should judge for itself whether a law was constitutional. No one branch, Jefferson believed, should have the power to determine constitutionality for the others. If Congress decided that an act was constitutional, and the president agreed and signed the bill, the Court should respect those judgments.

Marshall justified the Court's use of the power of judicial review with the following argument: When the people adopted the Constitution, they agreed that it would be the supreme law of the land. Therefore, they had consented to be governed by its rules, which included certain limitations on the powers of Congress. When Congress violates those limitations, it has violated the will of the people as expressed in the Constitution. If the Supreme Court did not have the power of judicial review, there would be no effective way to enforce the limitations placed on the powers of Congress in the Constitution. Its powers would be unlimited, and we would no longer have a constitutional government. The judiciary, therefore, is the guardian of the Constitution.

Why has judicial review remained controversial?

Most Americans recognize judicial review as a necessary power in our constitutional framework. They do not always agree, however, on how the courts should use this power. The Supreme Court often hears controversial cases about which there are strong feelings. Many of these cases involve disagreements about the proper role of government and the meaning of the Constitution. It is inevitable that some people will support the Court's decisions and some will criticize them. These disagreements are often over the methods used to interpret the Constitution.

What are four methods used to interpret the Constitution?

It is important to remember that judicial review is not an active power. That is, the Supreme Court cannot simply declare a law unconstitutional. The Court only hears "cases and controversies." That means that the parties to the case—like Marbury and Madison—must have a real dispute that the Court can settle. Most cases must go through the proper steps in lower courts before they are heard by the Supreme Court.

Once the Supreme Court agrees to hear a case on a constitutional issue, the justices face the difficult question of deciding whether the federal government or a state government has violated the Constitution. Understanding the meaning of some parts of the Constitution is fairly easy since they are quite specific. For example, there is little disagreement about what is meant in Article II by, "neither shall any person be eligible to that office [of president] who shall not have attained to the age of 35 years," or in Article I, "No tax or duty shall be laid on articles exported from any state."

Not all parts of the Constitution are so clear. For example, the Constitution is open to interpretation when it makes the following statements:

- Congress shall have the power to make laws that are "necessary and proper" to carry out its responsibilities.
- Citizens are protected against "unreasonable searches and seizures."
- No state shall "deprive any person of life, liberty, or property without due process of law."

Controversies over how the Constitution should be interpreted often focus on **methods of interpretation** such as the following:

1. Using the literal meaning of the words in the Constitution. With this method of interpretation, the justices should consider the literal or plain meaning of the words in the Constitution, or study what the words meant at the time they were written, and base their decisions upon them.

The Court's decisions should be based, as closely as possible, on how the Framers meant the Constitution to be interpreted. If the meaning of the words is clear, then this is the best way to find out what they meant. Also, by relying on the plain meaning, the law becomes certain and predictable.

The problem with this method, its critics say, is that Congress must still interpret the Constitution. Not only are phrases like "general welfare" vague, but some questions are not answered at all. For example, the Constitution gives Congress the power to establish an army and a navy. Does Congress not then have the power to establish an air force?

2. Using the intentions of those who wrote the Constitution. This method of interpretation is related to the "plain meaning" method. Unlike the plain meaning method, however, the "intention" method concedes that the Constitution, by itself, does not reveal its own meaning. Instead, we should look at the intentions of those who framed it. Judges should make decisions that are consistent with those intentions. They should not decide on the basis of their own understanding of what the Constitution's words mean.

What problems might arise in trying to discover the intentions of the Framers?

Critics argue that this method also asks judges to do something impossible. There were 39 signers of the Constitution, and each may have had different views of what its various provisions meant. Madison and Hamilton disagreed on the meaning of the "necessary and proper" clause in their dispute about setting up a national bank. Both were Framers. Which Framer was correct?

3. Using basic principles and values in the perspective of history. Besides its specific listing of powers, the Constitution is built upon some basic ideas about government. These include ideas of the natural rights philosophy, the principles of constitutionalism, and republican government. These ideas have a life of their own, and as the nation matures so does our understanding of these basic principles. People who hold this view believe that the justices should frame their decisions within the context of these principles and values without ignoring the realities of contemporary society. Judges have a responsibility not to hold back social progress by sticking to outmoded interpretations.

4. Using contemporary social values in terms of today's policy needs. This method argues that the justices should use contemporary social values in interpreting the Constitution to fit today's policy needs.

Critics say methods number 3 and 4 give judges too much power. The proper way to change interpretations of the Constitution is through the amending process. Controversial decisions are much better left in the hands of the elected branches, who represent the will of the majority.

Critical Thinking Exercise

EVALUATING, TAKING, AND DEFENDING POSITIONS ON JUDICIAL REVIEW

Your class should be divided into small groups. Each group should complete Parts I and II of the following exercise.

Part I: In light of what you have learned about judicial review, which of the following positions of the Founders do you agree with? Discuss the quotes with your group and be prepared to explain your answer to the class.

It is...of great importance...to examine...the judicial power, because those who are to be vested with it, are to be placed in a situation altogether unprecedented in a free country.... They are independent of the people, of the legislature, and of every power under heaven. Men placed in this situation will generally soon feel themselves independent of heaven itself.... If the legislature pass any laws, inconsistent with the sense the judges put on the constitution, they will declare it void; and therefore in this respect their power is superior to that of the legislature....

Letters of Brutus, 1787

...the judiciary, from the nature of its functions, will always be the least dangerous.... It may truly be said to have neither Force nor Will, but merely judgement.... A constitution is, in fact, and must be regarded by the judges, as a fundamental law. It therefore belongs to them to ascertain its meaning....

Alexander Hamilton, *The Federalist #78*, 1788

...the opinion which gives to the judges the right to decide what laws are constitutional and what not...would make the Judiciary a despotic branch.

Thomas Jefferson

The judiciary, therefore, is that department of the government to whom the protection of the rights of the individual is by the constitution especially confided, interposing it's shield between him and the sword of usurped authority, the darts of oppression, and the shafts of faction and violence.

St. George Tucker, 1803

Part II: Which of the following statements by former justices of the Supreme Court do you agree with? Discuss the quotes with your group and be prepared to explain your position to the class.

[The Constitution] is intended to endure for ages to come, and consequently, to be adapted to the various crises of human affairs.

Chief Justice John Marshall

We are under the Constitution, but the Constitution is what the judges say it is.

Chief Justice Charles Evans Hughes

As a member of this court I am not justified in writing my opinions into the Constitution, no matter how deeply I may cherish them.

Justice Felix Frankfurter

The case before us must be considered in the light of our whole experience and not merely in that of what was said a hundred years ago.

Justice Oliver Wendell Holmes

How has judicial review worked in practice?

In practice, justices tend to use all four methods of interpretation. They also are influenced by other considerations. These include the **precedents** courts have established in previous cases; current social policies; political and economic concerns; and, to greater or lesser degrees, their personal political, economic, and moral beliefs.

Despite these influences, the justices are conscious of their responsibility to take an objective view of the constitutional issues involved and not decide on the basis of their own personal feelings. This may mean that the Supreme Court will rule that a law is constitutional even if the justices feel that it is unwise.

While it would be unrealistic to pretend that the personal preferences of justices never affect the decisions of the Court, it is reasonable to claim that the continued authority of the Court depends on its being faithful to both the language and spirit of the Constitution.

Reviewing and Using the Lesson

1. How would you explain the power of "judicial review"? How did the Supreme Court acquire this power?

2. What were the circumstances that led to the Supreme Court's decision in the case of *Marbury v. Madison*? What were the important issues in this case? How did the Supreme Court's decision resolve these issues? Why is *Marbury v. Madison* a historically important decision?

3. What are some different approaches to interpreting the Constitution? What objections can be made to these approaches?

4. Explain the idea that courts should be guided by "precedents" in deciding cases.

5. Research each of the following cases: *Fletcher v. Peck*, 6 Cranch 87 (1810); *Dartmouth College v. Woodward*, 4 Wheaton 518 (1819); and *Gibbons v. Ogden*, 9 Wheaton 1 (1824). Report to the class the decision in each case and the significance of the decision to contemporary events.

LESSON 22

How Is Power Divided between the Federal and State Governments?

Purpose of Lesson

The purpose of this lesson is to increase your understanding of the federal system created by the Constitution. It also discusses important Supreme Court opinions that deal with the division of power between the federal and state governments. Finally, it introduces you to continuing problems in the relationship between the nation and the states as well as the expanded role of the federal government.

When you complete the lesson, you should be able to describe the basic characteristics of a federal system and give a brief explanation of the Supreme Court's opinion in *McCulloch v. Maryland* and its importance. You also should be able to describe some of the events which have led to the expanded power of the federal government.

Terms to Know

confederation
federal system
McCulloch v. Maryland
  (1819)

sovereignty
supremacy clause
unitary government

How was the federal system of government created by the Framers different from other governments of their time?

Our system of government is quite complicated. It differs in two important ways from other national systems in existence when the Constitution was written.

Sovereignty, or ultimate authority, is held by the people. In other nations, the ultimate authority was thought to be the government, even if its authority was received from the people. For example, in some nations the king was sovereign. In Great Britain, "king in Parliament" was sovereign. This meant that the king and Parliament, acting together, held the ultimate authority.

In the Preamble to the Constitution, the Framers set forth this new idea of sovereignty when they wrote, "We the People of the United States…do ordain and establish this Constitution for the United States of America." Under this new system, sovereignty remains in "the people,"

How do the people grant authority to government at all levels?

who delegate certain powers to the government. The government has the powers that the people give it, but the people retain the supreme authority.

Our government is a federal system. This means that the people have not delegated all the powers of governing to one national government. Instead, the people have delegated certain powers to their state governments, in their state constitutions. As citizens of the nation, they have delegated, in the United States Constitution, certain powers to the national government. Finally, certain powers have been kept by the people and not delegated to any government.

What kinds of governments existed before the federal system was established under the Constitution?

Before our government was established under the Constitution, most nations had been organized in one of two ways:

- unitary systems of government; or
- confederal systems of government known as confederations

Unitary governments are those in which a central government acts directly on the citizens. Local governments exercise powers granted to them by the central government. Great Britain has a unitary government.

In contrast, a **confederation** is a system of government in which sovereign states delegate power to a central government for specific purposes. States enter into a confederation for purposes such as defense and the regulation of trade.

The government of a confederation acts on the member states, not on the citizens of those states. American government under the Articles of Confederation was a confederation. Switzerland is a modern example of a confederation.

The Constitution established a system that is a combination of both unitary and confederate systems.

■ It is like a unitary government because the members of the House of Representatives are elected by the people from electoral districts of equal population. More important, it acts directly on the people in fulfilling the responsibilities it has been given by the Constitution.

■ It is like a confederation because it was ratified by state conventions, amendments are ratified by states, senators were originally chosen by state legislatures, and each state is represented by the same number of senators. In addition, the national government's power is limited to certain responsibilities.

The result of this complicated system is that both the federal and the state governments have certain powers over individual citizens, while sovereignty remains with the citizens. This system has many possibilities for disputes, most of which come down to the simple question, "Which powers have been delegated to which government?" This question was raised during the ratification debates and has remained one of the central issues in American politics ever since.

What do *you* think?

1. What are the advantages of a federal system over a confederate system? What are the disadvantages?

2. What did the Framers hope to achieve by establishing a federal system of government? Were they successful?

How did the Supreme Court gain the power of judicial review over state governments?

There were many disagreements at the Philadelphia Convention over what powers the federal government should have. There was no doubt, however, that whatever those powers were, they were superior to those of the state governments. Article VI says:

> *This constitution, and the laws of the United States which shall be made in pursuance thereof; and all treaties made…under the authority of the United States, **shall be the supreme law of the land;** and the judges in every state shall be bound thereby, anything in the constitution or laws of any state to the contrary notwithstanding.*

This section of the Constitution is known as the **supremacy clause**. It has been interpreted to mean that the United States Supreme Court can declare that state laws in violation of the Constitution or of federal laws "made in direct pursuance" of the Constitution should not be enforced. The First Congress also made this power clear in the Judiciary Act of 1789.

The Supreme Court first used its power of judicial review over **state** governments in 1796. After the Revolutionary War, the United States signed a peace treaty with the British that said all debts owed by Americans to British subjects would be paid. The state of Virginia had passed a law canceling all debts owed by Virginians to British subjects. Since this law clearly violated the peace treaty, the Supreme Court ruled that the law could not be enforced because the laws and treaties made by the federal government are the supreme law of the land. As a result, citizens of Virginia were responsible for paying their debts.

What was significant about the case of *McCulloch v. Maryland* (1819)?

The Supreme Court's decision that the national government had the power to make and enforce treaties did not provoke much controversy. After all, the national government had been created to take care of foreign affairs. Its domestic powers were more controversial. How far did the powers of Congress extend? What powers were reserved for the states? Were there areas where **both** governments had power?

A dispute over the powers of the state and federal governments came to the Supreme Court in 1819 in the case *McCulloch v. Maryland*. This case involved a bank created by the federal government, the Second Bank of the United States.

The Bank was extremely unpopular in the southern and western states. People there argued that the Bank favored the interests of wealthy shippers and merchants, and that it gave the federal government too much power. Some states attempted to prevent its operation.

In 1818, the Maryland legislature placed a heavy tax on all banks not chartered by the state. There was only one bank that fit the description: the Maryland branch of the Bank of the United States. James McCulloch, the cashier of the branch, refused to pay the tax and was sued by the state of Maryland. The state courts upheld the right of Maryland to tax the federal bank. McCulloch appealed to the Supreme Court.

McCulloch v. Maryland was one of the most important cases to be decided in the early days of the Supreme Court. Two key issues were involved. First, did Congress have the power to create a bank? Second, could the state of Maryland tax a branch of the federal bank?

The Supreme Court ruled that Congress did have the authority to create the bank. Chief Justice John Marshall said that this power was given to Congress by the "necessary and proper" clause of the Constitution. He used much the same reasoning Hamilton had used earlier to persuade President Washington to sign legislation creating the First Bank of the United States.

Turning to the second issue, Marshall insisted that the authority of the federal government comes from the people rather than from the state governments. The Constitution had not been adopted by state governments, but by people gathered in state conventions. Therefore, the Constitution gained its authority directly from the people. For this reason, the federal government, in fulfilling the responsibilities given it by the Constitution and ultimately by the people, is superior to the state governments. This is why the Framers included the supremacy clause, he argued.

Basing his argument on the supremacy clause, Marshall held that when a state law conflicts with a constitutional federal law, the federal law must be obeyed. Maryland's attempt to tax the federal bank, therefore, was illegal,

How did issues related to the creation of the Second Bank of the United States help define the authority of the federal government?

since "the power to tax involves the power to destroy." Marshall argued that if federal agencies could be taxed by the states, their existence would be dependent on the will of the states. The American people, Marshall claimed, did not design their federal government to be dependent on the states.

Marshall's ruling in *McCulloch v. Maryland* clearly established the supremacy of the federal government within its sphere of authority and increased the powers of Congress.

How has the commerce power been used to expand federal authority?

The Constitution gives Congress the power to "regulate Commerce…among the several states." What is "commerce"? In 1824, the Supreme Court gave a very wide definition of commerce in the case of *Gibbons v. Ogden.* The dispute was about whether a federal license to operate steamboats between New York and New Jersey took precedence over a state license issued by New York. The Court ruled that "navigation" was part of commerce, so the federal license took precedence.

In the late nineteenth century, the Supreme Court took a much more limited view of commerce. It also took a very limited view of "interstate." As a result, the Court denied Congress the power to regulate such things as child labor in factories. The Court ruled that manufacturing was not part of commerce. It was also something that was done entirely within a single state.

In a dramatic switch by the Court in *National Labor Relations Board v. Jones and Laughlin Steel Corp.* (1937), the previous reading limiting the commerce definition was abandoned. As a result, Congress has been able to regulate such things as minimum wages and job safety. It also has been able to enact laws regulating things that seem far removed from "commerce." For example, the Civil Rights Act of 1964 is partly based on the commerce power. The prohibitions against discrimination in employment and public accommodations are limited to employers and establishments affecting interstate commerce.

What power does the federal government have today?

Citizens demand more from the federal government today than they did in the past. In addition, the United States' political and military role in the world has greatly increased. As a result, the federal government now has far more power than anything the Framers could have imagined.

In some ways it can be argued that what the Anti-Federalists feared has indeed occurred—the federal government now has power over areas of people's lives that used to be controlled by the states or by the people themselves.

There are two important points to remember about federalism today:

1. Most of the decisions about how much power is left to the states are made by Congress, not by the Supreme Court. The Supreme Court has interpreted the Constitution to give federal government more power than it had in the past. Congress decides, on the basis of practical and political considerations, whether the federal or state governments should fulfill certain responsibilities.

2. In spite of the federal government's increased power, most of the laws that affect us directly are state laws. These include most property laws, contract laws, family laws, and criminal laws.

The power of the federal government is not limited, of course, to making laws. Indeed, it is increasingly common for the federal government to attempt to influence state law by the use of federal funds. For example, in the past the federal government used highway funds to encourage the states to set uniform speed limits. If a state did not agree to do this, it did not receive federal highway funds.

Two hundred years ago, the Framers could not have predicted the relationship today between the power of the states and the power of the federal government. The complexities of the new system of political organization they created, as well as the realities governments confront, make it equally unlikely that we can predict with a high degree of accuracy the nature of the relationship in the future.

What do *you* think?

1. Which government activities do you think are best handled at the national level and which at the state and local level? Why?

2. Explain a situation in which you think a state should be able to make a law without interference from the federal government.

3. What kinds of problems might be too difficult for state governments to handle alone?

4. The power of the federal government over the states has expanded during our history. Why do you think this has happened? Is this good or bad for the American people? Do you think there will ever be a shift back in the opposite direction?

Reviewing and Using the Lesson

1. What is "sovereignty"? In our system of government, who or what has sovereign authority?

2. How would you explain the difference between a "unitary" system of government and a "confederation"? In what ways does the government of the United States combine features of both unitary and confederate systems?

3. How would you explain the idea that our government is a "federal system"?

4. What is the "supremacy clause"? What does it mean? Why is it important?

5. How has the commerce power been used to expand the authority of the national government?

6. How did the Supreme Court interpret the "necessary and proper" clause in the case of *McCulloch v. Maryland*? Why is this case important?

7. What are some examples of the federal government's assumption of power over areas of people's lives that used to be controlled by the states or by the people themselves? How has this occurred?

Unit Four: *How Have the Protections of the Bill of Rights Been Developed and Expanded?*

Dred Scott decision (1857)	Emancipation Proclamation (1863)	13th Amendment (1865)			Plessy v. Ferguson (1896)		NAACP founded (1909)	19th Amendment (1920)				26th Amendment (1971) 24th Amendment (1964) Civil Rights Act of 1964 March on Washington (1963)
		14th Amendment (1868)										
		15th Amendment (1870)									Brown v. Board of Education (1954)	

1850s	1860s	1870s	1880s	1890s	1900s	1910s	1920s	1930s	1940s	1950s	1960s
	South Carolina is first state to secede from Union (1860)	Telephone invented (1876)		First piloted air flight (1903)	World War I begins (1914)	First woman elected to Congress (1916)	The Great Depression begins (1929)	U.S. enters World War II (1941)	First African American Supreme Court Justice (1967)		

Purpose of Unit

Chief Justice John Marshall called the Constitution a document "intended to endure for ages to come, and consequently, to be adapted to the various crises of human affairs." The Framers hoped to create a government with sufficient flexibility to assure the future of a young and growing nation and cope with circumstances that they themselves could not foresee.

In this unit you have the opportunity to study and evaluate the success of the Framers' efforts and the ability of the Constitution to be adapted to the "various crises of human affairs." You examine some important themes in the development of the Constitution from the founding era to the present day. The unit focuses on the expansion of constitutional rights as the nation tried to realize not only the principles of liberty and justice, but also equality for all Americans.

LESSON 23

What Were the Constitutional Issues That Led to the Civil War?

Purpose of Lesson

In this lesson you examine how sectional interests in the young nation created different interpretations of the Constitution. The issue of slavery widened those differences to a point that resulted in the Civil War which has been the greatest failure in America's history of constitutional government. By examining the great pre-Civil War debate over the meaning of the Constitution and the Union, you will have a better understanding of the nature of America's founding principles.

When you complete the lesson, you should be able to explain the major arguments that were made about the proper relationship between the nation and the states. You also learn how the institution of slavery forced a debate over the nation's most fundamental principles. Finally, you should be able to explain the significance of the Civil War and the Emancipation Proclamation for the development of the American political system.

How did the issue of the extension of slavery into the territories help bring about the Civil War?

Terms to Know

Dred Scott decision (1857)
Emancipation
   Proclamation

perpetual Union
secession
sectionalism

What problems were created by the growth of the United States after the founding era?

From 1789 to 1861, the population of the United States increased from 4 million to 30 million. Twenty-one new states joined the Union. By the 1850s, when California and Oregon were admitted to the Union, the United States had become a truly continental nation. Moreover, the growth in the size of the country was matched by economic development. The Northeast became a booming manufacturing center and the South the world's largest producer of cotton. The vast prairies of the Midwest were a new source of wheat, cattle, and corn. This dramatic growth, however, also created problems. Various sections of the country were divided by different economies and different ways of life. This gave rise to serious differences of opinion about the proper role of the national government and the relationship between the nation and the states. These disagreements were intensified by the issue of slavery.

How did early nineteenth-century Americans disagree about the relationship between the nation and the states?

Disagreements about the relationship between the nation and the states already existed during the writing, adoption, and ratification of the Constitution. These disagreements developed further with the rise of political parties in the early years of the nation. Jeffersonian Republicans emphasized state and local power in a strictly interpreted Constitution that granted the national government only specifically listed powers. Federalists like Alexander Hamilton and John Marshall argued for a broad interpretation of the Constitution that allowed for a strong national government possessing implied, as well as enumerated powers.

In time, **sectionalism**—economic and other conflicts among various sections of the country—intensified disagreements about the power of the national government and the relationship of the nation to the states. The Northern and Southern states were especially adamant about the question of tariffs, which the North favored and the South opposed.

Compromise was part of the American political tradition. It had been the key to the successful deliberations of the Constitutional Convention. The sectional interests of early nineteenth-century America might have been settled through political compromise, if it were not for the reemergence of an issue about which there could be no accommodation—slavery. The institution of slavery also had challenged the Framers. A majority of the Framers may have assumed that slavery would eventually disappear of its own accord, since they had provided an opportunity for Congress to act after 1808 to abolish the slave trade. This did not happen, however. Slavery was regarded as primarily a local matter for each state to decide.

Though slavery eventually disappeared in all the Northern states and was banned by law from the Northwest Territory, it survived in the South. In the South, growth in cotton production was used as a rationale for slavery's continued existence. Slavery became a symbol of the sectional rivalries between North and South.

Americans on both sides were forced to examine and debate the nation's most fundamental principles and identity. Do we believe in the principles of the Declaration of Independence or not? Are we one nation or a confederacy made up of the various states? These were the constitutional issues that were at stake at the outbreak of the Civil War.

Why was the Dred Scott decision important?

One of the most important and controversial Supreme Court decisions in American history was the **Dred Scott decision** of 1857. Dred Scott was an enslaved African who had been taken to the free state of Illinois and the free Wisconsin Territory and, later, back to Missouri, a slave state. In 1846 Scott sued the man who held him in servitude on the grounds that he had achieved his freedom by residing in free territory. When the Missouri Supreme Court ruled against him, Scott sued in the

Dred Scott (c. 1795–1858)
Why was the decision in the Dred Scott case a major defeat for antislavery forces?

federal Circuit Court in Missouri. When that court also ruled against him, Scott's attorney appealed the case to the U.S. Supreme Court.

Chief Justice Roger Taney wrote the Court's opinion, which reached several conclusions. Two were explosive in their significance:

- Blacks, whether slave or free, could not be citizens of the United States. Individual states might grant them state citizenship, but they could not enjoy the rights and protections of national citizenship under the Constitution. Taney reached this conclusion on the ground that blacks were not recognized as U.S. citizens when the Constitution was ratified.

- The federal government did not have the right to exclude slavery from the territories. Enslaved Africans, Taney argued, were property and property rights were protected under the due process clause of the Fifth Amendment to the Constitution. The right to own slaves, in other words, was protected by the Constitution. A slaveholder, therefore, had the right to take enslaved Africans into the territories.

Taney hoped that by invoking the authority and prestige of the Supreme Court in so definitive a ruling, he could peacefully resolve the conflict over slavery and avoid a civil war. His opinion, however, had exactly the opposite effect. Some believe that the Dred Scott decision was one of the principal causes of the Civil War.

In 1860 Abraham Lincoln was elected president in one of the nation's most significant elections. The election was marked by the controversy about slavery. Faced with the prospect of a national administration committed to the restriction and eventual abolition of slavery, the Southern states responded with **secession**. One by one, they voted to leave—secede from—the Union. They planned to form a new union called the Confederate States of America. The Southern secessionists believed they had a constitutional right to do this, based on their view of the Union as a compact of sovereign states. If the Union was only a federation of sovereign states, they could leave the Union to protect their basic rights.

President Lincoln and most Northerners, however, denied the constitutional right of any state to secede from the Union. Secession was not sanctioned by the Constitution and was, therefore, an act of rebellion or revolution. They believed that the Framers had created a **perpetual Union**, a national bond expressing the sovereign authority of the American people as a whole.

What do *you* think?

1. How did sectional rivalries in pre-Civil War America encourage different interpretations of the Constitution and the Union?

2. Which basic rights were in conflict in the Dred Scott case and what are some examples of similar conflicts today?

3. Why did the Southern states believe that secession was a constitutional action? Why did supporters of the Union believe that the South had no constitutional right to secede?

What was President Lincoln's view of the principle of secession?

How did the struggle to preserve the Union become a crusade for freedom?

At the outset of the Civil War, President Lincoln and most Northerners believed the war's objective was to preserve the Union. Though personally opposed to slavery, Lincoln believed his public duty as president was the defense of the existing Constitution, even if that meant the continued existence of slavery. Refusing to recognize the right of secession, he viewed the war as a "domestic insurrection." He hoped it would be concluded quickly and the Union would be preserved.

From its onset in April 1861, the war became a long and bloody conflict that hardened views on both sides. Eventually, supporters of the Union recognized that victory would require the conquest and destruction of much of the South.

The prolonged and bitter struggle opened the way for an expansion of the war's objectives. As the war dragged on, there was increased support in the North for demands that victory should mean the end of slavery. Only in this way, many believed, could the war find a purpose worthy enough to justify its terrible cost. As one long-time opponent of slavery declared

[T]his is not a war of geographic sections, nor political factions, but of principles and systems. [It is] a war for social equality, for rights, for justice, for freedom. Its outcome should not be the preservation of the old Union, but rather the creation of a new nation freed of slavery.

Why did Lincoln issue the Emancipation Proclamation?

For over a year President Lincoln resisted pressures to expand the war's aims to include the abolition of slavery. As he told the newspaper editor, Horace Greeley:

My paramount object...is to save the Union.... If I could save the Union without freeing any slave, I would do it; and if I could save it by freeing all the slaves, I would do it; and if I could do it by freeing some and leaving others alone, I would also do that.

Lincoln hoped to persuade the Southern states to cease their rebellion and he was worried about alienating those slave-holding states, like Kentucky, that had remained loyal to the Union. At most, Lincoln was prepared to support a gradual and voluntary ending of slavery.

By the summer of 1862, Lincoln had become convinced that winning the war required him to adopt the last of the three alternatives he had stated in his letter to Greeley—to free those enslaved Africans in the rebellious states. For Lincoln, this partial emancipation was a military necessity, and he was prepared to use his wartime powers as commander in chief to carry it out. He believed that the abolition of slavery would destroy the South's ability to make war.

Five days after the North's victory at Antietam (Sharpsburg) in September 1862, Lincoln issued his preliminary announcement of the **Emancipation Proclamation**. He announced that all enslaved Africans in states or parts of states still in rebellion on January 1, 1863, "shall be then, henceforward, and forever free." The president's action was a small step, justified only as a "fit and necessary war measure." Critics denounced it as an empty gesture. It left alone slavery in areas under federal control and abolished it only where the government then lacked the power to make emancipation a reality. Moreover, had all the Southern states ceased their rebellion before the January deadline, the war would have ended with slavery intact.

For all its limitations, the Emancipation Proclamation had a very important political and symbolic significance. The fight for the Union was now committed in principle to a partial ending of slavery by force of arms. Lincoln had taken the first step in making the war not only a struggle for the preservation of the Union but for its founding principles as well. In his annual message to Congress, issued a month before the Emancipation Proclamation was to take effect, Lincoln outlined a plan for the total abolition of slavery and declared:

Fellow-citizens, we cannot escape history.... The fiery trial through which we pass, will light us down, in honor or dishonor, to the latest generation.... In giving freedom to the slave, we assure freedom to the free—honoring alike in what we give, and what we preserve. We shall nobly save, or meanly lose, the last best hope of earth.

The Civil War finally resolved this great constitutional issue. The victory of the North also ended forever the idea of secession as a constitutional right and with it, the vision of the Union as a mere federation of states. Though states would continue to enjoy a significant amount of power and independence in the system of federalism created by the Constitution, the Civil War marked the beginning of a development that has continued to the present day. This is the supremacy of the national government, with powers sufficient to promote the "general welfare" of the people as a whole.

The nature of the Union was not the only issue to be resolved in the war's outcome. The issue of slavery had been settled as well. As Lincoln declared at Gettysburg, the war had made possible "a new birth of freedom."

What do *you* think?

1. Why do you suppose state governments posed greater threats to individual rights than did the federal government?

2. Why were the ideas of the natural rights philosophy as expressed in the Declaration of Independence used in the fight against slavery?

COME AND JOIN US BROTHERS.
PUBLISHED BY THE SUPERVISORY COMMITTEE FOR RECRUITING COLORED REGIMENTS

What roles did free blacks and slaves play in the Civil War?

Reviewing and Using the Lesson

1. What is the difference between "enumerated powers" and "implied powers"? How is this related to the conflict between "strict interpretation" and "broad interpretation" of the Constitution?

2. What was the Dred Scott case about? Why was the Supreme Court's decision in that case important?

3. How did Southern states justify their decision to secede from the Union? How did President Lincoln and other Northerners justify treating secession as an act of rebellion?

4. What was the Emancipation Proclamation? Why did Lincoln issue it?

5. Conduct research on how territorial expansion of the United States increased disagreements over slavery. Include in your research the Missouri Compromise of 1820, the Compromise of 1850, and the Kansas-Nebraska Act of 1854.

LESSON 24

What Amendments to the Constitution Were Added to Protect the Rights of African Americans?

Purpose of Lesson

In this lesson you examine the laws passed and the amendments added to the Constitution after the Civil War. These were intended to free enslaved Africans and give them the same rights other Americans had. These amendments, however, were not enough to guarantee the new citizens their rights. You learn how some states passed their own laws to deny African Americans their rights and prevent them from developing political power.

When you complete this lesson, you should be able to explain how the federal government attempted to use the Civil War Amendments to the Constitution to protect the rights of African Americans. You should be able to describe how the government used civil rights legislation to achieve the same end. You also should be able to explain how these attempts to end political discrimination against African Americans were limited at the state level.

Terms to Know

abridged
Black Codes
Civil Rights Act
  of 1866
Civil Rights Act
  of 1875
Civil War Amendments
grandfather clauses
Ku Klux Klan

literacy tests
Nineteenth Amendment
poll taxes
privileges and immunities
  clause
Reconstruction
Slaughterhouse Cases
vigilante

What was the Reconstruction period ?

The period after the Civil War is called **Reconstruction**. States that had seceded were being brought back into the Union. The Republican party, which got most of its support from the Northern states, continued to dominate the federal government. The Democratic party was strongly supported in the South. Many Confederate leaders were members of the Democratic party.

Since most slaveholders also had been members of the Democratic party, it was expected that the freed blacks would vote for the Republican party. As you shall see, this expectation strongly influenced some political battles fought over the rights of African Americans during Reconstruction.

Why were the Civil War Amendments added to the Constitution?

The Civil War ended more than 200 years of slavery in America. Shortly after the war, three amendments, commonly called the **Civil War Amendments**, were added to the Constitution.

- The **Thirteenth Amendment** (1865) abolished slavery "within the United States, or in any place subject to their jurisdiction."

- The **Fourteenth Amendment** (1868), among other things, made all persons born or naturalized within the United States citizens. It also prohibited any state from making or enforcing any law that abridged the privileges or immunities of citizens.

- The **Fifteenth Amendment** (1870) prohibited the national and state governments from denying citizens the right to vote because of their race, color, or status as former slaves.

The first session of Congress held after the Civil War was in December 1865. Congress and many state governments immediately passed laws designed to protect the rights of African Americans. When Congress tried vigorously to implement these laws, its efforts were strongly resisted by whites, especially in the South, who opposed racial equality. Eventually public support for protecting the rights of the newly freed people grew weaker and, by the late 1870s, the Fourteenth and Fifteenth Amendments had become useless as a tool for protecting their rights.

What was the effect of the Thirteenth Amendment?

The Thirteenth Amendment, ratified in 1865, was intended to end slavery and the unfair treatment of African Americans throughout the nation.

Several states did pass laws to expand the rights of African Americans. In 1865, both Illinois and California passed laws allowing blacks to testify against whites in trials. Massachusetts passed a law prohibiting racial discrimination in public accommodations. In 1868, both Minnesota and Iowa passed laws giving African American males the right to vote.

Some states refused to ratify the Thirteenth Amendment. Others demanded that the federal government pay their slaveholders for the loss of their laborers. Although some Southerners were in favor of freeing the enslaved Africans, many were not. Slavery had accustomed Southerners to seeing blacks as inferior. Plantation and farm owners had grown accustomed to using enslaved Africans as a cheap form of labor.

Many Northerners also were interested in cheap labor. White workers had been organizing into labor unions and were demanding better pay and working conditions. Owners of factories and other businesses saw the newly freed African Americans as a source of cheap labor.

Some workers in the North feared that black workers might compete for jobs by accepting lower wages. These Northerners wanted African Americans to stay in the South and West where they would not pose a threat to job availability or the power to organize for better working conditions.

Why did some people want to prevent African Americans from getting an education?

Whose political power did the Black Codes protect?

After the Civil War, the federal government kept Union troops in the South to protect African Americans. Southern legislatures passed laws called the **Black Codes** in an attempt to convince the federal government that they would treat African Americans fairly. Supposedly, these laws protected the rights of African Americans. The Black Codes were actually intended to prevent the former slaves from developing the political power they might have gained with education and the right to vote.

For example, the Black Codes protected the rights of African Americans to marry, own property, travel, work for pay, and sue in court. In fact, they severely limited these rights. African Americans could only marry other African Americans. They could own property, but few white people would sell it to them. They could travel, but only after dark and in the baggage cars of trains. They could work for pay, but few employers would pay them fair wages. They could sue for damages in court, but their right to sue white people was meaningless because cases were tried by white judges and juries who were hostile to black people.

In the Southern states, the educational opportunities for blacks were far fewer than those for whites. Schools for black students were usually inferior to those for white students. Black students could only go to school with other black children. People were discouraged from starting schools for African Americans and sometimes

such schools were burned. White supremacists did not want African Americans to be educated and those found with books were sometimes whipped.

Vigilante groups such as the **Ku Klux Klan** intimidated, terrorized, and sometimes killed black people and the whites who helped them claim their rights. African Americans could rarely look to their local or state governments for protection from such treatment. Law enforcement agencies and the courts were biased against black people and the whites who sympathized with them. African Americans were tried by all-white juries who rarely decided a case in their favor, no matter what the facts were.

When the Union troops withdrew, a reign of terror began in the South. Black people trying to gain their rights were assaulted and lynched. A white state senator who was sympathetic to the cause of African Americans was found with his throat slit. Others were lynched with signs hung around their necks saying such things as "beware, ye guilty, both white and black." Black Codes clearly placed the political power of the Southern states in the hands of white men.

Why did Congress pass the Civil Rights Act of 1866?

It became clear to members of Congress that the Thirteenth Amendment was not enough to protect the rights of African Americans. In an attempt to provide help, the **Civil Rights Act of 1866** was passed over the veto of President Andrew Johnson.

Despite the passing of this legislation, little changed. The president refused to enforce the laws and the Supreme Court refused to listen to people who complained that their rights, supposedly protected by the Civil Rights Act, had been violated.

Many political leaders in the North and elsewhere were outraged by the treatment of African Americans in the South. Republicans also were concerned that their power in the federal government might soon be endangered by the new Democratic representatives elected to Congress by the Southern states.

As a result of these concerns, Republicans in Congress drafted the Fourteenth and later the Fifteenth Amendment to be added to the Constitution. These amendments were written for both moral and political reasons. Many Republican leaders strongly believed in protecting the rights of African Americans. For this reason, they argued that only if Southern black people had the right to vote would the officials of their state and local governments be responsive to them and protect their rights.

In addition to protecting the rights of African Americans, Republicans also were interested in increasing the political power of black citizens in the Southern states. This was intended to keep the Republican party in power in the federal government and to limit the growing power of the Democratic party.

How well did the Civil War Amendments protect the rights of African Americans?

The Fourteenth Amendment. The Republicans had gained their objective and they dominated Congress. Strong laws were passed by Congress to enforce the Fourteenth Amendment. During the late 1860s and 1870s, state legislatures and courts in both the North and South tried to expand the rights of African Americans and enforce laws against discrimination. These efforts were not always successful.

The Fifteenth Amendment. The failure of the Fourteenth Amendment to protect adequately the rights of black citizens led to the adoption of the Fifteenth Amendment in 1870. This amendment contains the following two sections:

> *Section 1. The right of citizens of the United States to vote shall not be denied or abridged by the United States or by any state on account of race, color, or previous condition of servitude.*

> *Section 2. The Congress shall have the power to enforce this article by appropriate legislation.*

This amendment was clearly intended to protect the right of African Americans to vote. People believed that black citizens should have the same rights as all other citizens.

The immediate effect of this amendment and the legislation passed to support it was that, during the late 1860s through the 1880s, large numbers of African Americans voted. They gained considerable political power and they used it to protect their rights.

How did the Fifteenth Amendment protect the right to vote for African Americans?

Eliminating the African American power base in the South. After the Reconstruction period, Southern states began passing laws to destroy the political power of blacks in the South. The following are the major types of laws that were used to eliminate the participation of African Americans in politics in the Southern states.

- **Poll taxes.** Some states passed laws that required citizens to pay a tax before voting. Since most black people were desperately poor, these taxes greatly reduced the number who could vote.

- **Literacy tests**. Some states required citizens to take tests proving they could read or write before they were allowed to vote. Since most African Americans in the South had been prevented from learning how to read or write, these tests denied them the right to vote. Furthermore, these tests were administered by white people who prevented even literate African Americans from passing.

- **Grandfather clauses**. Laws were passed that allowed people in the South to vote, even if they could not read or write, if their grandfathers had voted. Since no African Americans had grandfathers who had voted, these laws denied African Americans the right to vote.

What do *you* think?

1. How did ratification of the Fourteenth Amendment reflect the failure of the original Constitution to achieve the goals stated in the Preamble?

2. In your opinion, have the goals of the Fourteenth Amendment as originally conceived been achieved? Explain.

Did the Bill of Rights, the Civil War Amendments, and the Civil Rights Act of 1875 accomplish their goals?

In the years following the Civil War, there was less and less talk about the rights and living conditions of African Americans. Unfortunately, the federal Bill of Rights offered little relief against injustice.

The Fourteenth Amendment contains the clause, "No state shall make or enforce any law which shall **abridge** the privileges or immunities of citizens of the United States." The Supreme Court was asked in the **Slaughterhouse Cases** of 1873 to rule that this clause protected the rights listed in the Bill of Rights from violation by state governments. The Court refused. The states still had the power to pass laws that violated the Bill of Rights. As a result of the Court's opinion in these cases, the **privileges and immunities clause** of the Fourteenth Amendment has been of little use in protecting individual rights to this day.

Congress passed the **Civil Rights Act of 1875** to give the federal government the power to enforce the protections of citizens' rights guaranteed under the Fourteenth Amendment. This act was not enforced by the executive branch. Later, the Supreme Court declared the Civil Rights Act of 1875 unconstitutional.

Rutherford B. Hayes of Ohio was the Republican candidate for president in 1876. Hayes won the election with a minority of the popular vote, but a majority of the electoral vote.

Hayes had campaigned under the promise that he would remove the remaining federal troops from the South. In 1877, soon after he was elected, he appointed a former Confederate leader to the cabinet. It was a symbolic gesture, but a clear signal. It was time to get on with expanding the economy and territory of the United States. Reconstruction was over.

In what ways did the laws in this illustration deny African Americans the right to vote?

Hayes and his supporters did not want to spend more time and money on the former slaves. They wanted to let Southern leaders handle their own problems. As the president told African Americans on a supposed "good will tour" of the South, "Your rights and interests would be safer if this great mass of intelligent white men were left alone by the federal government."

Hayes refused to enforce the Fourteenth and Fifteenth Amendments. One result of this failure was that African Americans learned to look to themselves and their own community institutions for help.

Ministers, teachers, and community leaders such as Sojourner Truth became the backbone of the continuing struggle for the rights of African Americans. They formed the leadership of the black community for the next hundred years.

Nevertheless, despite their limited effectiveness, the Civil War Amendments had created a constitutional basis for expanding the rights of individuals and minorities.

What do *you* think?

1. Was the failure of the Civil War Amendments primarily the responsibility of elected officials or private citizens?

2. Which of the Civil War Amendments has had the greatest impact on the protection of individual rights? Explain your reasoning.

3. What remedies, besides passing laws, might reduce or prevent discrimination? What are the advantages and disadvantages of each of these remedies?

4. Excluding laws, what remedies for discrimination are presently being used in your community or state? Explain them.

Critical Thinking Exercise
EXAMINING ALTERNATIVE MEANS OF PREVENTING DISCRIMINATION

You have seen that neither the Civil War Amendments nor the civil rights acts passed during the Reconstruction period achieved their goals. Work with a partner or in small groups to discuss and answer the following questions.

1. What were some reasons why these amendments and laws had so little effect?

Sojourner Truth (c. 1797–1883)
How did Sojourner Truth and other community leaders struggle to win rights for African Americans?

2. Suppose that Congress passed civil rights legislation today that was intended to protect racial and ethnic minorities from discrimination. Assume this legislation met resistance similar to that of the Reconstruction period. If you were a member of a group that wanted to see the goals of the legislation achieved, what are some actions your group could undertake to ensure its enforcement?

Reviewing and Using the Lesson

1. How would you describe the period after the Civil War known as Reconstruction?

2. What are the Civil War Amendments? What rights were they intended to secure? How effective were they when they were first adopted?

3. What are poll taxes, literacy tests, and grandfather clauses? How were they used to deny African Americans the right to vote?

4. What were the Black Codes? Why were they enacted?

5. What is the privileges and immunities clause? How important has it been in protecting individual rights?

6. Develop a time line illustrating the major events in the evolution of the civil rights movement from the Civil War to the present.

LESSON 25

How Did the Fourteenth Amendment Expand Constitutional Protections of Rights?

Purpose of Lesson

Next to the preservation of the Union and the abolition of slavery, the most important constitutional development of the post Civil War era was the passage of the Fourteenth Amendment. Originally intended to protect the rights of newly freed African Americans, the "Great Amendment," as it is sometimes called, has become a principal guarantee of the rights of all Americans, as important as the Bill of Rights itself.

In this lesson you examine those provisions of the Fourteenth Amendment that have made it so important. They gave new meaning to our concepts of citizenship, due process of law, and equal protection of the laws. You also examine the process of incorporation, by which many protections included in the Bill of Rights have been expanded to protect the rights of individuals against actions by state governments.

When you finish the lesson you should be able to explain the purpose of the Fourteenth Amendment and its three key provisions—privileges and immunities, due process of law, and equal protection of the laws. You also should be able to explain the distinctions between procedural and substantive due process; and different interpretations of the word "equality" in the principle of equal protection of the laws. Finally, you should be able to define incorporation and describe its effect on the federal system and the power of the states.

Terms to Know

double jeopardy
due process
equal protection of the laws
equality of condition
fair trial standard
Gitlow v. New York (1925)
Griswold v. Connecticut (1965)
incorporation
Palko v. Connecticut (1937)
Powell v. Alabama (1932)
preferred freedoms
procedural due process
selective incorporation
substantive due process

What parts of the Fourteenth Amendment remain important to us today?

The Fourteenth Amendment was initiated by Congress as part of its Reconstruction policy for the defeated South. The first and last sections of the amendment remain among the most important words in our Constitution.

> *Section 1. All persons born or naturalized in the United States and subject to the jurisdiction thereof, are citizens of the United States and of the State wherein they reside. No State shall make or enforce any law which shall abridge the privileges or immunities of citizens of the United States; nor shall any State deprive any person of life, liberty, or property, without due process of law; nor deny to any person within its jurisdiction the equal protection of the laws.*

> *Section 5. The Congress shall have power to enforce, by appropriate legislation, the provisions of this article.*

The constitutional guarantees expressed in Section 1 and the power of Congress to enforce them, as provided for in Section 5, are what make the Fourteenth Amendment important to us today.

Why is citizenship such an important status?

How does the Fourteenth Amendment change the definition of citizenship?

Section 1 of the Amendment first declares that "all persons born or naturalized in the United States and subject to the jurisdiction thereof, are citizens of the United States and of the State wherein they reside." To protect the rights of African Americans, the authors of the Fourteenth Amendment first of all had to establish that African Americans were citizens of the United States. The Dred Scott decision said that they were not. Among its other goals, the Fourteenth Amendment was intended to nullify this decision which had helped to cause the Civil War.

The Amendment also cleared up some confusion left by the Framers. The Constitution mentions citizenship but does not define it. During the decades before the Civil War, the relationship between citizenship rights in various states and the relationship between state and national citizenship was unclear.

Section 1 clarifies that United States citizenship is paramount to state citizenship, and that U.S. citizens have certain rights that no state government can take away.

How does the Fourteenth Amendment extend the meaning of due process of law?

[N]or shall any State deprive any person of life, liberty, or property, without due process of law.
Section 1, Fourteenth Amendment

Due process of law is one of the oldest constitutional principles. The concept appears in the Magna Carta, as well as in later landmarks of English and American constitutional history. The principle of due process of law is expressed in the Declaration of Independence and in the original Constitution. The words themselves were first added to the Constitution in 1791 when the Fifth Amendment was ratified.

The term **due process** refers to the requirement that the actions of government be conducted according to the rule of law. No government can be above the law. Both the lessons of history and the natural rights philosophy declare that each person possesses rights to life, liberty, and property. Government cannot interfere with these rights except according to established procedures of law. The principle of due process of law is one of the most important protections against arbitrary rule. The Fifth Amendment prevents the federal government from depriving any person of life, liberty, or property without due process of law. Many state declarations of rights provide the same protection against the actions of state governments. The Fourteenth Amendment **requires** state governments to respect due process of law and gives the federal government the power to enforce this requirement.

What do *you* think?

1. What is the relationship between due process and the natural rights philosophy?

2. How is the due process clause related to the principle of limited government?

What is the difference between procedural and substantive due process of law?

Due process originally meant that government must use fair procedures in fulfilling its responsibilities. This is known as **procedural due process**. It requires that the procedures used by government in making, applying, interpreting, and enforcing the law be reasonable and consistent.

Procedural due process limits the powers of government in order to protect individual rights. For example, police must use fair procedures in investigating crimes and in arresting and questioning suspects. Courts must use fair procedures in trying people suspected of crimes. The legislative and executive branches must treat people fairly, as well. Congress, for example, is required to follow due process when it conducts hearings.

How are you protected by your right to due process?

Over the years this traditional definition of due process of law has been expanded to include **substantive due process** as well. This is the requirement that government cannot make laws that apply to situations in which the government has no business interfering. It requires that the "substance" or purpose of laws be constitutional. For example, the right to substantive due process prohibits government from making laws or taking actions that interfere with certain areas of your life. These are areas, such as personal privacy, that the government has no right to regulate. It is not the business of government to interfere with what you believe, what friends you choose to associate with, the kind of work you want to do, where you want to travel, or whom you want to marry. Though not specifically mentioned in the Constitution or Bill of Rights, such basic freedoms are protected by substantive due process.

Before the Civil War, the Supreme Court used the idea of substantive due process several times in decisions regarding laws made by Congress. Chief Justice Taney used it in the Dred Scott decision to declare that Congress could not prohibit a slaveholder from taking slaves into the territories. Such a prohibition, Taney argued, was a violation of due process under the Fifth Amendment.

It was only after the adoption of the Fourteenth Amendment, however, that the idea of substantive due process became widely used. This was because the due process clause of the Fourteenth Amendment applied to the states. At that time state legislatures were more active than Congress in passing laws that affected the lives of citizens.

What do *you* think?

1. How might the rights of a criminal under the due process clause conflict with the common good? With freedom of the press? How should such conflicts be dealt with?

2. What is the difference between substantive and procedural due process? Give examples.

3. If a state law provided free counsel only for defendants in death penalty cases, would this be a violation of due process of law? Which concept of due process of law—procedural or substantive— would be involved? Explain your choice.

How does the Fourteenth Amendment promote equal protection of the laws?

Section 1 of the Fourteenth Amendment concludes by declaring that no state may "deny to any person within its jurisdiction the equal protection of the laws." By this provision the amendment gave a new importance to the principle of equality in the Constitution. As one of the Fourteenth Amendment's authors, Senator Jacob M. Howard of Michigan, declared,

It establishes equality before the law, and it gives, to the humblest, the poorest, the most despised...the same rights and the same protection before the law as it gives to the most

powerful, the most wealthy, or those most haughty.... Without this principle of equal justice to all men and equal protection under the shield of the law, there can be no republican government and none that is really worth maintaining.

The authors of the Fourteenth Amendment did not intend to protect a right to **equality of condition**. That would mean that government was responsible for guaranteeing that all its citizens were equal in the amount of property they possessed, their living standards, education, medical care, and working conditions. The authors of the Fourteenth Amendment wanted to create a society in which all people were treated equally before the law.

Equal protection of the laws meant that no individual or group was to receive special privileges or be deprived of certain rights under the law. The Fourteenth Amendment does not, however, prevent legislatures from passing laws that treat some people differently when there is a reasonable basis for doing so. For example, it does not prevent a legislature from passing a law granting the privilege of a driver's license only to those 16 or older, or denying the right to purchase alcoholic beverages to persons younger than 21. The equal protection clause was intended to prevent legislatures from passing laws that unreasonably and unfairly favor some groups over others.

What do *you* think?

1. What responsibilities, if any, are implied by the right to equal protection under the law?

2. Do you think the equal protection clause should be applied to require each state to spend the same amount per pupil on public education? Why or why not?

3. What are the differences between equality of condition and equal protection of the law?

4. In your opinion, is it ever just to treat people unequally? Explain.

How did incorporation make the protections of the Bill of Rights applicable to state governments?

Incorporation means the act of including one thing within something else. The Bill of Rights was originally intended to limit the powers of the federal government in order to protect the rights of the people and the states. The Bill of Rights did not protect the rights of individuals from state or local governments.

The Fourteenth Amendment provided a basis for removing this limitation by specifically prohibiting the states from violating a person's right to life, liberty, and property without due process of law. It also gave the federal government the authority to enforce this prohibition.

In a sense, incorporation turned the original intent of the Bill of Rights upside down. In addition to limiting the powers of the federal government in order to protect state and local rights, the incorporation of most of the Bill of Rights in the Fourteenth Amendment became a means by which the federal government prevented state and local governments from violating individual rights.

How did the Fourteenth Amendment incorporate the Bill of Rights?

During the first decades after the ratification of the Fourteenth Amendment the courts interpreted the amendment in a way that relied on the states to be the principal protectors of individual rights. Most judges at that time did not want to change the balance of power in the federal system. To do so would dramatically expand federal control over the criminal justice systems of the states, as well as over other areas that had been under local control since colonial times.

In *Gitlow v. New York* (1925) the Supreme Court began to identify certain fundamental rights protected by the due process clause of the Fourteenth Amendment. In that case the Court recognized the rights of free speech and

free press as among the personal rights to liberty protected by the due process clause of the Fourteenth Amendment. In a series of cases during the next two decades, the Court ruled that all the rights in the First Amendment—assembly, petition, and religion as well as speech and press—were protected from state action by the due process clause.

The Supreme Court was reluctant, however, to apply to the states those provisions in the Fourth through the Eighth Amendments that concerned criminal procedures. This was an area where state governments had been more active than the federal government and where procedural rights varied greatly from state to state. The justices did not find it reasonable, therefore, for the federal government to apply the specific procedural guarantees of the Bill of Rights as a "strait jacket" on the states.

Moreover, a majority of justices at this time did not believe that such specific procedural guarantees were as fundamentally important as the rights guaranteed by the First Amendment. First Amendment rights were considered **preferred freedoms**, without which a free society could not exist.

During the 1930s the Supreme Court did recognize certain rights of criminal procedure as being essential to protecting liberty under the due process clause. For example, in *Powell v. Alabama* (1932) it ruled that the right to counsel in death penalty trials was required by

Does equal protection of the law mean that all people have a right to equality of condition? Why? Why not?

What role does the Supreme Court play in the protection of individual rights?

the due process clause. But in ***Palko v. Connecticut*** (1937) the Court ruled that the Fifth Amendment's protection against **double jeopardy**—being tried twice for the same crime—was not essential to due process. Speaking for the Court, Justice Benjamin Cardozo tried to sharpen the distinction between fundamental and non-fundamental rights. The former, he said, were "of the very essence of a scheme of ordered liberty."

Most, but not all, of the Supreme Court justices at that time agreed with this position. One who did not was Justice Hugo Black. He argued that choosing between essential and nonessential rights in the Bill of Rights allowed judges to write their own subjective views into the law and caused too much confusion. Black believed that all the specific rights in the Bill of Rights should be incorporated into the due process clause of the Fourteenth Amendment. By this he meant that they should be applied to the states with exactly the same meaning and in exactly the same way as the Bill of Rights applied them to the federal government.

For a time, a majority of justices on the Supreme Court rejected Black's arguments for complete incorporation. State courts were not held accountable to most of the judicial protections in the Bill of Rights. The Supreme Court applied instead what Justice Felix Frankfurter called a **fair trial standard**. Decisions were based on whether the state in a given case had abided by those "canons of decency and fairness" fundamental to traditional notions of justice, but not necessarily in accord with the specific provisions of the Bill of Rights.

Then, in the 1960s, the Supreme Court changed course. It rejected the fair trial standard for a **selective incorporation** of most of the criminal procedure guarantees in the Bill of Rights. A general right to counsel, protection against self-incrimination and double jeopardy, and other procedural guarantees were found to be essential to due process under the Fourteenth Amendment.

Nonetheless, the Court avoided total incorporation. Certain specific provisions in the Bill of Rights have not yet been incorporated. These include the right to bear arms, to be protected against the quartering of troops in private homes, the right to an indictment by a grand jury, and the right to a jury trial as guaranteed by the Sixth and Seventh Amendments.

The Supreme Court has prohibited states from violating additional rights that do not specifically appear in the Bill of Rights. For example, in 1965 the Court ruled in ***Griswold v. Connecticut*** that the due process clause includes a right to marital privacy that forbids states from outlawing the use of contraceptives. In recent years the scope of the due process clause has become important in the constitutional debate about abortion.

What do *you* think?

1. Has incorporation undermined the Anti-Federalists' desire to protect state sovereignty through a bill of rights?

2. Why has the Supreme Court decided over the years to make most of the Bill of Rights' protections apply to state governments' actions?

3. What guidelines would you use to decide whether a right should be incorporated?

4. Why is the Fourteenth Amendment potentially a more important source of rights than the Bill of Rights?

What are the results of the incorporation of rights?

When the Bill of Rights only limited the power of the federal government, it was of almost no importance in protecting the rights of individuals. The great change occurred when the Supreme Court applied the protections of the Bill of Rights to the states through the due process clause of the Fourteenth Amendment. Instead of limiting only the power of the federal government, the Bill of Rights now also limits the power of state governments in an effort to achieve the fundamental purpose of the Constitution—protecting the rights of American citizens.

Reviewing and Using the Lesson

1. How did the Fourteenth Amendment change the definition of citizenship?

2. How would you explain the concept of due process of law? How does the Fourteenth Amendment extend the guarantee of due process of law?

3. How would you explain the difference between procedural due process of law and substantive due process of law?

4. How would you explain the Fourteenth Amendment's guarantee of equal protection of the laws? How is equal protection of the laws different from equality of condition?

5. How would you explain the doctrine of incorporation? What positions have been taken by Supreme Court justices regarding this doctrine?

6. How has the Fourteenth Amendment enhanced the importance of the Bill of Rights?

7. Research the Supreme Court cases *Gitlow v. New York*, 268 U.S. 652 (1925), *Powell v. Alabama*, 287 U.S. 45 (1932), and *Griswold v. Connecticut*, 381 U.S. 479 (1965) and report on how the decisions in these cases expanded individual rights.

LESSON 26

How Did the Civil Rights Movement Use the Constitution to Achieve Its Goals?

Purpose of Lesson

In this lesson you consider how the Fourteenth Amendment and other parts of the Constitution made it possible to secure and expand the rights of American citizens. The focus of the lesson is the Civil Rights era, a century after the Civil War. You examine Supreme Court decisions which interpreted the equal protection clause differently at different times in our history. You study the effects of the "separate but equal doctrine" and how the civil rights movement of the 1960s used both the protections of the Constitution and nonviolent direct action to end legal segregation.

When you finish the lesson, you should be able to explain how the Supreme Court's application of the equal protection clause has changed from the late nineteenth century to the present. You should be able to explain the "separate but equal doctrine" and the significance of the Supreme Court decisions in *Plessy v. Ferguson* and *Brown v. Board of Education*. You also should be able to describe the roles of the legislative, executive, and judicial branches of government in ending legal segregation. You should be able to describe how members of the civil rights movement used nonviolent direct action and their constitutional rights to oppose legal segregation and secure additional rights.

Terms to Know

Brown v. Board of
  Education of Topeka
  (1954)
civil disobedience
Civil Rights Act of 1964
commerce clause
Jim Crow laws
"Letter from
  Birmingham City Jail"
  (1963)
Montgomery bus
  boycott, 1955–56
National Association
  for the Advancement
  of Colored People
  (NAACP)

nonviolent direct action
Plessy v. Ferguson
  (1896)
segregation
separate but equal
  doctrine
sit-ins
Southern Christian
  Leadership
  Conference (SCLC)
Student Nonviolent
  Coordinating
  Committee (SNCC)
student placement laws
token integration
White Citizens Councils

What was the significance of the *Plessy v. Ferguson* decision?

The promised protection of rights under the Fourteenth Amendment did not last long. With the end of Reconstruction, Southern whites soon regained control of state governments and passed laws that once again reduced African Americans to second-class citizens.

Both state and federal courts upheld the right of states to pass such laws despite the equal protection clause. In the case of ***Plessy v. Ferguson*** (1896), the U.S. Supreme Court established the **separate but equal doctrine** that was to deny African Americans equal rights for more than half a century. It established the legal basis for racial **segregation**, which required African Americans to use separate schools and other public facilities. Louisiana had passed a law requiring railroad companies to provide separate but equal cars for black passengers and white passengers. African American leaders claimed this law violated their rights under the equal protection clause of the Fourteenth Amendment. They decided to challenge the constitutionality of the law in court and chose Homer Plessy to make the test case. Plessy bought a train ticket but insisted on riding in the "whites only" car. He was arrested and convicted. He then appealed his case to the Supreme Court.

How did "separate but equal" facilities deny African Americans equal protection of the law?

The question before the Supreme Court was whether the Louisiana law violated the equal protection clause. Claiming that the authors of the Fourteenth Amendment had never intended to enforce a social intermingling of the races, the Court held that to separate blacks and whites did not in itself suggest one race was inferior to the other. Since the law required that blacks and whites be provided equal facilities, the Court concluded that no unfair discrimination had occurred. The Louisiana law was declared constitutional.

Plessy v. Ferguson departed from the interpretation of the Fourteenth Amendment established in the post Reconstruction years. Even though the Supreme Court had interpreted the equal protection clause very narrowly, it had consistently forbidden states from officially discriminating between the races. The *Plessy* decision now allowed open discrimination.

Not all members of the Court agreed with the majority. Justice John Marshall Harlan, a white southerner, wrote a strong dissenting opinion. He argued that in allowing state-enforced segregation of the races, the Louisiana law implied that blacks were an inferior group or "caste," and thus violated the equal protection clause of the Fourteenth Amendment. Harlan declared:

> *Our Constitution is color-blind and neither knows nor tolerates classes among citizens. In respect of civil rights, all citizens are equal before the law....[T]he judgment this day rendered will prove to be quite as pernicious as...the* Dred Scott *case.*

What were the consequences of *Plessy v. Ferguson*?

As a result of the majority decision in *Plessy*, segregation and discrimination against African Americans became even more widespread in the South. A web of state laws and local ordinances soon segregated almost every area of public life: schools, hotels, restaurants, hospitals, streetcars, toilets, and drinking fountains. Courtrooms even kept separate Bibles for administering the oath.

The establishment of white supremacy required the destruction of African American political power. During the years following *Plessy* a variety of devices were adopted to evade the intent of the Fifteenth Amendment and deny African American citizens the right to vote. Legislative devices such as literacy tests, poll taxes, and grandfather clauses, took advantage of the poverty and lack of education among African Americans.

When such discriminatory regulations failed to keep African Americans from the polls, physical intimidation and threats of economic reprisals were used. As a result, voting by blacks declined dramatically. By 1910 fewer than 20 percent of African American citizens voted in most of the South, in the Deep South fewer than 2 percent voted. The white supremacy created through these laws and regulations became known as **Jim Crow**.

What do *you* think?

1. How did the *Plessy v. Ferguson* decision differ from earlier interpretations of the equal protection clause of the Fourteenth Amendment?

2. Evaluate the claim that emphasizing equality under the law has in fact promoted inequality in the United States.

What were the origins of the civil rights movement?

Despite the return of white supremacy in the decades following Reconstruction, the struggle for racial equality did not disappear altogether. Even during the height of Jim Crow many courageous African Americans, and their white allies, were able to chip away at the wall of discrimination.

How did segregated facilities undermine the intent of the Fourteenth Amendment?

In 1909 the **National Association for the Advancement of Colored People (NAACP)** was founded. The NAACP's team of able lawyers began to challenge Jim Crow laws in the courts and legislatures. The NAACP set as its primary goals the removal of segregation laws and the restoration of voting rights for African Americans.

All aspects of life for African Americans living in the South were tainted by segregation. In Montgomery, Alabama, on December 1, 1955, Rosa Parks, a black woman, was arrested when she refused to give up her bus seat to a white man. Local civil rights leaders convinced

Ms. Parks to fight the charges, and they called for a **boycott** of the Montgomery bus system. Some community leaders pledged their support for the action. Rev. Martin Luther King, Jr., a new minister at the Dexter Avenue Baptist Church, assumed a major leadership role in the boycott which lasted 400 days. Finally, the boycott ended in December 1956 when the Supreme Court forced Montgomery city officials to end segregation on city buses.

Rosa Parks (1913–)

How did Rosa Parks's refusal to give up her seat energize the civil rights movement?

What was the significance of Brown v. Board of Education?

The NAACP set as its priority the end of segregation in education. They developed a strategy of demonstrating through test cases that southern education was not living up to the conditions of "separate but equal" laid down in the *Plessy* decision. This was done through the efforts of a team of talented African American lawyers, including Charles Houston and Thurgood Marshall. They produced evidence to show that southern schools, though separate, were not equal in the facilities and advantages they offered African Americans.

Brown v. Board of Education of Topeka (1954) involved the schools in Topeka, Kansas. An African American girl was denied enrollment at the school in her neighborhood. She was forced to attend a school that was much farther from her home. Her father sued the board of education to allow her to attend the nearer school.

In appealing this case to the Supreme Court, the lawyers of the NAACP adopted a somewhat different strategy. They produced evidence to show the damaging effects of segregated schools on the psychological development of black children. The Court accepted this argument and, under the leadership of Chief Justice Earl Warren, handed down a unanimous decision, which declared:

> *To separate [children] from others of similar age and qualifications solely because of their race generates a feeling of inferiority as to their status in the community that may affect their hearts and minds in a way unlikely ever to be undone.... [Therefore] separate educational facilities are inherently unequal...[and deny] the equal protection of the laws guaranteed by the Fourteenth Amendment.*

Making a court decision was one thing; enforcing it was another. In 1955 the Court handed down a second *Brown* decision that concerned implementation of the Court's 1954 decision. It ordered an end to segregated schools "with all deliberate speed." Lower courts were authorized to approve desegregation plans and were allowed to take into account local conditions in approving such plans. In making this cautious and flexible decision, the Supreme Court acknowledged the serious impact the first *Brown* decision would have on American society.

As expected, reaction to the school desegregation decision among many white southerners was hostile. They viewed it as an attack on their "way of life," which had been accepted as legal under the Constitution for

George E.C. Hayes, Thurgood Marshall, and James M. Nabrit

What was the significance of Thurgood Marshall's victory in the Brown v. Board of Education case?

more than half a century. Southern leaders promised "massive resistance" and organized **White Citizens Councils** throughout the South. Resistance involved both legal and illegal tactics. They included delaying maneuvers in the courts and very limited or **token integration**. Southern state legislatures passed new laws making it possible for white students to attend private schools with state financial support. They also passed **student placement laws** allowing local school officials to impede integration through the use of placement tests and other administrative procedures. Some school districts closed their schools altogether rather than integrate.

When legal tactics failed, some resistant southerners resorted to violence and other forms of intimidation. This was evident in the first important confrontation over integration in Little Rock, Arkansas. The Arkansas governor allowed the state national guard and a local mob to prevent the court-ordered integration of a city high school in 1957. President Dwight Eisenhower responded by sending in units of the 101st Airborne Division of the U.S. Army.

The president had reservations about court-ordered integration. He feared quick implementation. "I don't believe," he said, "you can change the hearts of men with laws or decisions." President Eisenhower also realized, however, that the law of the land had to be upheld. His forceful response to the crisis in Little Rock was the first time since Reconstruction that federal troops had been used to defend the civil rights of American citizens.

Little Rock's high school was integrated under the protection of federal troops. Throughout the South, the pace of integration was slow. Neither the government nor organizations like the NAACP had the resources to challenge segregation everywhere. The task of implementing the Supreme Court's decision had to be fought school district by school district. In the 1960s, however, the federal government initiated a policy of withholding funding from schools that did not integrate and courts began to insist on positive results in school integration plans. Thereafter, the pace of school integration quickened. By the 1970s the South could rightly claim that it had the most integrated schools in the nation.

How did the civil rights movement use the tactics of nonviolent direct action?

Though encouraged by the Supreme Court's ending of legal segregation, African Americans became frustrated with the slow pace of implementing court decisions. Leaders realized they could not rely entirely on the government to further the cause of civil rights.

U.S. soldiers in front of Central High School, Little Rock, Arkansas, 1957

Why was it necessary to use federal troops to integrate schools in the South?

Following the success of the Montgomery bus boycott, Rev. Martin Luther King, Jr. organized a meeting of 60 southern ministers in Atlanta, Georgia. Out of this meeting the **Southern Christian Leadership Conference (SCLC)** was formed. King and the other leaders organized and conducted workshops throughout the South where people taught the principles of **nonviolent direct action**.

Nonviolent direct action sometimes used the tactics of **civil disobedience**. This involved the open violation of what were believed to be unjust laws, together with a willingness to accept the consequences through passive or nonviolent resistance. Those engaged in direct action would not resist arrest and imprisonment or respond with violence to the physical or other abuse they might suffer. The effectiveness of these tactics had been proven by the great Indian leader, Mohandas Gandhi, who used them to win independence for India from Great Britain.

African American students throughout the South had taken up the protest movement. In April 1960, leaders of the SCLC invited 100 student leaders to attend a conference in Raleigh, North Carolina, to discuss ways to coordinate their efforts to make them more effective. Out of this meeting emerged a new organization, the **Student Nonviolent Coordinating Committee (SNCC)**.

The energy and commitment of the members of SNCC led the organization to play an important role in helping achieve the goals of the civil rights movement. By September 1961, 70,000 black students and white students were staging **sit-ins** for social change. They conducted sit-ins, sleep-ins, pray-ins, and other actions to protest the segregation that existed in every type of facility open only to whites.

What do *you* think?

1. What do you think the respective roles of the executive, legislative, and judicial branches should be in promoting equal protection of the law?

2. Do you agree with President Eisenhower's views about the inability of law to change human attitudes and behavior? Support your answer with evidence.

3. Under what circumstances does a citizen in a representative democracy have a right to violate a law? Explain your position.

4. In your opinion, what is the most critical equal protection issue facing our nation today? What should be done to remedy it?

What were the origins of the Civil Rights Act of 1964?

Though President John F. Kennedy supported the enforcement of existing laws and court decisions on civil rights, he was reluctant at first to enlarge the government's authority by proposing new legislation. Events resulting from nonviolent direct action in 1963 changed his mind.

In the spring of that year, Rev. Martin Luther King, Jr. and other civil rights leaders decided to protest segregation and job discrimination in Birmingham, Alabama, known for its tough enforcement of Jim Crow laws. Sit-ins and protest marches prompted a brutal response by local police. Scenes of civil rights protesters being attacked by fire hoses and police dogs were carried on television and in newspapers around the world. The events in Birmingham shocked the consciences of many people and became an embarrassment to the country. They also set off a wave of protests in almost 200 other cities in the South.

These events persuaded President Kennedy that the time had come for the government to increase its commitment to civil rights. In a nationally televised address in June 1963, he told his fellow citizens:

Sit-in demonstration at a lunch counter in Mississippi, 1963

How did nonviolent direct action help achieve the goals of the civil rights movement?

We are confronted primarily with a moral issue. It is as old as the Scriptures and is as clear as the American Constitution. The heart of the question is whether all Americans are to be afforded equal rights and equal opportunities.... [T]he time has come for this nation to fulfill its promise.

Then on August 28, 1963, more than 200,000 people, most of them African Americans, converged on Washington, D.C., to demonstrate for a full and speedy program of civil rights and equal job opportunities.

President Kennedy announced that he would be asking Congress to enact major new civil rights legislation. Because he was assassinated, Kennedy did not see his proposed civil rights legislation enacted. Most of what he proposed became law in the **Civil Rights Act of 1964**. It included the most far-reaching civil rights legislation in history. It outlawed discrimination in hotels, restaurants, theaters, and other places of public accommodation. The act also gave the government new authority to bring about school integration and prohibited job discrimination by businesses and labor unions. Constitutional authority for the act came from the **commerce clause** of Article I, Section 8, which gave Congress the right to regulate activities having to do with interstate commerce.

Critical Thinking Exercise

EXAMINING CIVIL DISOBEDIENCE IN A CONSTITUTIONAL DEMOCRACY

While imprisoned during the protests in Birmingham, Alabama, in 1963, Rev. Martin Luther King, Jr. wrote the **Letter from Birmingham City Jail**. Nonviolent direct action, he said, forces a community to confront its unjust laws and customs. "It seeks so to dramatize the issue that it can no longer be ignored."

The letter defends civil disobedience by maintaining that "an individual who breaks a law that conscience tells him is unjust and who willingly accepts the possibility of imprisonment in order to arouse the conscience of the community…is in reality expressing the highest respect for law."

As Rev. King pointed out, civil disobedience is as old as the death of Socrates and the martyrdom of the early Christians. Its tactics were used by the American revolutionaries, by abolitionists, and by women's rights advocates. Civil disobedience was practiced by those opposed to the Vietnam War and even more recently by those opposed to abortion.

Even some early supporters of the civil rights movement, however, questioned the correctness of civil disobedience.

What limits, if any, should be placed on protests that use civil disobedience?

Such tactics, they argued, might be justified in a dictatorship or totalitarian state, but should not be used in a constitutional democracy where there is a "government of laws not men." In such a government there are other ways to seek a redress of grievances.

You should work with a study partner to read and discuss the "Letter from Birmingham City Jail" which is found in the Reference Section. Then answer the following questions and be prepared to share your position with the class.

1. What would happen to the rule of law and respect for the rights of other individuals if each person were free in conscience to defy the law?

2. How might Rev. Martin Luther King, Jr. respond to the charge that those who followed their consciences to defy local segregation laws were no different from white protesters who defied court orders to integrate?

3. How might Rev. King have used the natural rights philosophy to explain his position?

4. How does a society determine the difference between disobedience of unjust and disobedience of just laws?

5. Could it be argued that the tactics of civil disobedience are likely to be more effective in a constitutional democracy than in a totalitarian state? Why?

How did the civil rights movement use constitutional rights to achieve its objectives?

The civil rights movement is a good example of citizens using rights protected by the Constitution to secure other constitutional rights. Rev. Martin Luther King, Jr. reminded his followers in the Montgomery bus boycott that "One of the great glories of democracy is the right to protest for right."

The struggle to realize the ideals of the Fourteenth and Fifteenth Amendments would not have been possible without those rights of protest guaranteed in the First Amendment: freedom of speech, the press, assembly, and petitioning for the redress of grievances. As Rev. King said in 1965:

> *We march in the name of the Constitution, knowing that the Constitution is on our side. The right of people peaceably to assemble and to petition the government for the redress of grievances shall not be abridged. That's the First Amendment.*

In seeking their rights as citizens, civil rights organizations also created civic education programs across the South for the training of black leaders in the struggle.

How would you evaluate the contributions of Rev. Martin Luther King, Jr. to the civil rights movement?

How did court decisions during the 1950s and 60s extend constitutional due process protections?

During the 1950s and 60s, when the Supreme Court was particularly active in securing the rights of equality for racial minorities, it also was using the due process clause of the Fourteenth Amendment to secure procedural rights in criminal proceedings.

In the 1960s the Court greatly expanded the protections available to individuals suspected or charged with a crime. Most of the judicial protections in the Bill of Rights were incorporated in the due process clause of the Fourteenth Amendment. The Court's decisions reflected a change of attitude about criminal justice in American society.

Reviewing and Using the Lesson

1. How would you explain the "separate but equal" doctrine established by the Supreme Court in the case of *Plessy v. Ferguson*? What important consequences of this doctrine can you identify?

2. What is meant by "Jim Crow" laws? How did they affect everyday life?

3. What was the case of *Brown v. Board of Education* about? What was the Supreme Court's decision in this case? Why is this case important?

4. How would you describe the civil rights movement? What tactics were used by supporters of the movement to achieve their goals?

5. What was the Civil Rights Act of 1964? How has it been an important source of protection of rights?

6. How would you explain the idea of civil disobedience? How did Rev. Martin Luther King, Jr. justify its use?

7. How were the rights of assembly and petition, and freedom of speech and of the press used to help achieve the goals of the civil rights movement?

8. Research information about the use of civil disobedience by the abolition movement, the women's movement, or by civil rights leaders in other countries. Report your findings to the class.

LESSON 27

How Has the Right to Vote Expanded
Since the Adoption of the Constitution?

Purpose of Lesson

Suffrage, that is, the right to vote, has been a subject of controversy throughout our history. During the colonial period and the early years of our nation, voting was generally restricted to white men who owned property. While the majority of white males qualified for suffrage, other people, such as women, African Americans, Native Americans, and members of certain religious groups were usually denied the right to vote. In this lesson, you examine how the right to vote has been extended during the last 200 years to almost every citizen 18 years of age or older.

When you have completed this lesson, you should be able to describe the extension of voting rights as a result of changes in the voting laws in the various states, amendments to the Constitution, and decisions of the Supreme Court. You also should be able to describe how the extension of the right to vote is related to some fundamental ideas and principles about constitutional government that you have studied.

Terms to Know

Fifteenth Amendment
franchise
Nineteenth Amendment
referenda
suffrage

Twenty-fourth
Amendment
Twenty-sixth
Amendment

What is the difference between civil and political rights?

A distinction is sometimes made between civil and political rights in a free society. Civil rights usually refer to those rights that we enjoy as private individuals and that protect us from the unwarranted interference of government. Most of the provisions in the Bill of Rights are civil rights, including those rights that grant us due process of law.

Political rights refer to those rights that allow us to influence the actions of our government and to participate in government ourselves. The Constitution provides us with the right to vote and to hold public office. Those rights in the First Amendment that protect liberty in our private lives also give us the power to influence our government—through freedom of speech, the press, and the right to assemble and petition for the redress of grievances. These First Amendment freedoms, therefore, are both civil and political rights.

America is one of the world's oldest democracies, but that democracy has meant different things throughout our history. Our constitutional democracy is based on the sovereignty of the people, but the number of citizens entitled to exercise that sovereign power was once much smaller than it is today. The expansion of the right to vote to all citizens represents one of the great themes in our history, in some respects the most important theme. As the Supreme Court declared more than a century ago, the right to vote is "a fundamental right, because it is the preservative of all rights."

How has the right to vote become more inclusive in terms of economic status, gender, and age?

At the Philadelphia Convention, the Framers could not agree on who should be given the right to vote. As a result, the Constitution simply stated that members of the House of Representatives were to be elected by the people in each state who, under state law, were eligible to vote for the lower house of their state legislature.

The Constitution, therefore, left to each state government the power to decide who could vote. As a result, many of the early battles about voting rights took place at the state level.

Extending the right to vote to all white men. Since the founding of the country, white men have had the right to vote and take part in government, but usually they had to meet certain qualifications. In some states, the right to vote included the requirement that a person belong to a particular religious group.

During the Revolutionary War, six state governments eliminated all property requirements and gave the right to vote to all white males, rich or poor. At the same time, three other state governments increased the property requirements, limiting the right to vote.

Thomas Paine, in the following statement, clearly described the issue of linking the right to vote with the ownership of property.

> *You require that a man shall have sixty dollars worth of property, or he shall not vote. Very well, take an illustration. Here is a man who today owns a jackass, and the jackass is worth sixty dollars. Today the man is a voter and he goes to the polls and deposits his vote. Tomorrow the jackass dies. The next day the man comes to vote without his jackass and he cannot vote at all. Now tell me, which was the voter, the man or the jackass?*
>
> Thomas Paine

Following the election of Thomas Jefferson as president in 1800, many states began eliminating the property requirement for voting. Between 1812 and 1821, six new western states became part of the nation and they granted the vote to all white males. During the same period, four of the older states that had property requirements abolished them.

Andrew Jackson ran for president in 1828. His support came from many men who had just won the right to vote. In this election, three times more Americans voted than ever before. Jackson's election represented a new era in American politics, in which the spirit of democracy and equality began to influence the nation's political institutions. **Suffrage** continued to be extended to more white males.

As new states in the West entered the Union, they did so with nearly universal white male suffrage. One by one most of the older states amended their election laws by removing property qualifications. In most cases these reforms were accomplished peacefully. In Rhode Island, one of the last states to extend the right to vote to all white males, the issue resulted in a small civil war. In 1841 the leader of **franchise** reform in Rhode Island, Thomas Dorr, led his followers in an armed attack on the state capitol. By the time of the Civil War nearly universal white male suffrage had been realized in the United States.

Extending the right to vote to African American males. The **Fifteenth Amendment** was added to the Constitution in 1870, just after the Civil War. Although the Fifteenth Amendment guaranteed the right to vote to African American males, many states in the South passed laws that made it almost impossible for these new voters to exercise their right.

As a result of the civil rights movement of the 1950s and 1960s, the federal government began using its power to protect the rights of African Americans against political discrimination. In 1964, the **Twenty-fourth Amendment** was added to the Constitution prohibiting the use of poll taxes as a means of denying the right to vote in federal elections. The following year, Congress passed the Voting Rights Act. This act gave additional protection by authorizing the federal government to oversee the registration of voters in areas where state officials had regularly prevented African Americans from registering to vote. The Supreme Court ruled in *Harper v. Virginia Board of Elections* (1966) that the use of poll taxes in state elections was a violation of the equal protection clause of the Fourteenth Amendment. Thus, by the mid-60s, great progress had been made in ensuring that African American men could enjoy the right to vote as it had been guaranteed by the Fifteenth Amendment almost a century earlier.

Why was it important to extend voting rights to all Americans?

Extending the right to vote to women. Closely linked with the struggle of African Americans for freedom and equality was the struggle for women's rights. It took even longer for women to win the actual right to vote than it did for African American men.

For most of the history of the United States, women did not have the right to vote or take part in government. Women were the largest group of people ever denied the right to vote in our country. The struggle to gain this right was long and difficult because it challenged strongly held traditional beliefs about women's roles in society.

During the time Congress was considering the Civil War Amendments, leaders of the women's movement asked that the right to vote be expanded to include women. These leaders, including Susan B. Anthony, hoped their long support of the antislavery cause would be rewarded. Their appeal was denied. Male antislavery leaders refused to extend the vote to women. Instead, they specifically included the term "male citizen" for the first time in the Constitution. The Fourteenth Amendment prohibits any state from denying the right to vote to males.

The exclusion of women in the Fourteenth Amendment did not prevent states from granting women the right to vote. In 1874, people in favor of women's rights argued before the Supreme Court that the following clause gave women the right to vote.

> *All persons born or naturalized in the United States, and subject to the jurisdiction thereof, are citizens of the United States and of the State wherein they reside.*
>
> Fourteenth Amendment

The Supreme Court denied this claim. They ruled in *Minor v. Happersett* (1875) that being a citizen does not automatically give a person the right to vote. It was not unconstitutional for states to deny the vote to women.

In 1876, Susan B. Anthony led a delegation of women to the Philadelphia Centennial Celebration of the Declaration of Independence. Although no women had been invited to participate in the program, Anthony's protest included reading the Women's Declaration of Rights:

Why were women denied the right to vote until 1920?

Susan B. Anthony (1820–1906)

What methods did Susan B. Anthony and other leaders of the woman suffrage movement use in their efforts to secure the vote for women?

> *Yet we cannot forget, even in this glad hour, that while all men of every race...have been invested with the full rights of citizenship under our hospitable flag, all women still suffer the degradation of disfranchisement.*

Wyoming gave women the right to vote while it was still a territory. The story is told that when certain members of Congress argued against this "petticoat provision," the Wyoming legislature said it would rather stay out of the Union for 100 years than join it without allowing women to vote. Wyoming was admitted to the Union.

After Wyoming, other western states quickly extended the right of suffrage to women. By the end of World War I, more than half of the states had given women the right to vote.

In 1875 the Supreme Court had ruled that being a citizen did not automatically give a person the right to vote. States could deny this right to women if they chose. It was not until 1920, fifty years after African American men won the right to vote, that women were guaranteed the same right under the **Nineteenth Amendment**.

Pressure for a woman suffrage amendment mounted during World War I as women entered the work force in record numbers. The uncertainty and slowness of state-by-state victories encouraged women to push harder for an amendment to the Constitution giving them the right to vote. In 1918, President Woodrow Wilson announced his support for the proposed amendment. In

1920, even though there was still considerable opposition to granting suffrage to women, the Nineteenth Amendment was finally ratified. Women had the right to vote after being denied that right for more than 130 years. The Nineteenth Amendment says:

Section 1. The right of citizens of the United States to vote shall not be denied or abridged by the United States or by any State on account of sex.

Section 2. Congress shall have the power to enforce this article by appropriate legislation.

Extending the right to vote to Native Americans. The Constitution as originally adopted mentioned Indians twice. Under Article I, "Indians not taxed" were excluded from state populations for purposes of apportioning taxes and representatives in Congress. Also under Article I, Congress is accorded the power to "regulate commerce with foreign nations, among the several States, and with the Indian Tribes."

The implications of these provisions as interpreted by the Supreme Court are twofold:

- that Native Americans were not citizens of the United States or the states in which they resided and
- that Native American tribes were distinct political societies whose foreign and domestic relations were to be managed by the federal government of the United States

Their early relationship with the federal government affected the civil rights of Native Americans in profound ways. The most obvious is that Native American people, as citizens of distinct political communities, enjoyed none of the constitutional rights reserved to citizens.

Following the Snyder Act of 1924 all Native Americans were made United States citizens, although some had acquired citizenship earlier through other legislation. The assumption underlying this federal policy was that the tribes would eventually disappear and Native Americans would be citizens only of the federal and state governments. When that assumption proved false and the tribes did not disappear, what resulted was the dual citizenship that Native Americans have today.

Many states, however, continued to discriminate against Native Americans for purposes of voting, jury duty, and providing testimony in court. The Voting Rights Act of 1965 and its amendments were efforts to address the problem of discrimination against all minorities.

Extending the right to vote to eighteen-year-olds. Before 1971, only Alaska, Georgia, Hawaii, and Kentucky had allowed persons younger than twenty-one to participate in elections.

In 1970, Congress, in amending the Voting Rights Act, included a section that said no one should be denied the right to vote on the grounds of age who was eighteen-years-old or older. This law was challenged in the case of *Oregon v. Mitchell* (1970) and the Supreme Court was divided. Four justices felt that Congress had the power to lower the voting age to eighteen; four other justices concluded that Congress had no such power. Justice Hugo Black cast the decisive vote. He ruled that Congress could regulate the voting age in national elections but not in state elections. He argued that the Constitution leaves to the states the power to regulate the elections of their own public officials. The Congress does have the authority, however, to lower the voting age in federal elections.

Within six months of the Court decision, the **Twenty-sixth Amendment** was ratified by the required number of states. The Amendment states:

Section 1. The right of citizens of the United States, who are eighteen years of age or older, to vote shall not be denied or abridged by the United States or by any State on account of age.

Section 2. The Congress shall have the power to enforce this article by appropriate legislation.

What can be done to increase the number of eligible Americans who participate in elections?

What do *you* think?

1. Why is a constitutional democracy, more than any other form of government, dependent upon an informed, enlightened, and responsible citizenry?

2. Do you believe low voter turnout to be an important national problem? Why or why not?

3. Should all citizens eligible to vote be required to do so or be forced to pay a heavy fine? Why or why not?

4. If governing is left to representatives, why should citizens want or need to participate in the political life of the nation?

5. If you are not satisfied that any of the candidates will be a good representative, what should you do? Explain.

6. Young people between the ages of eighteen and twenty-five vote less frequently than any other age group. Why do you think this is so? Do you think this is an important problem? Why or why not? If so, explain what you think should be done to correct the problem.

Is the United States more or less democratic today?

Over the course of two centuries we have used our Constitution to achieve nearly universal adult suffrage. From a fraction of the country's population in 1789, "We the People" has grown to include nearly every American of voting age. In most respects the United States is the most democratic nation on earth. Americans can use the power of the ballot box to choose more public officials at more levels of government than do voters in any other democracy. Through special **referenda** we can even use our votes to make laws.

As the nation's democratic opportunities have expanded, though, the willingness of American citizens to participate has decreased. There has been a steady decline in voter turnout in recent years. Only 57 percent of eligible citizens voted in the 1992 presidential election. Fewer than 50 percent now vote in non-presidential or "off year" elections. A century ago more than 70 percent of eligible voters regularly went to the polls. The United States now ranks 11th among the world's democracies in the percentage of eligible voters who exercise that right.

One reason for this decline is the difficult and complicated registration procedures of many states. Citizens in most of the other democracies in the world find it easier to register to vote. Recent changes in registration laws have made it somewhat less difficult for potential voters in this country. The decline in voting also reflects the declining influence of political parties, especially at the local level. In the past, party organizations could be counted on to "get out the vote."

Whatever the causes, many people today worry about the unwillingness of so many Americans to use this most fundamental right of citizenship. They fear it may reflect a decline in civic-mindedness and a growing sense of alienation from government—the belief that "my vote doesn't count." By leaving the matter of governing entirely with bureaucrats and lobbyists, "We the People" may become less represented and less representative than we were 200 years ago. The future of democracy will be one of the great issues that America's younger citizens must face as the nation enters its third century.

Critical Thinking Exercise

EXAMINING THE REASONS WHY YOUNG AMERICANS DO NOT VOTE

Voter turnout is strongly influenced by socioeconomic status and education. Generally, better off and better educated American citizens use their right to vote to a much greater extent than do poor or uneducated citizens.

Are some Americans still denied the opportunity to vote? Explain.

Those who can understand and analyze public affairs are more likely to take an active interest in them. Completing the course of study in this book will probably increase the chance that you will participate in the democratic process in the years ahead.

Voting is also a function of age. Older Americans, those in middle age and retirement, have almost twice the voting percentage as young Americans aged 18–20. In 1992, although 80 percent of registered young people actually voted, this was only 40 percent of the young people eligible to vote. Some experts suggest that older citizens vote in greater percentages because they see more of a connection between government policies and the concerns of their individual lives.

1. Why do you think older Americans might be more interested in what government does than younger Americans?

2. What type of situation might make young citizens more interested in the affairs of government? Give examples?

3. If you have registered and voted, or are planning to do so, what are your motives for doing this?

4. Some European countries hold elections on Sunday and have eliminated formal voter registration procedures. Do you think similar measures would increase participation among younger voters in the United States? What other changes would increase participation?

Reviewing and Using the Lesson

1. How would you explain the difference between civil and political rights?

2. How did the Constitution deal with the right to vote? How has this been changed by amendments to the Constitution?

3. Why was the struggle to secure the right to vote for women so difficult?

4. What are some factors that affect voter turnout in the United States?

5. Prepare an oral report comparing the values, interests, and goals of the Declaration of Independence with the Declaration of Women's Rights drafted and presented by Elizabeth Cady Stanton at the Seneca Falls Convention in 1848.

LESSON 28

To What Extent Can the Law Correct Injustice and Other Problems in American Society?

Purpose of Lesson

To what extent can the Constitution and other laws be used in addressing injustice and other problems in modern-day America? This lesson focuses on that question, especially as it relates to the consequences of discrimination and inequality. One of the most controversial issues raised by the Fourteenth Amendment is affirmative action. This lesson discusses the history and rationale for affirmative action as well as some types of programs available. You also will consider the guidelines used to determine what affirmative action programs are acceptable under the equal protection clause.

When you finish the lesson, you should be able to explain the purpose of affirmative action programs, their relationship to the Fourteenth Amendment, and some issues they raise. You also should be able to take, defend, and evaluate positions on issues involving affirmative action and on the guidelines used to determine the constitutionality of these programs.

their problems in terms of law and constitutional principles. Our commitment to constitutional government provides the foundation for most of our attempts to resolve the problems in our society.

You have examined many examples of this American faith in constitutionalism. You have learned how we have used the Constitution to abolish slavery, restructure the Union, and expand equality in civil and political rights to minorities and women. With remarkably few changes in its content, the Constitution has proved itself capable of addressing these problems and adjusting to the vast changes in the nation during the last 200 years. To a large extent, Chief Justice Marshall's faith in a Constitution "intended to endure for ages to come...to be adapted to the various crises of human affairs" has been confirmed.

1. Do you agree with Alexis de Tocqueville's observation that most public issues eventually become legal questions? Why or why not?

2. What might be some advantages of relying on the legal system to resolve disputes about constitutional issues? What might be some disadvantages?

Terms to Know

affirmative action
aggressive recruitment
  programs
Education Amendment
  Act of 1972
Equal Employment
  Opportunities
  Commission
Equal Pay Act of 1963

preferential treatment
  programs
quotas and group
  entitlements
*Regents of the University of
  California v. Bakke*
  (1978)
remedial programs
reverse discrimination

Critical Thinking Exercise

EXAMINING THE ROLE OF LAW IN SOLVING PROBLEMS

The nineteenth-century observer of American democracy, Alexis de Tocqueville, observed that most public issues in the United States eventually become legal questions. What he meant was that Americans try to address and resolve

Should colleges guarantee that their student body is representative of the community?

3. Do you think the threat of a potential law suit is an effective means of safeguarding our interests and rights against the actions of public officials?

4. Some legal observers have accused Americans of "suing each other to death." Do you think this is detrimental to society? If so, what constitutional remedies might you propose?

What have been some recent efforts to end unfair discrimination in American society?

The most important legacy of the civil rights movement has been the sustained commitment to equality and protection of rights for all people in the United States. Both government policies and court decisions have continued the effort to eliminate discrimination, not only against African Americans, but against all "historically excluded groups." In recent years, the equal protection clause of the Fourteenth Amendment has been expanded to prevent discrimination on the basis of age, gender, and ethnic background as well as race.

Court decisions banning such discrimination have been reinforced by laws passed by Congress. The Civil Rights Act of 1964 outlawed job discrimination by private employers and labor unions. It also created an **Equal Employment Opportunities Commission** to monitor compliance. Subsequent legislation by Congress extended the protection to additional groups.

Women represent the largest group to benefit from these antidiscrimination efforts. The **Equal Pay Act of 1963** prohibited discrimination on the basis of gender in job pay. The **Equal Employment Opportunities Act of 1972** extended protection for women in the workplace by outlawing discrimination in the award of medical benefits. The **Education Amendment Act of 1972** outlawed gender discrimination in any educational program that received federal aid.

The nation's courts have wrestled with the problem of how to determine when discrimination exists. Should it be measured by the intent of the person or institution accused of discrimination or should it be determined by results, regardless of intent? Who should carry the burden of proving discrimination—those making the accusation or those being accused?

Why do some people claim that equality of opportunity is not enough to remedy past injustice?

There has been remarkable progress in recent years in providing equal protection of the laws to persons deprived of this right in the past. Some people argue, however, that the American emphasis on "equality of rights" instead of "equality of condition" results in an unacceptable inequality in our society. They argue that an emphasis on equal rights does nothing to address wide differences in wealth, power, and education. Consider three examples of how these differences in condition can make equality of rights meaningless.

Political influence. All persons have an equal right to participate in the political process by voting, expressing their views, and petitioning and lobbying government officials.

Despite this equal right, however, not all Americans have the same ability to influence the government. Many people are not well-educated and do not have the necessary understanding of how government works in order to influence its decisions. Many people without financial resources are more concerned with economic survival than with spending the time and energy required to influence their elected officials. On the other hand, people who are wealthy, well-educated, and have contact with powerful people often are able to use this knowledge and wealth to further their own political interests. As a result, despite equality of political rights, wealthy and more educated people generally have greater influence than undereducated people or those without adequate financial resources.

Rights of the accused. All persons accused of a crime have the right to be defended by a lawyer. If they cannot afford to hire a lawyer, the court will provide one. A wealthy person, however, can hire the best criminal lawyer available. In such a situation, the poorer person might have to depend on an overworked or less experienced lawyer to handle his or her defense.

Does the government have an obligation to provide a defendant with the best possible legal counsel?

Right to an education. Although the Constitution does not guarantee the right to education, every state offers free public education. The quality of education, however, varies widely. Public education is largely supported by property taxes. Children who live in poor communities often attend schools that have larger classes, fewer educational materials, fewer enrichment classes, lower teachers' salaries, and ill-kept buildings and equipment.

What do *you* think?

1. Does inequality of condition give some people a greater opportunity to enjoy their rights than others?

2. Does inequality of condition undermine the ideal of equality of rights?

3. Should the Constitution and the policies of government be used to provide remedies for inequality of condition? If so, what should they be?

Why were affirmative action programs started?

Many people believe that eliminating the legal barriers to equal opportunity is not enough. The effects of past discrimination and continued prejudice against women, racial and ethnic minorities, and others, still exist. Established patterns of prejudice and discrimination, some argue, hinder people from taking advantage of opportunities provided by law. It is not enough, they say, to sit back and passively wait for the effects of past legal discrimination to disappear. They believe that something positive or "affirmative," must be done to further the goal of equality of opportunity.

In the 1960s, as a result of such concerns, President Lyndon Johnson and others urged Congress to create programs that would go beyond merely removing legal barriers to equal opportunity. Such programs would open up opportunities in education and employment, provide remedial help, and, in some cases, preferential treatment for members of groups discriminated against in the past. These programs were called **affirmative action**.

Supporters of these programs claim that they are designed to make equality of opportunity a reality. They say affirmative action helps remedy the wrongs and reduce the handicaps caused by the unjust way women and minorities have been treated in the past. Affirmative action includes the following types of programs.

Aggressive recruitment programs. These are conducted by business, industry, and government to make sure that when opportunities in education and employment occur, women and members of minority groups are encouraged to apply for them. For example, it is common for many

Are affirmative action programs a justifiable means to correct the inequity of past discrimination? Explain.

people to learn of jobs from friends. Such practices may perpetuate existing patterns that deny equal employment opportunities to members of other groups. In this type of situation, providing equal opportunity would mean widely advertising the availability of jobs to members of all groups that might be interested.

Remedial programs. These include education programs in pre-schools and in elementary and secondary schools. These programs are designed to help students with particular educational and economic needs gain the basic skills to succeed in school and in the job market. Some help students to learn useful occupations. Others give remedial tutoring and assistance to students in college as well as to adults who want to improve their knowledge and skills. There has been little controversy about providing remedial programs, although some complain that there are not enough programs available for all children and adults who need them.

Preferential treatment programs. These are designed to compensate for the effects of past discrimination against women and minorities. These programs are designed to give members of these groups preferred treatment in gaining jobs and access to higher education. People argue that preferential treatment for such groups is required to

- balance the advantages white men have received from hundreds of years of preferential treatment

- promote diversity in colleges and universities in order to produce a less race-conscious and more racially fair society

- include people of different racial, religious, and ethnic groups whose perspectives help to improve educational programs for all

In what ways have preferential treatment programs helped some groups gain access to jobs and careers that were previously closed to them?

What issues are raised by affirmative action programs?

Affirmative action programs, particularly those calling for preferential treatment, are very controversial. Many events in the nation's constitutional history have produced tensions and conflicts between equally worthy ideals.

The debate about affirmative action programs involves such a conflict. Supporters of the programs point to America's historic commitment to equality of opportunity. Critics of affirmative action, on the other hand, appeal to another of this country's fundamental ideals—the rights of the individual. That is, each American should be rewarded according to his or her own merits, and not because of favoritism, privilege, or membership in a particular group.

Some opponents of affirmative action programs that involve preferential treatment believe that these programs violate the rights of the individual. In the interest of promoting equality the programs create new forms of inequality. To overcome past discrimination, some early preferential treatment programs called for setting aside a certain number of positions in colleges and businesses for qualified members of minority groups. Sometimes these programs established goals and timetables for filling positions to reflect the proportion of minorities and women in the community. For example, if 25 percent of a community belonged to a particular minority, a college might have set a goal of recruiting students from that group so that the student

body reflected that same percentage. Hiring or granting other benefits to individuals based on explicit racial **quotas**, however, is illegal except where justified to remedy the effects of demonstrated past discrimination.

The use of quotas and **group entitlements**—benefits provided by government to which recipients have a legally enforceable right—in education and employment has led to claims of unfairness from those who do not belong to groups receiving preferential treatment. Many people whose parents, grandparents, or in some cases themselves, had to overcome prejudice and hardship without the benefit of government programs resent what they see as government-supported favoritism of special groups.

Critics of affirmative action claim that such programs violate the ideals of the civil rights movement. Quotas and other forms of preferential treatment, they say, result in **reverse discrimination**. Just as it was wrong in the past to discriminate against people because of their gender, race, religion, or ethnic background, it is wrong now to discriminate in favor of people on the same basis. The equal protection clause of the Fourteenth Amendment was intended to remove racial and other discriminatory barriers, not create them.

Appealing to America's great traditions of individual rights and equality of opportunity, critics of affirmative action remind us of the long struggle to establish individual rights. This emphasis on individual rights distinguishes modern constitutionalism from the concept of rights in the ancient world and the Middle Ages.

Advocates of affirmative action respond by pointing out that the ideals of equality of opportunity and individual merit were never a reality in the past. For centuries a section of the population took advantage of privilege, social connections and the exclusion of women and non-whites. Some reverse discrimination is, therefore, necessary to remedy this past injustice by breaking down the legal and informal structures on which it was based.

Critical Thinking Exercise
EXAMINING A SUPREME COURT OPINION ON AFFIRMATIVE ACTION

The following exercise provides you with an opportunity to discuss a Supreme Court case that illustrates the difficulty of designing reasonable and fair programs to promote the goals of affirmative action while not violating the right of the individual to equal protection of the law.

Read the summary of the facts and opinions in this case. Be prepared to take a position and defend it.

Regents of the University of California v. Bakke **(1978).**
As part of its affirmative action program, the Medical
School of the University of California at Davis set aside
16 places for minorities out of its entering class of 100.
Alan Bakke, a non-minority applicant, was denied
admission even though his test scores were higher than
those of most of the minority applicants who were
accepted.

Bakke sued in the California courts claiming that the
admissions policy of the university violated the 1964
Civil Rights Act and denied him the right to equal
protection of the laws guaranteed by the Fourteenth
Amendment. The California Supreme Court agreed with
Bakke's claim. The case was appealed to the U.S.
Supreme Court which also ruled in Bakke's favor in a
5-4 decision. Bakke was accepted into the medical
school.

The five-member majority of the Court, however, was
not in agreement on why they voted in Bakke's favor.
Four of the justices said the university quota system
violated a prohibition of the 1964 Civil Rights Act—it
is unlawful to exclude anyone on the basis of race from
any program receiving federal funds. The university
received federal funds.

The fifth justice, Lewis F. Powell, concluded that the
racial quota was also a violation of the equal protection
clause of the Fourteenth Amendment. Powell's opinion
was based on the following points:

- He stated that it was a violation of the Constitution to
  place the burden of remedying the effects of past
  discrimination on individuals who had nothing to do
  with such discrimination.

**Allan Bakke, right, receiving his degree in medicine from
the Medical School at the University of California at Davis**

*What issues related to affirmative action are raised in the Bakke
case?*

- He rejected quotas.

- He approved, however, the consideration of race as a
  factor in an admissions policy meant to promote
  diversity in the student body. Such diversity is an
  acceptable goal for universities.

The four dissenting members of the Supreme Court
claimed that the university quota system was a
reasonable way to help remedy the effects of past
discrimination against racial and ethnic minorities.

1. What arguments could you make to support the
   majority opinion in this case? The minority opinion?

2. What values and interests underlie each position?

3. How could an admissions program meet Justice
   Powell's standards? Explain your position.

4. Should a university or college be allowed to have an
   admissions policy designed to promote racial,
   gender, ethnic, religious and other diversity on
   campus? Explain your position.

5. Is it possible to have an admissions policy based on
   sex, race, ethnicity, and religious beliefs that does not
   violate the right to equal protection of the laws as
   guaranteed by the Fourteenth Amendment? Explain
   your position.

What guidelines has the Supreme Court used
in dealing with issues of affirmative action?

The sharply divided opinions among the justices in the
Bakke decision indicate the problem the nation's courts
have faced in reconciling certain types of affirmative
action programs with the Constitution. Courts have had
little difficulty in approving remedial education and
minority recruitment programs. Preferential treatment of
minorities, however, has presented a more difficult issue.

Since the Bakke decision, the Supreme Court has ruled
on several cases involving preferential treatment. Its
decisions have not always been consistent, but they have
produced the following general guidelines:

- Affirmative action programs should be temporary
  arrangements to remedy the consequences of past
  discrimination.

- Any particular program should be designed to
  remedy the consequences of past discrimination in a
  specific situation rather than the more general
  problems of injustice in society at large.

- In applying an affirmative action program, the chance
  of unfair consequences for nonminority individuals
  should be minimized. The Supreme Court, however,

has ruled that even quotas may be used as a temporary remedy when the problems resulting from past discrimination are particularly serious.

What do *you* think?

1. Suppose a university set aside a number of positions in its first-year class for outstanding athletes who, though qualified for admission, have lower scores on entrance exams than others who were denied admission. Should this practice be considered a violation of equal protection of the law? Explain your position.

2. What current situations are you aware of in which affirmative action is an issue? Explain your position on the issues involved.

3. What might be the problems involved in an affirmative action policy requiring that every activity in the nation's life reflect the social composition of society at large? What might be the dangers or the benefits in structuring electoral processes and elected bodies according to proportional representation?

4. Should the Constitution be amended to protect group rights as well as individual rights? Explain your position.

Reviewing and Using the Lesson

1. How would you explain affirmative action programs? What purposes are they intended to serve? What constitutional issues do they raise?

2. What are some laws passed by Congress to end unfair discrimination?

3. What is meant by the term reverse discrimination? How is this idea used to argue against affirmative action programs?

4. What guidelines have been established in Supreme Court decisions with regard to affirmative action programs?

5. Research the arguments in the case *Fullilove v. Klutznick*, 448 U.S. 448 (1980), which focuses on the constitutionality of a federal law requiring that ten percent of federal funding for local public works projects be used to procure supplies and services from businesses owned by members of minority groups. Write a brief essay explaining whether you think such a law violates the equal protection clause of the Fourteenth Amendment.

Unit Five: *What Rights Does the Bill of Rights Protect?*

Purpose of Unit

The Bill of Rights contains 27 provisions protecting some fundamental rights. Originally, the Bill of Rights protected individuals only from the federal government. Through a process of incorporation it now applies to the states as well.

Some provisions of the Bill of Rights no longer seem very important. The Third Amendment's protection against quartering soldiers in the homes of civilians is one example. Other provisions, the First Amendment protection of freedom of speech, for example, have become more important. Many people argue that the rights protected in the First Amendment—to believe and worship, to speak and write, and to assemble—are the most important in the Bill of Rights.

Another important group of rights concerns people accused of crimes. These rights fall into two groups. The first group concerns protections against arbitrary and unreasonable law enforcement procedures. These protections are the subject of the Fourth and some provisions of the Fifth Amendments. The second group of rights concerns procedures within the court system. These rights are protected by the Fifth through Eighth Amendments.

After studying this unit, you will have a better idea of why these rights are so important, and why some remain controversial.

LESSON 29

Why Does the First Amendment Limit the Government's Power over Religion?

Purpose of Lesson

Two clauses in the First Amendment protect freedom of religion. These are the "establishment" and "free exercise" clauses. In this lesson you examine the Founders' belief that religion and government should be separate. Each clause deals with a different part of this separation. The "establishment" clause prohibits the federal government from establishing one or more official religions or churches for the nation. The "free exercise" clause prevents the government from putting unreasonable restrictions on particular religious practices.

When you complete this lesson, you should be able to explain the importance of freedom of religion, describe the differences between the establishment and free exercise clauses in the First Amendment. You also should be able to explain different interpretations of the establishment clause and the conflicts between the establishment and free exercise clauses. Finally you should be able to explain the issues and considerations involved in limiting the free exercise of religious beliefs.

Terms to Know

compelling state interest
established church
establishment clause
free exercise clause

Great Awakening
religious tests
separation of church
   and state

What is the historical background of religious freedom?

At the time of the first settlements in America, Europe was suffering from religious wars that had torn the continent apart since the early sixteenth century. This religious revolt, known as the Reformation, led to more than a century of bloodshed as Catholics and Protestants struggled for political power. Once in power, each group often attempted to eliminate its opponents through banishment, jail, torture or death.

Almost every nation in Europe had a government-sponsored Christian church, sometimes called an **established church**. In each nation there was only one

established church. The established church in England, for example, was the Church of England. In France and Spain, the Roman Catholic Church was established, while in some German states and in Sweden the Lutheran Church was the official church.

People who did not belong to the established church were denied certain rights. They were often excluded from universities and disqualified from civil and military offices. Sometimes they were persecuted or even killed for their beliefs.

Most Europeans in the seventeenth century accepted the idea of an established religion. The idea that several different religions could coexist was not yet widely accepted. In most of the early colonies there was little tolerance for religious differences. Not only did most colonies have an established church, but in many cases there was intolerance for nonmembers.

By the time of the American Revolution, people had become more tolerant. The religious revival of the mid-eighteenth century, known as the **Great Awakening**, drew many away from established religions and into new

How did the colonial experience shape the Founders' views on freedom of religion?

religious groups. This gave rise to the idea that all Protestant groups were equal. Diverse religious groups often existed in the same community, and people became used to living and working with others who had different beliefs. The large number of religious groups made it unlikely that one particular church could dominate all others.

It became increasingly difficult for one church to claim special privileges. As a result, even those colonies that had an established religion did not support only one church. Government assistance was given to several churches in an effort to support religion in general rather than a particular state church. Support, however, usually was given only to the Protestant form of the Christian religion. Catholics, Jews, and other groups were not supported and were sometimes discriminated against.

Eighteenth-century Americans generally thought that religion was important in developing the character needed to maintain a free society. Yet by the time the Constitution was written, most Americans also thought that freedom of belief was an essential right that needed protection. Americans considered freedom of religion to be something that strengthened both "church" and "state."

Why did the Founders believe in the separation of church and state?

There are two basic reasons why early Americans argued for the **separation of church and state**:

- to protect religion from being corrupted by the state
- to protect good government from corruption caused by religious conflict

People such as Roger Williams, the founder of Rhode Island, believed separation was essential so that religion would be safe from corruption by the state. He insisted that there should be a "wall of separation between the garden of the Church and the wilderness of the world." Thomas Jefferson thought that separation was important in keeping religious conflicts from corrupting government. James Madison combined these two views in his opposition to a religious establishment. He, of course, wrote the First Amendment.

Madison, like Jefferson, believed that individuals in a free society should have freedom of conscience—the right to decide for themselves what to believe. He worried that freedom of conscience would be threatened if government supported some religions but not others. Government should do only what is necessary to keep the peace and prevent one religious group from violating the rights of others. He concluded that to achieve this goal government should not interfere with religion in any way.

What do *you* think?

1. What experiences in England and the colonies contributed to the Framers' emphasis on the need to protect religious freedom?

2. What might be some common problems in protecting religious freedom? Explain how you think they should be dealt with.

3. What are the advantages and disadvantages of religious diversity in society?

How was religious freedom protected in the Constitution?

Before the Bill of Rights, the only mention of religion in the Constitution was the ban placed on **religious tests** for holding public office in the federal government stated in Article VI. This was a significant step in protecting religious freedom. In 1787, most states still had established religions or religious tests for office. Many Americans did not believe that non-Protestants could be trusted with public office. The Constitution opened the door to people of all religions.

Most but not all states followed the example of the federal government and abolished religious tests for holding state office. It was not until 1868 in North Carolina and 1946 in New Hampshire that such tests were abolished. A 1961 Supreme Court case held Maryland's religious test unconstitutional, and since then they have been prohibited entirely.

At the same time, a number of states still supported Protestant Christianity as an established religion. It was not until 1833, when Massachusetts changed its constitution to separate church and state, that established religion in America was eliminated.

How does the Bill of Rights prohibit state establishment of religion?

The First Amendment says "Congress shall make no law respecting an establishment of religion,..." It is clear that Madison wanted to end the practice of having the federal government declare an established church—a practice still prevalent in Europe at the time.

Some people supported the adoption of the First Amendment because they thought it would prevent Congress from interfering with their **state** religious establishments. Once the Fourteenth Amendment incorporated the First Amendment, however, the establishment clause was understood to prevent state establishment of religion as well.

How have the courts interpreted the establishment clause?

There is general agreement that the establishment clause means that government may not sponsor an official church. There is considerable disagreement, however, about the meaning of the **establishment clause** of the First Amendment. The disagreement can be summarized as follows:

1. The **broad interpretation**. People holding this position argue that the First Amendment prevents the government from providing any aid to any religion whatsoever. They believe that no tax money can be used to support any religious activity, practice, or institution. The government, however, may give religious groups the same services everyone else receives, such as police and fire protection. The government may provide assistance that makes it easier for people to exercise their religion. For example, schools may excuse students from classes during religious holidays.

2. The **narrow interpretation**. People holding this position argue that government is prohibited from giving one religious group preferential treatment. They believe the First Amendment does not prohibit government from supporting religion, as long as it does so impartially. This group supports placing the words "In God We Trust" on money and allowing nondenominational school prayer. People using a broad interpretation of the First Amendment often oppose these kinds of actions.

People who hold either the broad or narrow interpretation agree, however, that the First Amendment prohibits government acknowledgment of Christmas as a holiday if the holidays of other religious groups are not recognized.

3. The **literal interpretation**. People holding this position suggest that the First Amendment only prohibits the establishment of an official government religion. They would not prohibit the government's participation in particular religious practices. For example, the government may participate in Christmas celebrations as long as Christianity is not declared an official established religion.

In 1947 the Supreme Court made the establishment clause of the First Amendment applicable to the states through its incorporation into the Fourteenth Amendment. Since that time, the Court has heard many cases involving freedom of religion. These have involved such issues as prayer in schools, Christmas displays of Nativity scenes, and various kinds of support for religious education. While most people agree that church and state should be separate, we are no closer today to defining that separation than we were in 1791.

Does prayer in public schools violate the establishment clause?
Does a moment of silence violate the free exercise clause?

Critical Thinking Exercise
TAKING AND DEFENDING A POSITION ON THE ESTABLISHMENT CLAUSE

Each of the four situations below is based on a case that reached the Supreme Court. Your class should be divided into four groups. Each group should read one situation and answer the questions that follow. Be prepared to present and defend your position to the class.

Group 1. Under a Pennsylvania law, the state reimbursed private schools for teachers' salaries, textbooks, and instructional materials in math and science. Although the law generally applied to private schools, 96 percent of the money went to religious schools. Opponents argued that this kind of public support was unconstitutional. They felt it amounted to a subsidy for the schools' whole program, including religious instruction.

Group 2. New York City arranged a voluntary program permitting its public schools to release students during school hours to receive off-campus religious instruction. Opponents complained that this violated the establishment clause.

Group 3. The New York State Board of Regents required teachers to begin each school day by leading their class in a nondenominational prayer written by state officials. Students who did not wish to participate were permitted to remain silent or be excused from the classroom. The parents of ten students claimed the prayer was against their religious beliefs and violated the establishment clause.

Group 4. The city of Pawtucket, Rhode Island, put up a Christmas display that included a Santa Claus house, reindeer pulling Santa's sleigh, a Christmas tree, and a large banner reading "Season's Greetings." It also contained a creche with the figures of the infant Jesus, Mary, Joseph, angels, shepherds, kings, and animals. Opponents complained that this violated the establishment clause.

1. What position would people who hold the broad interpretation of the establishment clause take on this issue? The narrow interpretation? The literal interpretation? Explain your answers.

2. What arguments can you make for permitting the government to do what it did? What values and interests are involved?

3. What arguments can you make for prohibiting the government from doing what it did? What values and interests are involved?

4. Be prepared to evaluate the other positions presented.

What rights are protected by the free exercise clause?

The establishment clause prevents the government from requiring citizens to practice a particular religion. The **free exercise clause** is intended to make sure that people who want to practice their religion will be permitted to do so.

There are two parts to freedom of religion: the freedom to believe and the freedom to practice religious beliefs. The Supreme Court has said that individuals have an absolute right to freedom of belief or conscience. The government may not interfere with this right. Under certain conditions, however, the right to practice one's beliefs may be limited to protect other important values and interests. The problem is deciding which religious practices should be protected by the First Amendment and which practices government may limit.

What are the conflicts between the free exercise and establishment clauses?

There are times when the free exercise clause and the establishment clause of the First Amendment come into conflict. For example, consider the following situations:

■ If the government pays to provide for chaplains in the armed forces and in prisons, is it violating the establishment clause? If the government failed to provide chaplains, would it be limiting the free exercise of beliefs by persons in the armed forces or in prison?

■ If public school officials excuse Jewish students from attending classes on Yom Kippur to attend religious services, are they creating a preference for a particular group that violates the establishment clause? If they deny students the right to be absent, are they prohibiting the free exercise of their religion?

■ On August 11, 1984, President Reagan signed into law the Equal Access Act. It requires secondary schools to allow student religious groups to hold meetings in school buildings if other groups or social clubs are given the same opportunity. If schools do not provide meeting facilities for student religious groups, are they limiting their free exercise? If they do, are they violating the establishment clause?

Is it possible to balance the rights of "free exercise" against other interests of society?

The justices of the Supreme Court often have held differing opinions on the issues you have been discussing. Sometimes they have overruled earlier decisions. The justices have continually attempted to refine the "tests" or considerations used to make a decision.

The Court has considered some issues several times. For example, when the health of the community must be balanced against the religious beliefs of an individual or group, public health is considered to be more important.

By contrast, when the life, health, or safety of individuals, rather than the community, is involved, the Court has upheld the right of mentally competent adults to make their own decisions based on their religious beliefs. For example, an adult may refuse to receive a blood transfusion even if his or her life is at risk. Parents, however, may not refuse a transfusion for their children, and the courts may step in to protect the rights of minors.

The Court also has protected the right of students to refuse to salute the flag or attend high school if this is against their religious beliefs. In deciding such cases, the Court asked whether the government had a **compelling state interest**, one that was great enough to justify limiting the individual's free exercise of religion. For example, the justices considered the government's requiring a student to salute the flag to be an unreasonable attempt to force a student to accept a belief.

Should public school officials be allowed to require inoculations against communicable diseases for students whose parents argue against them on religious grounds?

What do *you* think?

1. How might the establishment and free exercise clauses come into conflict, and what criteria do you think should be used to ease this conflict?

2. In cases involving the right of individuals to freely exercise their beliefs versus the common good, which interests should be given preference and why? Give examples to support your work.

3. How can individuals help protect freedom of belief and the exercise of those beliefs?

Critical Thinking Exercise
EVALUATING THE FREE EXERCISE CLAUSE

Read the following selection dealing with an attempt by Santeria practitioners to build a new church in a Florida city. After discussing the issues involved in the case, your class will be divided into groups of three so that you can hold a simulated court hearing. One person in each group will present the case of the Santeria congregation, one will present the city's argument, and one will act as judge. Answer the questions following the selection, then be prepared to explain and defend your arguments and decisions.

The Santeria religion is practiced by the descendants of enslaved Africans in Cuba, and was brought to the United States by Cuban exiles. Santeria practices animal sacrifice in some of its rituals, including rites for birth and marriage, for healing, and for the initiation of new members and priests. Animals sacrificed include chickens, goats, sheep, and turtles; in most rituals the animals are cooked and eaten.

When a congregation of Santeria adherents announced plans to build a church in a Florida city, the city responded by passing ordinances forbidding the unnecessary or cruel killing of animals. The city explicitly prohibited killing or slaughtering an animal if the killing is part of a ritual and the animal is to be eaten. Members of the Santeria congregation sued the city, arguing that the ordinances were specifically directed at their religious practices and interfered with the free exercise of their religion.

Reasonable people may differ on the following questions. It is the right of each person to develop his or her own answers. Under our system of government, the Supreme Court determines if a government action has violated a person's religious liberty. Such laws would not be passed in the first place if at least some people did not want them. Therefore, it is important for each of us to recognize the importance of the religious liberty protected by the First Amendment. If we insist that everyone's religious liberty needs to be respected, laws that violate the First Amendment are less likely to be passed.

1. What interests of society might be promoted by a ban on animal sacrifice for religious purposes?

2. What principles might be promoted by permitting the church to continue its rituals?

3. If you were a member of the Supreme Court, how would you have decided this case? Explain your reasoning.

Reviewing and Using the Lesson

1. What is an "established church"? What was the "Great Awakening" and what effect did it have on established churches?

2. How would you explain the principle of "separation of church and state"? What reasons can you identify to support this principle?

3. What are "religious tests" for public office? What does the Constitution say about them?

4. What is the "establishment clause"? What disagreements have arisen over how courts should interpret it?

5. What is the "free exercise clause"? How have courts tried to balance the individual's right to free exercise of religion with the interests of society?

6. What examples can you give of situations in which the free exercise clause and the establishment clause seem to come into conflict?

7. Interview a spiritual leader about whether he or she supports legislation permitting prayer in public schools. Ask for reasons supporting his or her position. Report your findings to the class.

LESSON 30

How Does the First Amendment Protect Freedom of Expression?

Purpose of Lesson

The First Amendment says that "Congress shall make no law...abridging the freedom of speech, or of the press, or the right of the people peaceably to assemble, and to petition the Government for a redress of grievances." Together these four rights may be considered as one—the right to freedom of expression.

In this lesson you examine the benefits that freedom of speech and freedom of the press offer to the individual and society, why they were important to the Founders, and the circumstances under which the government should be able to limit them.

When you finish this lesson, you should be able to explain the importance of freedom of expression to both the individual and society and its historical significance. You should be able to explain considerations useful in deciding when to place limits on freedom of speech and press and be able to take, defend, and evaluate positions on issues involving the right to freedom of expression.

Terms to Know

libel
clear and present danger
Sedition Act of 1798

seditious libel
time, place, and manner
    restrictions

Why is protecting the right to freedom of expression important?

The First Amendment was written because the Founders believed that the freedom to express personal opinions is essential to a free government. The Founders knew from their own experience and knowledge of history that the freedom to write and publish must be protected from government interference.

It is not easy for anyone to tolerate the speech or writings of those with whom they strongly disagree. In a democracy, the danger to freedom of speech comes not only from government officials but also from majorities intolerant of minority opinions.

The pressures to suppress freedom of expression are widespread and powerful in any society. It is important, therefore, to remind ourselves constantly of the important benefits of freedom of expression to the individual and society. Among the arguments that favor free speech are the following:

- **Freedom of expression promotes individual growth and human dignity**. The right to think about and arrive at your own conclusions concerning morality, politics, or anything else, is part of individual freedom. That right would be meaningless without the freedom to speak and write about your opinions, and without the freedom to test those opinions by comparing them with the views of others.

- **Freedom of expression is important for the advancement of knowledge**. New ideas are more likely to be developed in a community that allows free discussion. As the British philosopher John Stuart Mill (1806–1873) said, progress is possible only when all points of view can be expressed and considered. This way, scientific or other discoveries can form the basis for future discoveries and inventions.

- **Freedom of expression is a necessary part of our representative government**. In our system of government, the government responds to the will of the people. If the people are to instruct government properly, they must have access to information, ideas, and different points of view. Freedom of expression is crucial both in determining policy and in monitoring how well the government is carrying out its responsibilities.

- **Freedom of expression is vital to bringing about peaceful social change**. The right to express one's ideas freely provides a "safety valve" for strongly held opinions. Freedom of expression allows you to try to influence public opinion through persuasion rather than by resorting to violence.

- **Freedom of expression is essential for the protection of all individual rights**. The free expression of ideas and the right to speak against the violation of one's rights by others or by the government are essential for the protection of all the other rights of the individual.

How was freedom of expression protected in early America?

Many ideas about the importance of freedom of speech and of the press were brought to America from England. In the seventeenth century, the English won the right to speak and publish without prior censorship. They could still be prosecuted afterward for what they said or wrote, however, under the common law of **seditious libel**. This law made it a crime to publish anything that might be injurious to the reputation of the government.

There is no indication that the Framers intended the Constitution or the Bill of Rights to prevent prosecution for seditious libel. The common view, in both America and Britain, was that no one should be able to make false or malicious accusations against the government.

The Constitution makes no mention of a free press, however, because the Framers believed, as Roger Sherman of Connecticut declared, "The power of Congress does not extend to the Press." The First Amendment was designed to quiet fears that Congress might interfere with the press anyway. These fears seemed to be confirmed by the passage of the **Sedition Act** in 1798. This act, passed by some of the same people who approved the Bill of Rights, indicates that some Americans still had a narrow view of free expression.

Many people, however, opposed such limitations. One reason the Republicans won the election of 1800 was that they were viewed as supporters of political freedom. By 1800, freedom of speech and press were beginning to be considered an essential part of free government.

How did the trial of John Peter Zenger help establish freedom of the press?

What is "seditious libel"? The common law definition was vague. In general, it meant defaming or ridiculing officers of the government, or the constitution, laws, or government policies, in a way that might jeopardize "public peace." This included not only things that were false and malicious, but also things that were true.

In 1735, John Peter Zenger, a New York printer, was charged with seditious libel by the colonial authorities. Zenger's lawyer argued that what Zenger had published was true, and therefore could not be libelous.

The judge told the jury that the common law did not permit truth as a defense. It was the judge's prerogative to decide, as a matter of law, whether the articles met the definition of seditious libel. He instructed the jury that

the only thing they could decide was the "fact" of whether Zenger was the publisher of the articles in question. If he was the publisher, which Zenger did not deny, then he was guilty—pure and simple.

The jury ignored the judge's instructions and found Zenger not guilty because the information he reported in the articles was true. Many Americans believed that this case not only established an important right of freedom of the press, but also proved the importance of the jury as a check on arbitrary government.

When has freedom of expression been suppressed?

There has been pressure at many times throughout history to suppress unpopular ideas. Restrictions generally have been imposed during times of war or when the government has felt threatened. Before the Civil War, for example, Congress made it a federal offense to send abolitionist literature through the mail. The early years of the twentieth century were marked by fears of the growing labor movement, socialism, communism, and anarchy. From World War I through the McCarthy era of the 1950s, state and federal governments prosecuted many suspected anarchists, socialists, and communists for advocating draft resistance, mass strikes, or overthrow of the government. These actions raised serious questions about the right of free speech and led to a number of Supreme Court cases. Since the 1960s, however, there have been fewer attempts to prosecute those who advocate their beliefs including belief in the benefits of a different form of government.

How might government persecution of dissidents, which occurred during the McCarthy era, endanger a free society?

Critical Thinking Exercise
EVALUATING AND DEVELOPING POSITIONS ON THE SCOPE AND LIMITS OF FREEDOM OF EXPRESSION

Judges, professors of constitutional law, and other students of the Constitution have tried to develop standards that will help us decide when freedom of expression may be limited. The following are two positions that judges and others have proposed. Your class will be divided into two groups to debate the opposing positions described below. Make sure your position addresses the questions at the end of the exercise.

Group 1. The freedom of expression of groups that advocate anti-democratic ideas may be limited. People have argued that the rights of certain groups to express their ideas should not be protected by the First Amendment. Typically, these are groups that advocate overthrowing our representative government. They may also be groups that express malicious ideas that violate the dignity and feelings of other people in the community.

People often conclude this position by arguing that only people who agree to abide by the rules of our society, such as those in the Constitution and the Bill of Rights, should be allowed to participate in free and open discussion.

Group 2. All persons should be allowed freedom of expression no matter how dangerous or obnoxious their ideas. People holding this position say that rarely, if ever, should the government be allowed to limit the freedom of expression. For example, if public order is jeopardized, limitations on free expression could be justified. They claim that even totalitarian, racist, and other obnoxious ideas may serve to make people defend and better understand their own values. To suppress such expression only makes those people who were denied the right to express their ideas become more hostile. It eliminates the safety-valve function of free speech and weakens society.

They also argue that to give government the power to suppress the expression of ideas that some people find unacceptable is too dangerous. It gives government the power to decide what beliefs and opinions are acceptable and unacceptable. A quotation attributed to Voltaire, the eighteenth-century French author most noted for his criticism of tyranny and bigotry, summarizes this position, "I may disapprove of what you say, but will defend to the death your right to say it."

1. What rights, values, and interests of individuals and society might be promoted or endangered by the position that advocates limiting the freedom to express anti-democratic ideas?

2. What rights, values, and interests of individuals and society might be promoted or endangered by the position which advocates limiting freedom of expression rarely, if ever, no matter how dangerous or obnoxious these ideas may be?

What are commonly accepted limitations on freedom of expression?

Despite the statement in the First Amendment that "Congress shall make no law...abridging the freedom of speech," most people argue in favor of limiting freedom of expression in certain specific situations.

Suppose the First Amendment were interpreted to mean that there could be no laws at all limiting speech. If so, people would be able to say anything they wanted at any time they wanted. People could lie in court and deprive others of their right to a fair trial. People could scream in libraries, give political speeches in the middle of church sermons, or speak through loudspeakers in neighborhoods in the middle of the night.

Most judges and legal scholars believe the First Amendment should not be interpreted to protect freedom of expression in situations such as those above. In some situations, limiting freedom to speak may actually increase a person's ability to be heard. For example, there are rules governing when someone may talk at a meeting or debate. You may have the right to protest a government policy you do not like, but you do not have the right to do so with a loudspeaker in a residential area in the middle of the night.

These limitations on freedom of expression are referred to as **time**, **place**, **and manner restrictions**. They govern when, where, and how you may speak, not what you may say. Most people agree that these limitations do not violate the right to free expression so long as they do not make it difficult or impossible for you to express your ideas to others. These regulations must not favor some opinions over others. For example, one group may not be given a permit to speak in a public park when other groups are forbidden to do so.

What considerations has the Supreme Court used to limit freedom of expression?

The difficult question for the Court to decide is when freedom of expression should be limited to protect other important social goals. The Supreme Court has upheld time, place, and manner restrictions, so long as they are neutral and applied fairly.

The idea of **neutrality** is important, for the Court has generally taken the position that no matter how dangerous or obnoxious the ideas, people should be allowed to express their views freely.

Yet the Court will sometimes allow speech to be limited based on its **content**. Over the years, the courts have developed guidelines to use in balancing the right to free expression against other important rights and interests of society. For example, suppose your right to free expression could endanger the public safety or national security. If the danger is considered great enough, the courts will decide that your right to free speech must be limited. No one has the right to publish secret military information, or the names of U.S. intelligence agents overseas, for example.

How would you define speech that presents a clear and present danger to society?

Does the First Amendment protect all forms of expression?

The courts have upheld laws prohibiting speech or writings that present a **clear and present danger** to others or to society. Examples include giving away national security secrets, lying under oath, or **libel**—ruining other people's reputations by knowingly spreading lies about them. The courts also have said that you may not engage in speech that could directly lead to violence or cause a riot.

Some judges and scholars have argued that the authors of the First Amendment did not intend it to protect all kinds of speech and press. Their belief in the need to protect free expression was based on the idea that the free exchange of political ideas was essential to democracy. It was not their intention to protect speech that was blasphemous, obscene, or libelous.

To some degree the courts still maintain that the speech protections of the First Amendment only apply to certain kinds of speech. Obscenity, for example, is not protected.

The Supreme Court, however, in a series of decisions, has made it increasingly difficult to determine what is "obscene." Consequently, although obscene speech is not protected there are fewer successful prosecutions of obscene speech because of changing community and legal standards.

Commercial speech, such as advertising, also receives less protection by the courts. Regulations that prevent consumer fraud and false advertising, for example, are permitted. In addition, commercial speech may be regulated for reasons of public health. This is why the government can ban cigarette advertising on television.

When the rights of free press come into conflict with the right to a fair trial, the courts have generally upheld the right of reporters to cover trials. Judges have been told to find other ways to protect the defendant's right to a fair trial.

What do *you* think?

1. When, if ever, does the right of free speech come into conflict with the common good and how should such conflicts be addressed?

2. Would a law restricting the amount of money an individual or group can give to a political party or candidate violate freedom of expression?

3. Describe how you would seek to weigh the sometimes conflicting rights of citizens to a free press and to a fair trial.

4. Do you think freedom of expression should extend to racist speech designed to engender hatred or contempt? Why or why not?

Critical Thinking Exercise
TAKING AND DEFENDING POSITIONS ON AN ISSUE OF FREEDOM OF EXPRESSION

Read the description of issues regarding freedom of expression on college and university campuses. Then follow directions for the exercise.

Colleges and universities are places where free inquiry, debate, and expression are highly valued. Professors and students are supposed to have great freedom to explore, express, debate, and discuss both popular and unpopular ideas. The university ideal is a place where all ideas are worthy of exploration.

In years past, most students at major colleges and universities were white. Today, student bodies of colleges and universities better reflect the diversity of our nation.

What limitations, if any, should be placed on speakers on college campuses?

Despite the increased understanding of diversity in the United States, conflicts among students along racial, ethnic, and religious lines have occurred on college campuses. As a result, university administrators and student governments have attempted to promote civility and understanding on campus by various means.

Recently, at more than 200 colleges and universities across the nation, student codes of conduct or "speech codes" were established. They are designed to prevent statements or comments about race, gender, religion, national origin, or sexual orientation that might offend some people. The goal of such codes is to discourage prejudice and create a more comfortable learning environment for all students.

Supporters of the codes explain that "freedom of expression is no more sacred than freedom from intolerance or bigotry." Critics charge that the result has been to violate students' and teachers' right to free expression. They refer to various instances in which students have been suspended or expelled for comments that were offensive to others.

Your class should be divided into small groups. Assume that you and your group are college students asked to determine what policy should be established to deal with the issue of what limitations, if any, should be placed on freedom of expression for students on campus? Develop a proposed policy and be prepared to present it to the class. Explain whether your position is based on philosophical principles, constitutional principles, specific circumstances, or on some or all of these.

Issue: On a typical college campus, a large number of students of relatively diverse backgrounds are thrown together in crowded living conditions.

1. Do you think these conditions distinguish the campus from the larger society? If so, do you think this would support the claim that different rules governing speech are needed on campus than those that apply to the society at large?

2. Should any limits be placed on the freedom of expression of professors whose courses are required of all students for graduation?

3. What issues of freedom of expression are involved in this situation?

4. What values and interests are involved?

5. What arguments might be presented by persons holding the position that the right to free expression by people expressing undemocratic ideas can be limited?

6. What arguments might be presented by persons holding the position that the right to free expression should not be limited, even for those expressing dangerous or obnoxious ideas?

Reviewing and Using the Lesson

1. What rights, considered together, make up "freedom of expression"?

2. Why is it important to protect freedom of expression?

3. What is "seditious libel"? What examples can you give of circumstances in which laws against seditious libel were used to try to suppress criticism of the government?

4. How would you explain "time, place, and manner" restrictions on freedom of expression? What conditions must such restrictions meet in order to be valid?

5. Under what circumstances may limitations on expression be based upon its content?

6. What is meant by the term "libel"?

7. Research the following cases related to free speech in a school setting: *Tinker v. Des Moines School District*, 393, U.S. 503 (1963) and *Bethel School District v. Fraser*, 54 U.S.L.W. 5054 (1986). Report your findings to the class.

LESSON 31

How Does the First Amendment Protect Freedom of Assembly, Petition, and Association?

Purpose of Lesson

The First Amendment says that "Congress shall make no law...abridging...the right of the people peaceably to assemble, and to petition the government for a redress of grievances." In this lesson you examine the importance and historical background of these rights. You also discuss an important related right—freedom of association.

When you finish this lesson, you should be able to explain the importance of the rights to freedom of assembly, petition, and association. You should also be able to describe the history of these rights and in what types of situations they might be limited. Finally, you should be able to take and defend a position on an issue involving these rights.

Terms to Know

gag rule
lobby
public forum
redress of grievances

right to assembly
right of association
right of petition

What is the importance of the rights to assembly, petition, and association?

As we have seen, the First Amendment protects our rights to form our own opinions including those about politics and religion. It also protects our right to communicate those opinions to others. These rights would not mean very much, though, if the government had the power to prevent people from getting together to express their views. The people's freedom to **assemble** and **petition** the government—to ask the government to take action or change its policies—enhances the First Amendment's protection of our political rights.

A related right that has been recognized by courts is the right to freedom of **association**. We are free to associate with others who share our opinions. These associations include political groups, church groups, professional associations, social clubs, and community service organizations. All are protected by the right to associate freely.

Why were the rights of assembly and petition important to the Founders?

The rights of assembly and petition were part of English common law for hundreds of years and were seen by Americans as fundamental to a constitutional democracy. Historically these two rights have been associated with each other. People thought that the purpose of the right to assemble was to petition the government. The right of petition was recognized in the Magna Carta; in fact, the Magna Carta itself was a petition addressed to the king demanding that he correct certain wrongs. A resolution of the House of Commons in 1669, along with the English Bill of Rights of 1689, guaranteed English subjects the right to petition both the House of Commons and the monarch.

The American colonists considered the right to petition a basic right of Englishmen and used it often. Since they could not send representatives to Parliament, they saw the right of petition as an important means of communication with the British government. One of the colonists' frustrations in the years before the Revolution was the feeling that Parliament was ignoring their petitions.

During and after the Revolution, most states protected the rights of assembly and petition, either within their state constitutions or in their state bills of rights. Today, the rights of assembly and petition have been included in all but two of the fifty state constitutions.

How have the rights of assembly and petition been used?

From the beginning, Americans have felt free to ask the government for action on issues that were important to them. In the 1790s, one task that faced the First Congress was acting on thousands of petitions for pensions or for back pay promised to the widows and orphans of soldiers in the Revolutionary War. Often, as with the Revolutionary War widows, people were asking the government to keep its promises.

In the 1830s, Congress received numerous petitions urging that slavery be abolished in the District of Columbia. The feeling against abolitionists was so strong that in 1836 Congress passed a **gag rule** to prevent debate on all petitions related to slavery. This rule not only prevented any discussion of ending slavery, it limited the ways nonvoters could express their views. The use of the right to petition was an important way for women, African Americans, and others who were denied the right to vote to communicate with public officials. The gag rule was finally repealed in 1844, thanks to the leadership of former president John Quincy Adams, a member of Congress at that time.

How has the right to petition been used by Americans to influence their elected representatives?

There are other instances when the United States government has tried to silence its critics. For example, during the Great Depression, a "Bonus Army" of World War I veterans converged on the nation's capital in the summer of 1932 to petition Congress for early payment of their military bonuses. Congress refused to support the bill and half the veterans returned home. Several thousand, however, remained in a camp outside the city. President Herbert Hoover ordered General Douglas MacArthur and the Army to drive the veterans out of the

camp. General MacArthur did so with tanks, guns, and tear gas, killing two veterans and wounding several others.

The importance of the right to assemble is nowhere better illustrated than in the civil rights movement of the 1950s and 1960s. Under the leadership of the Reverend Martin Luther King, Jr., thousands participated in the march for "Jobs and Freedom."

Today, the right to petition is widely used at the local, state, and federal levels. Groups that do not have the money to buy advertising often use the freedom to assemble and petition to make their views known by attracting the attention of the mass media.

The right to petition, however, includes much more than formal petitions. Faxes, e-mail, phone calls, and letters to public officials are methods of petitioning the government. The right to petition is not limited to people wishing the government to correct wrongs. It is used by individuals, groups, and corporations to **lobby** government officials to try to persuade them to adopt policies that will benefit their interests or the interests of the country as a whole.

What do *you* think?

1. Should the right of association be interpreted to mean that organizations cannot impose any limits on their membership? Explain your position.

2. Do you think that the moves by some cities and towns to prohibit gangs from peacefully gathering in public parks violates the freedom of assembly and association? Why?

3. What conflicts might occur between the right of freedom of assembly and other values and interests of society? How should these conflicts be managed?

Why is the right to assemble fundamental to a democratic society?

What limitations may be placed on the right of assembly?

The rights of free speech and assembly protect the rights of people to march and demonstrate. It is expected that these rights will result in activities where people express strongly held views on political, economic, and social issues. The government is responsible for making sure that demonstrations are "peaceable" and do not endanger community safety or unreasonably inconvenience the public.

Public property is owned by the people. It would appear, therefore, that people have a right to assemble on public property to speak and in other ways demonstrate their views on different issues. As with all other rights, in some situations it may be reasonable and fair to limit this right.

Judges and other students of the Constitution have taken different positions on this question. Some argue that people should be able to assemble on any public property so long as it does not disrupt the normal use of that property. Others argue that the right to use public property should be limited to only those places, such as street corners and parks, that are traditionally associated with free speech.

Critical Thinking Exercise

DEVELOPING STANDARDS TO USE IN LIMITING FREEDOM OF ASSEMBLY

The following seven situations raise questions about when people should be able to assemble and demonstrate on public property. Work in small groups to examine the situations and answer the questions that follow them.

1. Demonstrators are marching in front of a private home to protest the actions of the person who lives there.

2. People are assembling to march through a shopping mall.

3. People are marching through a public school while it is in session.

4. Pickets are blocking the entrance to a factory.

5. Pickets are blocking the entrance to an abortion clinic.

6. A group is demonstrating by sitting on the floors of the hallways of government buildings such as city hall, the university, and the courts.

7. A group is demonstrating during rush hour on a bridge over an expressway.

Examining the Issues. List the rights, values, and interests involved in each situation. Then, develop one or more considerations that should be used in balancing these factors. For example, what considerations should be used in deciding when public safety should outweigh the right to demonstrate? Be prepared to present and defend your group's position before the class.

1. What arguments might be given in each situation by people supporting the right to assemble and to demonstrate?

2. What arguments might be given by those opposing the assembly and demonstration?

3. What competing values and interests are involved in each situation?

What limits has the Supreme Court placed on freedom of assembly?

In general, it has been assumed that the government has the power to impose time, place and manner restrictions on the right to assemble just as it does on the right of freedom of expression. The courts have said that any regulation must

- be designed to protect a legitimate government interest and not be intended to suppress free speech or assembly
- it must be applied in a non-discriminatory manner. That is, it cannot put restrictions on assembly that only apply to certain groups or only because of theme or subject.

The courts have ruled that the right of assembly extends to meetings held in **public forums** such as streets, parks, and sidewalks. Free access to public property has historically been especially important for people who cannot afford more costly ways to communicate, such as advertising in newspapers or on television.

How is the right of association protected?

Although the right of association is not mentioned in the Constitution, courts have said that it is implied by the other rights in the First Amendment—in particular, by the rights of free speech and assembly. The right to associate freely with one's fellow citizens is part of living in a free society. The government should not interfere with your right to join with others, it is argued, whether it be in private clubs, college fraternities, political parties, professional organizations, or labor unions.

The first time the Supreme Court dealt with an issue regarding the freedom of association was in 1958. The state of Alabama had ordered the **National Association for the Advancement of Colored People (NAACP)** to disclose its membership lists. During this time, the NAACP was engaged in a bitter civil rights struggle. The Supreme Court thought that if the NAACP membership lists were made public, this might lead to hostile acts against its members. The Court ruled in *NAACP v. Alabama* (1958) that freedom of association is protected by the First Amendment and that Alabama's demand for the membership lists violated this right.

Soon after the Alabama ruling, however, the Court upheld laws that required disclosure of membership lists of the Communist party. In *Barenblatt v. U.S.* (1959) the Court justified their decision on the ground that the organization advocated the violent overthrow of the government.

One question that this raises is whether the right of association means you have the right **not** to associate with certain people. Should private organizations be able to prohibit some people from becoming members? For example, should the government be able to require private golf courses to admit African Americans or private men's clubs to admit women? This question involves the right of equal protection as well as that of association.

In cases involving this question, the Supreme Court has ruled that the government cannot interfere in a person's choices about whom to associate with in private life. On the other hand, the court has ruled that in some situations that go beyond close personal relationships and involve larger social purposes, the government may force private organizations not to discriminate on the basis of race, gender, or ethnic background.

These issues can be very difficult. The difficulties reflect the tension between two important ideals:

- eliminating unfair discrimination in American life
- the right of each individual to live his or her own life as free as possible from government interference

Do people have a right to join in private associations which exclude others on the basis of gender, race, religion, or ethnicity?

One hundred fifty years ago, Alexis de Tocqueville (1805–1859) commented on the Americans' tendency to join together to solve common problems. The exercise of freedom of association was, Tocqueville thought, one of the outstanding characteristics of American citizenship. It is difficult to imagine the development of American labor unions and political parties, as well as a host of other organizations that play important roles in our civic life, without the exercise of this right.

Tocqueville believed that the freedom to associate was essential for preserving free government. Americans did not need to rely on the government to solve all their problems because private groups could organize themselves quickly to respond to common concerns or needs. Tocqueville thought that this helped to make Americans more public-spirited. Americans were aware that they were responsible for helping to achieve the common good, and that they could each do something to help achieve it.

Critical Thinking Exercise
TAKING AND DEFENDING A POSITION ON A FIRST AMENDMENT ISSUE

Board of Education of the Westside Community Schools v. Mergens (1990) involves most of the First Amendment rights you have been studying—religion, speech, and association. Read the summary of the case below. Then to complete this exercise your class should be divided into three groups. All groups should be sure to address the questions following the case summary.

In 1984, Congress passed the Equal Access Act, which prohibits any public secondary school that receives federal funds and provides facilities for extracurricular organizations from discriminating against student clubs because of their religious or philosophical orientation.

Westside High School is a public school in Omaha, Nebraska, with about 1,500 students. Students have the opportunity to participate in a number of groups and clubs, all of which meet after school on the school's premises. Among these groups are the Creative Writing Club, the Math Club, and the Future Medical Assistants. School board policy requires that each group have a faculty sponsor and none can be sponsored by any organization that denies membership based on race, color, creed, gender, or political belief.

In January, 1985, Bridget Mergens met with the Westside principal to request permission to form a Christian Club whose purpose would be "to permit students to read and discuss the Bible, to have fellowship, and to pray together." The club would be open to all students, regardless of religious beliefs. There would be no faculty sponsor.

Both the principal and the district superintendent denied the request. They said, first of all, the sponsor requirement was not met. More importantly, permitting the religious club to meet on school property would be unconstitutional. The school board upheld the denial.

Mergens and her parents sued the school for violating the Equal Access Act and the First Amendment protections of free speech, association, and free exercise of religion.

The trial judge ruled in favor of the school saying that the Equal Access Act did not apply because all the other clubs at school were related to curriculum and linked to the school's educational function.

The U.S. Court of Appeals reversed the lower court ruling because it said there were other school clubs, such as the Chess Club and the Surfing Club, that were not directly related to the school's educational function. The school district appealed to the Supreme Court.

Group 1. Your group should develop arguments for Westside High School's position.

Group 2. Your group should develop arguments for the position of Bridget Mergens.

Group 3. Your group should act as judges, listen to both arguments, and decide whether the Christian Club should be able to meet after school at Westside. The judges should be able to explain the basis for their decisions and defend them before the class.

1. What First Amendment issues are raised in this case?

2. What values and interests are in conflict in this case?

3. What arguments can you make for allowing the group to meet?

4. What arguments can you make for prohibiting the group from meeting?

Reviewing and Using the Lesson

1. How would you explain the rights of assembly, petition, and association?

2. How would you describe the historical origins of the rights of assembly and petition?

3. How have the rights of assembly and petition been important in American history?

4. What restrictions have been imposed on the right of assembly, and how have these restrictions been justified?

5. Since the right of association is not mentioned in the First Amendment, how have courts justified treating it as a constitutional right?

LESSON 32

What Is the Importance of Procedural Due Process?

Purpose of Lesson

In this lesson you further examine one of the key provisions of the Fourteenth Amendment raised in Lesson 25—due process. You will discuss how it protects individuals from possible abuses of power, the difference between procedural and substantive due process, and the history of due process. Finally, you examine some violations of due process in a contemporary situation.

When you finish this lesson, you should be able to explain why the Founders considered this right so important. You also should be able to explain the purpose and importance of procedural due process and to identify violations of due process in a specific situation.

How does the right to a trial by jury provide a check on the power of the state?

Terms to Know

adversary system
general warrants
inquisitorial system
oath
perjury

procedural due process
reasonable doubt
substantive due process
writs of assistance

What is the difference between procedural and substantive due process of law?

Substantive due process, limits the **degree** to which government can interfere with a person's life, liberty or property.

Procedural due process, on the other hand, limits the procedures that may be used by government when interfering with life, liberty, or property. It requires the government to use fair procedures when investigating, trying, or punishing someone for a crime.

Procedural due process limits the powers of law enforcement agencies and courts. These limits protect both the innocent and the guilty against possible abuses of official power.

Certain due process rights are protected in the body of the Constitution. For example, it guarantees the right to a writ of habeas corpus and trial by jury in criminal cases.

The Fourth through Eighth Amendments protect rights of people who are suspected of, charged with, or convicted of crimes. These Amendments also guide judges in conducting trials, appeals, and sentencing.

What is the historical background of procedural due process?

In English law one of the first procedural due process rights to develop was that to a "speedy and public trial." The Magna Carta helped to establish this right in Article 40: "To no one will we sell, to none will we refuse or delay, right or justice." In the centuries that followed, trial by jury also became a right of procedural due process as the jury system spread throughout England with the expansion of royal courts and the common law. This right is guaranteed in our Bill of Rights by the Sixth Amendment.

Many other procedural rights valued by Americans were first asserted in England during the religious strife of the sixteenth and seventeenth centuries. In those days, following the "wrong" religion was usually a very serious crime—either treason or heresy, or both. The right against self-incrimination grew out of the practices of the infamous Court of High Commission and Court of the Star Chamber. People could be forced to appear before these courts, and required to take an **oath**—call on God to witness their truthfulness. Lying under oath meant not only committing the crime of **perjury**—lying to the court—but also committing a sin.

In what ways did the Framers' knowledge of history and their experiences influence the writing of the Bill of Rights as it relates to due process?

It was not uncommon for authorities to use torture to compel people to confess to crimes. Even after torture was banned, the government continued to punish people for refusing to answer questions at their trials. The practice of torture also led to the Eighth Amendment provision that bans "cruel and unusual punishments." This provision, which was taken almost word for word from the English Bill of Rights, still did not prevent some punishments that we would not allow today.

The Fourth Amendment requirement that law enforcement officers obtain a warrant before searching someone's home stems from the common law principle that "a man's home is his castle." Common law prevented judges from giving law enforcement officials **general warrants.** A general warrant did not describe specifically the places to be searched, or the persons or things to be seized. The American colonists experienced the injustice of both general warrants and **writs of assistance**, which were issued by British officials enforcing customs laws. The officials often used warrants and writs to harass and intimidate innocent people.

Why are procedural rights important in an adversary legal system?

The legal system in England and the United States is known as an **adversary system**. This means that in most legal cases, civil or criminal, there are two opposing, or "adverse" parties, and each party does its best to prove its case before an impartial judge or jury.

An adversary system may be contrasted with an **inquisitorial system**, which is the system that prevails in France and other European countries. In these systems, the judge acts as a kind of combination judge and prosecutor. The accused is expected to answer the judge's questions truthfully and may not invoke a right against self-incrimination. The judge examines witnesses and evidence, and if the judge decides that there is enough proof of guilt, the case goes to a panel of presiding judges who review the evidence and make a final decision. There are no jury trials, fewer lawyers, and court proceedings are usually much shorter. In spite of the lack of procedural guarantees, it does not appear that there is a greater number of unfair convictions in countries that have an inquisitorial system.

The adversary system is characteristic of English law and the systems that developed from it. Because each side must do its best to prove its case, we consider it important that neither side has any unfair advantage. Over the years, due process rights have been expanded to try to equalize the power of the individual and the power of the government.

An important procedural right that does not appear in our Constitution is the requirement that in criminal cases the government must prove its case "beyond a **reasonable doubt**." The government must prove that the defendant is guilty, the defendant is not required to prove his or her innocence. The idea of "innocent until proven guilty" is the foundation of all other due process rights.

Most of the time we do not think about what kind of legal system we have, or what alternative legal systems might be like. The adversary system is often defended because it seems to be more likely to get to the truth. If each side can develop its evidence, present its witnesses, and make its arguments, it gives the judge or jury a clear-cut decision to make. Critics, however, charge that an adversary system is wasteful and inefficient, and does more to increase the influence of lawyers than to uncover the truth.

Whether or not the inquisitorial system produces results that are as fair as those in an adversary system, it is unlikely that there will be a movement away from the current system in the United States. The adversary system is consistent with Americans' long-standing suspicion of government power, and with our basic ideas of fairness.

What guarantees of due process appear in the Bill of Rights?

The important guarantees of due process appear in the Fourth through the Eighth Amendments. The Fourth and the Fifth Amendments protect rights that apply to people who are being investigated as criminal suspects, but have not necessarily been charged with a crime. Thus, they limit the government's power to search private homes and papers, conduct wire taps, seize evidence, and charge people with crimes.

The Fifth through Eighth Amendments protect rights of people who are on trial for crimes, those who wish to appeal a sentence or verdict, or those who have received a sentence after conviction. The Seventh Amendment also guarantees a right of trial by jury in **civil** cases. That means that in a federal lawsuit between two people, or between a person and a corporation, a jury trial can be requested.

What do *you* think?

1. Describe provisions of the Constitution designed to protect individuals who are accused of crimes before trial, during trial, and after trial.

   What purposes are served by such protections?

2. In your opinion, what is the most important right protected by the due process clause? Explain.

3. Do you think laws should be passed to require minors accused of committing particularly heinous crimes to be treated as adults before, during, and after trial? Why?

What is the importance of the protection provided by procedural due process?

The individual's right to procedural due process has been called the greatest protection in the Constitution from the abuse of power by government. The amendments guaranteeing procedural due process are the most important of all the amendments. These amendments were based on centuries of experience in which governments routinely violated due process rights.

Many people question why the Founders placed such importance on rights that are designed to protect individuals accused of breaking the law. Many Americans before and during the Revolution suffered from the violation of their procedural rights by Great Britain, although these rights were a part of the British constitution. The colonists knew that just because a person was accused of a crime did not mean that the person was guilty.

The protection of procedural rights is just as important and difficult today as it was in colonial America. This is why an understanding of the principles of due process should be the responsibility of every citizen. Studies have shown that many Americans do not understand due process of law or do not even think it is important unless they have personally suffered a violation of their rights. As a result, the public often does not support due process rights, and public debate on issues of due process is often misinformed.

Why is it important for the courts to try to balance the rights of a person accused of a crime against the rights of the rest of the community?

Critical Thinking Exercise
IDENTIFYING VIOLATIONS OF DUE PROCESS

The following situation is an actual case. Fortunately, it is not typical of our criminal justice system. Yet for such a situation to occur, even infrequently, confirms that there is a constant need to ensure that all rights that constitute due process are respected.

Work in small groups, read the events of the case and respond to the questions and instructions that follow it. Be prepared to present and explain your responses to the class.

In 1980 in a small town, a sixteen-year-old white girl disappeared while looking for a restroom at a high school. Two custodians later found her body hidden in the loft of the school auditorium. She had been raped and strangled. The community in which this crime occurred was one with a history of racial prejudice and conflict.

The custodians were Jones, a white man, and Smith, an African American. Both were questioned by the police and made to sign statements explaining where they had been and how they had found the body. They were taken to a hospital and were made to give samples of their saliva, blood, and hair. Then a police officer drove them back to the high school. As he dropped them off, he said, "One of you two is gonna hang for this." Then he turned to Smith and said, "Since you're the black, you're elected." One week later, Smith was arrested for raping and murdering the girl. He was tried and convicted by an all white jury from which qualified blacks had been excluded, and he was sentenced to death.

A writ of **habeas corpus** to the state supreme court was filed, and a hearing was held seven years later. The appeals court judge found that the arresting officer and district attorney suppressed evidence favorable to Smith. They had lied and created false testimony to have Smith charged and convicted.

At Smith's trial, the medical evidence that would have shown that Smith was innocent was "lost." The medical examiner "forgot" the results of the autopsy, "lost" his notes on his findings, and "lost" the samples he had taken from the victim's body.

A police officer threatened witnesses whose testimony supported Smith's innocence, then coached witnesses to lie in court. The officer also falsified the findings of the lie-detector test that supported Smith's innocence.

The sheriff defied the original trial court's order to release Smith on bail. The judge, rather than enforcing his order, changed it and denied bail. Smith's defense lawyer won two stays of execution, which saved his life while he waited for his case to be heard by the appeals court.

The judge who presided over the 1987 hearing stated in his findings that Smith "did not receive a fair trial, was denied the basic fundamental rights of due process of law, and did not commit the crime for which he now resides on death row."

At the end of the hearing the judge stated, "In the thirty years this court has presided...no case has presented a more shocking scenario of the effects of racial prejudice, perjured testimony, [and] witness intimidation.... The continued incarceration of [Smith] under these circumstances is an affront to the basic notions of fairness and justice."

It took two more years for the state supreme court to uphold the order of the appeals court judge and to set Smith free. The court stated, "Due process of law is the cornerstone of a civilized system of justice. Our society wins not only when the guilty are convicted but when criminal trials are fair; our system of justice suffers when an accused is treated unfairly."

1. In what ways was Smith denied a fair trial?

2. In what ways were Smith's rights violated?

3. Although some law enforcement officers and judges appear to have tried to deprive Smith of his rights, what were the actions of certain people to ensure that his procedural rights were honored? Explain your answer.

4. What fundamental values and interests of our society were endangered in this situation?

5. What ways can you suggest to prevent the injustices in this case from happening to someone else in the future?

6. What do you think should happen in a case like this, if the defendant is indeed guilty?

What do *you* think?

1. Why is procedural due process called the cornerstone of a civilized system of justice?

2. What limits, if any, would you put on the number of times a person could use the right to a writ of habeas corpus to appeal a case to a higher court? Explain your position.

3. Why is procedural due process as important and difficult today as in colonial times?

4. The statement by the British jurist Sir William Blackstone (1723–1780) is often quoted "Better that nine guilty men go free than one innocent man be convicted." Do you agree or disagree? Would you agree if the figures were "ninety-nine" and "one"?

How does the rule of law protect the rights of individuals?

Due process includes the basic idea that government officials must obey the law. This idea is hundreds of years old. Today, no one who has the power to make laws, enforce them, or interpret them can be excused from obeying the law.

In our system, we believe it is fundamentally important that any decision about taking away someone's rights be made according to fair, established procedures. By insisting that procedures be followed carefully, we hope to reduce the risk that mistakes, prejudices, or the personal beliefs of government officials will lead to innocent people being accused or convicted of crimes. The government can best encourage the people to respect the law by obeying the law itself.

Many people believe that the Fourth, Fifth, Sixth, and Eighth Amendments are the very heart of the Bill of Rights and the whole theory behind rule of law. These amendments and the Supreme Court's extensions of them distinguish our society from many others. Great Britain still does not allow a citizen accused of a crime the full range of rights Americans enjoy.

Although we have not always lived up to the ideal of due process, as Frederick Douglass once said,

> There is hope for a people when their laws are righteous, whether for the moment they conform to them or not.

Reviewing and Using the Lesson

1. How would you explain the concept of "procedural due process"? Why is procedural due process important?

2. What are the historical origins of procedural due process? What guarantees of procedural due process are contained in the Bill of Rights?

3. How would you define the following terms:

   - habeas corpus
   - perjury
   - general warrants
   - writs of assistance

4. What are the important differences between an "adversary system" of justice and an "inquisitorial system" of justice?

5. How would you explain the requirement in criminal cases that to obtain a conviction, the government must prove its case "beyond a reasonable doubt"?

6. How is procedural due process related to the idea of "the rule of law"?

7. Examine due process issues in a public school setting by researching the landmark Supreme Court case *Goss v. Lopez*, 419 U.S. 565 (1975). Report your findings to the class.

LESSON 33

How Do the Fourth and Fifth Amendments Protect Us against Unreasonable Law Enforcement Procedures?

Purpose of Lesson

Both the Fourth and Fifth Amendments put limits on the methods used by law enforcement officials investigating crimes. The idea behind both amendments is that the government must respect the principle that people are innocent until they are proven guilty.

The Fourth Amendment limits the powers of law enforcement officials to enter and search people's houses or to stop and search someone without reasonable cause. The Fifth Amendment contains several other important protections. This lesson focuses on protecting individuals from being forced to confess to a crime. You examine the history of these rights and their importance to the Framers.

When you finish this lesson, you should be able to explain the purpose and history of the Fourth Amendment, issues raised in its interpretation, and the importance of the Fifth Amendment provision against self-incrimination. Finally you should be able to take, defend, and evaluate positions on cases involving the right against self-incrimination.

How do search warrants protect every person's right to be secure?

Terms to Know

contempt of court
exclusionary rule
immunity
misdemeanor
probable cause

right against
    self-incrimination
right to privacy
warrant

What is the purpose of the Fourth Amendment?

Although the Fourth Amendment originally limited only the powers of the federal government, it has been applied to state and local governments by its incorporation into the Fourteenth Amendment. The intent of the amendment can be discovered fairly easily by reading it, even though the authors used several legal terms, as well as phrases that are not defined and now require interpretation.

The right of the people to be secure in their persons, houses, papers, and effects, against unreasonable searches and seizures, shall not be violated, and no Warrants shall issue, but upon probable cause, supported by oath or affirmation, and particularly describing the place to be searched, and the persons or things to be seized.

Fourth Amendment

Although the Fourth Amendment does not specifically state that it protects the **right to privacy**, it has been interpreted to protect this right, which is one of the most significant protections of human freedom and dignity found in the Bill of Rights.

The protection of privacy from invasion by government officials is highly valued for its own sake. It also is important to the right to freedom of conscience, thought, religion, expression, and property. Without the right to privacy, these other valued rights could be violated by government officials. Such a danger is particularly acute today with advanced surveillance technology and computers available to the government. If people were under constant or periodic observation by government, how free would they be to discuss differing opinions about our political system?

The importance to a free society of the protections against unreasonable searches and seizures was stressed by Justice Robert Jackson soon after he served as a judge at the Nuremberg trials of Nazi war criminals in 1949. He said:

> *Among the deprivations of rights, none is so effective in cowing a population, crushing the spirit of the individual and putting terror in every heart as uncontrolled search and seizure. It is one of the first and most effective weapons in the arsenal of every arbitrary government.*

The Fourth Amendment prohibits law enforcement officers from searching or seizing people or their property unless there is **probable cause**—a good reason for suspecting a person of breaking a law. Its authors, however, decided not to allow police officers themselves to decide what constitutes probable cause. The amendment requires police officers to present their reasons for a search or seizure to a judge of a magistrate. If the judge or magistrate agrees there is probable cause to suspect a violation of law, the law enforcement officer is given a **warrant**—a written document giving permission for a search or seizure.

The Fourth Amendment has, however, been interpreted to allow searches and arrests without a warrant under certain circumstances. The Fourth Amendment provides further protection for individuals by limiting the power of judges to issue warrants. Warrants must specifically describe "the place to be searched and the persons or things to be seized." A judge cannot give law enforcement officers a warrant that enables them to search anything they please.

In recent times the Fourth Amendment's protections have not been limited to physical intrusions by government on an individual's person or property. The Fourth Amendment's language does refer only to "persons, houses, papers, and effects," and for many years the Supreme Court gave those words a literal interpretation.

Today, however, the Court gives the Amendment a broader interpretation and extends the Amendment's coverage to wiretapping, "bugging", and other forms of eavesdropping. The courts have stated in these cases that persons, not places, are to be protected and, therefore, wiretapping can only occur after a warrant is issued.

How is the right to privacy different today from what it was when the Framers wrote the Constitution?

What is the history of the Fourth Amendment?

We inherited from British history the saying that "a man's home is his castle." The right to privacy and its importance to a free society have been understood for generations. English common law protected the right to privacy by prohibiting judges from giving law enforcement officials **general warrants** that did not describe in detail the places to be searched and the things or persons to be seized. General warrants have been referred to as open-ended "hunting licenses" authorizing government officials to search people, their businesses, homes, and property indiscriminately.

Despite the common law, royal commissions and Parliament had sometimes authorized the use of general warrants by government officials. At times these searches were directed at violent criminals. Often they were used to harass and persecute individuals who were critical of the government or who dissented from the Church of England.

As early as 1589, in a case involving a general search of Puritans and their property, English lawyers argued that the Magna Carta protected the personal privacy of individuals. Nevertheless, in 1662 Parliament passed a law that permitted general warrants called **writs of assistance**. These writs gave government officials the power to search for goods that had entered the country in violation of custom laws.

Officials did not need to convince a judge that they had reason to suspect an individual of committing a crime or that illegal goods were being hidden in a particular place. Without having to show good reason to suspect that a crime had been committed, unscrupulous government officials found it easy to use the writs of assistance to persecute individuals for their political and religious beliefs, or often, just to seek revenge against someone for personal reasons.

In the eighteenth century, Parliament again passed laws that authorized writs of assistance. These were used by British authorities in the American colonies to enforce the Trade Acts that taxed and limited the colonists' right to trade with other nations. Writs of assistance were generally used to collect taxes and to recover stolen goods, including enslaved Africans.

Colonial legislatures tried unsuccessfully to outlaw the writs by requiring warrants specifying who and what was to be searched and why. During the time just before the Revolution, the writs were used more and more frequently against colonists who were critical of British policy. They also were used against those believed to be violating the British restrictions on trade by smuggling tea and other products into Massachusetts and other colonies. The colonists' strong objections to the trade laws and writs of assistance contributed to the American Revolution.

What is the importance of the right to be secure in one's home from unreasonable searches and seizures?

The British were not entirely wrong in suspecting the colonists of smuggling. Some famous Americans violated the trade restrictions. For example, John Hancock's father had made a great deal of money smuggling tea into Boston. A writ of assistance enabled the British to discover that John Hancock himself was smuggling wine. As you can imagine, there was more than one reason why the Founders protested against such general warrants.

After the Revolution, many state declarations of rights outlawed unreasonable searches and seizures. Anti-Federalists later criticized the Constitution for not placing similar limitations on the federal government. A delegate to the Massachusetts ratifying convention said, "There is no provision made in the Constitution to prevent...the most innocent person...being taken by virtue of a general warrant...and dragged from his home." It was in response to such concerns that the Fourth Amendment was included in the Bill of Rights. Today every state constitution contains a clause similar to the Fourth Amendment.

What controversies are raised in the interpretation and application of the Fourth Amendment?

Three of the most important questions raised by the Fourth Amendment are

- When is a warrant not required?
- What is probable cause?
- How can the Fourth Amendment be enforced?

We will look briefly at the first two questions. The last question requires a more careful examination, as it has been a constant source of controversy. The next two sections focus on that issue.

When is a warrant not required? Whenever there is time to do so, law enforcement officers must convince a judge that they have probable cause to justify a search or arrest. If the judge accepts the officers' facts and reasoning, the judge will issue a warrant for an arrest, a search, or both.

There are times, however, when law enforcement officers cannot wait for a warrant. For example, police may be on the scene of a violent crime or a robbery in progress. If they do not arrest the suspect immediately, the person might injure a police officer or bystanders, or escape. Under these emergency circumstances, it is necessary for officers to be able to arrest a person or search property without a warrant. Later, however, the officers must convince a judge that they had probable cause and did not have time to obtain a warrant.

What are some situations when police officers should be able to make an arrest without a warrant?

What is probable cause? What evidence must law enforcement officers have to justify a search or seizure of a person or property? Generally, at the moment a law enforcement officer decides to arrest a person, he or she must have reliable knowledge that the suspect either has already committed a crime or is doing so at the time of arrest.

The specific criteria for probable cause are constantly being refined by the Supreme Court in the light of experience. This process reveals a commitment to protecting the rights of individuals while at the same time protecting society from those who break the law.

Critical Thinking Exercise
EVALUATING, TAKING, AND DEFENDING A POSITION ON PROBABLE CAUSE

Work with a study partner to consider the following situations which are based on actual incidents. Read the Fourth Amendment in reference to probable cause. Then with your partner decide whether the Amendment was violated in each incident. Be prepared to share your position with the class.

1. Tom Alvin was suspected of being an armed and dangerous drug dealer. The entrance to his apartment was by a very narrow staircase over which video cameras were installed. Police officers armed with a search warrant decided it was too dangerous to enter the apartment by normal means. Therefore, they placed ladders against the side of the building, climbed up to Alvin's apartment, smashed in the windows, entered, searched for, and seized cocaine.

2. A consumer organization is lobbying Congress to pass a law to prohibit the selling of a phone gadget which reveals the caller's phone number. They claim that using the product is an unlawful invasion of privacy.

3. Lucy Briggs was laid off her job as a flight attendant as the result of testing positive for drug use. The test was part of a new company policy requiring all airline employees to undergo surprise drug tests. Lucy claims that the mandatory urine test violates the "right of the people to be secure in their persons."

4. Acting quickly before a murder suspect could wash his hands, the police seized him and took skin scrapings from beneath his fingernails. They say the warrantless search was legal because there was no time to get a warrant before the suspect destroyed the evidence.

5. A student completed certain forms to apply for a government college loan. The confidential, personal information was stored on a computer network. It was later accessed by a different government agency and used without the student's knowledge or permission as part of a survey on college-age Americans.

What are means of enforcing the Fourth Amendment?

We must give law enforcement officers enough power to protect us from criminals. This means that we must trust them with the power, in certain situations, to limit some of our most valuable rights. Under certain circumstances, law enforcement officers have the power to

- stop and question us
- use force, if necessary, to restrain us
- search our person, homes, cars, garbage cans, and other property
- arrest us and place us in jail
- question us while we are in jail

These powers are easily open to abuse. The question is how to keep law enforcement officials from violating constitutional rights. Below are brief descriptions of several policies that are being used to check the abuse of power by police officers.

Departmental discipline. Some law enforcement agencies have a board of officers responsible for investigating claims that an officer has violated a due process right. The board conducts a hearing and, if it finds the officer guilty, takes appropriate action to prevent that person from breaking the law again.

Civilian review boards. Law enforcement agencies are sometimes supervised by a civilian review board appointed by local government. This board has the authority to investigate charges against officers accused of breaking the law or violating rules and procedures. It also has the responsibility to provide the officer a fair hearing. If the board reaches the conclusion that the officer is guilty, it recommends appropriate action to the law enforcement agency or suggests criminal prosecution.

Civil suits. Civilians who think their rights have been violated by law enforcement officers sometimes have the right to sue individual officers and the agency for damages in a civil court or under the Civil Rights Act.

Exclusionary rule. Any evidence gained by law enforcement officers as a result of breaking the law may not be used as evidence in court against the defendant. This evidence is said to be "excluded" by the judge at the trial.

What do *you* think?

1. What should be done if law enforcement officers break the law and violate individual rights protected by the Fourth Amendment?

2. Suppose officers arbitrarily and unfairly search a person's home or other property or arrest a person without having a good reason for doing so?

3. What can be done to prevent law enforcement officers from violating people's constitutional rights?

What is the significance of the exclusionary rule?

Perhaps the most controversial of these policies is the **exclusionary rule**. The rule is most often used to exclude evidence attained from illegal searches and seizures. It also is used to exclude evidence gathered in violation of the Fifth Amendment right against self-incrimination and the Sixth Amendment right to counsel.

The exclusionary rule was created by judges to discourage law enforcement officers from breaking the law. The courts have argued that it is the most effective way of preventing violations of individual rights.

The exclusionary rule has been used since 1914 to limit the powers of federal law enforcement agencies such as the F.B.I. It was not until 1961, however, that the Supreme Court applied the exclusionary rule to criminal prosecutions at the state and local levels in the case *Mapp v. Ohio*. Since that time there has been continual controversy about its use.

What do *you* think?

1. What might be the advantages and disadvantages of each of the policies described on page 178 and above?

2. Which policies would you support? Why?

What is the purpose of the Fifth Amendment provision against self-incrimination?

The **right against self-incrimination** is a protection of both the innocent and the guilty alike from the potential abuse of government power. The Fifth Amendment provides that, "No person...shall be compelled in any criminal case to be a witness against himself." Its primary purpose is to prohibit the government from threatening, mistreating, or even torturing people to gain evidence against them or their associates.

A confession is powerful evidence. If a prosecutor or police can obtain a confession from a suspect, it often eliminates the need for a costly or careful search for other evidence. The Framers were aware of the problems that could arise from the "third degree" and other forms of improper pressure.

Refusing to testify by "taking the Fifth" is one of the most familiar provisions of the Bill of Rights. It is controversial because many people see the refusal to testify as a right that only benefits those who are guilty. The right not to testify against oneself, however, is essential to uphold the principle that a person is presumed innocent until proven guilty beyond a reasonable doubt.

This clause of the Fifth Amendment protects persons accused of crimes. It also protects witnesses from being forced to incriminate themselves.

Critical Thinking Exercise
EXAMINING ISSUES OF SELF-INCRIMINATION

This exercise provides you an opportunity to examine both a historical and a contemporary case involving the right against self-incrimination. Your class should be divided into six groups. Three groups should be assigned to the 1791 case and three to the 1991 case. Students in the first group assigned to each case will play the role of justices. The other two groups assigned for each case will argue for or against the position that the Fifth Amendment prohibition against self-incrimination has been violated. After two-minute oral arguments have been made for each side in each case, the justices should deliberate. Then they should issue their opinions on the question, "Has the self-incrimination clause of the Fifth Amendment been violated?"

Afterward, your entire class should compare the cases and discuss your views using the following questions as a guide:

1. In what ways are the two cases similar or dissimilar?

2. What values and interests are involved in each case?

3. Under what conditions, if any, should the right against self-incrimination be applied and limited? Explain your reasoning.

***Commonwealth v. Dillon* (1791)**. On the 18th of December, Dillon, a twelve-year-old Philadelphia apprentice, was arrested for arson, a crime punishable by death. He was accused of burning several stables containing hay and other goods. According to court records, the boy was visited by his minister, master, and other "respectable citizens". They urged him to confess for the good of his "mortal body and soul". He said he was not guilty.

> *The inspectors of the prison...[then] carried him into the dungeon; they displayed it in all its gloom and horror; they said that he would be confined in it, dark and cold and hungry, unless he made full disclosure [confession]; but if he did...he would be well accommodated with room, fire, and victuals [food], and might expect pity and favour from the court.*

Dillon continued to deny his guilt, even when kept in the dungeon without heat, food, or water. After about forty-eight hours, however, the boy confessed in front of the mayor, his master, and law enforcement officials.

When the case came to trial, Dillon's attorney argued that the charges should be dismissed. He said that the main evidence against Dillon was his confession, which was forced by keeping him in the dungeon, threatening him, and promising him he could expect pity and good treatment by the court. He claimed that such confessions were unreliable and illegal.

The state's attorney, however, argued that the confession was freely made in public. Therefore, it could be used as evidence at his trial. The attorney admitted that the interference of the inspectors at the prison was slightly irregular, but the way in which Dillon was encouraged to confess was not threatening. Therefore, his confession was not forced and should not be excluded at the trial. To do so would be to excuse the fact that he had committed a serious crime. The boy had confessed to a crime which had endangered lives and destroyed the property of others.

The state's attorney said that confessions freely given, as everyone knows, are the best evidence of guilt. The point to be considered was whether Dillon falsely accused himself of a crime. If there was any possibility that he had done so, he should not be executed. But since Dillon had never retracted his statement, he should be found guilty.

***Fulminante v. Arizona* (1991)**. The Arizona police lacked enough evidence to prove that Orestes Fulminante, a convicted child molester, had murdered his eleven-year-old stepdaughter. He was sent to prison on a weapons charge. The murder case, however, remained unsolved. In prison, Fulminante was threatened by several inmates who had heard rumors that he was a child killer. A fellow inmate, with a reputation for mob connections, offered to protect him. But first, the inmate insisted on knowing the details of the murder.

Fearing for his life, Fulminante admitted that he had driven the young girl to the desert. There he abused her, forced her to beg for her life, and then shot her twice in the head.

What Fulminante didn't know was that his fellow inmate was an FBI informer. After being freed on the gun charge, Fulminante was arrested, tried, and convicted of murder. The main evidence against him was his confession to the inmate and a similar confession made to the informant's fiancee at a later date.

Fulminante's attorney appealed the conviction. He argued that the prison confession was forced. Its use to convict Fulminante was a violation of the Fifth Amendment right against self-incrimination. Since the confessions were the only real evidence against Fulminante, he deserved a new trial with a jury that would not hear about the confessions.

The state's attorney argued that even if the first confession was forced, the second was not forced. It was freely made. At most, introducing the confession as evidence should be considered a harmless error, made in good faith by officers and prosecutors in a brutal child sexual assault and murder case.

What happened to Dillon and Fulminante?

The cases you have examined illustrate how issues involving the right against self-incrimination have been debated for centuries. In 1791, the judge ruled that because arson was a crime punishable by death, benefit of the doubt should be given to twelve-year-old Dillon. The arson charge was dropped and he was retried on a **misdemeanor** charge—a less serious crime. The judge said:

> *Though it is the province [of the court] to administer justice, and not to bestow mercy; and though it is better not to err at all...in a doubtful case, error on the side of mercy if safer...than error on the side of rigid justice.*

In 1991, the Supreme Court also sent back the Fulminante case for retrial. The majority of justices said that the confession in prison was made under a believable threat of physical violence. Thus it was the product of coercion and was the main evidence against Fulminante.

Without the confession, the prosecution probably would not have had enough evidence to get a conviction. Therefore, Fulminante was entitled to a new trial.

How have protections against self-incrimination developed?

There are a number of contemporary issues involving the right against self-incrimination. Originally, the right was limited to proceedings during a trial and did not limit the power of law enforcement officers to question persons they had arrested. This allowed the police to force people to confess or give evidence against themselves.

After hearing numerous cases in which the right against self-incrimination had been violated, the Supreme Court ruled, in *Miranda v. Arizona* (1966), that law enforcement officers must warn suspects that they may remain silent and that they have the right to have an attorney with them when being questioned. Suspects must also be told that anything they say can and will be used against them and that if they cannot afford an attorney, one will be appointed for them. This warning has become known as the "Miranda warning." The Court has ruled, however, that the right to remain silent does not mean that officers cannot take a voluntary statement from the accused.

What are common limitations on the right against self-incrimination?

The exercise of the right against self-incrimination is, however, subject to some limitations. For example:

- **Personal right.** Because the right against self-incrimination is intended to protect individuals, it cannot be used to protect organizations such as businesses or trade unions. Nor may someone refuse to testify if the testimony would incriminate a friend or family member. Witnesses, as well as defendants, may refuse to answer questions if their answers might incriminate them personally.

- **Immunity.** Under certain circumstances, a person may be compelled to testify if the court offers **immunity**. For example, if the court states that nothing the person says can be used in a trial against him or her, the person must testify or be charged with **contempt of court**.

What do *you* think?

1. What position would you take on the recent Supreme Court decision that allows forced confessions to be used in court if there is enough other evidence to convict a person? Explain your position.

2. If someone refuses to answer questions by the police, or to be a witness in his or her own defense at a trial, are we entitled to assume that the person is hiding something, and must be guilty? Would it be constitutional for a prosecutor to remind the jury that the defendant had an opportunity to speak in his or her own defense, and chose not to?

Reviewing and Using the Lesson

1. How would you define the "right to privacy"? How does the Fourth Amendment protect this right?

2. How would you explain the term "probable cause"? Why does the Fourth Amendment require "probable cause" before a warrant can be issued?

3. Why does the Fourth Amendment generally require a warrant before a search can be conducted? Why does the Fourth Amendment require warrants to "particularly describ[e] the place to be searched, and the persons or things to be seized"? Under what circumstances is a warrant not required? Why?

4. How would you explain the right against self-incrimination? What purposes does this right serve?

5. What are some limitations on the right against self-incrimination?

6. Research search and seizure issues in a school setting by examining the case *New Jersey v. T.L.O.*, 469 U.S. 325 (1985). Report your findings to the class.

LESSON 34

How Do the Fifth through Eighth Amendments Protect Our Rights within the Judicial System?

Purpose of Lesson

In this lesson, you examine how provisions of the Fifth through Eighth Amendments protect the rights of people accused of crimes and put on trial. After a brief examination of some provisions of the Fifth Amendment, you survey the Sixth Amendment and take a close look at the right to counsel. In addition, you look at the Eighth Amendment, which protects people who are being held for trial, and protects persons convicted of crimes from receiving unjust treatment. Finally, you examine the continuing controversy about whether the death penalty should be prohibited under the Eighth Amendment.

When you finish this lesson, you should be able to identify the rights protected by the Fifth, Sixth, and Eighth Amendments to the Constitution. You also should be able to describe the issues involved in capital punishment and evaluate positions on its use.

Terms to Know

acquitted	felony
bail	guided discretion
capital punishment	indicted
cruel and unusual punishment	right to counsel
double jeopardy	unguided discretion

How do provisions of the Fifth Amendment protect an individual's rights after arrest?

Once a person has been arrested for a crime, the next step is usually to charge the person formally in a judicial proceeding. In the federal system, anyone who is to be tried for a crime must be **indicted** by a grand jury. The military, however is an exception to this rule. A grand jury, unlike a trial jury, does not decide whether someone is innocent or guilty, but instead decides whether there is enough evidence to go to trial. This is an important safeguard, because it ensures that the government cannot bring formal charges against people on the basis of weak evidence, or no evidence. A similar purpose lies behind the **double jeopardy** provision of the Fifth Amendment.

The government cannot wear someone out with repeated charges and trials. Usually, someone who is **acquitted**—found innocent—by a jury may not be tried for that crime again.

What limitations does the Sixth Amendment place on the government?

The Sixth Amendment contains a number of additional procedural rights that are part of due process of law. Almost all the protections of the Sixth Amendment have been incorporated into the Fourteenth Amendment, making them applicable to the states.

The amendment's provisions are intended to provide a fair hearing in court for persons accused of crimes. Briefly examine each of these provisions before looking at their history and focusing on the right to counsel.

- **Speedy trial.** The federal government cannot hold you in jail for a long period of time without bringing you to trial if you demand that the trial be held as soon as possible.

- **Public trial.** The government cannot try you in secret. Your trial must be open to the public and there must be a public record of the proceedings.

- **Impartial jury.** The government must try you before a jury. It cannot try you before a jury that is prejudiced. For example, if you were on trial for a drug-related crime and jurors admitted to having angry and violent reactions because they had been victims of similar crimes, the jury could not be impartial.

- **Location of the trial.** The government must try you in the state, district or community where the crime was committed. You may, however, have the right to have the trial moved if you can show that the community is prejudiced.

- **Information on charges.** The government cannot arrest you and hold you for trial without telling you why it is doing so. Government lawyers also must present in open court enough evidence to justify holding you for trial.

- **Confronting witnesses.** You and your lawyer have the right to confront and cross-examine all witnesses against you. The government cannot present the testimony of secret witnesses who do not appear in court against you.

- **Favorable witnesses.** The government cannot prevent you from presenting witnesses who might testify for you. In fact, if such witnesses do not want to testify and you want them to, the court must force them to appear.

- **Assistance of counsel.** The government cannot prevent you from having a lawyer defend you from the time you are named as a suspect. If you are charged with a serious crime and cannot afford a lawyer, the government must provide one free of charge.

What is the importance of the right to counsel?

The American criminal justice system is an adversary system as opposed to the inquisitorial system used in some other countries. In an adversary system there are two sides that present their positions before an impartial third party—a jury, a judge, or both. The prosecuting attorney presents the government's side; the defense attorney presents arguments for the accused person.

Why is the right to counsel so important?

The complexity of our adversary system requires the use of lawyers to represent defendants. Even well-educated people and many lawyers who do not specialize in criminal law, are not competent to conduct an adequate defense in today's courts.

In the twentieth century, the Supreme Court and Congress have extended the right to counsel to people to whom it had not been provided in the past. This right is now interpreted to guarantee

- that every person accused of a **felony**—a major crime—may have a lawyer and

- that those too poor to afford to hire a lawyer will have one appointed by the court

The right also has been extended by decisions in such cases as *Miranda v. Arizona* (1966) to apply not only to criminal trials, but to other critical stages in the criminal justice process, such as questioning of suspects by police.

Critical Thinking Exercise
EXAMINING CURRENT CONTROVERSIES ABOUT THE RIGHT TO COUNSEL

A number of issues are currently raised regarding the right to counsel. Two of the most frequently mentioned are discussed below. Read about these issues and develop positions on the questions they raise.

1. The right to effective counsel. Wealthy people can afford to hire lawyers of their choice; usually the poor must accept the lawyers assigned to them. Lawyers serving the poor may be excellent, but often they are overworked and do not have sufficient time or the resources to prepare the best defense possible.

   Question: How can the government provide effective counsel to represent the poor? If a poor person is represented ineffectively by a lawyer and found guilty, should this be the basis for a retrial? Explain your position.

2. Limiting the right to counsel for poor defendants. The law requires that poor defendants be provided counsel at public expense. Counsel may be attorneys from the community selected by judges to defend the poor. They may also be volunteers or public defenders employed by the government. Sometimes poor defendants appeal their cases numerous times, costing the taxpayers millions of dollars each year.

   Question: Should some limit be placed on how many times or under what circumstances poor people should be provided this assistance? Explain your position.

How are the rights of the Sixth Amendment enforced?

Suppose you are tried in a criminal court, found guilty, and imprisoned. You believe that one or more of your Sixth Amendment rights have been violated by the government during your trial. For example, suppose you believe that the jury was prejudiced against you.

The right to appeal your case to a higher court is available to you if you can show that your constitutional rights have been violated. Each state has a system of appellate courts, and so does the federal government, with the Supreme Court being the highest court of appeals in the nation. If, after reviewing the trial record, an appellate court decides the trial has been unfair, it can overturn the lower court's verdict. If that happens, the prosecution can usually choose whether or not to retry the case.

What limitations does the Eighth Amendment place on the government?

The Eighth Amendment protects people accused of crimes and awaiting trial, and people found guilty of crimes. Its protections, incorporated by the Fourteenth Amendment, limit the powers of the judicial and legislative branches of federal and state government in the following ways:

- **Limitations on the judiciary**. Judges usually have the power to decide whether a person arrested for a crime should be held in jail or set free on bail while awaiting trial. They also have the right to decide how much bail should be required. This amendment says that judges cannot require excessive bail.

- **Limitations of the legislature**. Congress and state legislatures establish the range of punishments for breaking laws. This amendment says legislatures cannot pass laws that impose excessive fines or inflict **cruel and unusual punishments**. The power of judges and juries to decide punishments is limited by the laws passed by the legislatures that, in turn, are limited by the Eighth Amendment.

Critical Thinking Exercise

EXAMINING EARLY POSITIONS ON PUNISHMENT

The French philosopher Montesquieu greatly influenced Americans' views on law and punishment. Below is a quotation from his writings followed by an excerpt from a letter by Thomas Jefferson. Read the selections and answer the questions that follow.

Experience shows that in countries remarkable for the leniency of their laws the spirit of the inhabitants is as much affected by slight penalties as in other countries by severer punishments.... Mankind must not be governed with too much severity...if we inquire into the cause of all human corruptions, we shall find that they proceed from the impunity [exemption from punishment] of criminals, and not from the moderation of punishments.... It is [also] an essential point, that there should be a certain proportion in punishments.... It is a great abuse amongst us to condemn to the same punishment a person that only robs on the highway and another who robs and murders.

Baron de Montesquieu, "Of the Power of Punishments," *The Spirit of the Laws, 1748*

The fantastical idea of virtue and the public good being sufficient security to the state against the commission of crimes, which you say you have heard insisted on by some, I assure you was never mine. It is only the sanguinary [bloodthirsty] hue of our penal laws which I meant to object to. Punishments I know are necessary, and I would provide them, strict and inflexible, but proportioned to the crime.... Let mercy be the character of the law-giver, but let the judge be a mere machine. The mercies of the law will be dispensed equally and impartially to every description of men.

Thomas Jefferson to Edmund Pendleton, August 26, 1776

1. What position does Montesquieu take on the effects of lenient and severe punishments?

2. What does Montesquieu say is a major cause of crime?

3. In what ways do Montesquieu and Jefferson appear to be in agreement?

4. What idea is expressed in Jefferson's statement that is not in Montesquieu's?

5. Do you agree or disagree with the positions stated by Montesquieu and Jefferson? Explain your position.

What are the purposes of the Eighth Amendment rights?

The right to be free on bail pending trial. Although persons accused of crimes have the right to a speedy trial after they have been arrested, there are usually delays while both the prosecution and defense prepare for trial. Since a person is presumed innocent until proven guilty, one might argue that suspects should go free until the time of their trial. Not all suspects can be trusted to appear in court when they are supposed to. Some suspects may be dangerous, and it is reasonable to think that those accused of crimes for which there are severe penalties might not appear.

The government's main responsibility in this regard is to make sure suspects appear in court to be tried. This may be accomplished by

- keeping suspects in jail while awaiting trial, or
- having them place **bail**—money or property—in the hands of the government to ensure that they will appear in court rather than forfeit it

The right to bail allows suspects to be free while preparing their defense, which is often difficult to do from jail. It also avoids punishing suspects by holding them in jail before they are found guilty or innocent.

How does the right to bail help protect an accused person's due process right?

This is particularly important for innocent persons who would otherwise suffer unfair punishment while awaiting trial. The sentencing of persons found guilty takes into account how much time they have spent in jail awaiting trial.

Problems arising from the implementation of the right to bail include the following:

- **Unfair treatment of the poor.** Wealthy people can afford bail; the poor often cannot. Therefore, the poor are more likely to remain in jail awaiting trial, lose income, and not be able to do as much to prepare for their defense.

- **Punishment of innocent poor.** Poor people who are innocent and cannot afford bail are kept in jail and then released after their trial. This means that innocent people are punished by imprisonment and rarely compensated for the time they have lost or the wrongs done to them.

- **Increased chances of conviction and more severe sentences**. Studies have shown that being held in jail prior to a trial seems to have a negative influence on judges and juries. It results in a greater possibility of convicting such people of crimes and giving them more severe sentences.

One remedy for the inequitable aspects of the bail system is to release defendants without bail on their own recognizance, that is, on their promise to return to court for trial. This procedure is being used more and more when defendants have families or other ties to the community that would make it unlikely they would flee. It is used when a suspect's release would not seem to present a danger to the community.

The right to be free from excessive fines. The purpose of this provision is to require courts to levy fines that are reasonable in relation to whatever crime has been committed. If a fine was extremely high in proportion to the seriousness of the crime, a person could claim the excessive fine violates his or her rights under the Eighth Amendment.

The right to be free from cruel and unusual punishment. This right is based on the belief that the law should treat even the most horrible criminal with dignity. Punishments should not violate society's standards of decency.

The question raised by this right is to determine what is meant by the terms "cruel" and "unusual." What the Framers meant by "cruel and unusual punishments" is not at all clear. Part of the problem is that what is considered cruel and unusual has changed over the years. The most difficult issues, however, have been raised by the issue of the death penalty.

What is the history of capital punishment in the United States?

Capital punishment has been used in the United States from colonial times to the present, and the Supreme Court has never held that it is prohibited by the Eighth Amendment. The Constitution appears to accept the legitimacy of the death penalty. Both the Fifth and Fourteenth Amendments forbid the government to deprive someone of "life" without due process of law. These clauses seem to suggest that if due process is provided, people may be deprived of their lives by the government.

At one time, execution was the automatic penalty for murder or other serious crimes. By the early twentieth century, most states developed laws that allowed juries a choice between the death penalty and other forms of punishment. In most states, however, the juries were not given much guidance in making these decisions. This policy of allowing juries **unguided discretion** was common until 1972.

What are the major arguments for and against the death penalty?

What is the basis of opposition to the death penalty?

Executions of murderers and rapists were common in the United States until the 1960s when moral and political opposition developed because of a number of factors:

- Information on how the death penalty was chosen revealed that juries often acted randomly and capriciously in deciding who should be executed and who should not.

- Studies showed that the race of the defendant and the victim appeared to be the most important factors in whether a jury inflicted the death penalty.

- Studies did not confirm the belief that capital punishment deterred crime.

- Often, the cost of capital punishment, considering appeals, is more expensive than sentencing a person to life in prison without parole.

What issues are involved in allowing capital punishment?

Studies indicating unfairness in the imposition of the death penalty led to widespread debate and increasing opposition to its use. Courts and legislatures faced growing pressure to develop clear, reasonable, and fair standards to be used by juries in making their decisions.

Since 1972 the Supreme Court and legislatures have been attempting to develop such standards. This process resulted from a decision made by the Court in the case of *Furman v. Georgia* (1972). In that case, a five-to-four majority struck down a statute giving juries unguided discretion in the imposition of the death penalty.

The *Furman* decision did not result in the prohibition of the death penalty. The majority argued that while the death penalty was constitutional, state laws permitting unguided discretion were unconstitutional. The result of this decision was that all executions in the United States were suspended. State legislatures were faced with the task of developing new laws with standards to avoid the arbitrary and discriminatory imposition of the death penalty, which was characteristic of the past.

Some states attempted to solve the problem by going back to the practice of automatic death penalties for certain serious crimes. Others developed new **guided discretion** laws. These laws called for juries or judges to decide whether to impose life or death sentences at a hearing held for this purpose after the trial in which a person was found guilty.

In 1976, the Supreme Court heard five cases on the new state laws. It upheld the new practice of guided discretion and declared that the automatic sentencing law was unconstitutional. Thus, the Court upheld the constitutionality of the death penalty once again. No clear standards were set to implement the policy of guided discretion, however. As a result, the courts have been flooded with appeals of death penalty sentences claiming that unfair standards have been used.

Recent studies have found that, despite the efforts of state legislatures and the courts to develop fair and reasonable standards, the system may still result in inconsistent and racially biased sentences. Murderers of whites are far more likely to be sentenced to death than murderers of blacks. Such studies have given new impetus to the question of the constitutionality of the death penalty.

It is important to note that whether or not the Supreme Court says the Constitution prohibits the death penalty is an altogether different issue from the question of whether or not society ought to execute individuals who have committed certain kinds of crimes. Even if the death penalty is constitutional, states are free to abolish it. It is quite possible to argue that while the Constitution does not prevent the government from imposing the death penalty, the government should not use it.

What is the relationship of procedural justice and a republican form of government?

The Framers had personal experience with arbitrary government. They understood that rights would not be secure if the government had an unlimited ability to investigate people, accuse them of crimes, and hold them in jail or punish them in some other way. They also understood that republican or popular governments were capable of acting just as arbitrarily as monarchies. Thus the Framers addressed the Bill of Rights to all three branches of the federal government.

The Framers set out a careful process by which the innocence or guilt of a person could be decided. It is important to remember that procedural due process is designed to protect the innocent. In doing their job, they also can be used as "loopholes" by those who are guilty. Many have argued that this is a small price to pay for the protection we often take for granted. Above all, they argue, it is a reminder of our commitment to the idea that the actions of the government must be limited by the rule of law.

Reviewing and Using the Lesson

1. What are some of the procedural rights contained in the Sixth Amendment? How do these rights help guarantee a fair trial for people accused of crimes?

2. How would you explain the right to counsel? Why is this right important in an adversary system of justice?

3. What is "bail"? Why are people charged with crimes allowed to remain free on bail before trial?

4. How would you explain the Eighth Amendment right to be free from "cruel and unusual punishment"?

5. What is "capital punishment"? What arguments have been made to limit or abolish it?

6. The United States imprisons more people than any other nation. Yet, our crime rate remains very high. Do research and find alternative forms of punishment or programs that we, as a society, should explore to reduce the crime rate.

Unit Six: *What Are the Roles of the Citizen in American Democracy?*

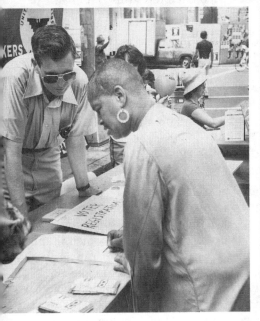

United Nations founded (1945)		Universal Declaration of Human Rights (1948)					
FDR delivers "Four Freedoms" speech (1941)		European Convention on Human Rights (1950)		*Griswold v. Connecticut* (1965)		Voting Rights Act (1975)	Berlin Wall falls (1989)
1930s	**1940s**	**1950s**		**1960s**		**1970s**	**1980s**
First female senator elected (1932)	U.S. tests world's first atomic bomb (1945)	First African American major league baseball player (1947)		First commercial nuclear power plant opens (1957)	Watergate burglars arrested (1972)	First female Supreme Court Justice (1981)	Equal Rights Amendment is defeated (1982)

Purpose of Unit

Justice Louis Brandeis called citizenship the "most important office" in the land. Brandeis was acknowledging one of the oldest principles of American democracy, part of the nation's legacy of classical republicanism. Our nation's experiment in self-government depends foremost not upon presidents, members of Congress, or justices, but upon each of us as "citizens." The unit begins with a discussion of influences of classical republicanism and natural rights philosophy on Americans' ideals about citizenship. It concludes by offering you the opportunity to discuss some of the most fundamental questions of citizenship.

LESSON 35

What Does It Mean to Be a Citizen?

Purpose of Lesson

In previous units you were asked to focus on the history and nature of our legacy as a constitutional democracy. In this lesson you examine what this legacy means for us as individual citizens.

When you finish this lesson you should be able to explain how Americans have viewed citizenship and its rights and responsibilities. You also should be able to distinguish between a citizen and a resident alien. Finally, you should be able to explain the special importance the idea of citizenship has in America as a land of immigrants from many nations.

Terms to Know

commonwealth	naturalized citizen
enlightened self-interest	orthodoxy
melting pot	resident alien
nation of nations	spirit of association

How have Americans thought of citizenship?

From its beginnings, America was strongly influenced by the ideals of classical republicanism. The early American colonies of the seventeenth century were political communities in which civic virtue could be exercised. Many of these colonies were called **commonwealths**, a word that meant something like a republic, that is, self-governing communities of equals whose members were expected to help serve the good of all. In the Mayflower Compact, the Pilgrims declared their intent to "covenant and combine themselves together into a civil body politic."

The American Founders admired the civic virtue of the ancients and the classical models of republican government. They also were influenced by the natural rights philosophy of John Locke. The natural rights philosophy conflicted in several important ways with the ideals of classical republicanism. Instead of the common good, it stressed the importance of individual rights and self-interest. Society and government, according to Locke, were established to protect the rights of the individual. Human communities did not exist for their own sake, but rather to protect the individuals belonging to them, each of whom is free to pursue his or her own interest so long as it does not interfere with the interests of others.

The Founders were influenced by both these theories of government. They had to compromise in adapting this intellectual inheritance to the conditions in America. They established a limited government of checks and balances that allowed civic virtue to flourish, but also could prevent abuses of self-interest when it did not.

The Founders realized that the classical republicanism of the ancient city states could not be easily adapted to a country as large and diverse as America. They also recognized that republican self-government required a greater measure of civic virtue than did other forms of government. Civic virtue, therefore, was essential. But how was civic virtue to be promoted in this new experiment in republican self-government?

In general, the Founders looked to two solutions: religion and education. The Founders themselves had different religious beliefs. Many were wary of the dangers that religious **orthodoxy** posed to individual freedom. At the same time, however, they acknowledged the value of organized religion in promoting virtue. Virtuous behavior, which enabled people to control their passions, would produce upright, responsible citizens.

The second solution that the Founders recognized was the importance of education to good citizenship. For the American experiment in republican self-government to succeed, each of its citizens had to be schooled in the ideals and principles upon which that experiment was based. Formal schooling, together with a free press, became a priority in the early years of the new republic. Public or "common schools" developed rapidly to prepare Americans not only as workers in a growing economy, but also as citizens committed to the principles of self-government. As nineteenth-century American educator Horace Mann observed, "schoolhouses are the republican line of fortifications."

How did Tocqueville connect good citizenship with self-interest in the American democracy?

Alexis de Tocqueville was a young French aristocrat who visited the United States in the 1830s, at a time when the spirit of Jacksonian democracy was helping to bring about greater equality and more widespread participation in the nation's political life. He was curious about and impressed by America's experiment in democracy and how well it worked. After finishing his tour of the United

States, he recorded his impressions in a very influential book, *Democracy in America*.

Tocqueville found much both to admire and to criticize as he traveled the country. Though impressed by the equality of opportunity in the American democracy, he wondered how a society so devoted to materialism and the pursuit of individual self-interest could produce the civic spirit needed for self-government.

He believed the answer was to be found in the qualities he admired in American democracy: traditions of local self-government and habits of free association.

The New England townships were tiny models of classical republicanism, where the habits of citizenship were developed. Tocqueville observed that a citizen of one of these American towns

> takes part in every affair of the place; he practices the act of government in the small sphere within his reach...and collects clear practical notions on the nature of his duties and the extent of his rights.

This tradition of local self-government also encouraged voluntary association. Nothing so impressed de Tocqueville about America as the fondness American citizens had for banding together to address problems of common interest. While Europeans would prefer to let government address all public problems, Americans preferred to do it themselves, as citizens. This **spirit of association** remains a distinctive characteristic of American society today.

Such traditions of local self-government and habits of free association, Tocqueville concluded, provided a way for teaching citizenship in the American democracy. He wrote,

> The most powerful and perhaps the only means that we still possess of interesting men in the welfare of their country is to make them participate in the government. At the present time civic zeal seems to be inseparable from the exercise of political rights.

Like the Founders, Tocqueville realized that the civic virtue of the ancients was not practical in the United States. Democratic citizenship, he believed, would have to depend on something else. He did not believe there had to be a contradiction between self-interest and civic-mindedness. In a land of equality and widespread participation in political life, each citizen could see a connection between self-interest and the common good. American citizens are willing to devote themselves to public ends, Tocqueville believed, because they realize that the fulfillment of their private ambitions depends in large part on the success of the democratic society. Good citizenship for Tocqueville, therefore, was nothing other than **enlightened self-interest**.

Town meeting in Laguna Niguel, California

How does the tradition of local self-government embody Tocqueville's concept of "spirit of association"?

What do *you* think?

1. Some people claim that the best way to achieve the common good is for each person to work for his or her self-interest. Do you agree? Why or why not?

2. The common good is a principle originally practiced in relatively small and homogeneous societies. Do you think there is a common good in a nation as large and diverse as the Unites States? Why or why not?

3. What should voters do if their representative votes for a bill that is good for the entire country but damages their particular interest?

Who is a citizen?

In our country, anyone who is born in the United States, or is born to citizens of the United States, is a citizen. The term used for noncitizens who legally reside in the United States is **resident aliens**. By satisfying certain requirements, resident aliens may become **naturalized citizens**.

Both resident aliens and citizens who live in the United States must obey the laws of the United States. They also receive the protection of those laws. Resident aliens are guaranteed most of the rights possessed by citizens. If they are tried in a court of law, for example, they are guaranteed the same rights to due process that are provided for citizens in the Constitution.

There are two important rights, however, that citizens have and aliens do not: the rights to vote and to hold public office. Possessing these rights, many people have argued, is what distinguishes the citizen from the noncitizen. Some people also argue that in possessing these important rights, citizens also have special responsibilities toward their country that noncitizens do not.

Critical Thinking Exercise

EVALUATING, TAKING, AND DEFENDING A POSITION ON EXTENDING THE RIGHT TO VOTE FOR SCHOOL BOARD MEMBERS TO RESIDENT ALIENS

Your class should be divided into four groups—two for the issue and two against. Each group should choose a spokesperson to present the group's views to the class. Groups on the same side of the issue should compare ideas and not make duplicate points. After the four presentations are made the class should vote on whether to pass the proposed legislation.

In some communities in our nation, there is growing interest in extending to resident aliens the right to vote in local school board elections. Proponents of such a law argue that resident aliens pay state and local taxes to support public education and that all taxpayers should have a representative voice influencing policies that directly affect them or their children. In addition, resident aliens have met all the criteria for being in this country legally. Opponents argue that because resident aliens are not citizens, they lack a long-term interest in the welfare of the community, and granting them voting rights in school board elections blurs the distinction between rights of citizens and noncitizens. It is the first step, they argue, in the demise of meaningful citizenship.

1. Do you think that resident aliens who must pay taxes and obey the government's laws should have a voice in local government by being permitted to vote? Why or why not?

2. Do you think that resident aliens should have the right to serve as elected members of local government?

3. What political obligations or responsibilities should resident aliens or noncitizens have? Explain your position.

How has the American ideal of citizenship adapted itself to an increasingly diverse society?

From its beginnings, America has been what the poet Walt Whitman called a "**nation of nations**," peopled by millions of immigrants of different races, religions,

How has the diversity of new citizens enriched America?

languages, and ethnic backgrounds. One of the greatest challenges to the American experiment in republican government has been to form a common bond out of such diversity. That common bond is provided by the ideal of American citizenship and a commitment to the Constitution and its ideals and principles. Though they could not foresee how diverse the immigration to this country would become, many of the Founders recognized that the new country would continue to take in people of different origins. For them, becoming American was primarily a matter of allegiance to the political ideals of the new land. In the early nineteenth century, Congress established five years as the minimum time required for immigrants to learn these ideals and to become naturalized citizens.

As George Washington told the members of the Touro Synagogue of Newport, Rhode Island, in 1790,

> *Happily, the government of the United States that gives to bigotry no sanction, to persecution no assistance, requires only that they who live under its protection should demean themselves as good citizens in giving it their effectual support.*

How can you apply the phrase "to give to bigotry no sanction" to your daily life?

For Washington and other Founders, good citizenship meant responsible conduct and acceptance of the nation's political principles.

For much of our nation's history, however, becoming an American meant something more. It represented a fresh start, a new beginning, leaving the injustices and prejudices of the old world behind.

"What then is this American, this new man?" asked Crevecoeur, the eighteenth-century French immigrant to America. Americans, Crevecoeur believed, had left the values and lifestyles of their different origins behind to become "a new race of men." Perhaps the most famous metaphor for this ideal of Americanization was expressed by Israel Zangwell in his 1908 play, *The Melting Pot*, "America is God's crucible, the great **melting pot** where all the races of men are melting and re-forming."

Has America been a melting pot? Not entirely. Throughout our history the assimilation of different people into a new American identity has been only partially successful in achieving the classical republican ideal of a common culture. Many immigrants to the new land were reluctant to give up the heritages they brought with them. They were proud of both their "Americaness" and the cultural inheritance they carried to the New World.

As a nation of immigrants we have come to appreciate the benefits of the great mixture of heritages transplanted to America. They have enriched American life in many ways. The diversity of the nation's cultural inheritance also has placed a heavy responsibility on our ideal of citizenship. The unity of American society depends very largely on the ability of that ideal—the civic culture all Americans, whatever their particular origins, share in common—to hold us together as a nation. Throughout our history there has been tension between the diversity of backgrounds and the common ideal of citizenship. The need to balance unity with diversity remains a challenging goal for your generation.

Critical Thinking Exercise

EVALUATING THE RELATIONSHIP BETWEEN THE IDEALS OF CLASSICAL REPUBLICANISM AND CONTEMPORARY AMERICAN CITIZENSHIP

Some observers of American society today are worried about the future health of America's experiment in self-government. They believe we have inherited too much of the self-interest of the natural rights philosophy and not enough of the public spirit of classical republicanism. These critics see contemporary America as a fragmented society, in which individuals are preoccupied with the pursuit of economic self-interest.

How can America be a "nation of nations" and still have a common civic culture?

Some feel that government is disconnected from people's lives. Americans see fewer opportunities to exercise their responsibilities as citizens than they did in the past.

Some critics believe a return to the principles of classical republicanism is the solution to this problem. The nation's schools, they say, should improve civics education, and our democratic institutions must create new ways to involve citizens in public affairs.

Work in small groups to develop positions on the following questions. Be prepared to present and defend your positions before the class.

1. Do you think the observations in the exercise about contemporary American society are accurate? Explain your position.

2. Do you think the classical republican sense of community is possible in American society today? What forces work against it? What resources might encourage its development?

3. What ways can you think of to involve citizens in public affairs? What reforms would you propose to the political process? To the Constitution? To our education system?

Reviewing and Using the Lesson

1. How would you explain the term "commonwealth"?

2. How did the Founders expect to promote civic virtue in a country as large and diverse as the United States?

3. How would you explain the term "enlightened self-interest"?

4. What is the difference between citizens and resident aliens? What rights and responsibilities do both citizens and resident aliens have? What rights and responsibilities do citizens have that resident aliens do not?

5. Given the diversity of American society, what provides a common bond to us as Americans?

6. Write an editorial on the role of citizens in a constitutional democracy based on the following quotation from Adlai Stevenson: "As citizens of this democracy, you are the rulers and the ruled, the lawgivers and the law abiding, the beginning and the end."

LESSON 36

How Do We Use Our Citizenship?

Purpose of Lesson

In this lesson you examine the characteristics of citizenship in a constitutional democracy. Citizens sometimes disagree about what their role should be. It is your right in a free society to decide how you wish to exercise the rights and responsibilities of citizenship. What you have learned in this text and elsewhere about your heritage of constitutional democracy will help you in making this decision. How you conduct yourself as a citizen also will depend on your own interests and abilities.

When you complete this lesson you should be able to evaluate, take, and defend positions on the role of citizens in a constitutional democracy.

Terms to Know

civic values,
   principles, skills,
   and dispositions
civil rights
civility
common good

empowerment
greatest happiness of the
   greatest number
political action
political rights
social action

How do citizens in a constitutional democracy differ from those in a dictatorship or totalitarian state?

Citizenship has meant different things at different times in history and in different places. Totalitarian states and dictatorships also refer to those they govern as citizens—though they may lack the rights and responsibilities associated with American citizenship. Your role as a citizen of a constitutional democracy differs in fundamental respects from the role of a citizen living under unlimited or arbitrary government. While passive obedience and unquestioning loyalty are demanded by unlimited regimes, the citizen of a constitutional democracy is expected to be a critical and participating member of the political community. Citizens of constitutional democracies should have a reasoned loyalty and obedience to law not based on unquestioning deference to authority.

Criticism of one's government may carry with it a right, and perhaps even a duty, to disobey laws you believe are unjust laws—the civil rights movement provides a contemporary example.

Is it possible to generate reasoned loyalty and obedience in a system that demands unquestioned deference to authority? Why?

What do *you* think?

1. Is civil disobedience ever a justified form of political participation? Give two examples to support your position.

2. Under what circumstances do you think a citizen in a representative democracy has a right to violate a law? Explain your position.

3. What would be a proper response of the government to someone, who for reasons of conscience, breaks a law?

4. Do you agree with Thomas Jefferson that "a little rebellion" now and then is healthy for the political system? If so, what form might a little rebellion take?

What types of rights and responsibilities do citizens have?

As you consider the rights of citizenship, it is important to distinguish between civil rights and political rights.

- **Civil rights** protect us in our private lives from the arbitrary and unfair actions of government.

- **Political rights** allow us to participate in our own governance.

Since noncitizens living in this country are granted the same civil rights that citizens enjoy, political rights are to a large extent what define our status as citizens. You must be a citizen to exercise the rights to vote or serve in government.

Many of our rights suggest a corresponding obligation. In exercising our rights as individuals, we must respect other citizens' use of those same rights. Some obligations are legal, imposed by laws commonly agreed upon. For example, we have an obligation to obey the law, including those laws that require us to pay taxes, serve on juries, and meet the other responsibilities that help government operate.

Most of us would agree that we also have certain moral obligations as citizens. For example, some argue we have a duty, as well as a right, to vote. Even though the law no longer requires American citizens to perform military service, many Americans believe it is a duty to defend one's country or to assist it in other emergencies.

What do *you* think

1. How does Voltaire's statement "I may detest what you say, but will defend to the death your right to say it," relate to the responsibilities of citizenship?

2. Why is it important to speak up for the rights of others even if your own rights are not endangered?

Does U.S. citizenship carry with it an obligation to perform national service? Explain.

Why should we try to be effective citizens?

The natural rights philosophy and classical republicanism provide different answers to this question.

The natural rights philosophy emphasizes the elective nature of citizenship. Each citizen has a choice whether to remain a citizen of the United States. Each citizen possesses certain natural rights and it is the primary purpose of government to protect these rights. In choosing a government to protect these rights, citizens follow their self-interest in making sure that government does its job. We pay attention to how well the people we choose to govern us are doing their jobs. We participate as citizens, therefore, to ensure that government complies with its contractual obligations to us as individuals.

The classical republican philosophy, on the other hand, emphasizes our obligation to the society into which we were born or naturalized. Classical republicanism emphasizes the **common good** and the obligation of each citizen to serve the good of the whole community. Citizenship requires that we put this general good before our own self-interest, especially when the two conflict.

In practice, of course, the American civic tradition includes both concepts of citizenship. One of the enduring challenges you face as a citizen is sorting out for yourself the conflict between them in many different situations.

Critical Thinking Exercise

RECONCILING THE COMMON GOOD AND INDIVIDUAL SELF-INTEREST

Your class will be divided into small groups to discuss the issue of conflict between the good of the whole society and individual self-interest. Discuss and take a position on the questions at the end of the exercise. Be prepared to share your opinions with the class.

The conflict between the common good and self-interest is not the only problem you face as citizens. Sometimes it is difficult to determine what the common good or your own self-interest actually is. In some situations the common good may be quite clear as, for example, the need to protect the community from criminals, foreign enemies, and air pollution. In other situations, however, citizens strongly disagree about what the common good is and what policies are needed to serve it. For example, some would argue that laws strictly limiting human activity in environmentally sensitive areas are necessary to preserve the future well-being of our natural resources. Others claim that such restrictive policies can endanger the economy and may violate property rights.

It is not always easy to know how our individual interests are served. What may appear to be self-interest in the short-run might not be in our best long-term interest. Some aspects of this problem are raised in the following questions.

1. Is the common good **the greatest happiness of the greatest number**? If so, what does that phrase mean? Should the measurement of the greatest number be a minimum of 51 percent or should the percentage be higher? What would be the danger in determining the common good according to this principle?

2. Is the common good the goals that all people in the nation share? If so, how do we find out what those goals are?

3. If you find that you and your fellow citizens cannot agree on what the common good is, should you just pursue your own interests and forget about what is good for all? What alternatives might there be?

What do we need to understand to become effective citizens in a constitutional democracy?

However defined, the effective use of rights and responsibilities in a constitutional democracy requires certain beliefs, commitments, and skills. They can be described as follows:

Civic values. These express our most fundamental beliefs about the purpose of government within a society and the goals that we expect a government to achieve. They are ideals expressed or implied in some of the nation's founding documents, including the Declaration of Independence and the Preamble to the Constitution. They include such ideals as the dignity of the individual, equality, and justice. Though we as citizens might disagree about the meaning and relative importance of each specific value, we share a broad agreement about their significance in defining the ultimate ends of the society we have established.

Civic principles. These can be defined as those principles of government that best enable society to realize its civic values. Included among these essential principles would be the rule of law, popular sovereignty, and freedom of expression. Such principles define our commitment to constitutional government and democracy.

Civic skills. These describe the abilities we need as individuals to help realize civic values and make civic principles work. To be effective citizens we must have knowledge of our government's history and how it operates. We also must develop our intellectual abilities: analytical skills for the solving of problems, and communication skills to express our opinions and understand the opinions of others.

Civic dispositions. Effective citizenship is not possible if we do not adopt those dispositions or qualities of behavior that sustain a civic culture in a free society. Such a culture depends on tolerance, fairness, a respect for the opinions of others, and a commitment to truth. The word **civility** suggests the decency and integrity that are essential to a constitutional democracy.

What do *you* think?

1. What do you consider to be the principle obligations of good citizenship?

2. Does civic responsibility imply that citizens not only obey laws, but report lawbreakers to the authorities? For example, if you saw a friend shoplifting, are you morally obligated to report him or her?

3. What arguments can you make to convince a friend or classmate to become a more active citizen?

4. What means should a good citizens use to promote his or her own social and political views?

What do we mean by empowerment?

By developing an informed commitment to the values, principles, and dispositions of our civic culture and by acquiring the knowledge and skills necessary to play a role in it, we become "empowered" as citizens. **Empowerment** is a word we sometimes use today to describe the ability to "make one's voice heard" in public

Town meeting in Charlotte, Vermont

How does participation in public affairs "empower" citizens?

affairs. With empowerment, each of us knows that we have the potential to be effective as citizens when the need and opportunity arise.

You have more empowerment than you may realize. In 1991, at the time our country was celebrating the 200th anniversary of the Bill of Rights, a group of high school students in North Carolina discovered that their state had never ratified the Twenty-fourth Amendment, which abolished the poll tax and other taxes that had been used to discriminate against African Americans. As a project, the students investigated the legal requirements for ratification. They then petitioned the North Carolina state legislature to formally ratify the amendment. The students visited the state capitol and lobbied their legislators. After the legislature complied, the students carried the official notice of ratification to Washington, D.C., where they presented it to the Archivist of the United States. Through this school project, the students demonstrated their empowerment as citizens.

How do we learn to become effective citizens?

Citizenship in a free society is not always easy. Freedom requires us to live as self-reliant individuals, to think for ourselves, to solve our own problems, to cope with uncertainty and change, and to assist and respect others.

Citizens are made, not born. Like the ancient Greeks and Romans, the Founders placed great importance on the role of education in preparing each generation for citizenship. Your education will help provide you with the knowledge and skills to function effectively as citizens of a constitutional democracy. Practical experience has been as important as formal schooling in preparing Americans for citizenship. Americans learn the skills of citizenship through the many opportunities to participate in public affairs.

We begin the process of learning to be citizens in early childhood. At home and in the classroom, we begin to think for ourselves, to express our own opinions, and to respect the opinions of others. Through such activities as student government, school projects, sports, and community and club activities, we begin to acquire the skills of teamwork, organization, and debate. In short, many of the qualities that we need for citizenship begin to develop early in our lives.

How do we exercise our rights and responsibilities as citizens?

In dealing with the problems of our communities and the nation, we have different possibilities. We may engage in **social action** or we may engage in **political action.** We may, of course, choose to engage in both. For example, in dealing with the problems of crime in the community, we might join a neighborhood watch. Alternatively, we might organize other members of the community to present the problem to the city council in an effort to get more police officers on the streets. The first is an example of social action, the second an example of political action. These two courses of action are not mutually exclusive. We might decide to engage in both at the same time.

One of the issues we must decide as citizens is how a particular problem is most effectively solved. The decision we make depends on our analysis of the problem, our estimate of the possible solutions, and our own values. Making these decisions lies at the heart of the practice of responsible citizenship.

Critical Thinking Exercise
EXAMINING THE RESPONSIBILITIES OF CITIZENSHIP AND DECIDING ON HOW THEY CAN BE FULFILLED

In contemporary urban and rural America, violence by and against young people is receiving increased social and political attention, as well as daily coverage on television and in newspapers. Statistically, the incidence of youth violence has not increased during the last decade, the deadliness of it has. More young people carry guns or other weapons and use them as a means of settling disputes or intimidating others.

1. What responsibilities, if any, do you as a citizen have to promote sound political and social policies designed to decrease or prevent the problem of violence?

2. What social actions can you, as a citizen of your school and community, become involved in to help prevent the problem?

3. What political actions can you become involved in?

4. What values and interests do you think are important for you as a citizen to promote in connection with prevention of violence by and against young people?

Reviewing and Using the Lesson

1. How would you describe the role of citizens in a constitutional democracy?

2. How might a classical republican explain the duty to be an active citizen? How might a natural rights philosopher explain this duty?

3. How would you define the "common good"? Why might people seek to promote the common good instead of their own interests?

4. What are civic values, civic principles, civic skills, and civic dispositions?

5. How would you explain the difference between "social action" and "political action"?

Does citizenship obligate a person to participate in social and political actions? Why?

LESSON 37

How May Citizenship Change in the Nation's Third Century?

Purpose of Lesson

This lesson looks to the future. You focus on some major developments taking place in our society that are likely to affect the very nature of citizenship during your lifetime.

When you complete this lesson, you should be able to explain how the increased diversity of our society, technological progress, and closer international relationships are likely to affect your life as a citizen. You should be able to describe how diversity has challenged our civic culture, how the computer and modern telecommunications are expanding the possibilities of citizenship, and how our nation's greater interdependence with the rest of the world is changing the pattern of civic loyalties.

Terms to Know

cosmopolitan
E Pluribus Unum
e-mail
electronic city state
futurist
global village

international
internet
plebiscites
telecommunications
teledemocracy

What are some developments now taking place in the world that will likely affect the future of American citizenship?

Three developments promise to shape the future of American citizenship in important ways:

■ the increasing diversity of American society

■ the impact of modern technology, especially the computer and electronic **telecommunications**

■ America's growing interdependence with the rest of the world

How is diversity in American society creating new challenges for the ideal of American citizenship?

You know how Americans have adapted the idea of citizenship to a nation of immigrants, people from many lands and cultures, bound together by a commitment to a common set of political values. The American ideal of *E Pluribus Unum*—Out of Many, One—has usually been able to balance the benefits of a diverse society with the unifying influence of a common civic culture. One of the major challenges you face as an American citizen is to sustain that balance in a society that is becoming far more diverse and complex.

America in the founding era was a nation of 3.5 million inhabitants—3 million free whites and half a million enslaved Africans. Most of the white population were northern European in ancestry. The young republic also was overwhelmingly Protestant. Today America is a microcosm of the world. It has become one of the most ethnically diverse countries on earth. You may see evidence of this diversity in your school. More than 100 languages are spoken by students in the Los Angeles school district. The results of recent immigration to this country have been dramatic. Of the 14 million immigrants since 1965, 85 percent have come from non-European countries. During the 1980s, immigrants to the United States came from 164 different lands. By the turn of the century, one in every four Americans will be either Hispanic, African American, or Asian. By the year 2030, one-half of the country's population will belong to one minority group or another. In a sense, there

What strengths can immigrants bring to a society? What problems can arise as a result of large-scale immigration?

will no longer be a traditional majority group. In 1995 only 15 percent of Americans identify themselves as descendants of British immigrants, who once comprised a large majority of the population. The faces of "We the People" have changed considerably in the course of 200 years and will continue to change during your lifetime.

What consequences will the change toward a more diverse society have for us as citizens?

Americans today disagree about the answers to this question. To some the diversity brought about by recent immigration is no different from what has happened throughout American history. The mix of people has strengthened American society and reaffirmed our commitment to ideals that are the property of all humanity, not a particular ethnic group. As with their predecessors, most recent immigrants have adapted to American society, enriching the nation's economic life, culture, and educational institutions.

Others worry that there are limits to how much diversity the country can absorb without losing the common bonds that unite us. They fear that in an increasingly diverse society, self-interests may prevail over the common good. A challenge for your generation as for all previous generations is balancing the *unum* with the *pluribus* in America.

What do *you* think?

1. What advantages does our political system gain from diversity of people and ideas? What might be some disadvantages?

2. When does diversity become an issue in a free society? Is there such a thing as too much diversity? What effects—good or bad—do you think groups and "cliques" have on the life of your school community?

3. Do you agree with Woodrow Wilson that "a man who thinks of himself as belonging to a particular group in America has not yet become an American?" Why or why not?

4. What obligations, if any, do you think you should have as a citizen toward people who hold social, religious, or political beliefs with which you strongly disagree? Explain your position.

How is citizenship being changed by modern technology?

Modern technology has expanded the possibilities for participatory citizenship. Audio and video teleconferencing has become a familiar way for citizens to discuss issues of common concern. So has talk radio.

Some state legislatures have begun to use such telecommunications on a regular basis as a way of staying in touch with their constituents. Advocacy groups of all kinds use the research and communication tools of the internet, including e-mail, to inform and organize their members.

Some **futurists**—theorists who consider possibilities for the future based on current information and trends—see revolutionary implications in this technology. They envision the possibility of a **teledemocracy** in the years ahead. This term means a new version of direct democracy, where citizens can participate to a much greater extent in the affairs of government with less reliance on their elected representatives.

Does modern technology help or hinder American citizenship?

National **plebiscites** also have become a practical option. By use of on-line computerized voting, each citizen could register his or her views on particular issues, with the results instantly tabulated. "Going to the polls" could become an outmoded custom. Citizens could exercise their political rights from a computer work station at home or in public facilities like libraries or the post office.

The Framers believed that classical republicanism in its purest form was impractical in a country as large and diverse as the American republic. Some people believe that teledemocracy overcomes many of these impracticalities. The computer makes possible an **electronic city-state** in which citizens scattered across the country can join together to participate more effectively in public affairs.

Whatever its potential implications, the computer is forcing us to reexamine the most basic principles and institutions in our constitutional democracy.

Critical Thinking Exercise
ROLE PLAYING JAMES MADISON IN THE THIRD CENTURY OF GOVERNMENT UNDER THE CONSTITUTION

Imagine, for a moment, that you are James Madison, brought back to life in the year 2000. What would be your assessment of teledemocracy and the electronic city-state? To help develop your position answer the following questions.

1. What are the dangers of direct democracy? Why did the Framers of the Constitution distrust it? Why did they prefer representative democracy instead?

2. To what extent is "public opinion" synonymous with the "will of the people"?

3. What should be the role of political leadership in a democracy? To what extent should leaders influence and to what extent should they be influenced by popular opinion? Can government in a democracy be too much in touch with the sentiments of the people?

4. In what ways is computer technology a threat to individual liberty as well as a tool on its behalf?

5. What expectations does teledemocracy place on citizens? To what extent are those expectations realistic?

6. The advancements of technology show us what we have the capability of doing, not what we necessarily have to do or should do. What other considerations about citizenship and civic culture might argue against the creation of teledemocracy?

How is internationalism affecting American citizenship?

One important consequence of the communications revolution has been America's increased interaction and interdependence with the rest of the world. Issues of national importance in the United States have an impact beyond our borders. Conversely, events and developments elsewhere in the world are becoming more significant in the lives of American citizens.

The achievements of modern technology are turning the world into a **global village**, with shared cultural, economic, and environmental concerns. National corporations have become international. Economic decisions made in Tokyo or London affect the things Americans buy and the jobs they seek. Environmental concerns also transcend national boundaries. Entertainment—music, sports, and film—command worldwide markets. The culture that we live in is becoming **cosmopolitan**, that is, belonging to the whole world.

The movement of people, as well as information, has helped bring about global interdependence. Improved transportation has been a key factor in increased immigration to the United States. People go where there is economic opportunity and they can go more easily and much farther than in the past. The movement of people across national borders will continue to increase. Such migrations help to reduce cultural and other differences that have historically divided nations. They also create new problems for governments which have the responsibility for providing for the well-being of citizens and other residents.

In what ways does the internationalization of business affect tradition and culture?

Citizenship in modern history has been defined largely in terms of nation-states. The idea of being a citizen, however, developed in many different political contexts throughout history, from tiny city-states to large empires. In the American experience, citizenship has changed in its patterns of allegiance and loyalty. Before the Civil War, many Americans would have defined their citizenship in terms of loyalty to their respective states rather than to the United States.

Although national citizenship is likely to remain fundamentally important in the future, the issues confronting American citizens are increasingly **international**. Issues of economic competition, the environment, and the movement of peoples around the world require an awareness of political associations that are larger in scope than the nation-state.

What do *you* think?

1. In *The Federalist* essays Madison argued that two conditions would help to prevent a tyranny of the majority in America. One was the diversity of interests in the new nation. The other was geographic distance making it difficult for these different interests to combine. As you evaluate the significant changes now taking place in American society, do you think the threat of such a democratic tyranny has increased or decreased? What trends may have increased the danger? What trends decreased it?

2. In his observations about American democracy, Tocqueville warned of the danger of individual isolation in a society where everyone was equal. Democracy, he said, "throws [each individual] back forever upon himself alone and threatens in the end to confine him entirely within the solitude of his own heart." Has computer technology made such individual isolation more or less likely today? Explain your answer.

3. What advantages might be offered by world citizenship? What disadvantages? Do you think that world citizenship will be possible in your lifetime?

Reviewing and Using the Lesson

1. How would you describe the challenges and opportunities created by the increasing diversity of American society?

2. How might modern technology expand the opportunities for direct participation by citizens in self-government?

3. In what ways has America become increasingly interdependent with the rest of the world? What might be some consequences of this interdependence?

4. Locate newspaper and magazine articles about DNA research and the impact of genetic fingerprinting on privacy and due process rights. Report your findings to the class.

What Can American Citizens Learn about Constitutionalism from Other Countries?

Purpose of Lesson

We often examine constitutionalism primarily within the context of the American experience. By itself this perspective is too narrow, especially in today's world. In this lesson you look at other traditions of constitutional government and at the many experiments in constitutionalism now taking place in the world. You examine the historical impact of American constitutionalism on other countries. The lesson focuses on the subject of human rights and its increasing importance in current international affairs.

When you finish the lesson, you should be able to explain why some aspects of the U.S. Constitution have been adopted by emerging democracies while others have not. You should be able to explain the differences between the United States' form of constitutional government and other forms of constitutional government, such as parliamentary systems. Finally, you should be able to explain the differences between the American understanding of constitutional rights and rights guarantees as they have been developed in other parts of the world.

Fall of the Berlin Wall, 1989
Did the principles and values of American constitutional democracy influence world events in the 1980s and 90s? If so, how?

Terms to Know

civil and political rights
European Convention
  on Human Rights
federalism
Four Freedoms, 1941
human rights
independent judiciary
negative and positive rights

parliamentary government
prime minister
rights of solidarity
social and economic rights
United Nations Charter,
  1945
Universal Declaration of
  Human Rights, 1948

What has been the influence of American ideals about government and human rights on the rest of the world?

America's constitutional ideals are perhaps this country's greatest contribution to the world. Few historic documents have had the impact of the Declaration of Independence and the U.S. Constitution, whose words have been copied and paraphrased in numerous other charters of freedom.

The American republic, product of the world's first democratic revolution, influenced many other countries during the first decades of its existence. The French Revolution of 1789 was inspired by the American Revolution and the French Constitution of 1791 copied many elements from America's first state constitutions. The world's second-oldest written constitution, the Polish Constitution of 1791, also was influenced by the American example. When Latin American countries won their independence from Spain in the early nineteenth century, they looked to the U.S. Constitution as a model for republican government. In 1825 the first demands for constitutional government in Russia, though unsuccessful, were inspired by American ideals.

The influence of American constitutionalism has expanded in this century because of the position of the United States as a world power. During the American occupation of Japan and Germany after World War II, a committee of Americans drafted the Japanese Constitution of 1947, and similarly, the new German Constitution of 1949 incorporated elements from the American model.

As the United States celebrated the bicentennial of its Constitution in 1987–1991, other nations were writing new chapters in the history of constitutional government. The 1980s and early 1990s saw the collapse of Soviet Communism and the emergence of democratic governments in Eastern Europe. In 1989 students in China staged a challenge to totalitarian government. These dramatic developments could signal the beginning of a new era of constitutionalism with important implications for American citizens.

There has been renewed interest in the heritage of American ideals in the aftermath of the Cold War, as many former Communist states have begun to experiment with their own forms of constitutionalism. Some of the most eloquent tributes to our Constitution's bicentennial were expressed by the leaders of these newly independent countries. The president of Czechoslovakia, Vaclav Havel, remarked in a speech before the U.S. Congress in 1990,

> *Wasn't it the best minds of your country...who wrote your famous Declaration of Independence, your Bill of Human Rights, and your Constitution?... Those great documents...inspire us all; they inspire us despite the fact that they are over 200 years old. They inspire us to be citizens.*

Vaclav Havel addressing the United States Congress
How might constitutionalism change in the post Cold War period?

What elements of American constitutionalism have been most widely adopted by other countries?

As the world's first written framework of national government, the U.S. Constitution established an important precedent. Nearly all countries today either have or are in the process of drafting written constitutions. Totalitarian systems also felt it necessary to produce written constitutions, although in no way did they restrict the real exercise of power. The process by which the U.S. Constitution was drafted and adopted also established a precedent—the use of constitutional conventions and popular ratifications.

Key principles of the U.S. Constitution were spread throughout the world by *The Federalist*, America's greatest contribution to political thought. Many of these principles have been adopted in other constitutions.

Perhaps the most widely admired and imitated feature of the U.S. Constitution, after the Bill of Rights, has been the establishment of an **independent judiciary**. An inviolate—secure from outside influence—judicial branch acts as the watchdog of the Constitution and prevents the executive and legislative branches of government from disregarding it. The judicial branch helps to ensure that the words of the Constitution will be obeyed by the government.

Another aspect of American constitutionalism that is of great interest in the world today is **federalism**. By combining a central government with a large measure of autonomy for the states the Framers were able to solve the problem of how to establish effective national and local governments in a large country. America's federal system has interested the former Communist states of Eastern Europe, where decades of centralized control all but destroyed local government. Federalism also has influenced the democracies of Western Europe in their creation of a European union.

What do *you* think?

1. What responsibilities, if any, do Americans have to promote representative democracy and constitutional government in other nations? Explain your reasoning.

2. What responsibilities, if any, do Americans have to promote respect for human rights in other nations? Explain your position.

How have other constitutional democracies differed from the American model?

The U.S. Constitution, however, is not the world's only source of ideas about constitutional democracy. Nations have looked to other traditions and to their own particular circumstances and historical legacies to find a form of constitutionalism that will be effective for them. However much we value our own political ideals and institutions, we must realize that they cannot always be transplanted.

Some elements in the U.S. Constitution have been adopted by other nations only with substantial modification; other elements have been rejected altogether in favor of different constitutional models. For example, the office of the presidency was another of the great innovations of the Framers. It was their solution to the need for a strong executive to replace a monarchy. Elected independently of the legislature, the president possesses those powers described in the Constitution itself.

The title of "President" to describe the constitutional chief executive has been widely adopted since that time, though usually not with the same powers and responsibilities U.S. presidents have. Because of their own historical experiences, many countries have been fearful of a strong executive. Freed from Communist dictatorships, the countries in the former Soviet bloc have provided for weak executives in their new constitutional arrangements, much like some of the first state constitutions in this country.

Perhaps the most distinguishing characteristic of the American system of government has been its separation and sharing of powers among three co-equal branches. Few other constitutional democracies, however, use that system today. Its critics consider our arrangement of divided powers inefficient and undemocratic. Most of the world's democracies have adopted instead some form of **parliamentary government**.

How does parliamentary government differ from a constitutional system based on separation of powers?

The Framers were very much influenced by the British constitution, even though it differed in important respects from the model they eventually adopted. The British constitution featured a system of checks and balances, but its executive, legislative, and judicial branches were not separated. Parliament, for example, was considered an instrument of the Crown, rather than an independent branch of government.

During the last two centuries a system of government modeled on the British constitution has been widely imitated, not only in Britain's former colonies but in many other countries as well. In a parliamentary system, government ministers are also members of the legislature. The head of the executive branch, usually called a **prime minister,** is determined by whatever party or combination of parties has a majority in the parliament or legislature.

Unlike the American system, in a parliamentary arrangement the majority in the legislative branch decides who will head the executive branch. Many nations prefer the parliamentary system because they see the closer linkage of the executive and legislative branches as a more efficient form of government and one that is more reflective of the popular will.

British Prime Minister John Major speaking in Parliament
What advantages might be enjoyed under the British constitution as compared with the U.S. Constitution?

What has been the influence of the U.S. Bill of Rights on constitutional government elsewhere?

Probably the single greatest contribution of American constitutionalism to the world has been its example of incorporating fundamental guarantees of individual rights into a written constitution. Nearly all national constitutions adopted since have included similar guarantees. The inspiring model of the U.S. Bill of Rights has become especially important during the latter half of this century, when interest in basic rights has increased around the world. As President Jimmy Carter observed in 1977:

The basic thrust of human affairs points toward a more universal demand for fundamental human rights.

Before this century, individual rights were generally regarded as an internal matter, to be left to each nation to decide. The world-wide economic depression of the 1930s, and the unprecedented crimes against humanity committed by totalitarian governments before and during World War II, gave the issue of human rights a new importance.

It was an American president, Franklin D. Roosevelt, who anticipated a new era in the history of basic rights. In a speech to Congress in 1941, the president defined the **Four Freedoms** worth fighting for: freedom of speech and expression, freedom of worship, freedom from want, and freedom from fear. The charter that founded the **United Nations** in 1945, and subsequently led to the **United Nations Universal Declaration of Human Rights of 1948**, followed President Roosevelt's example. The Declaration and the charter proclaimed universal standards of basic rights, called **human rights,** because they were considered essential to the dignity of each human being.

In the decades since, the concern for human rights has become an issue of importance in the relations among nations. Regional agreements have expanded the United Nations Declaration. For example, in 1950 the countries of Western Europe agreed to a **European Convention on Human Rights**. They established a European Court to which the citizens of these countries could appeal when they believed their rights had been violated.

Increasingly, the protection of rights is also an important diplomatic issue among nations. The United States, for example, has sometimes restricted trade with countries considered to be violating human rights. In recent years our relations with the Republic of South Africa were influenced to a large extent by the issue of rights violations in that country.

How do other national guarantees of rights differ from the U.S. Bill of Rights?

As fundamental and lasting as its guarantees have been, the U.S. Bill of Rights is a document of the eighteenth century, reflecting the issues and concerns of the age in which it was written. The rights guaranteed to Americans are **civil** and **political rights**. They express a fear of government power. They protect the individual from wrongful acts by government and provide each citizen with ways to participate in public affairs.

Other national guarantees of rights also reflect the cultures that created them. Many of these cultures have values and priorities different from our own. In many Asian countries, for example, the rights of the individual are secondary to the interests of the whole community. Islamic countries take their code of laws from the teachings of the Koran, the book of sacred writings accepted by Muslims as revelations made to the prophet Muhammad by God.

In some countries freedom of conscience is considered less important than it is in the United States and other Western democracies. What constitutes cruel and unusual punishment, which is forbidden by our Eighth Amendment, differs greatly from country to country, depending on its particular history and culture.

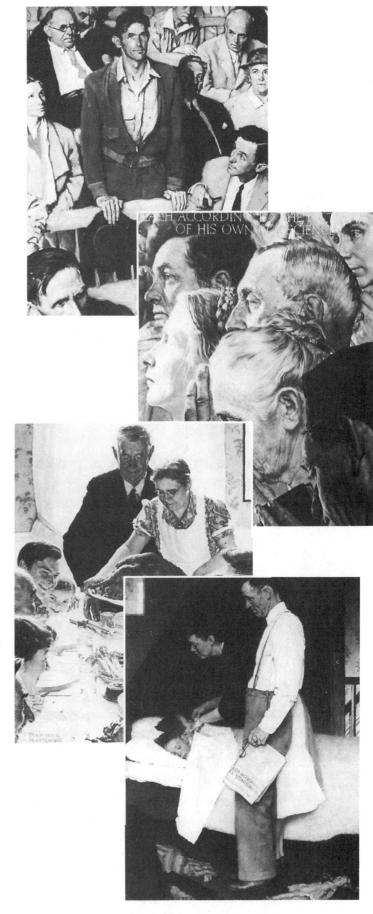

Four Freedoms by Norman Rockwell
In what ways are Roosevelt's Four Freedoms essential to maintaining basic human rights for people everywhere?

Contemporary charters of basic rights also reflect the changes that have taken place in government and society during the last 200 years. Many guarantees of rights adopted since World War II have been modeled on the United Nations' Universal Declaration of Human Rights. They include many of the civil and political rights represented in our Bill of Rights. Most go further to include **social** and **economic rights.**

Examples of social and economic rights would be the right to choose a career, secure employment, health care, and education. Others might include certain societal rights, such as the right to responsible management of nonrenewable resources or a clean environment. The inclusion of such provisions in guaranteed rights reflects a change in the role government plays in society and the expectations its citizens place on it.

The Founders considered the role of government in people's lives to be very limited, as indeed it was in the eighteenth century. Governments play a much larger role today and that role has expanded the meaning of basic rights in most societies. The people in the former Communist states of Europe, for example, may appreciate their newfound civic and political rights, but many are reluctant to give up the economic security and social rights their former Communist governments provided.

What is the difference between negative and positive rights?

In the natural rights tradition, which provides the foundation of the United States Constitution, rights are seen as restraints on the power of government. They are sometimes called **negative rights** because they prevent government from acting in a certain way. The Bill of Rights generally requires the government not to act. For example, the First Amendment says, "Government shall make no law…"

The social, economic, and **solidarity rights** included in the United Nations' Universal Declaration of Rights, and in many national guarantees of rights adopted since, are what are sometimes called **positive rights**. Instead of preventing the government from acting, they require it to act, to ensure such things as economic security, health care, and a clean environment for its citizens.

There are other important differences between negative and positive rights. Negative rights prevent the government from taking away something its citizens already possess, for example, freedom of expression. Many positive rights, on the other hand, describe certain benefits that citizens should have. These rights express the objectives worthy of any just society.

EXAMINING THE UNIVERSAL DECLARATION OF HUMAN RIGHTS

Review the Universal Declaration of Human Rights found in the Reference Section and answer the following questions:

1. What rights does the Universal Declaration of Human Rights proclaim that are in the U.S. Constitution and Bill of Rights?

2. What rights in our Constitution and Bill of Rights are not included in the Universal Declaration of Human Rights? Why do you suppose they are not included?

3. What appears to be the purposes of the rights in the Universal Declaration of Human Rights that are not protected by our Constitution or Bill of Rights?

4. Examine each of the rights in the Universal Declaration of Human Rights that is not protected specifically in our Constitution. Is the right you have identified protected in the United States by other means, such as civil rights legislation; civil or criminal law contracts between private parties; labor and manage-ment agreements on employment benefits, vacation pay, and sick leave; custom or tradition; other means not listed above?

5. What rights, if any, in the Universal Declaration of Human Rights should be established in the United States? How should they be established? Explain your position.

6. How do the rights listed in the Universal Declaration of Human Rights appear to reflect the history and experiences of the time in which it was written?

Reviewing and Using the Lesson

1. Which aspects of American constitutional democracy have been particularly influential in other countries?

2. How would you describe the important features of a parliamentary form of government?

3. What is the difference between civil and political rights, on one hand, and social and economic rights, on the other? How is this difference related to the difference between "negative rights" and "positive rights"?

4. What are some important differences between the Bill of Rights and the Universal Declaration of Human Rights?

5. Research the work Eleanor Roosevelt did on behalf of passage of the United Nations' Universal Declaration of Human Rights.

LESSON 39

What Are Some Constitutional Issues Facing United States Citizens in the Nation's Third Century?

Purpose of Lesson

In this lesson you focus on some constitutional issues being raised by our changing roles as citizens and the influence of many developments in modern society. You examine how these issues have challenged our understanding of group rights, the rights to life and to privacy, and the conflict between individual rights and the general good.

When you finish this lesson, you should be able to describe and give examples of how changes in our society have raised new constitutional issues. You should be able to evaluate, take, and defend positions on the different philosophies of judicial interpretation of the Constitution.

Terms to Know

broad construction
emanations
judicial activism
judicial restraint

penumbras
strict construction
unenumerated rights

Why has the Constitution been changed so infrequently?

Some critics believe the system of government created by the Framers for the world of the eighteenth century has proven itself unsuited for the more complex, faster-paced world of the twenty-first century. Others, however, respond by noting that any system that has managed to adapt itself to the changes of 200 years deserves the benefit of the doubt. Tampering with the Constitution, they say, should always err on the side of caution.

Americans have never been reluctant to tinker with the Constitution. More than 10,000 constitutional amendments have been introduced; but only 33 have been approved by Congress and submitted to the states for ratification; and only 27 of these have been adopted. Changing the Constitution has proven to be difficult, which is what the Framers intended when they outlined the requirements for amendment in Article V. After all, it took two

centuries for the Twenty-seventh Amendment to the Constitution to be adopted.

The Framers wanted the Constitution to remain the nation's fundamental law, not to be confused, as a result of frequent changes, with ordinary laws and regulations. Because it has proven difficult to amend, the Constitution remains one of the oldest and shortest written constitutions, with a total of 7,591 words.

What are some constitutional rights issues being raised by changes in American society?

Progress and change have created new issues for the Constitution. Their complexity challenges the nation's historic commitment to resolve its problems through constitutional means. Among the issues likely to be important in the years ahead are the following:

- Group rights
- Right to life and death
- Right to privacy
- Rights of the individual and providing for the common good
- Rights of citizens and rights of resident aliens

Group rights. America's increasingly pluralistic society and the nation's ongoing commitment to equality have forced Americans to recognize the differences that exist between groups. How far should constitutional guarantees go, for example, in providing for favored treatment of historically excluded groups? In a multilingual society to what extent should the government be obliged to provide ballots, income tax returns, and other government forms in languages other than English?

Right to life and death. The accomplishments of modern science in sustaining life before full-term pregnancy and into old age have made our society reexamine both the legal and ethical meaning of life itself. To some, high tech life support systems have created a distinction between **life** and **existence**. When does life begin? When does it end? Does an individual have a right to take his or her own life? Does an individual have the right to assist someone else's suicide?

Right to privacy. Electronic communications pose new potential threats to individual privacy. Federal, state, and local governments now keep vast computer databases on individual citizens. In the computer age, to what extent do the constitutional protections of personal "papers and effects" under the Fourth Amendment extend beyond one's home into these government files? Who has access to these records and for what purposes?

Moreover, Fourth Amendment protections do not apply to the actions of the private sector of our society. Corporations, hospitals, and other private agencies also keep computer records. Both private and public institutions can invade the privacy of individuals through "electronic snooping"—using video cameras, audio "bugs", and microwave technology to spy on individuals. The constitutional limitations on such activity have yet to be developed.

Rights of the individual and providing for the common good. The enduring tension between these two conflicting values in our constitutional democracy is being tested once again by environmental and other issues in modern society. How will our constitutional arrangements balance the rights of the individual to property and pursuit of happiness with the responsibility to provide for the general good of the larger society by guaranteeing such things as clean air and the preservation of natural habitats? Controversies surrounding the protection of old-growth forests, preservation of the spotted owl, and the effects of cigarette smoking exemplify this tension.

Right of citizens and rights of resident aliens. The increasing movement of peoples across national borders is likely to raise new constitutional issues regarding the meaning of citizenship and the status of aliens in the United States. Aliens enjoy many of the civil rights that the Constitution accords to "persons" as distinguished from citizens. These include most provisions of the Bill of Rights and freedom from arbitrary discrimination. Aliens are subject to the laws of the United States and must pay taxes. If immigration continues in future years new issues are likely to arise regarding the rights of both citizens and aliens under our Constitution.

What are unenumerated rights?

The perplexing constitutional issues of modern life have not only prompted reinterpretations of well established rights, they also have given new importance to a largely unexplored frontier of our Constitution: **unenumerated rights**. Unenumerated rights are rights possessed by every American that are not listed or enumerated in the Constitution. They are unspecified rights.

One of the principal objections to a federal bill of rights was that such a document could not possibly list all the rights of the people. Leaving some rights unlisted, or unenumerated, might imply that they did not exist. Omission also could be interpreted to mean that such rights, even if they did exist, were not important.

How can government agencies best mediate the conflict between legitimate individual rights and the common good?

It was probably as a result of these concerns that the Ninth Amendment was included in the Bill of Rights. It says,

> The enumeration in the Constitution of certain rights shall not be construed to deny or disparage others retained by the people.

The Ninth Amendment embodies that great principle that can be traced back through the history of constitutional government to the Magna Carta—the principle that there exist certain fundamental rights that we take for granted, not just those rights that happen to be specified in a particular document. Justice William O. Douglas stated,

> It well may be that guarantees which must be written are less secure than those so embedded in the hearts of men that they need not be written.

What do *you* think?

1. Which of the changes taking place in contemporary American society do you think is likely to present the greatest challenge to constitutional rights in the years ahead?

2. Which do you think might require a constitutional amendment? Explain your position.

Who should have the power to identify unenumerated rights?

Who should decide what is an unenumerated right protected by the Constitution? There are differences of opinion on how this question should be answered. At issue is a basic principle of constitutional government that requires the powers of all the agencies of government be limited by law.

The Supreme Court has the power according to the principle of judicial review to decide whether a legislative act or executive order violates a right protected by the Constitution. This task is difficult enough with issues involving rights explicitly listed in the Constitution, such as the rights to a writ of habeas corpus or protection against unlawful entry by the authorities. The task becomes even more difficult when the issue involves unenumerated rights. What standard, if any, can justices use to avoid reading their own prejudices into the Constitution?

Critics of judicial power have claimed that anyone can find any right they want through a subjective interpretation of the Constitution. These critics often refer to the language of the majority opinion in *Griswold v. Connecticut* (1965), written by Justice Douglas. The case involved a Connecticut law that prohibited the use of contraceptives in all circumstances. A physician had

Who should determine which matters of personal privacy should remain free from government regulation?

been arrested for giving information on contraception to a married couple.

Douglas's opinion claimed that the Connecticut law violated the right of marital privacy. This right is not specifically referred to anywhere in the Constitution. In his opinion, however, Douglas argued that the right was protected by **"penumbras**, formed by **emanations"** from other enumerated rights, specifically those in the First, Third, Fourth, and Fifth Amendments. By this, he meant that some provisions of the Bill of Rights **implied** a right to marital privacy. In terms of his colorful metaphor, unenumerated rights were to be found in the shadows cast by the light of enumerated rights.

Should judges be given the freedom to decide what rights are to be discovered in the shadows of the Constitution's emanations? Some critics believe that to allow such latitude gives the Court almost unlimited power, not only to interpret the law but by doing so to create new law.

There has been, and will continue to be, disagreement about the role judges should play in a constitutional democracy. There is disagreement about how the Constitution should be interpreted, with some believing in a **strict construction**, adhering as closely as possible to the original intent of the Framers. Others believe in **broad construction**, giving judges considerable leeway in applying the words of the Constitution to the circumstances of a changing world.

There also is disagreement about the degree to which judges should intercede in the activities of the legislative and executive branches. Some believe in a philosophy of **judicial restraint**, that places strong limitations on the discretionary powers of judges and relies instead on the political process to influence legislators to pass laws that protect rights. In the words of former Chief Justice Warren Burger,

> *In a democratic society, legislatures, not courts, are constituted to respond to the will, and consequently the moral values, of the people.*

Others have argued for **judicial activism** by pointing out that the nation's courts, as watchdogs of the Constitution, have always had a special role to play in the identification, definition, and protection of individual rights.

It was an advocate of judicial activism and broad construction, Justice William J. Brennan, who said,

> *We current Justices read the Constitution in the only way we can, as Twentieth Century Americans. We look to the history of the time of framing and to the intervening history of interpretation. The ultimate question must be, what do the words of the text mean for our time? For the genius of the Constitution rests not in any static meaning it might have had in a world that is dead and gone, but in the adaptability of its great principles to cope with current problems and current needs.*

In a sense, what Justice Brennan said applies to every citizen called on to make sense of the Constitution—we cannot escape altogether the context and perspective of our own time. The challenge, as always, will be to apply the principles of the Constitution to changing circumstances without losing its basic principles in the process.

Reviewing and Using the Lesson

1. How would you explain the fact that thousands of constitutional amendments have been proposed, but only 27 have been adopted?

2. What are "enumerated rights"? Why have Supreme Court decisions protecting unenumerated rights been controversial?

3. How would you describe "strict construction" and "broad construction" of the Constitution?

4. What is meant by "judicial restraint"? What is meant by "judicial activism"? What arguments have been made in support of these two approaches to fulfilling the responsibilities of being a judge?

5. Examine the following U.S. Supreme Court cases regarding the right to travel in the United States and abroad: *Crandall v. Nevada*, 73 U.S. 35 (1869); *Kent v. Dulles*, 357 U.S. 16 (1958); *Aptheher v. Secretary of State*, 378 U.S. 500 (1964); and *Regan v. Wald*, 468 U.S. 222 (1984).

LESSON 40

What Is Meant by Returning to Fundamental Principles?

Purpose of Lesson

Founder George Mason said, "No free government, or the blessings of liberty can be preserved to any people, but by frequent recurrence to fundamental principles." In this concluding lesson, you have the opportunity of relating some fundamental principles and ideas of our government to contemporary issues.

The format of this lesson differs from the others. Critical Thinking Exercises, similar to those you have done throughout the book, present a series of quotations representing many great ideas and principles that have shaped our constitutional heritage. Some of these ideas contradict each other. American constitutional history has witnessed many conflicts between competing principles of equal merit, for example, the conflict between majority rule and minority rights, between sovereign power and fundamental rights, liberty and order, unity and diversity.

You encounter once again some of these conflicts in the following exercises. In each case you are asked to apply the principles and ideas suggested in the quotations to a contemporary issue, to work through the issue on your own, or in small groups, and to reach your own conclusions.

In so doing, you use the skills of citizenship—observation, analysis, and value judgments to reach an opinion, to express that opinion and to be prepared to defend it. The exercises provides practice for the responsibilities you will encounter in the years ahead.

The English economist, John Maynard Keynes, once remarked that "in the long run it is ideas and not men who rule the world." If the upheavals of this century have taught us anything, it is that ideas have consequences, sometimes for good, sometimes for evil. We like to believe that in the end, good ideas will prevail over bad. Whatever the case, ideas do matter. One of the twentieth century's most compelling images comes from the Chinese student uprising of 1989. It was the photograph below of a young man, armed only with the moral authority of his cause, confronting a column of armored tanks. The picture moved and inspired the world.

Do you have an obligation as a citizen and a human being to exercise your moral authority when injustice occurs?

Why are fundamental principles important?

You will remember that this book began with the observation that the American experiment in self-government was an adventure in ideas. The individuals who founded our government cherished and respected ideas. They were excited about them. Ours is a nation that was created by ideas. It is not the product of a common culture or geography or centuries of tradition. The United States began as an experiment to see if certain ideas about government—never before tried on such a scale and in such a way—would work.

The Soviet dictator, Joseph Stalin, once disparaged the influence of religion by asking, "How many divisions does the Pope have?" It is one of the great ironies of this century that the fall of Stalin's Communist empire began in Poland, in a revolution inspired in large part by the religious faith of the Polish people and supported throughout by the moral influence of the papacy. "An invasion of armies can be resisted," said the French novelist Victor Hugo, "but not an idea whose time has come."

What did the Founders mean by returning to first principles?

When George Mason spoke of the importance of a frequent recurrence to fundamental principles, he was invoking an old idea associated with republican government. The ancient Greeks and Romans believed that a government established with the purpose of serving the public good and involving the participation of all citizens could not survive unless each generation was reminded of that government's reason for being and the principles by which it operated.

"If a nation means its systems, religious or political, shall have duration," said another of the Founders, "it ought to recognize the leading principles of them in the front page of every family book. What is the usefulness of a truth in theory, unless it exists constantly in the minds of the people and has their assent?"

It is doubtful that these Founders had in mind an uncritical acceptance of the "wisdom of the past." In revisiting these principles, each generation must examine and evaluate them anew. Indeed, it is probable that the Founders would be somewhat surprised at the reverence in which they and their writings have been held by subsequent generations of Americans.

The Founders, themselves, were vigorous critics of the wisdom they inherited and the principles in which they believed. They were articulate, opinionated individuals who loved to examine ideas, to analyze, argue, and debate them. They expected no less of future generations. They would expect no less of you. To go back in thought or discussion to first principles requires us to make principled arguments and ground our opinions in ideas of enduring value. It is what citizenship in a free society is all about.

Critical Thinking Exercise #1

LIBERTY V. ORDER

One of the most enduring and important challenges in our constitutional system of government is how to balance order with liberty. Today, this challenge is focused on the issue of crime. Violent crime is widespread in the nation's inner cities, but few areas of our society feel safe. Violence even has become a problem for our schools.

Recently, in response to the crime problem in a housing project of one of the nation's largest cities, officials in that city proposed large-scale police "sweeps" of apartments to search for illegal weapons. These searches would not use a search warrant or provide evidence of probable cause. After a judge struck down the proposal as an unconstitutional violation of the Fourth Amendment, the city then proposed a new policy: requiring prospective tenants in public housing projects to waive their Fourth Amendment rights as a condition of their leases.

Critics of this proposal doubt its constitutionality and worry about the consequences of a policy that would require a citizen to give up any of the liberties protected by the Bill of Rights. Those supporting the proposal point to the dangerous conditions that such tenants must live in. What's the point of worrying about procedural rights in a world that has, in effect, become a lawless state? Government's first obligation, they say, is to provide the security of an orderly society.

What is your position on this issue? Justify it in terms of the situation itself and in terms of constitutional principles.

1. How do the following statements apply to this situation? What principles and ideals are implied in each statement? How, if at all, do these principles conflict with each other?

    a. "The right of the people to be secure in their persons, houses, papers, and effects, against unreasonable searches and seizures, shall not be violated, and no warrants shall issue, but upon probable cause…" Fourth Amendment

    b. "The good of the people is the highest law." Cicero

    c. "Authority without wisdom is like a heavy axe without an edge, fitter to bruise than polish." Anne Bradstreet

    d. "For a man's house is his castle." Edward Coke

    e. "They that can give up essential liberty to obtain a little temporary safety deserve neither liberty nor safety." Benjamin Franklin

    f. "Since the general civilization of mankind, I believe there are more instances of the abridgment of the freedom of the people by gradual and silent encroachments of those in power, than by violent and sudden usurpation." James Madison

    g. "Every successful revolution puts on in time the robe of the tyrant it has deposed." Barbara Tuchman

    h. "Liberty, too, must be limited in order to be possessed." Edmund Burke

    i. "The great and chief end, therefore, of men's uniting into Commonwealths, and putting themselves under Government, is the preservation of property [i.e., life, liberty, and estate]." John Locke

2. Which, if any, of these statements do you find most persuasive? Why?

3. What is your position on this issue? Explain the reasons for your position in terms of the situation itself and in terms of the principles involved.

Critical Thinking Exercise #2

RIGHTS OF THE ACCUSED

Americans are worried about the drug problem. A recent poll indicated that a substantial percentage of American citizens would be willing to give up some protections of the Bill of Rights in order to control illegal drug use.

Several years ago Congress passed a law authorizing federal authorities to confiscate the property of individuals suspected of trafficking in drugs. Such property could be seized on mere suspicion. Individuals whose property had been seized could appeal and seek a return of their property, but the burden of proof rested on them to prove their innocence.

Advocates of this law argued its constitutionality on the grounds that the government was not acting against the suspected individuals, only against their property. Since only individuals, and not property, enjoy the protection of the Bill of Rights, they said, the law did not violate the Constitution.

Since going into effect the law has proved controversial. Congress may repeal it. Do you think it should be repealed? Even if the constitutionality of such a law is upheld, should the government have such power? How would you determine the circumstances in which protections guaranteed by the Constitution should be curtailed by the government?

1. How do the following statements apply to this situation? What principles and ideals are implied in each statement? How, if at all, do these principles conflict with each other?

    a. "No person shall be...deprived of life, liberty, or property, without due process of law...." Fifth Amendment

    b. "It is better that ten guilty persons escape than one innocent person suffer." William Blackstone

    c. "Man's capacity for justice makes democracy possible, but man's inclination to injustice makes democracy necessary." Reinhold Niebuhr

---

d. "The mood and temper of the public in the treatment of crime and criminals is one of the most unfailing tests of civilization of any country." Winston Churchill

2. Which, if any, of these statements do you find most persuasive? Why?

3. What is your position on this issue? Explain the reasons for your position in terms of the situation itself and in terms of the principles involved.

Critical Thinking Exercise #3

UNITY V. DIVERSITY

Is a common language essential to the survival of American democracy? One of the most controversial aspects of diversity in America has to do with language. Throughout our history English has been the principal language of the country. For millions of immigrants, learning English was an important first step to becoming a U.S. citizen.

Schools must teach immigrant children who speak languages other than English. Educators differ about how best to accomplish their tasks. Moreover, a large percentage of recent immigrants use Spanish as their first language. In certain areas of the country Spanish is as commonly spoken as English. We are becoming, many believe, a bilingual nation.

1. How do the following statements apply to this situation? What principles and ideals are implied in each statement? How, if at all, do these principles conflict with each other?

    a. "America is God's crucible, the great melting pot where all the races of Europe are melting and re-forming!" Israel Zangwell

    b. "Immigrants are not refuse; rather, they are the sinew and bone of all nations.... Education is the essence of American opportunity, the treasure that no thief could touch, not even misfortune or poverty." Mary Antin

    c. "Our political harmony is therefore concerned in a uniformity of language." Noah Webster

    d. "We have room for but one language here, and that is the English language, and we intend to see that the crucible turns our people out as Americans, and not as dwellers of a polyglot boarding-house." Theodore Roosevelt

    e. "In world history, those who have helped to build the same culture are not necessarily of one race, and those of the same race have not all participated in one culture." Ruth Fulton Benedict

f. "We have become not a melting pot but a beautiful mosaic. Different people, different beliefs, different yearnings, different hopes, different dreams." Jimmy Carter

g. "America is not a melting pot. It is a sizzling cauldron." Barbara Mikulski

i. "Unless you speak English and read well, you'll never become a first-class citizen…but when you say 'official', that becomes a racial slur." Barbara Bush

j. "The individual…does not exist for the State, nor for that abstraction called 'society,' or the 'nation,' which is only a collection of individuals." Emma Goldman

2. Which, if any, of these statements do you find most persuasive? Why?

3. Is a common language necessary to American citizenship? Explain your position in terms of the principles involved.

Critical Thinking Skill #4

INDIVIDUAL RIGHTS V. THE SOVEREIGNTY OF THE PEOPLE

One of the great conflicts of principles you have encountered in reading this text is that which exists between fundamental rights on the one hand and sovereign power on the other. This conflict was an important factor in the American Revolution and in the Civil War. A fundamental right, as you remember, is one that cannot be revised or taken away by any power. Sovereignty is that power within a state beyond which there is no appeal—whoever has the sovereign power has the final say.

In 1990 the Supreme Court ruled in *Texas v. Johnson* that the burning of an American flag as a political protest, however distasteful an act to many Americans, was protected under the free speech provision of the First Amendment. The Court's decision prompted demands for a constitutional amendment prohibiting the desecration of "Old Glory." President George Bush publicly endorsed such an amendment.

Were the proposed amendment adopted, it would have added to the Constitution for the first time the prohibition of a particular form of expression. It would also have represented a limitation on one of the essential freedoms guaranteed in the Bill of Rights.

This incident reminds us that it is within the sovereign authority of the American people to revise or abolish entirely the Bill of Rights. What do you think the incident suggests about the protection of rights in a constitutional democracy? Does it suggest that the theory of fundamental rights is irrelevant? What does it suggest about the relevance of the natural rights philosophy?

1. How do the following statements apply to this situation? What principles and ideals are implied in each statement? How, if at all, do these principles conflict with each other?

a. "We the People of the United States…do ordain and establish this Constitution…." Preamble to the Constitution

b. "Congress shall make no law…abridging the freedom of speech." First Amendment

c. "All lawful authority, legislative, and executive, originates from the people. Power in the people is like light in the sun, native, original, inherent, and unlimited by any thing human." James Burgh

d. "No written law has ever been more binding than unwritten custom supported by popular opinion." Carrie Chapman Catt

e. "You have rights antecedent to all earthly governments; rights that cannot be repealed or restrained by human law; rights derived from the Great Legislator of the Universe." John Adams

f. "The people made the Constitution and the people can unmake it. It is the creature of their own will, and lives only by their will." John Marshall

g. "…No one cause is left but the most ancient of all, the one, in fact, that from the beginning of our history has determined the very existence of politics, the cause of freedom versus tyranny." Hannah Arendt

h. "When I refuse to obey an unjust law, I do not contest the right of the majority to command, but I simply appeal from the sovereignty of the people to the sovereignty of mankind." Alexis de Tocqueville

2. Which, if any, of these statements do you find most persuasive? Why?

3. What is your position on this issue? Explain the reasons for your position in terms of the situation itself and in terms of the principles involved.

Critical Thinking Exercise #5

THE DANGERS AND BENEFITS OF ENERGETIC GOVERNMENT

One of the major issues of the 1990s is health care reform. In addition to the many, complex aspects of health care itself, there also is a constitutional aspect to this issue: the benefits and dangers of government power. A national health care plan would mean a substantial expansion of the federal government's involvement in the private sector. Health care services now comprise about one-seventh of the nation's economy.

Advocates of comprehensive health care reform argue the need for government to take charge of what has become a serious problem in contemporary America. They would point to precedents such as the Social Security System, that was created in 1935 as part of the New Deal. Critics of a national health care plan, on the other hand, express concern about any substantial increase in government bureaucracy. A national health care system administered by the government, they believe, constitutes a potential threat to individual liberty.

With the complexities and demands of modern American society, what are the proper limits to an energetic government? What criteria should the citizen employ in evaluating the benefits and dangers of government regulation?

1. How do the following statements apply to this situation? What principles and ideals are implied in each statement? How, if at all, do these principles conflict with each other?

   a. "…[to] promote the general Welfare." Preamble to the Constitution

   b. "To make all Laws which are necessary and proper for carrying into Execution the foregoing Powers." Constitution, Article I, Sec. 7

   c. "If, my countrymen, you wait for a constitution which absolutely bars a power of doing evil, you must wait long, and when obtained it will have no power of doing good." Oliver Ellsworth

   d. "A government ought to contain in itself every power requisite to the full accomplishment of the objects committed to its care, and to the complete execution of the trusts for which it is responsible, free from every other control, but a regard to the public good and to the sense of the people." Alexander Hamilton

   e. "I own I am not a friend to a very energetic government. It is always oppressive." Thomas Jefferson

2. With the complexities and demands of modern American society, what are the proper limits to an energetic government?

3. Which, if any, of these statements do you find most persuasive? Why?

4. What is your position on this issue? Explain the reasons for your position in terms of the situation itself and in terms of the principles involved.

Critical Thinking Exercise #6

CAPITAL PUNISHMENT AND THE CONSTITUTION

With the exception of the issue of separation of church and state, no issue has focused so sharply the question of constitutional interpretation and the role of the judiciary in making such interpretation as the death penalty. Shortly before his retirement in 1994, Justice Harry Blackmun announced that he would no longer vote in favor of implementation of the death penalty. While he did not exactly say that capital punishment was unconstitutional, his remarks suggested that because the death penalty had become so repugnant to him, he would no longer have anything to do with its enforcement.

Justice Blackmun's remarks were controversial, in part because of the strong opinions on the death penalty issue in the United States. They also were controversial because of what they suggested about how the words of the Constitution should be interpreted and the degree to which a judge's subjectivity should influence that interpretation.

Is the death penalty constitutional? Its opponents say no. They maintain that the penalty itself violates the "cruel and unusual punishment" of the Eighth Amendment—both the manner of taking life and the long delays that usually accompany it. Opponents also have argued that implementation of capital punishment violates the equal protection clause of the Fourteenth Amendment, since its application falls disproportionately on the poor and minorities.

Other citizens, including some who are opposed to the death penalty as a policy, say it is constitutional. The text of the Constitution, they argue, makes clear that the Framers clearly intended to allow for capital punishment. It is up to the people through their representatives—and not to judges—to decide on whether or not to employ this option.

If you were a justice on the Supreme Court, how would you approach this issue? What outlook and criteria would you use to interpret the words of the Framers? What would you consider to be the proper role of judges in addressing this issue? Would you take a different position if you were a legislator?

1. How do the following statements apply to this situation? What principles and ideals are implied in each statement? How, if at all, do these principles conflict with each other?

    a. "…nor cruel and unusual punishments inflicted." Eighth Amendment

    b. "No punishment has ever possessed enough power of deterrence to prevent the commission of crimes." Hannah Arendt

    c. "No person shall be…deprived of life, liberty, or property, without due process of law…" Fifth Amendment

    d. "Then thou shall give for a life, eye for eye, tooth for tooth…." *Exodus*, 21:23-24

    e. "Thou shalt not kill" *Exodus*, 20:13

2. What is the difference between the constitutional principles, a and c, and the passages from the Bible, d and e? What is it about these ideas that allows people to reach opposing points of view? Because something is legal, does that make it moral?

3. Which, if any, of these statements do you find most persuasive? Why?

4. What is your position on this issue? Explain the reasons for your position in terms of the situation itself and in terms of the principles involved.

Postscript

"Our Constitution is a covenant running from the first generation of Americans to us and then to future generations. It is a coherent succession. Each generation must learn anew that the Constitution's written terms embody ideas and aspirations that must survive more ages than one."

Justices O'Connor, Kennedy, and Souter

REFERENCE SECTION

Virginia Declaration of Rights

June 12, 1776

A **DECLARATION OF RIGHTS** made by the Representatives of the good people of VIRGINIA, assembled in full and free Convention; which rights do pertain to them and their posterity, as the basis and foundation of Government.

1. That all men are by nature equally free and independent, and have certain inherent rights, of which, when they enter into a state of society, they cannot, by any compact, deprive or divest their posterity; namely, the enjoyment of life and liberty, with the means of acquiring and possessing property, and pursuing and obtaining happiness and safety.

2. That all power is vested in, and consequently derived from, the People; that magistrates are their trustees and servants, and at all times amenable to them.

3. That Government is, or ought to be, instituted for the common benefit, protection, and security of the people, nation, or community;—of all the various modes and forms of Government that is best which is capable of producing the greatest degree of happiness and safety, and is most effectually secured against the danger of mal-administration;—and that, whenever any Government shall be found inadequate or contrary to these purposes, a majority of the community hath an indubitable, unalienable, and indefeasible right, to reform, alter, or abolish it, in such manner as shall be judged most conducive to the publick weal.

4. That no man, or set of men, are entitled to exclusive or separate emoluments and privileges from the community, but in consideration of publick services; which, not being descendible, neither ought the offices of Magistrate, Legislator, or Judge, to be hereditary.

5. That the Legislative and Executive powers of the State should be separate and distinct from the Judicative; and, that the members of the two first may be restrained from oppression, by feeling and participating the burdens of the people, they should, at fixed periods, be reduced to a private station, return into that body from which they were originally taken, and the vacancies be supplied by frequent, certain, and regular elections, in which all, or any part of the former members, to be again eligible, or ineligible, as the law shall direct.

6. That elections of members to serve as Representatives of the people, in Assembly, ought to be free; and that all men, having sufficient evidence of permanent common interest with, and attachment to, the community, have the right of suffrage, and cannot be taxed or deprived of their property for publick uses without their own consent or that of their Representative so elected, nor bound by any law to which they have not, in like manner, assented, for the publick good.

7. That all power of suspending laws, or the execution of laws, by any authority, without consent of the Representatives of the people, is injurious to their rights, and ought not to be exercised.

8. That in all capital or criminal prosecutions a man hath a right to demand the cause and nature of his accusation, to be confronted with the accusers and witnesses, to call for evidence in his favour, and to a speedy trial by an impartial jury of his vicinage, without whose unanimous consent he cannot be found guilty, nor can he be compelled to give evidence against himself; that no man be deprived of his liberty except by the law of the land, or the judgment of his peers.

9. That excessive bail ought not to be required, nor excessive fines imposed, nor cruel and unusual punishments inflicted.

10. That general warrants, whereby any officer or messenger may be commanded to search suspected places without evidence of a fact committed, or to seize any person or persons not named, or whose offence is not particularly described and supported by evidence, are grievous and oppressive, and ought not to be granted.

11. That in controversies respecting property, and in suits between man and man, the ancient trial by Jury is preferable to any other, and ought to be held sacred.

12. That the freedom of the Press is one of the greatest bulwarks of liberty, and can never be restrained but by despotick Governments.

13. That a well-regulated Militia, composed of the body of the people, trained to arms, is the proper, natural, and safe defence of a free State; that Standing Armies, in time

of peace, should be avoided as dangerous to liberty; and that, in all cases, the military should be under strict subordination to, and governed by, the civil power.

14. That the people have a right to uniform Government; and, therefore, that no Government separate from, or independent of, the Government of Virginia, ought to be erected or established within the limits thereof.

15. That no free Government, or the blessing of liberty, can be preserved to any people but by a firm adherence to justice, moderation, temperance, frugality, and virtue, and by frequent recurrence to fundamental principles.

16. That Religion, or the duty which we owe to our Creator, and the manner of discharging it, can be directed only by reason and conviction, not by force or violence; and, therefore, all men are equally entitled to the free exercise of religion, according to the dictates of conscience; and that it is the mutual duty of all to practice Christian forbearance, love, and charity, towards each other.

Declaration of Independence

IN CONGRESS JULY 4, 1776.

A DECLARATION

BY THE REPRESENTATIVES OF THE

UNITED STATES OF AMERICA,

IN GENERAL CONGRESS ASSEMBLED

WHEN in the Course of human Events, it becomes necessary for one People to dissolve the Political Bands which have connected them with another, and to assume among the Powers of the Earth, the separate and equal Station to which the Laws of Nature and of Nature's God entitle them, a decent Respect to the Opinions of Mankind requires that they should declare the causes which impel them to the Separation.

We hold these Truths to be self-evident, that all Men are created equal, that they are endowed by their Creator with certain unalienable Rights, that among these are Life, Liberty, and the Pursuit of Happiness—That to secure these Rights, Governments are instituted among Men, deriving their just Powers from the Consent of the Governed, that whenever any Form of Government becomes destructive of these Ends it is the Right of the People to alter or to abolish it, and to institute new Government, laying its Foundation on such Principles, and organizing its Powers in such Form, as to them shall seem most likely to effect their Safety and Happiness. Prudence, indeed, will dictate that Governments long established should not be changed for light and transient Causes; and accordingly all Experience hath shewn, that Mankind are more disposed to suffer, while Evils are sufferable, than to right themselves by abolishing the Forms to which they are accustomed. But when a long Train of Abuses and Usurpations, pursuing invariably the same Object, evinces a Design to reduce them under absolute Despotism, it is their Right, it is their Duty, to throw off such Government, and to provide new Guards for their future Security. Such has been the patient Sufferance of these Colonies; and such is now the Necessity which constrains them to alter their former Systems of Government. The History of the present King of Great-Britain is a History of repeated Injuries and Usurpations, all having in direct Object the Establishment of an absolute Tyranny over these States. To prove this, let Facts be submitted to a candid World.

He has refused his Assent to Laws, the most wholesome and necessary for the public Good.

He has forbidden his Governors to pass Laws of immediate and pressing Importance, unless suspended in their Operation till his Assent should be obtained; and when so suspended, he has utterly neglected to attend to them.

He has refused to pass other Laws for the Accommodation of large Districts of People, unless those People would relinquish the Right of Representation in the Legislature, a Right inestimable to them, and formidable to Tyrants only.

He has called together Legislative Bodies at Places unusual, uncomfortable, and distant from the Depository of their public Records, for the sole Purpose of fatiguing them into Compliance with his Measures.

He has dissolved Representative Houses repeatedly, for opposing with manly Firmness his Invasions on the Rights of the People.

He has refused for a long Time, after such Dissolutions, to cause others to be elected; whereby the Legislative Powers, incapable of Annihilation, have returned to the People at large for their exercise; the State remaining in the mean time exposed to all the Dangers of Invasions from without, and Convulsions within.

He has endeavored to prevent the Population of these States; for that Purpose obstructing the Laws for Naturalization of Foreigners; refusing to pass others to encourage their Migrations hither, and raising the Conditions of new Appropriations of Lands.

He has obstructed the Administration of Justice, by refusing his Assent to Laws for establishing Judiciary Powers.

He has made Judges dependent on his Will alone, for the Tenure of their Offices, and the Amount and Payment of their Salaries.

He has erected a Multitude of new Offices, and sent hither Swarms of Officers to harass our People and eat out their Substance.

He has kept among us, in Times of Peace, Standing Armies, without the consent of our Legislatures.

He has affected to render the Military independent of and superior to the Civil Power.

He has combined with others to subject us to a Jurisdiction foreign to our Constitution, and unacknowledged by our Laws; giving his Assent to their Acts of pretended Legislation:

For quartering large Bodies of Armed Troops among us:

For protecting them, by a mock Trial, from Punishment for any Murders which they should commit on the Inhabitants of these States:

For cutting off our Trade with all Parts of the World:

For imposing Taxes on us without our Consent:

For depriving us, in many Cases, of the Benefits of Trial by Jury:

For transporting us beyond Seas to be tried for pretended Offenses:

For abolishing the free System of English Laws in a neighbouring Province, establishing therein an Arbitrary Government, and enlarging its Boundaries, so as to render it at once an Example and fit Instrument for introducing the same absolute Rule into these Colonies:

For taking away our Charters, abolishing our most valuable Laws, and altering fundamentally the Forms of our Governments:

For suspending our own Legislatures, and declaring themselves invested with Power to legislate for us in all Cases whatsoever.

He has abdicated Government here, by declaring us out of his Protection and waging War against us.

He has plundered our Seas, ravaged our Coasts, burnt our Towns, and destroyed the Lives of our People.

He is, at this Time, transporting large Armies of foreign Mercenaries to compleat the Works of Death, Desolation, and Tyranny, already begun with circumstances of Cruelty and Perfidy, scarcely paralleled in the most barbarous Ages, and totally unworthy the Head of a civilized Nation.

He has constrained our fellow Citizens taken Captive on the high Seas to bear Arms against their Country, to become the Executioners of their Friends and Brethren, or to fall themselves by their Hands.

He has excited domestic Insurrections amongst us, and has endeavoured to bring on the Inhabitants of our Frontiers, the merciless Indian Savages, whose known Rule of Warfare, is an undistinguished Destruction, of all Ages, Sexes and Conditions.

In every stage of these Oppressions we have Petitioned for Redress in the most humble Terms: Our repeated Petitions have been answered only by repeated Injury. A Prince, whose Character is thus marked by every act which may define a Tyrant, is unfit to be the Ruler of a free People.

Nor have we been wanting in Attentions to our British Brethren. We have warned them from Time to Time of Attempts by their Legislature to extend an unwarrantable Jurisdiction over us. We have reminded them of the Circumstances of our Emigration and Settlement here. We have appealed to their native Justice and Magnanimity, and we have conjured them by the Ties of our common Kindred to disavow these Usurpations, which, would inevitably interrupt our Connections and Correspondence. They too have been deaf to the Voice of Justice and of Consanguinity. We must, therefore, acquiesce in the Necessity, which denounces our Separation, and hold them, as we hold the rest of Mankind, Enemies in War, in Peace, Friends.

We, therefore, the Representatives of the UNITED STATES OF AMERICA, in GENERAL CONGRESS, Assembled, appealing to the Supreme Judge of the World for the Rectitude of our Intentions, do, in the Name, and by Authority of the good People of these Colonies, solemnly Publish and Declare, That these United Colonies are, and of Right ought to be, FREE AND INDEPENDENT STATES; that they are absolved from all Allegiance to the British Crown, and that all political Connection between them and the State of Great-Britain, is and ought to be totally dissolved; and that as FREE AND INDEPENDENT STATES, they have full Power to levy War, conclude Peace, contract Alliances, establish Commerce, and to do all other Acts and Things which INDEPENDENT STATES may of right do. And for the support of this Declaration, with a firm Reliance on the Protection of divine Providence, we mutually pledge to each other our Lives, our Fortunes, and our sacred Honor.

Signed by ORDER and in BEHALF of the CONGRESS,

JOHN HANCOCK, PRESIDENT.

Signers of the Declaration of Independence

New-Hampshire
Josiah Bartlett,
Wm. Whipple,
Matthew Thornton.

Massachusetts-Bay
Saml. Adams,
John Adams,
Robt. Treat Paine,
Elbridge Gerry.

Rhode-Island and Providence, &c.
Step. Hopkins,
William Ellery.

Connecticut
Roger Sherman,
Saml. Huntington,
Wm. Williams,
Oliver Wolcott.

New-York
Wm. Floyd,
Phil. Livingston,
Frans. Lewis,
Lewis Morris.

New-Jersey
Richd. Stockton,
Jno. Witherspoon,
Fras. Hopkinson,
John Hart,
Abra. Clark.

Pennsylvania
Robt. Morris,
Benjamin Rush,
Benja. Franklin,
John Morton,
Geo. Clymer,
Jas. Smith,
Geo. Taylor,
James Wilson,
Geo. Ross.

Delaware
Casar Rodney,
Geo. Read,
(Tho M:Kean.)

Maryland
Samuel Chase,
Wm. Paca,
Thos. Stone,
Charles Carroll, of Carrollton.

Virginia
George Wythe,
Richard Henry Lee,
Ths. Jefferson,
Benja. Harrison,
Thos. Nelson, jr.
Francis Lightfoot Lee,
Carter Braxton.

North-Carolina.
Wm. Hooper
Joseph Hewes,
John Penn.

South-Carolina.
Edward Rutledge,
Thos. Heyward, junr.
Thomas Lynch, junr.
Arthur Middleton.

Georgia.
Button Gwinnett,
Lyman Hall,
Geo. Walton.

According to the authenticated list printed by order of Congress of January 18, 1777.
Braces, spelling, and abbreviations of names conform to original printed list.

The Articles of Confederation

Agreed to by Congress November 15, 1777;
ratified and in force, March 1, 1781

TO ALL TO WHOM these Presents shall come, we the undersigned Delegates of the States affixed to our Names send greeting. Whereas the Delegates of the United States of America in Congress assembled did on the fifteenth day of November in the Year of our Lord One Thousand Seven Hundred and Seventy seven, and in the Second Year of the Independence of America agree to certain articles of Confederation and perpetual Union between the States of Newhampshire, Massachusetts-bay, Rhodeisland and Providence Plantations, Connecticut, New York, New Jersey, Pennsylvania, Delaware, Maryland, Virginia, North-Carolina, South Carolina and Georgia in the Words following, viz. "Articles of Confederation and perpetual Union between the states of Newhampshire, Massachusetts-bay, Rhodeisland and Providence Plantations, Connecticut, New-York, New-Jersey, Pennsylvania, Delaware, Maryland, Virginia, North-Carolina, South-Carolina and Georgia.

Art. I. The Stile of this confederacy shall be "The United States of America."

Art. II. Each state retains its sovereignty, freedom and independence, and every Power, Jurisdiction and right, which is not by this confederation expressly delegated to the United States, in Congress assembled.

Art. III. The said states hereby severally enter into a firm league of friendship with each other, for their common defence, the security of their Liberties, and their mutual and general welfare, binding themselves to assist each other, against all force offered to, or attacks made upon them, or any of them, on account of religion, sovereignty, trade, or any other pretence whatever.

Art. IV. The better to secure and perpetuate mutual friendship and intercourse among the people of the different states in this union, the free inhabitants of each of these states, paupers, vagabonds and fugitives from Justice excepted, shall be entitled to all privileges and immunities of free citizens in the several states; and the people of each state shall have free ingress and regress to and from any other state, and shall enjoy therein all the privileges of trade and commerce, subject to the same duties, impositions and restrictions as the inhabitants thereof respectively, provided that such restriction shall not extend so far as to prevent the removal of property imported into any state, to any other state of which the Owner is an inhabitant; provided also that no imposition, duties or restriction shall be laid by any state, on the property of the united states, or either of them.

If any Person guilty of, or charged with treason, felony, or other high misdemeanor in any state, shall flee from Justice, and be found in any of the united states, he shall upon demand of the Governor or executive power, of the state from which he fled, be delivered up and removed to the state having jurisdiction of his offence.

Full faith and credit shall be given in each of these states to the records, acts and judicial proceedings of the courts and magistrates of every other state.

Art. V. For the more convenient management of the general interests of the united states, delegates shall be annually appointed in such manner as the legislature of each state shall direct, to meet in Congress on the first Monday in November, in every year, with a power reserved to each state, to recal its delegates, or any of them, at any time within the year, and to send others in their stead, for the remainder of the Year.

No state shall be represented in Congress by less than two, nor by more than seven Members; and no person shall be capable of being a delegate for more than three years in any term of six years; nor shall any person, being a delegate, be capable of holding any office under the united states, for which he, or another for his benefit receives any salary, fees or emolument of any kind.

Each state shall maintain its own delegates in a meeting of the states, and while they act as members of the committee of the states.

In determining questions in the united states, in Congress assembled, each state shall have one vote.

Freedom of speech and debate in Congress shall not be impeached or questioned in any Court, or place out of Congress, and the members of congress shall be protected in their persons from arrests and imprisonments, during the time of their going to and from, and attendance on congress, except for treason, felony, or breach of the peace.

Art. VI. No state without the Consent of the united states in congress assembled, shall send any embassy to, or receive any embassy from, or enter into any conference, agreement, or alliance or treaty with any King, prince or state; nor shall any person holding any office of profit or trust under the united states, or any of them, accept of any present, emolument, office or title of any kind whatever from any king, prince or foreign state; nor shall the united states in congress assembled, or any of them, grant any title of nobility.

No two or more states shall enter into any treaty, confederation or alliance whatever between them, without the consent of the united states in congress assembled, specifying accurately the purposes for which the same is to be entered into, and how long it shall continue.

No state shall lay any imposts or duties, which may interfere with any stipulations in treaties, entered into by the united states in congress assembled, with any king, prince or state, in pursuance of any treaties already proposed by congress, to the courts of France and Spain.

No vessels of war shall be kept up in time of peace by any state, except such number only, as shall be deemed necessary by the united states in congress assembled, for the defence of such state, or its trade; nor shall any body of forces be kept up by any state, in time of peace, except such number only, as in the judgment of the united states, in congress assembled, shall be deemed requisite to garrison the forts necessary for the defence of such state; but every state shall always keep up a well regulated and disciplined militia, sufficiently armed and accoutred, and shall provide and constantly have ready for use, in public stores, a due number of field pieces and tents, and a proper quantity of arms, ammunition and camp equipage.

No state shall engage in any war without the consent of the united states in congress assembled, unless such state be actually invaded by enemies, or shall have received certain advice of a resolution being formed by some nation of Indians to invade such state, and the danger is so imminent as not to admit of a delay, till the united states in congress assembled can be consulted: nor shall any state grant commissions to any ships or vessels of war, nor letters of marque or reprisal, except it be after a declaration of war by the united states in congress assembled, and then only against the kingdom or state and the subjects thereof, against which war has been so declared, and under such regulations as shall be established by the united states in congress assembled, unless such state be infested by pirates, in which case vessels of war may be fitted out for that occasion, and kept so long as the danger shall continue, or until the united states in congress assembled shall determine otherwise.

Art. VII. When land-forces are raised by any state for the common defence, all officers of or under the rank of colonel, shall be appointed by the legislature of each state respectively by whom such forces shall be raised, or in such manner as such state shall direct, and all vacancies shall be filled up by the state which first made the appointment.

Art. VIII. All charges of war, and all other expences that shall be incurred for the common defence or general welfare, and allowed by the united states in congress assembled, shall be defrayed out of a common treasury, which shall be supplied by the several states, in proportion to the value of all land within each state, granted to or surveyed for any Person, as such land and the buildings and improvements thereon shall be estimated according to such mode as the united states in congress assembled, shall from time to time direct and appoint. The taxes for paying that proportion shall be laid and levied by the authority and direction of the legislatures of the several states within the time agreed upon by the united states in congress assembled.

Art. IX. The united states in congress assembled, shall have the sole and exclusive right and power of determining on peace and war, except in the cases mentioned in the sixth article—of sending and receiving ambassadors—entering into treaties and alliances, provided that no treaty of commerce shall be made whereby the legislative power of the respective states shall be restrained from imposing such imposts and duties on foreigners, as their own people are subjected to, or from prohibiting the exportation or importation of any species of goods or commodities whatsoever—of establishing rules for deciding in all cases, what captures on land or water shall be legal, and in what manner prizes taken by land or naval forces in the service of the united states shall be divided or appropriated—of granting letters of marque and reprisal in times of peace—appointing courts for the trial of piracies and felonies committed on the high seas and establishing courts for receiving and determining finally appeals in all cases of captures, provided that no member of congress shall be appointed a judge of any of the said courts.

The united states in congress assembled shall also be the last resort on appeal in all disputes and differences now subsisting or that hereafter may arise between two or more states concerning boundary, jurisdiction or any other cause whatever; which authority shall always be exercised in the manner following. Whenever the legislative or executive authority or lawful agent of any state in controversy with another shall present a petition to congress, stating the matter in question and praying for a hearing, notice thereof shall be given by order of congress to the legislative or executive authority of the other state in controversy, and a day assigned for the appearance of the parties by their lawful agents, who shall then be directed to appoint by joint consent, commissioners or judges to constitute a court for hearing and determining the matter in question: but if they cannot agree, congress shall name three persons out of each of the united states, and from the list of such persons each party shall alternately strike out one, the petitioners beginning, until the number shall be reduced to thirteen; and from that number not less than seven, nor more than nine names as congress shall direct, shall in the presence of congress be drawn out by lot, and the persons whose names shall be so drawn or any five of them, shall be commissioners or judges, to hear and finally determine the controversy, so always as a major part of the judges who shall hear the cause shall agree in the determination: and if either party shall neglect to attend at the day appointed, without shewing reasons, which congress shall judge sufficient, or being present shall refuse to strike, the congress shall proceed to nominate three persons out of each state, and the secretary of congress shall strike in behalf of such party absent or refusing; and the judgment and sentence of the court to be appointed, in the manner before prescribed, shall be final and conclusive; and if any of the parties shall refuse to submit to the authority of such court, or to appear to defend their claim or cause, the court shall nevertheless proceed to pronounce sentence, or judgment, which shall in like manner be final and decisive, the judgment or sentence and other proceedings being in either case transmitted to congress, and lodged among the acts of congress for the security of the parties concerned: provided that every commissioner, before he sits in judgment, shall take an oath to be administered by one of the judges of the supreme or superior court of the state, where the cause shall be tried, "well and truly to hear and determine the matter in question, according to the best of his judgment, without favour, affection or hope of reward:" provided also that no state shall be deprived of territory for the benefit of the united states.

All controversies concerning the private right of soil claimed under different grants of two or more states, whose jurisdictions as they may respect such lands, and the states which passed such grants are adjusted, the said grants or either of them being at the same time claimed to have originated antecedent to such settlement of jurisdiction, shall on the petition of either party to the congress of the united states, be finally determined as near as may be in the same manner as is before prescribed for deciding disputes respecting territorial jurisdiction between different states.

The united states in congress assembled shall also have the sole and exclusive right and power of regulating the alloy and value of coin struck by their own authority, or by that of the respective states—fixing the standard of weights and measures throughout the united states—regulating the trade and managing all affairs with the Indians, not members of any of the states,

provided that the legislative right of any state within its own limits be not infringed or violated—establishing and regulating post-offices from one state to another throughout all the united states, and exacting such postage on the papers passing thro' the same as may be requisite to defray the expences of the said office—appointing all officers of the land forces, in the service of the united states, excepting regimental officers.—appointing all the officers of the naval forces, and commissioning all officers whatever in the service of the united states—making rules for the government and regulation of the said land and naval forces, and directing their operations.

The united states in congress assembled shall have authority to appoint a committee, to sit in the recess of congress, to be denominated "A Committee of the States," and to consist of one delegate from each state; and to appoint such other committees and civil officers as may be necessary for managing the general affairs of the united states under their direction—to appoint one of their number to preside, provided that no person be allowed to serve in the office of president more than one year in any term of three years; to ascertain the necessary sums of Money to be raised for the service of the united states, and to appropriate and apply the same for defraying the public expences—to borrow money, or emit bills on the credit of the united states, transmitting every half year to the respective states an account of the sums of money so borrowed or emitted,—to build and equip a navy—to agree upon the number of land forces, and to make requisitions from each state for its quota, in proportion to the number of white inhabitants in such state; which requisition shall be binding, and thereupon the legislature of each state shall appoint the regimental officers, raise the men and cloath, arm and equip them in a soldier like manner, at the expence of the united states, and the officers and men so cloathed, armed and equipped shall march to the place appointed, and within the time agreed on by the united states in congress assembled: But if the united states in congress assembled shall, on consideration of circumstances judge proper that any state should not raise men, or should raise a smaller number than its quota, and that any other state should raise a greater number of men than the quota thereof, such extra number shall be raised, officered, cloathed, armed and equipped in the same manner as the quota of such state, unless the legislature of such state shall judge that such extra number cannot be safely spared out of the same, in which case they shall raise officer, cloath, arm and equip as many of such extra number as they judge can be safely spared. And the officers and men so cloathed, armed and equipped, shall march to the place appointed, and within the time agreed on by the united states in congress assembled.

The united states in congress assembled shall never engage in a war, nor grant letters of marque and reprisal in time of peace, nor enter into any treaties or alliances, nor coin money, nor regulate the value thereof, nor ascertain the sums and expences necessary for the defence and welfare of the united states, or any of them, nor emit bills, nor borrow money on the credit of the united states, nor appropriate money, nor agree upon the number of vessels of war, to be built or purchased, or the number of land or sea forces to be raised, nor appoint a commander in chief of the army or navy, unless nine states assent to the same: nor shall a question on any other point, except for adjourning from day to day be determined unless by the votes of a majority of the united states in congress assembled.

The Congress of the United States shall have power to adjourn to any time within the year, and to any place within the united states, so that no period of adjournment be for a longer duration than the space of six Months, and shall publish the Journal of their proceedings monthly, except such parts thereof relating to treaties, alliances or military operations as in their judgement require secresy; and the yeas and nays of the delegates of each state on any question shall be entered on the Journal, when it is desired by any delegate; and the delegates of a state, or any of them, at his or their request shall be furnished with a transcript of the said Journal, except such parts as are above excepted, to lay before the legislatures of the several states.

Art. X. The committee of the states, or any nine of them, shall be authorized to execute, in the recess of congress, such of the powers of congress as the United States in congress assembled, by the consent of nine states, shall from time to time think expedient to vest them with; provided that no power be delegated to the said committee, for the exercise of which, by the articles of confederation, the voice of nine states in the congress of the united states assembled is requisite.

Art. XI. Canada acceding to this confederation, and joining in the measures of the united states, shall be admitted into, and entitled to all the advantages of this union: but no other colony shall be admitted into the same, unless such admission be agreed to by nine states.

Art. XII. All bills of credit emitted, monies borrowed and debts contracted by, or under the authority of congress, before the assembling of the united states, in pursuance of the present confederation, shall be deemed and considered as a charge against the united states, for payment and satisfaction whereof the said united states, and the public faith are hereby solemnly pledged.

Art. XIII. Every state shall abide by the determinations of the united states in congress assembled, on all questions which by this confederation are submitted to them. And the Articles of this confederation shall be inviolably observed by every state, and the union shall be perpetual; nor shall any alteration at any time hereafter be made in any of them; unless such alteration be agreed to in a congress of the united states, and be afterwards confirmed by the legislatures of every state.

AND WHEREAS it hath pleased the Great Governor of the World to incline the hearts of the legislatures we respectively represent in congress, to approve of, and to authorize us to ratify the said articles of confederation and perpetual union. KNOW YE that we the under-signed delegates, by virtue of the power and authority to us given for that purpose, do by these presents, in the name and in behalf of our respective constituents, fully and entirely ratify and confirm each and every of the said articles of confederation and perpetual union, and all and singular the matters and things therein contained: And we do further solemnly plight and engage the faith of our respective constituents, that they shall abide by the determinations of the united states in congress assembled, on all questions, which by the said confederation are submitted to them. And that the articles thereof shall be inviolably observed by the states we respectively represent, and that the union shall be perpetual. In Witness whereof we have hereunto set our hands in Congress. Done at Philadelphia in the state of Pennsylvania the ninth Day of July in the Year of our Lord one Thousand seven Hundred and Seventy-eight, and in the third year of the independence of America.

Signers of the Articles of Confederation

Josiah Bartlett
John Wentworth, junr
August 8th 1778
On the part & behalf of the State of New Hampshire

John Hancock
Samuel Adams
Elbridge Gerry
Francis Dana
James Lovell
Samuel Holten
On the part and behalf of The State of Massachusetts Bay

William Ellery
Henry Marchant
John Collins
On the part and behalf of the State of Rhode-Island and Providence Plantations

Roger Sherman
Samuel Huntington
Oliver Wolcott
Titus Hosmer
Andrew Adams
On the part and behalf of the State of Connecticut

Jas Duane
Fras Lewis
Wm Duer
Gouvr Morris
On the Part and Behalf of the State of New York

Jno Witherspoon
Nathl Scudder
On the Part and in Behalf of the State of New Jersey, November 26, 1778.

Robert Morris
Daniel Roberdeau
Jon. Bayard Smith
William Clingan
Joseph Reed,
22d July 1778
On the part and behalf of the State of Pennsylvania

Thos McKean,
Feby 12d, 1779
John Dickinson,
May 5th, 1779
Nicholas Van Dyke
On the part & behalf of the State of Delaware

John Hanson,
March 1, 1781
Daniel Carroll, do
On the part and behalf of the State of Maryland

Richard Henry Lee
John Banister
Thomas Adams
Jno Harvie
Francis Lightfoot Lee
On the Part and Behalf of the State of Virginia

John Penn,
July 21st, 1778
Corns Harnett
Jno Williams
On the part and behalf of the State of North Carolina

Henry Laurens
William Henry Drayton
Jno Mathews
Richd Hutson
Thos Heywar, Junr
On the part & behalf of the State of South Carolina

Jno Walton,
24th July 1778
Edwd Telfair
Edwd Langworthy
On the part & behalf of the State of Georgia

The Constitution of the United States of America

PREAMBLE

We the People of the United States, in Order to form a more perfect Union, establish Justice, insure domestic Tranquility, provide for the common defence, promote the general Welfare, and secure the Blessings of Liberty to ourselves and our Posterity, do ordain and establish this Constitution for the United States of America.

ARTICLE I

Section 1

All legislative Powers herein granted shall be vested in a Congress of the United States, which shall consist of a Senate and House of Representatives.

Section 2

1. The House of Representatives shall be composed of Members chosen every second Year by the People of the several States, and the Electors in each State shall have the Qualifications requisite for Electors of the most numerous Branch of the State Legislature.

2. No Person shall be a Representative who shall not have attained to the Age of twenty five Years, and been seven Years a Citizen of the United States, and who shall not, when elected, be an Inhabitant of that State in which he shall be chosen.

3. [Representatives and direct Taxes shall be apportioned among the several States which may be included within this Union, according to their respective Numbers, which shall be determined by adding to the whole Number of free Persons, including those bound to Service for a Term of Years, and excluding Indians not taxed, three fifths of all other Persons.]* The actual Enumeration shall be made within three Years after the first Meeting of the Congress of the United States, and within every subsequent Term of ten Years, in such Manner as they shall by Law direct. The number of Representatives shall not exceed one for every thirty Thousand, but each State shall have at Least one Representative; and until such enumeration shall be made, the State of New Hampshire shall be entitled to choose three, Massachusetts eight, Rhode-Island and Providence Plantations one, Connecticut five, New York six, New Jersey four, Pennsylvania eight, Delaware one, Maryland six, Virginia ten, North Carolina five, South Carolina five, and Georgia three.

4. When vacancies happen in the Representation from any State, the Executive Authority thereof shall issue Writs of Election to fill such Vacancies.

5. The House of Representatives shall choose their Speaker and other Officers; and shall have the sole Power of Impeachment.

Section 3

1. The Senate of the United States shall be composed of two Senators from each State, [chosen by the Legislature thereof,]** for six Years; and each Senator shall have one Vote.

2. Immediately after they shall be assembled in consequence of the first Election, they shall be divided as equally as may be into three Classes. The Seats of the Senators of the first Class shall be vacated at the Expiration of the second Year, of the second Class at the Expiration of the fourth Year, and of the third Class at the Expiration of the sixth Year, so that one third may be chosen every second Year; [and if Vacancies happen by Resignation, or otherwise, during the Recess of the Legislature of any State, the Executive thereof may make temporary Appointments until the next Meeting of the Legislature, which shall then fill such Vacancies.]***

3. No Person shall be a Senator who shall not have attained to the Age of thirty Years, and been nine Years a Citizen of the United States, and who shall not, when elected, be an inhabitant of that State for which he shall be chosen.

4. The Vice President of the United States shall be President of the Senate, but shall have no vote, unless they be equally divided.

5. The Senate shall choose their other Officers, and also a President pro tempore, in the Absence of the Vice President, or when he shall exercise the Office of President of the United States.

6. The Senate shall have the sole Power to try all Impeachments. When sitting for that Purpose, they shall be on Oath or Affirmation. When the President of the United States is tried, the Chief Justice shall preside; and no Person shall be convicted without the Concurrence of two thirds of the Members present.

---

*Changed by Section 2 of the Fourteenth Amendment.

**Changed by the Seventeenth Amendment.
***Changed by the Seventeenth Amendment.

7. Judgment in Cases of Impeachment shall not extend further than to removal from Office, and disqualification to hold and enjoy any Office of Honor, Trust or Profit under the United States; but the Party convicted shall nevertheless be liable and subject to Indictment, Trial, Judgment and Punishment, according to Law.

Section 4

1. The Times, Places and Manner of holding Elections for Senators and Representatives shall be prescribed in each State by the legislature thereof; but the Congress may at any time by Law make or alter such Regulations, except as to the Places of choosing Senators.

2. The Congress shall assemble at least once in every Year, and such Meeting shall be [on the first Monday in December,]* unless they shall by Law appoint a different Day.

Section 5

1. Each House shall be the Judge of the Elections, Returns and Qualifications of its own Members, and a Majority of each shall constitute a Quorum to do Business; but a smaller Number may adjourn from day to day, and may be authorized to compel the Attendance of absent Members, in such Manner, and under such Penalties as each House may provide.

2. Each House may determine the Rules of its Proceedings, punish its Members for disorderly Behavior, and, with the Concurrence of two thirds, expel a Member.

3. Each House shall keep a journal of its Proceedings, and from time to time publish the same, excepting such Parts as may in their Judgment require Secrecy; and the Yeas and Nays of the Members of either House on any question shall, at the Desire of one fifth of those Present, be entered on the Journal.

4. Neither House, during the Session of Congress, shall, without the Consent of the other, adjourn for more than three days, nor to any other Place than that in which the two Houses shall be sitting.

Section 6

1. The Senators and Representatives shall receive a Compensation for their Services, to be ascertained by Law, and paid out of the Treasury of the United States. They shall in all Cases, except Treason, Felony, and Breach of the Peace be privileged from Arrest during their Attendance at the Session of their respective Houses, and in going to and returning from the same; and

*Changed by Section 2 of the Twentieth Amendment.

for any Speech or Debate in either House, they shall not be questioned in any other Place.

2. No Senator or Representative shall, during the Time for which he was elected, be appointed to any civil Office under the Authority of the United States, which shall have been created, or the Emoluments whereof shall have been increased during such time; and no Person holding any Office under the United States, shall be a Member of either House during his continuance in Office.

Section 7

1. All Bills for raising Revenue shall originate in the House of Representatives; but the Senate may propose or concur with Amendments as on other Bills.

2. Every Bill which shall have passed the House of Representatives and the Senate, shall, before it becomes a Law, be presented to the President of the United States; if he approves he shall sign it, but if not he shall return it, with his Objections, to that House in which it shall have originated, who shall enter the Objections at large on their Journal, and proceed to Reconsider it. If after such reconsideration two thirds of that House shall agree to pass the Bill, it shall be sent, together with the Objections, to the other House, by which it shall likewise be reconsidered, and if approved by two thirds of that House, it shall become a Law. But in all such cases the votes of both Houses shall be determined by Yeas and Nays, and the Names of the Persons voting for and against the Bill shall be entered on the Journal of each House respectively. If any Bill shall not be returned by the President within ten Days (Sundays excepted) after it shall have been presented to him, the Same shall be a Law, in like Manner as if he had signed it, unless the Congress by their Adjournment prevent its Return, in which Case it shall not be a Law.

3. Every Order, Resolution, or Vote to which the Concurrence of the Senate and House of Representatives may be necessary (except on a question of Adjournment) shall be presented to the President of the United States; and before the Same shall take Effect, shall be approved by him, or being disapproved by him, shall be repassed by two thirds of the Senate and House of Representatives, according to the Rules and Limitations prescribed in the Case of a Bill.

Section 8

The Congress shall have power:

1. To lay and collect Taxes, Duties, Imposts and Excises, to pay the Debts and provide for the common Defence and general Welfare of the United States; but

all duties, imposts and excises shall be uniform throughout the United States;

2. To borrow Money on the credit of the United States;

3. To regulate Commerce with foreign Nations, and among the several States, and with the Indian Tribes;

4. To establish a uniform Rule of Naturalization, and uniform Laws on the subject of Bankruptcies throughout the United States;

5. To coin Money, regulate the Value thereof, and of foreign Coin, and fix the Standard of Weights and Measures;

6. To provide for the Punishment of counterfeiting the Securities and current Coin of the United States;

7. To establish Post Offices and post Roads;

8. To promote the Progress of Science and useful Arts, by securing for limited Times to Authors and Inventors the exclusive Right to their respective Writings and Discoveries;

9. To constitute Tribunals inferior to the Supreme Court;

10. To define and punish Piracies and Felonies committed on the high Seas, and Offenses against the Law of Nations;

11. To declare War, grant Letters of Marque and Reprisal, and make Rules concerning Captures on Land and Water;

12. To raise and support Armies, but no Appropriation of Money to that Use shall be for a longer Term than two Years;

13. To provide and maintain a Navy;

14. To make Rules for the Government and Regulation of the land and naval Forces;

15. To provide for calling forth the Militia to execute the Laws of the Union, suppress Insurrections and repel Invasions;

16. To provide for organizing, arming, and disciplining the Militia, and for governing such Part of them as may be employed in the Service of the United States, reserving to the States respectively, the Appointment of the Officers, and the Authority of training the Militia according to the discipline prescribed by Congress;

17. To exercise exclusive Legislation in all Cases whatsoever, over such District (not exceeding ten Miles square) as may, by Session of particular States, and the Acceptance of Congress, become the Seat of the Government of the United States, and to exercise like Authority over all Places purchased by the Consent of the Legislature of the State in which the Same shall be, for the Erection of Forts, Magazines, Arsenals, dock-Yards and other needful Buildings;—and

18. To make all Laws which shall be necessary and proper for carrying into Execution the foregoing Powers, and all other Powers vested by this Constitution in the Government of the United States, or in any Department or Officer thereof.

Section 9

1. The Migration or Importation of such Persons as any of the States now existing shall think proper to admit, shall not be prohibited by the Congress prior to the Year one thousand eight hundred and eight, but a Tax or duty may be imposed on such Importation, not exceeding ten dollars for each Person.

2. The Privilege of the Writ of Habeas Corpus shall not be suspended, unless when in Cases of Rebellion or Invasion the public Safety may require it.

3. No Bill of Attainder or ex post facto Law shall be passed.

4. [No Capitation, or other direct, Tax shall be laid, unless in Proportion to the Census or Enumeration herein before directed to be taken.]*

5. No Tax or Duty shall be laid on Articles exported from any State.

6. No Preference shall be given by any Regulation of Commerce or Revenue to the Ports of one State over those of another; nor shall Vessels bound to, or from, one State, be obliged to enter, clear, or pay Duties in another.

7. No Money shall be drawn from the Treasury, but in Consequence of Appropriations made by Law; and a regular Statement and Account of the Receipts and Expenditures of all public Money shall be published from time to time.

8. No Title of Nobility shall be granted by the United States: And no Person holding any Office of Profit or Trust under them, shall, without the Consent of the Congress, accept of any present, Emolument, Office, or Title, of any kind whatever, from any King, Prince, or foreign State.

Section 10

1. No State shall enter into any Treaty, Alliance, or

---

*Changed by the Sixteenth Amendment.

Confederation; grant Letters of Marque and Reprisal; coin Money; emit Bills of Credit; make any Thing but gold and silver Coin a Tender in Payment of Debts; pass any Bill of Attainder, ex post facto Law, or Law impairing the Obligation of Contracts, or grant any Title of Nobility.

2.   No State shall, without the Consent of the Congress, lay any Imposts or Duties on Imports or Exports, except what may be absolutely necessary for executing its inspection Laws: and the net Produce of all Duties and Imposts, laid by any State on Imports or Exports, shall be for the Use of the Treasury of the United States; and all such Laws shall be subject to the Revision and Control of the Congress.

3.   No State shall, without the Consent of Congress, lay any Duty of Tonnage, keep Troops, or Ships of War in time of Peace, enter into any Agreement or Compact with another State, or with a foreign Power, or engage in War, unless actually invaded, or in such imminent Danger as will not admit of delay.

ARTICLE II

Section 1

1.   The executive Power shall be vested in a President of the United States of America. He shall hold his Office during the term of four Years, and, together with the Vice President, chosen for the same Term, be elected, as follows.

2.   Each State shall appoint, in such Manner as the Legislature thereof may direct, a Number of Electors, equal to the whole Number of Senators and Representatives to which the State may be entitled in the Congress: but no Senator or Representative, or Person holding an Office of Trust or Profit under the United States, shall be appointed an Elector.

3.   [The Electors shall meet in their respective states, and vote by Ballot for two Persons, of whom one at least shall not be an Inhabitant of the same State with themselves. And they shall make a List of all the Persons voted for, and of the Number of Votes for each; which List they shall sign and certify, and transmit sealed to the Seat of the Government of the United States, directed to the President of the Senate. The President of the Senate shall, in the Presence of the Senate and House of Representatives, open all the Certificates, and the Votes shall then be counted. The Person having the greatest Number of Votes shall be the President, if such Number be a Majority of the whole Number of Electors appointed; and if there be more than one who have such Majority, and have an equal Number of Votes, then the House of Representatives shall immediately choose by Ballot one of them for President; and if no Person have a Majority, then from the five highest on the List the said House shall in like manner choose the President. But in choosing the President, the Votes shall be taken by States, the Representation from each State having one Vote; A quorum for this Purpose shall consist of a Member or Members from two thirds of the States, and a Majority of all the States shall be necessary to a Choice. In every Case, after the Choice of the President, the Person having the greatest Number of Votes of the Electors shall be the Vice President. But if there should remain two or more who have equal Votes, the Senate shall choose from them by Ballot the Vice President.]*

4.   The Congress may determine the Time of choosing the Electors, and the day on which they shall give their Votes; which Day shall be the same throughout the United States.

5.   No Person except a natural born Citizen, or a Citizen of the United States at the time of the Adoption of this Constitution, shall be eligible to the Office of the President; neither shall any person be eligible to that Office who shall not have attained to the Age of thirty five Years, and been fourteen Years a Resident within the United States.

6.   [In Case of the Removal of the President from Office, or of his Death, Resignation, or Inability to discharge the Powers and Duties of the said Office, the Same shall devolve on the Vice President, and the Congress may by Law provide for the Case of Removal, Death, Resignation or Inability, both of the President and Vice President, declaring what Officer shall then act as President, and such Officer shall act accordingly, until the Disability be removed, or a President shall be elected.]**

7.   The President shall, at stated Times, receive for his Services, a Compensation, which shall neither be increased nor diminished during the Period for which he shall have been elected, and he shall not receive within that Period any other Emolument from the United States, or any of them.

8.   Before he enter the Execution of his Office, he shall take the following Oath or Affirmation:—"I do solemnly swear (or affirm) that I will faithfully execute the Office of President of the United States, and will to the best of my ability, preserve, protect, and defend the Constitution of the United States."

---

*Changed by the Twelfth Amendment.
**Changed by the Twenty-fifth Amendment.

Section 2

1. The President shall be Commander in Chief of the Army and Navy of the United States, and of the Militia of the several States, when called into the actual Service of the United States; he may require the Opinion, in writing, of the principal Officer in each of the executive Departments, upon any Subject relating to the Duties of their respective Offices, and he shall have Power to grant Reprieves and Pardons for Offenses against the United States, except in Cases of Impeachment.

2. He shall have Power, by and with the Advice and Consent of the Senate, to make Treaties, provided two thirds of the Senators present concur; and he shall nominate, and by and with the Advice and Consent of the Senate, shall appoint Ambassadors, other public Ministers and Consuls, Judges of the supreme Court, and all other Officers of the United States, whose Appointments are not herein otherwise provided for, and which shall be established by Law; but the Congress may by Law vest the Appointment of such inferior Officers, as they think proper, in the President alone, in the Courts of Law, or in the Heads of Departments.

3. The President shall have Power to fill up all Vacancies that may happen during the Recess of the Senate, by granting Commissions which shall expire at the End of their next Session.

Section 3

He shall from time to time give to the Congress Information of the State of the Union, and recommend to their Consideration such Measures as he shall judge necessary and expedient; he may, on extraordinary Occasions, convene both Houses, or either of them, and in Case of Disagreement between them, with Respect to the Time of Adjournment, he may adjourn them to such Time as he shall think proper; he shall receive Ambassadors and other public Ministers; he shall take Care that the Laws be faithfully executed, and shall Commission all the Officers of the United States.

Section 4

The President, Vice President and all civil Officers of the United States, shall be removed from Office on Impeachment for, and Conviction of, Treason, Bribery, or other high Crimes and Misdemeanors.

ARTICLE III

Section 1

The judicial Power of the United States, shall be vested in one supreme Court, and in such inferior Courts as the Congress may from time to time ordain and establish. The Judges, both of the supreme and inferior Courts, shall hold their Offices during good Behavior, and shall, at stated Times, receive for their Services a Compensation, which shall not be diminished during their Continuance in Office.

Section 2

1. The judicial Power shall extend to all Cases, in Law and Equity, arising under this Constitution, the Laws of the United States, and Treaties made, or which shall be made, under their Authority;— to all Cases affecting Ambassadors, other public Ministers and Consuls;—to all Cases of admiralty and maritime Jurisdiction;—to Controversies to which the United States shall be a Party;—to Controversies between two or more States; [between a State and Citizens of another State;] between Citizens of different States;—between Citizens of the same State claiming Lands under Grants of different States;—[and between a State, or the Citizens thereof, and foreign States, Citizens or Subjects.]*

2. In all Cases affecting Ambassadors, other public Ministers and Consuls, and those in which a State shall be Party, the supreme Court shall have original Jurisdiction. In all the other Cases before mentioned, the supreme Court shall have appellate Jurisdiction, both as to Law and Fact, with such Exceptions, and under such Regulations as the Congress shall make.

3. The Trial of all Crimes, except in Cases of Impeachment, shall be by Jury; and such Trial shall be held in the State where said Crimes shall have been committed; but when not committed within any State, the Trial shall be at such Place or Places as the Congress may by Law have directed.

Section 3

1. Treason against the United States shall consist only in levying War against them, or in adhering to their Enemies, giving them Aid and Comfort. No Person shall be convicted of Treason unless on the Testimony of two Witnesses to the same overt Act, or on Confession in open Court.

2. The Congress shall have Power to declare the Punishment of Treason, but no Attainder of Treason shall work Corruption of Blood, or Forfeiture except during the Life of the Person attainted.

ARTICLE IV

Section 1

Full Faith and Credit shall be given in each State to the public Acts, Records, and judicial Proceedings of every

---

*Changed by the Eleventh Amendment.

other State; And the Congress may by general Laws prescribe the manner in which such Acts, Records and Proceedings shall be proved, and the Effect thereof.

Section 2

1. The Citizens of each State shall be entitled to all Privileges and Immunities of Citizens in the several States.

2. A Person charged in any State with Treason, Felony, or other Crime, who shall flee from Justice, and be found in another State, shall on Demand of the executive Authority of the State from which he fled, be delivered up, to be removed to the State having Jurisdiction of the Crime.

3. [No person held to Service or Labour in one State, under the Laws thereof, escaping into another, shall, in Consequence of any Law or Regulation therein, be discharged from such Service or Labour, but shall be delivered up on Claim of the Party to whom such Service or Labour may be due.]*

Section 3

1. New States may be admitted by the Congress into this Union; but no new State shall be formed or erected within the Jurisdiction of any other State; nor any State be formed by the Junction of two or more States, or parts of States, without the Consent of the Legislatures of the States concerned as well as of the Congress.

2. The Congress shall have Power to dispose of and make all needful Rules and Regulations respecting the territory or other Property belonging to the United States; and nothing in this Constitution shall be so construed as to Prejudice any Claims of the United States, or of any particular State.

Section 4

The United States shall guarantee to every State in this Union a Republican Form of Government, and shall protect each of them against Invasion; and on Application of the Legislature, or of the Executive (when the Legislature cannot be convened) against domestic Violence.

ARTICLE V

The Congress, whenever two thirds of both Houses shall deem it necessary, shall propose Amendments to this Constitution, or, on the Application of the Legislatures

---

*Changed by the Thirteenth Amendment.

of two thirds of the several States, shall call a Convention for proposing Amendments, which, in either Case, shall be valid to all Intents and Purposes, as Part of this Constitution, when ratified by the Legislatures of three fourths of the several States, or by Conventions in three fourths thereof, as the one or the other Mode of Ratification may be proposed by the Congress; Provided that no Amendment which may be made prior to the Year One thousand eight hundred and eight shall in any Manner affect the first and fourth Clauses in the Ninth Section of the first Article; and that no State, without its Consent, shall be deprived of its equal Suffrage in the Senate.

ARTICLE VI

1. All debts contracted and Engagements entered into, before the Adoption of this Constitution, shall be as valid against the United States under this Constitution, as under the Confederation.

2. This Constitution, and the Laws of the United States which shall be made in Pursuance thereof; and all Treaties made, or which shall be made, under the Authority of the United States, shall be the supreme Law of the Land; and the Judges in every State shall be bound thereby, any Thing in the Constitution or Laws of any State to the Contrary notwithstanding.

3. The Senators and Representatives before mentioned, and the Members of the several State Legislatures, and all executive and judicial Officers, both of the United States and of the several States, shall be bound by Oath or Affirmation, to support this Constitution; but no religious Test shall ever be required as a Qualification to any Office or public Trust under the United States.

ARTICLE VII

The Ratification of the Conventions of nine States, shall be sufficient for the Establishment of this Constitution between the States so ratifying the Same.

Done in Convention by the unanimous consent of the States present the seventeenth day of September in the year of our Lord one thousand seven hundred and eighty seven and of the Independence of the United States of America the Twelfth. In witness whereof we have hereunto subscribed our Names,

George Washington—President
and deputy from Virginia

(This Constitution was adopted on September 17, 1787 by the Constitutional Convention, and was declared ratified on July 2, 1788)

Signers of the Constitution

New-Hampshire
John Langdon
Nicholas Gilman

Massachusetts
Nathaniel Gorham
Rufus King

Connecticut
William Samuel Johnson
Roger Sherman

New York
Alexander Hamilton

New Jersey
William Livingston
David Brearley
William Paterson
Jonathan Dayton

Pennsylvania
Benjamin Franklin
Thomas Mifflin
Robert Morris
George Clymer
Thomas Fitzsimons
Jared Ingersoll
James Wilson
Gouverneur Morris

Delaware
George Read
Gunning Bedford, Jr.
John Dickinson
Richard Bassett
Jacob Broom

Maryland
James McHenry
Daniel of St. Tho. Jenifer
Daniel Carroll

Virginia
John Blair
James Madison, Junior

North Carolina
William Blount
Richard Dobbs Spaight
Hugh Williamson

South Carolina
John Ruthledge
Charles Cotesworth Pinckney
Charles Pinckney
Pierce Butler

Georgia
William Few
Abraham Baldwin

Attest: William Jackson, Secretary

AMENDMENTS TO THE CONSTITUTION OF THE UNITED STATES OF AMERICA

AMENDMENT I

Congress shall make no law respecting an establishment of religion, or prohibiting the free exercise thereof; or abridging the freedom of speech, or of the press, or the right of the people peaceably to assemble, and to petition the Government for a redress of grievances. (Ratified December, 1791.)

AMENDMENT II

A well regulated Militia, being necessary to the security of a free State, the right of the people to keep and bear Arms, shall not be infringed. (Ratified December, 1791.)

AMENDMENT III

No Soldier shall, in time of peace be quartered in any house, without the consent of the Owner, nor in time of war, but in a manner to be prescribed by law. (Ratified December, 1791.)

AMENDMENT IV

The right of the people to be secure in their persons, houses, papers, and effects, against unreasonable searches and seizures, shall not be violated, and no Warrants shall issue, but upon probable cause, supported by Oath or affirmation, and particularly describing the place to be searched, and the persons or things to be seized. (Ratified December, 1791.)

AMENDMENT V

No person shall be held to answer for a capital, or otherwise infamous crime, unless on a presentment or indictment of a Grand Jury, except in cases arising in the land or naval forces, or in the Militia, when in actual service in time of War or public danger; nor shall any person be subject for the same offence to be twice put in jeopardy of life or limb, nor shall be compelled in any criminal case to be a witness against himself, nor be deprived of life, liberty, or property, without due process of law; nor shall private property be taken for public use without just compensation. (Ratified December, 1791.)

AMENDMENT VI

In all criminal prosecutions, the accused shall enjoy the right to a speedy and public trial, by an impartial jury of the State and district wherein the crime shall have been committed; which district shall have been previously ascertained by law, and to be informed of the nature and cause of the accusation; to be confronted with the witnesses against him; to have compulsory process for obtaining witnesses in his favor, and to have the assistance of counsel for his defence. (Ratified December, 1791.)

AMENDMENT VII

In Suits at common law, where the value in controversy shall exceed twenty dollars, the right of trial by jury shall be preserved, and no fact tried by a jury shall be otherwise re-examined in any Court of the United States, than according to the rules of the common law. (Ratified December, 1791.)

AMENDMENT VIII

Excessive bail shall not be required, nor excessive fines imposed, nor cruel and unusual punishments inflicted. (Ratified December, 1791.)

AMENDMENT IX

The enumeration in the Constitution of certain rights shall not be construed to deny or disparage others retained by the people. (Ratified December, 1791.)

AMENDMENT X

The powers not delegated to the United States by the Constitution, nor prohibited by it to the States, are reserved to the States respectively, or to the people. (Ratified December, 1791.)

AMENDMENT XI

The Judicial power of the United States shall not be construed to extend to any suit in law or equity, commenced or prosecuted against one of the United States by Citizens of another State, or by Citizens or Subjects of any Foreign State. (Ratified February, 1795.)

AMENDMENT XII

The Electors shall meet in their respective states, and vote by ballot for President and Vice President, one of whom, at least, shall not be an inhabitant of the same state with themselves; they shall name in their ballots the person voted for as President, and in distinct ballots the person voted for as Vice-President, and they shall make distinct lists of all persons voted for as President, and of all persons voted for as Vice-President, and of the number of votes for each, which lists they shall sign and certify, and transmit sealed to the seat of the government of the United States, directed to the President of the Senate;—The President of the Senate shall, in the presence of the Senate and House of Representatives, open all the certificates and the votes shall then be counted;—The person having the greatest number of votes for President, shall be the President, if such number be a majority of the whole number of Electors appointed; and if no person have such majority, then from the persons having the highest numbers not exceeding three on the list of those voted for as President, the House of Representatives shall choose immediately, by ballot, the President. But in choosing the President, the votes shall be taken by states, the representation from each state having one vote; a quorum for this purpose shall consist of a member or members from two-thirds of the states, and a majority of all the states shall be necessary to a choice. [And if the House of Representatives shall not choose a President whenever the right of choice shall devolve upon them, before the fourth day of March next following, then the Vice-President shall act as President, as in the case of the death or other constitutional disability of the President—]* The person having the greatest number of votes as Vice-President, shall be the Vice-President, if such number be a majority of the whole number of Electors appointed, and if no person have a majority, then from the two highest numbers on the list, the Senate shall choose the Vice-President; a quorum for the purpose shall consist of two-thirds of the whole number of Senators, and a majority of the whole number shall be necessary to a choice. But no person constitutionally ineligible to the office of President shall be eligible to that of Vice-President of the United States. (Ratified June, 1804.)

AMENDMENT XIII

Section 1

Neither slavery nor involuntary servitude, except as a punishment for crime whereof the party shall have been duly convicted, shall exist within the United States, or any place subject to their jurisdiction.

Section 2

Congress shall have power to enforce this article by appropriate legislation. (Ratified December, 1865.)

AMENDMENT XIV

Section 1

All persons born or naturalized in the United States and subject to the jurisdiction thereof, are citizens of the United States and of the State wherein they reside. No State shall make or enforce any law which shall abridge the privileges or immunities of citizens of the United States; nor shall any State deprive any person of life,

liberty, or property, without due process of law; nor deny to any person within its jurisdiction the equal protection of the laws.

Section 2

Representatives shall be apportioned among the several States according to their respective numbers, counting the whole number of persons in each State, excluding Indians not taxed. But when the right to vote at any election for the choice of electors for President and Vice President of the United States, Representatives in Congress, the Executive and Judicial officers of a State, or the members of the Legislature thereof, is denied to any of the male inhabitants of such State, being twenty-one years of age, and citizens of the United States, or in any way abridged, except for participation in rebellion, or other crime, the basis of representation therein shall be reduced in the proportion which the number of such male citizens shall bear to the whole number of male citizens twenty-one years of age in such State.

Section 3

No person shall be a Senator or a Representative in Congress, or elector of President and Vice President, or hold any office, civil or military, under the United States, or under any State, who, having previously taken an oath, as a member of Congress, or as an officer of the United States, or as a member of any State legislature, or as an executive or judicial officer of any State, to support the Constitution of the United States, shall have engaged in insurrection or rebellion against the same, or given aid or comfort to the enemies thereof. But Congress may by a vote of two-thirds of each House, remove such disability.

Section 4

The validity of the public debt of the United States, authorized by law, including debts incurred for payment of pensions and bounties for services in suppressing insurrection or rebellion, shall not be questioned. But neither the United States nor any State shall assume or pay any debt or obligation incurred in aid of insurrection or rebellion against the United States, or any claim for the loss or emancipation of any slave; but all such debts, obligations and claims shall be held illegal and void.

Section 5

The Congress shall have power to enforce, by appropriate legislation, the provisions of this article. (Ratified July, 1868.)

---

*Superseded by Section 3 of the Twentieth Amendment.

AMENDMENT XV

Section 1

The right of citizens of the United States to vote shall not be denied or abridged by the United States or by any State on account of race, color, or previous condition of servitude.

Section 2

The Congress shall have power to enforce this article by appropriate legislation. (Ratified February, 1870.)

AMENDMENT XVI

The Congress shall have power to lay and collect taxes on incomes, from whatever source derived, without apportionment among the several States, and without regard to any census or enumeration. (Ratified February, 1913.)

AMENDMENT XVII

The Senate of the United States shall be composed of two Senators from each State, elected by the people thereof, for six years; and each Senator shall have one vote. The electors in each State shall have the qualifications requisite for electors of the most numerous branch of the State legislatures.

When vacancies happen in the representation of any State in the Senate, the executive authority of such State shall issue writs of election to fill such vacancies: Provided, That the legislature of any State may empower the executive thereof to make temporary appointments until the people fill the vacancies by election as the legislature may direct.

This amendment shall not be so construed as to affect the election or term of any Senator chosen before it becomes valid as part of the Constitution. (Ratified April, 1913.)

AMENDMENT XVIII

[Section 1

After one year from the ratification of this article the manufacture, sale, or transportation of intoxicating liquors within, the importation thereof into, or the exportation thereof from the United States and all territory subject to the jurisdiction thereof for beverage purposes is hereby prohibited.

Section 2

The Congress and the several States shall have concurrent power to enforce this article by appropriate legislation.

Section 3

This article shall be inoperative unless it shall have been ratified as an amendment to the Constitution by the legislatures of the several States, as provided in the Constitution, within seven years from the date of the submission hereof to the States by the Congress.]* (Ratified January, 1919.)

AMENDMENT XIX

The right of citizens of the United States to vote shall not be denied or abridged by the United States or by any State on account of sex.

Congress shall have power to enforce this article by appropriate legislation.(Ratified August, 1920.)

AMENDMENT XX

Section 1

The terms of the President and Vice President shall end at noon on the 20th day of January, and the terms of Senators and Representatives at noon on the 3d day of January, of the years in which such terms would have ended if this article had not been ratified; and the terms of their successors shall then begin.

Section 2

The Congress shall assemble at least once in every year, and such meeting shall begin at noon on the 3d day of January, unless they shall by law appoint a different day.

Section 3

If, at the time fixed for the beginning of the term of the President, the President elect shall have died, the Vice President elect shall become President. If a President shall not have been chosen before the time fixed for the beginning of his term, or if the President elect shall have failed to qualify, then the Vice President elect shall act as President until a President shall have qualified; and the Congress may by law provide for the case wherein neither a President elect nor a Vice President elect shall have qualified, declaring who shall then act as President, or the manner in which one who is to act shall be selected, and such person shall act accordingly until a President or Vice President shall have qualified.

Section 4

The Congress may by law provide for the case of the death of any of the persons from whom the House of Representatives may choose a President whenever the right of choice shall have devolved upon them, and for the case of the death of any of the persons from whom the Senate may choose a Vice President whenever the right of choice shall have devolved upon them.

---

*Repealed by the Twenty-first Amendment.

Section 5

Sections 1 and 2 shall take effect on the 15th day of October following the ratification of this article.

Section 6

This article shall be inoperative unless it shall have been ratified as an amendment to the Constitution by the legislatures of three-fourths of the several States within seven years from the date of its submission. (Ratified January, 1933.)

AMENDMENT XXI

Section 1

The eighteenth article of amendment to the Constitution of the United States is hereby repealed.

Section 2

The transportation or importation into any State, Territory, or possession of the United States for delivery or use therein of intoxicating liquors, in violation of the laws thereof, is hereby prohibited.

Section 3

This article shall be inoperative unless it shall have been ratified as an amendment to the Constitution by conventions in the several States, as provided in the Constitution, within seven years from the date of the submission hereof to the States by the Congress. (Ratified December, 1933.)

AMENDMENT XXII

Section 1

No person shall be elected to the office of the President more than twice, and no person who has held the office of President, or acted as President, for more than two years of a term to which some other person was elected President shall be elected to the office of the President more than once. But this Article shall not apply to any person holding the office of President when this Article was proposed by the Congress, and shall not prevent any person who may be holding the office of President, or acting as President, during the term within which this Article becomes operative from holding the office of President or acting as President during the remainder of such term.

Section 2

This article shall be inoperative unless it shall have been ratified as an amendment to the Constitution by the legislatures of three-fourths of the several States within seven years from the date of its submission to the States by the Congress. (Ratified February, 1951.)

AMENDMENT XXIII

Section 1

The District constituting the seat of Government of the United States shall appoint in such manner as the Congress may direct:

A number of electors of President and Vice President equal to the whole number of Senators and Representatives in Congress to which the District would be entitled if it were a State, but in no event more than the least populous State; they shall be in addition to those appointed by the States, but they shall be considered, for the purposes of the election of President and Vice President, to be electors appointed by a State; and they shall meet in the District and perform such duties as provided by the twelfth article of amendment.

Section 2

The Congress shall have power to enforce this article by appropriate legislation. (Ratified March, 1961.)

AMENDMENT XXIV

Section 1

The right of citizens of the United States to vote in any primary or other election for President or Vice President, for electors for President or Vice President, or for Senator or Representative in Congress, shall not be denied or abridged by the United States or any State by reason of failure to pay any poll tax or other tax.

Section 2

The Congress shall have power to enforce this article by appropriate legislation. (Ratified January, 1964.)

AMENDMENT XXV

Section 1

In case of the removal of the President from office or of his death or resignation, the Vice President shall become President.

Section 2

Whenever there is a vacancy in the office of the Vice President, the President shall nominate a Vice President who shall take office upon confirmation by a majority vote of both Houses of Congress.

Section 3

Whenever the President transmits to the President pro tempore of the Senate and the Speaker of the House of Representatives his written declaration that he is unable to discharge the powers and duties of his office, and until he transmits to them a written declaration to the contrary, such powers and duties shall be discharged by the Vice President as Acting President.

Section 4

Whenever the Vice President and a majority of either the principal officers of the executive departments or of such other body as Congress may by law provide, transmit to the President pro tempore of the Senate and the Speaker of the House of Representatives their written declaration that the President is unable to discharge the powers and duties of his office, the Vice President shall immediately assume the powers and duties of the office as Acting President.

Thereafter, when the President transmits to the President pro tempore of the Senate and the Speaker of the House of Representatives his written declaration that no inability exists, he shall resume the powers and duties of his office unless the Vice President and a majority of either the principal officers of the executive department or of such other body as Congress may by law provide, transmit within four days to the President pro tempore of the Senate and the Speaker of the House of Representatives their written declaration that the President is unable to discharge the powers and duties of his office. Thereupon Congress shall decide the issue, assembling within forty-eight hours for that purpose if not in session. If the Congress, within twenty-one days after receipt of the latter written declaration, or, if Congress is not in session, within twenty-one days after Congress is required to assemble, determines by two-thirds vote of both Houses that the President is unable to discharge the powers and duties of his office, the Vice President shall continue to discharge the same as Acting President; otherwise, the President shall resume the powers and duties of his office. (Ratified February, 1967.)

AMENDMENT XXVI

Section 1

The right of citizens of the United States, who are eighteen years of age or older, to vote shall not be denied or abridged by the United States or by any State on account of age.

Section 2

The Congress shall have power to enforce this article by appropriate legislation. (Ratified July, 1971.)

AMENDMENT XXVII

No law varying the compensation for the services of the Senators or Representatives, shall take effect, until an election of Representatives shall have intervened. (Ratified May, 1992.)

Descriptive headings have been added by editors. Passages in brackets marked by an asterisk indicate that they were changed by amendment.

The Emancipation Proclamation

Whereas on the 22nd day of September, A.D. 1862, a proclamation was issued by the President of the United States, containing, among other things, the following, to wit:

"That on the 1st day of January, A.D. 1863, all persons held as slaves within any State or designated part of a State the people whereof shall then be in rebellion against the United States shall be then, thenceforward, and forever free; and the executive government of the United States, including the military and naval authority thereof, will recognize and maintain the freedom of such persons and will do no act or acts to repress such persons, or any of them, in any efforts they may make for their actual freedom.

"That the executive will on the 1st day of January aforesaid, by proclamation, designate the States and parts of States, if any, in which the people thereof, respectively, shall then be in rebellion against the United States; and the fact that any State or the people thereof shall on that day be in good faith represented in the Congress of the United States by members chosen thereto at elections wherein a majority of the qualified voters of such States shall have participated shall, in the absence of strong countervailing testimony, be deemed conclusive evidence that such State and the people thereof are not then in rebellion against the United States."

Now, therefore, I, Abraham Lincoln, President of the United States, by virtue of the power in me vested as Commander-In-Chief of the Army and Navy of the United States in time of actual armed rebellion against the authority and government of the United States, and as a fit and necessary war measure for supressing said rebellion, do, on this 1st day of January, A.D. 1863, and in accordance with my purpose so to do, publicly proclaimed for the full period of one hundred days from the first day above mentioned, order and designate as the States and parts of States wherein the people thereof, respectively, are this day in rebellion against the United States the following, to wit:

Arkansas, Texas, Louisiana (except the parishes of St. Bernard, Palquemines, Jefferson, St. John, St. Charles, St. James, Ascension, Assumption, Terrebone, Lafourche, St. Mary, St. Martin, and Orleans, including the city of New Orleans), Mississippi, Alabama, Florida, Georgia, South Carolina, North Carolina, and Virginia (except the forty-eight counties designated as West Virginia, and also the counties of Berkeley, Accomac, Morthhampton, Elizabeth City, York, Princess Anne, and Norfolk, including the cities of Norfolk and Portsmouth), and which excepted parts are for the present left precisely as if this proclamation were not issued.

And by virtue of the power and for the purpose aforesaid, I do order and declare that all persons held as slaves within said designated States and parts of States are, and henceforward shall be, free; and that the Executive Government of the United States, including the military and naval authorities thereof, will recognize and maintain the freedom of said persons.

And I hereby enjoin upon the people so declared to be free to abstain from all violence, unless in necessary self-defence; and I recommend to them that, in all case when allowed, they labor faithfully for reasonable wages.

And I further declare and make known that such persons of suitable condition will be received into the armed service of the United States to garrison forts, positions, stations, and other places, and to man vessels of all sorts in said service.

And upon this act, sincerely believed to be an act of justice, warranted by the Constitution upon military necessity, I invoke the considerate judgment of mankind and the gracious favor of Almighty God.

Universal Declaration of Human Rights [1948]

PREAMBLE

Whereas recognition of the inherent dignity and of the equal and inalienable rights of all members of the human family is the foundation of freedom, justice and peace in the world,

Whereas disregard and contempt for human rights have resulted in barbarous acts which have outraged the conscience of mankind, and the advent of a world in which human beings shall enjoy freedom of speech and belief and freedom from fear and want has been proclaimed as the highest aspiration of the common people,

Whereas it is essential, if man is not to be compelled to have recourse, as a last resort, to rebellion against tyranny and oppression, that human rights should be protected by the rule of law,

Whereas it is essential to promote the development of friendly relations between nations,

Whereas the peoples of the United Nations have in the Charter reaffirmed their faith in fundamental human rights, in the dignity and worth of the human person and in the equal rights of men and women and have determined to promote social progress and better standards of life in larger freedom,

Whereas Member States have pledged themselves to achieve, in co-operation with the United Nations, the promotion of universal respect for and observance of human rights and fundamental freedoms,

Whereas a common understanding of these rights and freedoms is of the greatest importance for the full realization of this pledge,

Now, therefore,

The General Assembly

Proclaims this Universal Declaration of Human Rights as a common standard of achievement for all peoples and all nations, to the end that every individual and every organ of society, keeping this Declaration constantly in mind, shall strive by teaching and education to promote respect for these rights and freedoms and by progressive measures, national and international, to secure their universal and effective recognition and observance, both among the peoples of Member States themselves and among the peoples of territories under their jurisdiction.

Article 1

All human beings are born free and equal in dignity and rights. They are endowed with reason and conscience and should act towards one another in a spirit of brotherhood.

Article 2

Everyone is entitled to all the rights and freedoms set forth in this Declaration, without distinction of any kind, such as race, colour, sex, language, religion, political or other opinion, national or social origin, property, birth or other status.

Furthermore, no distinction shall be made on the basis of the political, jurisdictional or international status of the country or territory to which a person belongs, whether it be independent, trust, non-self-governing or under any other limitation of sovereignty.

Article 3

Everyone has the right to life, liberty and the security of person.

Article 4

No one shall be held in slavery or servitude; slavery and the slave trade shall be prohibited in all their forms.

Article 5

No one shall be subjected to torture or to cruel, inhuman or degrading treatment or punishment.

Article 6

Everyone has the right to recognition everywhere as a person before the law.

Article 7

All are equal before the law and are entitled without any discrimination to equal protection of the law. All are entitled to equal protection against any discrimination in violation of this Declaration and against any incitement to such discrimination.

Article 8

Everyone has the right to an effective remedy by the competent national tribunals for acts violating the fundamental rights granted him by the constitution or by law.

Article 9

No one shall be subjected to arbitrary arrest, detention or exile.

Article 10

Everyone is entitled in full equality to a fair, and public hearing by an independent and impartial tribunal, in the determination of his rights and obligations and of any criminal charge against him.

Article 11

1. Everyone charged with a penal offence has the right to be presumed innocent until proved guilty according to law in a public trail at which he has had all the guarantees necessary for his defence.

2. No one shall be held guilty of any penal offence on account of any act or omission which did not constitute a penal offence, under national or international law, at the time when it was committed. Nor shall a heavier penalty be imposed than the one that was applicable at the time the penal offence was committed.

Article 12

No one shall be subjected to arbitrary interference with his privacy, family, home or correspondence, nor to attacks upon his honour and reputation. Everyone has the right to the protection of the law against such interference or attacks.

Article 13

1. Everyone has the right to freedom of movement and residence within the borders of each State.

2. Everyone has the right to leave any country, including his own, and to return to his country.

Article 14

1. Everyone has the right to seek and to enjoy in other countries asylum from persecution.

2. This right may not be invoked in the case of prosecutions genuinely arising from non-political crimes or from acts contrary to the purposes and principles of the United Nations.

Article 15

1. Everyone has the right to a nationality.

2. No one shall be arbitrarily deprived of his nationality nor denied the right to change his nationality.

Article 16

1. Men and women of full age, without any limitation due to race, nationality or religion, have the right to marry and to found a family. They are entitled to equal rights as to marriage, during marriage and at its dissolution.

2. Marriage shall be entered into only with the free and full consent of the intending spouses.

3. The family is the natural and fundamental group unit of society and is entitled to protection by society and the State.

Article 17

1. Everyone has the right to own property alone as well as in association with others.

2. No one shall be arbitrarily deprived of his property.

Article 18

Everyone has the right to freedom of thought, conscience and religion; this right includes freedom to change his religion or belief, and freedom, either alone or in community with others and in public or private, to manifest his religion or belief in teaching, practice, worship and observance.

Article 19

Everyone has the right to freedom of opinion and expression; this right includes freedom to hold opinions without interference and to seek, receive and impart information and ideas through any media and regardless of frontiers.

Article 20

1. Everyone has the right to freedom of peaceful assembly and association.

2. No one may be compelled to belong to an association.

Article 21

1. Everyone has the right to take part in the government of his country, directly or through freely chosen representatives.

2. Everyone has the right of equal access to public service in his country.

3. The will of the people shall be the basis of the authority of government; this will shall be expressed in periodic and genuine elections which shall be by universal and equal suffrage and shall be held by secret vote or by equivalent free voting procedures.

Article 22

Everyone, as a member of society, has the right to social security and is entitled to realization, through national effort and international co-operation and in accordance with the organization and resources of each State, of the economic, social and cultural rights indispensable for his dignity and the free development of his personality.

Article 23

1. Everyone has the right to work, to free choice of employment, to just and favourable conditions of work and to protection against unemployment.

2. Everyone, without any discrimination, has the right to equal pay for equal work.

3. Everyone who works has the right to just and favourable remuneration ensuring for himself and his family an existence worthy of human dignity, and supplemented, if necessary, by other means of social protection.

4. Everyone has the right to form and to join trade unions for the protection of his interests.

Article 24

Everyone has the right to rest and leisure, including reasonable limitation of working hours and periodic holidays with pay.

Article 25

1. Everyone has the right to a standard of living adequate for the health and well-being of himself and of his family, including food, clothing, housing and medical care and necessary social services, and the right to security in the event of unemployment, sickness, disability, widowhood, old age or other lack of livelihood in circumstances beyond his control.

2. Motherhood and childhood are entitled to special care and assistance. All children, whether born in or out of wedlock, shall enjoy the same social protection.

Article 26

1. Everyone has the right to education. Education shall be free, at least in the elementary and fundamental stages. Elementary education shall be compulsory. Technical and professional education shall be made generally available and higher education shall be equally accessible to all on the basis of merit.

2. Education shall be directed to the full development of the human personality and to the strengthening of respect for human rights and fundamental freedoms. It shall promote understanding, tolerance and friendship among all nations, racial or religious groups, and shall further the activities of the United Nations for the maintenance of peace.

3. Parents have a prior right to choose the kind of education that shall be given to their children.

Article 27

1. Everyone has the right freely to participate in the cultural life of the community, to enjoy the arts and to share in scientific advancement and its benefits.

2. Everyone has the right to the protection of the moral and material interests resulting from any scientific, literary or artistic production of which he is the author.

Article 28

Everyone is entitled to a social and international order in which the rights and freedoms set forth in this Declaration can be fully realized.

Article 29

1. Everyone has duties to the community in which alone the free and full development of his personality is possible.

2. In the exercise of his rights and freedoms, everyone shall be subject only to such limitations as are determined by law solely for the purpose of securing due recognition and respect for the rights and freedoms of others and of meeting the just requirements of morality, public order and the general welfare in a democratic society.

3. These rights and freedoms may in no case be exercised contrary to the purposes and principles of the United Nations.

Article 30

Nothing in this Declaration may be interpreted as implying for any State, group or person any right to engage in any activity or to perform any act aimed at the destruction of any of the rights and freedoms set forth herein.

Martin Luther King, Jr.
Letter from Birmingham City Jail

...I am in Birmingham because injustice is here. Just as the prophets of the eighth century B.C. left their villages and carried their "thus saith the Lord" far beyond the boundaries of their home towns, and just as the Apostle Paul left his village of Tarsus and carried the gospel of Jesus Christ to the far corners of the Greco-Roman world, so am I compelled to carry the gospel of freedom beyond my own home town. Like Paul, I must constantly respond to the Macedonian call for aid.

Moreover, I am cognizant of the interrelatedness of all communities and states. I cannot sit idly by in Atlanta and not be concerned about what happens in Birmingham. Injustice anywhere is a threat to justice everywhere. We are caught in an inescapable network of mutuality, tied in a single garment of destiny. Whatever affects one directly, affects all indirectly. Never again can we afford to live with the narrow, provincial "outside agitator" idea. Anyone who lives inside the United States can never be considered an outsider anywhere within its bounds.

You deplore the demonstrations taking place in Birmingham. But your statement, I am sorry to say, fails to express a similar concern for the conditions that brought about the demonstrations....

Birmingham is probably the most thoroughly segregated city in the United States. Its ugly record of brutality is widely known. Negroes have experienced grossly unjust treatment in the courts. There have been more unsolved bombings of Negro homes and churches in Birmingham than in any other city in the nation. These are the hard, brutal facts of the case. On the basis of these conditions, Negro leaders sought to negotiate with the city fathers. But the latter consistently refused to engage in good-faith negotiation.

Then, last September, came the opportunity to talk with leaders of Birmingham's economic community. In the course of the negotiations, certain promises were made by the merchants—for example, to remove the stores' humiliating racial signs....[But a] few signs, briefly removed, returned; the others remained.

As in so many past experiences, our hopes had been blasted, and the shadow of deep disappointment settled upon us. We had no alternative except to prepare for direct action, whereby we would present our very bodies as a means of laying our case before the conscience of the local and the national community. Mindful of the difficulties involved, we decided to undertake a process of self-purification. We began a series of workshops on nonviolence, and we repeatedly asked ourselves: "Are you able to accept blows without retaliating?" "Are you able to endure the ordeal of jail?"...

You may well ask: "Why direct action? Why sit-ins, marches and so forth? Isn't negotiation a better path?" You are quite right in calling for negotiation. Indeed, this is the very purpose of direct action. Nonviolent direct action seeks to create such a crisis and foster such a tension that a community which has constantly refused to negotiate is forced to confront the issue. It seeks so to dramatize the issue that it can no longer be ignored. My citing the creation of tension as part of the work of the nonviolent-resister may sound rather shocking. But I must confess that I am not afraid of the word "tension." I have earnestly opposed violent tension, but there is a type of constructive, nonviolent tension which is necessary for growth. Just as Socrates felt that it was necessary to create a tension in the mind so that individuals could rise from the bondage of myths and half-truths to the unfettered realm of creative analysis and objective appraisal, so must we see the need for nonviolent gadflies to create the kind of tension in society that will help men rise from the dark depths of prejudice and racism to the majestic heights of understanding and brotherhood.

The purpose of our direct-action program is to create a situation so crisis-packed that it will inevitably open the door to negotiation. I therefore concur with you in your call for negotiation. Too long has our beloved Southland been bogged down in a tragic effort to live in monologue rather than dialogue....

My friends, I must say to you that we have not made a single gain in civil rights without determined legal and nonviolent pressure. Lamentably, it is an historical fact that privileged groups seldom give up their privileges voluntarily. Individuals may see the moral light and voluntarily give up their unjust posture; but, as Reinhold Niebuhr has reminded us, groups tend to be more immoral than individuals.

We know through painful experience that freedom is never voluntarily given by the oppressor; it must be demanded by the oppressed. Frankly, I have yet to engage in a direct-action campaign that was "well timed" in the view of those who have not suffered unduly from the disease of segregation. For years now I have heard the word "Wait!" It rings in the ear of every Negro with piercing familiarity. This "Wait" has almost always meant "Never." We must come to see, with one of our distinguished jurists, that "justice too long delayed is justice denied."

We have waited for more than 340 years for our constitutional and God-given rights. The nations of Asia and Africa are moving with jet-like speed toward gaining political independence, but we still creep at horse-and-buggy pace toward gaining a cup of coffee at a lunch counter. Perhaps it is easy for those who have never felt the stinging darts of segregation to say, "Wait." But when you have seen vicious mobs lynch your mothers and fathers at will and drown your sisters and brothers at whim; when you have seen hate-filled policemen curse, kick and even kill your black brothers and sisters; when you see the vast majority of your twenty million Negro brothers smothering in an airtight cage of poverty in the midst of an affluent society; when you suddenly find your tongue twisted and your speech stammering as you seek to explain to your six-year-old daughter why she can't go to the public amusement park that has just been advertised on television, and see tears welling up in her eyes when she is told that Funtown is closed to colored children, and see ominous clouds of inferiority beginning to form in her little mental sky, and see her beginning to distort her personality by developing an unconscious bitterness toward white people; when you have to concoct an answer for a five-year-old son who is asking: "Daddy, why do white people treat colored people so mean?"; when you take a cross-country drive and find it necessary to sleep night after night in the uncomfortable corners of your automobile because no motel will accept you; when you are humiliated day in and day out by nagging signs reading "white" and "colored"; when your first name becomes "nigger," your middle name becomes "boy" (however old you are) and your last name becomes "John," and your wife and mother are never given the respected title "Mrs."; when you are harried by day and haunted by night by the fact that you are a Negro, living constantly at tiptoe stance, never quite knowing what to expect next, and are plagued with inner fears and outer resentments; when you are forever fighting a degenerating sense of "nobodiness"—then you will understand why we find it difficult to wait. There comes a time when the cup of endurance runs over, and men are no longer willing to be plunged into the abyss of despair. I hope, sirs, you can understand our legitimate and unavoidable impatience.

You express a great deal of anxiety over our willingness to break laws. This is certainly a legitimate concern. Since we so diligently urge people to obey the Supreme Court's decision of 1954 outlawing segregation in the public schools, at first glance it may seem rather paradoxical for us consciously to break laws. One may well ask, "How can you advocate breaking some laws and obeying others?" The answer lies in the fact that there are two types of laws: just and unjust. I would be the first to advocate obeying just laws. One has not only a legal but a moral responsibility to obey just laws.

Conversely, one has a moral responsibility to disobey unjust laws. I would agree with St. Augustine that "an unjust law is no law at all."

Now, what is the difference between the two? How does one determine whether a law is just or unjust? A just law is a man-made code that squares with the moral law or the law of God. An unjust law is a code that is out of harmony with the moral law. To put it in the terms of St. Thomas Aquinas: An unjust law is a human law that is not rooted in eternal law and natural law. Any law that uplifts human personality is just. Any law that degrades human personality is unjust. All segregation statutes are unjust because segregation distorts the soul and damages the personality. It gives the segregator a false sense of superiority and the segregated a false sense of inferiority. Segregation, to use the terminology of the Jewish philosopher Martin Buber, substitutes an "I—it" relationship for an "I—thou" relationship and ends up relegating persons to the status of things. Hence segregation is not only politically, economically and sociologically unsound, it is morally wrong and sinful. Paul Tillich has said that sin is separation. Is not segregation an existential expression of man's tragic separation, his awful estrangement, his terrible sinfulness? Thus it is that I can urge men to obey the 1954 decision of the Supreme Court, for it is morally right; and I can urge them to disobey segregation ordinances, for they are morally wrong.

Let us consider a more concrete example of just and unjust laws. An unjust law is a code that a numerical or power majority group compels a minority group to obey but does not make binding on itself. This is difference made legal. By the same token, a just law is a code that a majority compels a minority to follow and that is willing to follow itself. This is sameness made legal.

Let me give another explanation. A law is unjust if it is inflicted on a minority that, as a result of being denied the right to vote, had no part in enacting or devising the law. Who can say that the legislature of Alabama which set up that state's segregation laws was democratically elected? Throughout Alabama all sorts of devious methods are used to prevent Negroes from becoming registered voters, and there are some counties in which, even though Negroes constitute a majority of the population, not a single Negro is registered. Can any law enacted under such circumstances be considered democratically structured?

Sometimes a law is just on its face and unjust in its application. For instance, I have been arrested on a charge of parading without a permit. Now, there is nothing wrong in having an ordinance which requires a permit for a parade. But such an ordinance becomes unjust when it is used to maintain segregation and to deny citizens the First-Amendment privilege of peaceful assembly and protest.

I hope you are able to see the distinction I am trying to point out. In no sense do I advocate evading or defying the law, as would the rabid segregationist. That would lead to anarchy. One who breaks an unjust law must do so openly, lovingly, and with a willingness to accept the penalty. I submit that an individual who breaks a law that conscience tells him is unjust, and who willingly accepts the penalty of imprisonment in order to arouse the conscience of the community over its injustice, is in reality expressing the highest respect for law.

Of course, there is nothing new about this kind of civil disobedience. It was evidenced sublimely in the refusal of Shadrach, Meshach and Abednego to obey the laws of Nebuchadnezzar, on the ground that a higher moral law was at stake. It was practiced superbly by the early Christians, who were willing to face hungry lions and the excruciating pain of chopping blocks rather than submit to certain unjust laws of the Roman Empire. To a degree, academic freedom is a reality today because Socrates practiced civil disobedience. In our own nation, the Boston Tea Party represented a massive act of civil disobedience.

We should never forget that everything Adolf Hitler did in Germany was "legal" and everything the Hungarian freedom fighters did in Hungary was "illegal." It was "illegal" to aid and comfort a Jew in Hitler's Germany. Even so, I am sure that, had I lived in Germany at the time, I would have aided and comforted my Jewish brothers. If today I lived in a Communist country where certain principles dear to the Christian faith are suppressed, I would openly advocate disobeying that country's antireligious laws....

Like a boil that can never be cured so long as it is covered up but must be opened with all its ugliness to the natural medicines of air and light, injustice must be exposed, with all the tension its exposure creates, to the light of human conscience and the air of national opinion before it can be cured.

In your statement you assert that our actions, even though peaceful, must be condemned because they precipitate violence. But is this a logical assertion? Isn't this like condemning a robbed man because his possession of money precipitated the evil act of robbery? Isn't this like condemning Socrates because his unswerving commitment to truth and his philosophical inquiries precipitated the act by the misguided populace in which they made him drink hemlock? Isn't this like condemning Jesus because his unique God consciousness and never ceasing devotion to God's will precipitated the evil act of crucifixion? We must come to see that, as the federal courts have consistently affirmed, it is wrong to urge an individual to cease his efforts to gain his basic constitutional rights because the quest may precipitate violence. Society must protect the robbed and punish the robber....

Oppressed people cannot remain oppressed forever. The yearning for freedom eventually manifests itself, and that is what has happened to the American Negro. Something within has reminded him of his birthright of freedom, and something without has reminded him that it can be gained. Consciously or unconsciously, he has been caught up by the Zeitgeist, and with his black brothers of Africa and his brown and yellow brothers of Asia, South America and the Caribbean, the United States Negro is moving with a sense of great urgency toward the promised land of racial justice. If one recognizes this vital urge that has engulfed the Negro community, one should readily understand why public demonstrations are taking place. The Negro has many pent-up resentments and latent frustrations, and he must release them. So let him march; let him make prayer pilgrimages to the city hall; let him go on freedom rides—and try to understand why he must do so. If his repressed emotions are not released in nonviolent ways, they will seek expression through violence; this is not a threat but a fact of history. So I have not said to my people: "Get rid of your discontent." Rather, I have tried to say that this normal and healthy discontent can be channeled into the creative outlet of nonviolent direct action. And now this approach is being termed extremist.

But though I was initially disappointed at being categorized as an extremist, as I continued to think about the matter I gradually gained a measure of satisfaction from the label. Was not Jesus an extremist for love: "Love your enemies, bless them that curse you, do good to them that hate you, and pray for them which despitefully use you, and persecute you." Was not Amos an extremist for justice: "Let justice roll down like waters and righteousness like an ever-flowing stream." Was not Paul an extremist for the Christian gospel: "I bear in my body the marks of the Lord Jesus." Was not Martin Luther an extremist: "Here I stand; I cannot do otherwise, so help me God." And John Bunyan: "I will stay in jail to the end of my days before I make a butchery of my conscience." And Abraham Lincoln: "This nation cannot survive half slave and half free." And Thomas Jefferson: "We hold these truths to be self-evident, that all men are created equal..." So the question is not whether we will be extremists, but what kind of extremists we will be. Will we be extremists for hate or for love? Will we be extremists for the preservation of injustice or for the extension of justice? In that dramatic scene on Calvary's hill three men were crucified. We must never forget that all three were crucified for the same crime—the crime of extremism. Two were extremists for immorality, and thus fell below their environment. The other, Jesus Christ, was an extremist for love, truth and goodness, and thereby rose above his environment. Perhaps the South, the nation and the world are in dire need of creative extremists....

I have no fear about the outcome of our struggle in Birmingham, even if our motives are at present misunderstood. We will reach the goal of freedom in Birmingham and all over the nation, because the goal of America is freedom. Abused and scorned though we may be, our destiny is tied up with America's destiny. Before the pilgrims landed at Plymouth, we were here. Before the pen of Jefferson etched the majestic words of the Declaration of Independence across the pages of history, we were here. For more than two centuries our forebears labored in this country without wages; they made cotton king; they built the homes of their masters while suffering gross injustice and shameful humiliation—and yet out of a bottomless vitality they continued to thrive and develop. If the inexpressible cruelties of slavery could not stop us, the opposition we now face will surely fail. We will win our freedom because the sacred heritage of our nation and the eternal will of God are embodied in our echoing demands....

Over the past few years I have consistently preached that nonviolence demands that the means we use must be as pure as the ends we seek. I have tried to make clear that it is wrong to use immoral means to attain moral ends. But now I must affirm that it is just as wrong, or perhaps even more so, to use moral means to preserve immoral ends....

I wish you had commended the Negro sit-inners and demonstrators of Birmingham for their sublime courage, their willingness to suffer and their amazing discipline in the midst of great provocation. One day the South will recognize its real heroes. They will be the James Merediths, with the noble sense of purpose that enables them to face jeering and hostile mobs, and with the agonizing loneliness that characterizes the life of the pioneer. They will be old, oppressed, battered Negro women, symbolized in a seventy-two-year-old woman in Montgomery, Alabama, who rose up with a sense of dignity and with her people decided not to ride segregated buses, and who responded with ungrammatical profundity to one who inquired about her weariness: "My feets is tired, but my soul is at rest." They will be the young high school and college students, the young ministers of the gospel and a host of their elders, courageously and nonviolently sitting in at lunch counters and willingly going to jail for conscience' sake. One day the South will know that when these disinherited children of God sat down at lunch counters, they were in reality standing up for what is best in the American dream and for the most sacred values in our Judaeo-Christian heritage, thereby bringing our nation back to those great wells of democracy which were dug deep by the founding fathers in their formulation of the Constitution and the Declaration of Independence....

If I have said anything in this letter that overstates the truth and indicates an unreasonable impatience, I beg you to forgive me. If I have said anything that understates the truth and indicates my having a patience that allows me to settle for anything less than brotherhood, I beg God to forgive me.

I hope this letter finds you strong in the faith. I also hope that circumstances will soon make it possible for me to meet each of you, not as an integrationist or a civil-rights leader but as a fellow clergyman and a Christian brother. Let us all hope that the dark clouds of racial prejudice will soon pass away and the deep fog of misunderstanding will be lifted from our fear-drenched communities, and in some not too distant tomorrow the radiant stars of love and brotherhood will shine over our great nation with all their scintillating beauty.

Biographical Notes

ADAMS, ABIGAIL (1744–1818). Wife of President John Adams. Supported her husband in the revolutionary cause. Well known for her letters which have been a rich source of social history.

ADAMS, JOHN (1735–1826). Second president of the United States. Lawyer, revolutionary leader, and leading Federalist. As a member of the Continental Congress, he served on the committee to draft the Declaration of Independence. Minister to the Netherlands and Great Britain. Elected vice president in 1789 and president in 1796.

ANTHONY, SUSAN B. (1820–1906). Social reformer involved in both the abolitionist and woman suffrage movements. President of National American Woman Suffrage Association. Wrote and lectured in both the United States and Europe for women's right to vote.

BALDWIN, ABRAHAM (1745–1815). Baldwin was born in Connecticut. He attended Yale, where he studied the classics and law. He moved to Georgia in 1784. He served Georgia as a state legislator, in the Continental Congress, at the Philadelphia Convention, in the House of Representatives, and in the U.S. Senate. He also founded the University of Georgia. As a national legislator, Baldwin supported states' rights, though he had argued for a strong national government at the Philadelphia Convention.

BASSETT, RICHARD (1745–1815). Bassett was born in Maryland. He studied law in Philadelphia and set up his law practice in Delaware. He was also a planter, owning three homes in Delaware and Maryland. Bassett served in the Continental Army during the Revolutionary War and participated in Delaware's constitutional convention and state legislature. At the Philadelphia Convention, Bassett made no speeches. Bassett later served as a U.S. Senator, a judge, and governor of Delaware.

BEDFORD, GUNNING (1747–1812). Like many of the Framers, Bedford was born into a large family. A roommate of James Madison at the College of New Jersey, Bedford later studied law in Philadelphia. Bedford moved to Delaware, where he practiced law and served the state as a legislator, representative to the Continental Congress, and attorney general. Bedford was a member of the committee that drafted the Great Compromise, representing the small states' point of view. After the Convention, Bedford spent many years as a federal district judge.

BLACK, HUGO (1886–1971). Supreme Court justice from 1937 to 1971. Served in the Senate and was appointed to the Supreme Court by President Roosevelt.

BLAIR, JOHN (1732–1800). Blair was born into a prominent Virginia family. He graduated from the College of William and Mary and studied law in London. Blair was active in the movement to gain independence from Great Britain. He was active in Virginia state government after independence was declared. At Philadelphia, Blair never spoke, usually going along with the Virginia delegation. He later served on the Supreme Court.

BLOUNT, WILLIAM (1749–1800). Blount was the eldest son of a well-established North Carolina family. He served in the Continental Army, the North Carolina state government, and the Continental Congress. Blount missed more than a month of the Philadelphia Convention and did not say much while he was there. In 1790, he moved, settling in what is now Tennessee, and was one of its first U.S. senators.

BREARLY, DAVID (1745–1790). Brearly was born and raised in New Jersey. Although he dropped out of college, he practiced law in New Jersey. He was an avid patriot. Arrested by the British for treason, Brearly was freed by a group of patriots. Brearly fought in the Revolutionary War. From 1779 to 1789, he served as the chief justice of the New Jersey supreme court. Brearly argued for the interests of the small states at the Philadelphia Convention. He served as the president of the New Jersey ratifying convention. Appointed a federal district judge in 1789, Brearly died the next year at age 45.

BROOM, JACOB (1752–1810). Broom was born in Delaware. His career was varied, including farming, surveying and map-making, shipping, importing, real estate, and city government. Broom attended every session of the Philadelphia Convention.

BURGER, WARREN E. (1907–). Chief Justice of the United States from 1969 to 1986. Appointed by President Nixon. Named as assistant attorney general in 1953; three years later was appointed to U.S. Court of Appeals for the District of Columbia. Retired in 1986 to head the Commission on the Bicentennial of the United States Constitution.

BURR, AARON (1756–1836). Public official and political leader. Served in Continental Army, New York Assembly, and U.S. Senate. Elected as vice president in 1800.

BUTLER, PIERCE (1744–1822). Butler was born in Ireland, the son of a member of the House of Lords. He served in the British Army until 1771, when he resigned after marrying a colonial girl. He served with the South Carolina militia in the Revolutionary War, during which he lost much of his property. Butler spoke often at the Philadelphia Convention, arguing for a strong national government and for the interests of southern slaveholders. Although he later served in the U.S. Senate, he devoted most of his time to his plantation.

CARROLL, DANIEL (1730–1796). Carroll was one of only two Roman Catholics to sign the Constitution. He was a member of a prominent Maryland family. He studied in Europe, returning to the United States to live the life of a planter. In 1781, Carroll was elected to the Continental Congress. He also served in the Maryland senate. Carroll arrived late at the Philadelphia Convention but attended regularly once he got there. He participated in the debates and campaigned for ratification in Maryland. Carroll served in the House of Representatives and as one of the first commissioners of the District of Columbia.

CHARLES I (1600–1649). King of England 1625–1649. Believed in the divine right of kings and absolute power of the monarch. Clashed with the House of Commons and ruled seven years without Parliament. Forced to assent to the Petition of Right in 1628. Struggle with Parliament led to Civil War and his execution for high treason.

CHARLES II (1630–1685). King of England. Son of Charles I, he restored the monarchy in 1660 but continued to have problems with Parliament. He agreed to the Habeas Corpus Act in 1678.

CLINTON, GEORGE (1739–1812). Revolutionary soldier and public official. Member of the Continental Congress, governor of New York, general in the Continental Army. Had a profound distrust of centralized government and opposed ratification of the Constitution. Supporter of Jefferson, he served as vice president in 1804 and 1808.

CLYMER, GEORGE (1739–1813). Clymer inherited his uncle's business, which suffered as a result of British restrictions on colonial trade. He was, nevertheless, a patriot who worked hard for independence. Clymer served in the Pennsylvania legislature and the Continental Congress. Although he did not speak often at the Philadelphia Convention, his speeches were well planned and effective. Clymer was elected to the First Congress and later served as a member of the commission that negotiated a treaty with Native Americans in Georgia.

CROMWELL, OLIVER (1599–1658). Lord Protector of England, 1653-1658. Puritan. Military leader in the English Civil War, he upheld the Parliamentary cause and led the army to victory. He united the kingdom, dissolved Parliament, and established himself as ruler until his death.

DAVIE, WILLIAM R. (1756–1820). Davie was born in England, moving to South Carolina in 1763. He attended college in North Carolina and New Jersey, graduating with honors. He studied law in North Carolina and practiced there until 1787. During the 1780s, he also served in the military, a career he enjoyed. Davie favored the Great Compromise, the indirect election of senators and the president, and representation for slave property. Davie did not sign the Constitution but did work for ratification. After the convention, he served as governor of North Carolina, as a state legislator, and as a peace commissioner to France, among other offices. Davie was one of the founders of the University of North Carolina.

DAWES, WILLIAM (1745–1799). Tradesman, active in the Revolutionary movement in Boston. Gave the warning, with Paul Revere, before the battles of Lexington and Concord. Joined the Continental Army.

DAYTON, JONATHAN (1760–1824). Dayton, a native of New Jersey, was the youngest man to sign the Constitution. As soon as he graduated from the College of New Jersey, he entered the Continental Army. After the war, Dayton studied law and set up his practice. He also served in the New Jersey legislature. Dayton was chosen to attend the Philadelphia Convention because his father and another associate decided not to go. He participated in the debates and signed the Constitution, even though there were some parts of it he did not like. Dayton later served in the House of Representatives and Senate.

DICKINSON, JOHN (1732–1808). Dickinson was born in Maryland, the son of a wealthy farm family. He was educated by private tutors, then studied law in Philadelphia and London. He set up his first law practice in Philadelphia, where he served in the Pennsylvania legislature. Dickinson became famous throughout the colonies for opposing British taxation. However, he voted against independence in 1776 and did not sign the Declaration. He did enlist in the Continental Army. He headed the committee that drafted the Articles of Confederation but by 1786 believed they needed to be changed. Dickinson had the reputation of a scholar and was highly respected. He made important contributions to the Philadelphia Convention but left early due to illness. He spent his later years writing about politics.

DOUGLAS, WILLIAM (1898–1980). Supreme Court Justice from 1939 to 1975. Appointed to the Supreme Court by President Franklin D. Roosevelt.

DYER, MARY (?–1660). Religious martyr. Born in England and came to Boston in 1635. As a Quaker who preached ideas unpopular with the Puritan leaders of Boston, she was banned from that city under threat of death. When she returned, she was arrested and hanged publicly on June 1, 1660.

EISENHOWER, DWIGHT (1890–1969). Thirty-fourth president. Commander of U.S. Forces in Europe during World War II and then elevated to Allied commander in chief. Elected president in 1952 and reelected four years later. In 1957, ordered federal troops into Little Rock to enforce integration order.

ELLSWORTH, OLIVER (1745–1807). Ellsworth was a member of a well-to-do Connecticut family. He graduated from the College of New Jersey, taught school, and served as a minister before going into law. He was soon considered one of Connecticut's best lawyers. Ellsworth served in the Continental Congress and was a delegate to the Philadelphia Convention. He played an important role at the convention and was one of the authors of the Great Compromise. Elected to the U.S. Senate, he was responsible for the Judiciary Act of 1789. In 1796 Ellsworth was appointed Chief Justice of the United States.

FEW, WILLIAM (1748–1828). Few was born in Maryland but moved to North Carolina when he was ten. In 1771, William, his father, and a brother were involved with a group of frontiersmen who opposed the Royal Governor of North Carolina. As a result, his brother was hanged and the family had to flee to Georgia. Few served in the Georgia state legislature and the Continental Congress. He missed much of the Philadelphia Convention because he was in Congress. Few became one of Georgia's first U.S. senators. In 1799, he moved to New York, where he was active in New York state politics and banking.

FITZSIMONS, THOMAS (1741–1811). Fitzsimons was born in Ireland, moving to America about 1760. He lived in Philadelphia, where he was a prominent businessman. He fought in the Revolutionary War, donating money to the patriots' cause. Fitzsimons served in the Continental Congress and as a Pennsylvania state legislator. He did not say much at the Philadelphia Convention, although he attended regularly and favored a strong national government. Fitzsimons served three terms in the House of Representatives but spent most of the rest of his life attending to his business interests.

FRANKLIN, BENJAMIN (1706–1790). Franklin was the oldest delegate to the Philadelphia Convention. With the possible exception of George Washington, Franklin was the best-known man in America. Born into a poor family, Franklin became an inventor, scientist, diplomat, and publisher. His *Poor Richard's Almanac* was read nationwide. His career in public service was a long and varied one, including service as an ambassador to England and France and as governor of Pennsylvania. At the Philadelphia Convention, Franklin was a compromiser, using wit to bring delegates together. He played an important role in creating the Great Compromise. He favored a strong national government and argued that the Framers should trust the judgment of the people. Although he was in poor health in 1787, he missed few sessions, being carried to and from the meeting place in a special chair. Although he did not agree with everything in the Constitution, he believed that no other convention could come up with a better document.

GERRY, ELBRIDGE (1744–1814). Gerry was born to a wealthy merchant family in Massachusetts. He graduated from Harvard and was a staunch supporter of Samuel Adams. Gerry was active in protests against British policies and was one of the signers of the Declaration of Independence. He often changed his mind about political issues. For example, after Shays' Rebellion, he spoke against giving the common people too much power, but he still argued for yearly elections and against giving the Senate, which was not accountable to the people, too much power. Gerry refused to sign the Constitution and worked against ratification. Throughout his life, he served in a variety of offices including that of vice president.

GILMAN, NICHOLAS (1755–1814). Gilman was born into a large and distinguished New Hampshire family. He served in the Continental Army, returning home after the war to work in his father's store and take part in state politics. He served in the Continental Congress, although he had a poor attendance record. Gilman arrived late at the Philadelphia Convention and made no speeches. He was important in getting New Hampshire to ratify the Constitution. He served in the House of Representatives as a Federalist and later won election to the Senate as a Republican.

GORHAM, NATHANIEL (1738–1796). Gorham was born in Massachusetts. He received little formal education, becoming an apprentice to a merchant at age 15. He was active in state politics and supported the revolutionary cause. He served in the Continental Congress and was an important member of the Philadelphia Convention, speaking often and serving on various committees. He worked to gain approval of the Constitution in Massachusetts. Gorham is one of the few delegates to the convention who did not serve in the new government.

HAMILTON, ALEXANDER (1755–1804). Alexander Hamilton was one of the most brilliant thinkers at the Philadelphia Convention. His origins were modest, having been born to unmarried parents in the British West Indies. As a young man, he traveled to New York City with the help of people who recognized his intelligence. He attended college until the Revolution, in which he was very active, interrupted his studies. After the war, he studied law and entered practice. He served in the Continental Congress and was one of the leaders in calling for a constitutional convention. As a delegate to the Philadelphia Convention, he played a rather small role, partly because he had to miss many sessions due to legal business, partly because he wanted a much stronger national government than did most delegates, and partly because he did not get along with the other delegates from New York. He was one of the authors of *The Federalist* and worked hard for ratification in New York. He served in Washington's government as Secretary of the Treasury and was a leader of the Federalist Party. In 1804, Hamilton was killed in a duel with Aaron Burr.

HARLAN, JOHN MARSHALL (1899–1971). Justice of the Supreme Court from 1955 to 1971. Appointed by President Eisenhower.

HAROLD, KING OF ENGLAND (1022?–1066). Elected on January 6, 1066. Defeated by William, Duke of Normandy, at the Battle of Hastings on October 14, 1066.

HENRY, PATRICK (1736–1799). Political leader. Supporter of the revolutionary cause. Opposed the Philadelphia Convention and refused to attend. Led opposition in Virginia to ratification of the Constitution. Worked to include the Bill of Rights in the Constitution.

HENRY III (1207–1272). King of England from 1216 to 1272. Provoked rebellion of nobles who forced him to accept a series of reforms, an important step toward constitutional monarchy. During King Henry's reign, Commons became part of Parliament.

HOLMES, OLIVER WENDELL, JR. (1841–1935). Justice of the Supreme Court from 1902 to 1932. Appointed by President Theodore Roosevelt. Served 19 years on the Massachusetts Supreme Court.

HOOKER, THOMAS (1586–1647). Religious leader. Puritan. Born and educated in England, he fled to Holland and then to Massachusetts. In 1636, he led a group of followers to Connecticut to enjoy religious freedom.

HOUSTON, WILLIAM C. (1746–1788). William C. Houston studied at the College of New Jersey, where he later taught. He served in the military during the Revolutionary War and represented New Jersey in the Continental Congress. He also served as a collector of continental taxes in New Jersey, not a rewarding job during the time the Articles of Confederation were in effect. Houston did not sign the Constitution.

HOUSTON, WILLIAM (1757–?). Not a great deal is known about William Houston of Georgia. He was a member of the Continental Congress and represented Georgia in a boundary dispute with South Carolina in 1785. One of his fellow delegates to the Philadelphia Convention described him as a "gentleman of family" with little or no legal or political knowledge. He did not sign the Constitution.

INGERSOLL, JARED (1749–1822). Ingersoll was born in Connecticut, the son of a British colonial official. He graduated from Yale and then managed his father's business affairs. He followed his father to Philadelphia, where he studied law. Ingersoll attended every session of the Philadelphia Convention, although he said little. His service after the convention was extensive, holding such jobs as attorney general of Pennsylvania and presiding judge of the Philadelphia District Court. He once ran for vice president, but lost. In his successful law practice, he argued several important cases before the Supreme Court.

JACKSON, ANDREW (1767–1845). Seventh president of the United States. General and hero of the War of 1812. Served in the House and Senate. Came from frontier origins and was seen as representative of the growing democratic spirit in the South and West. Elected president in 1828 and reelected in 1832.

JAMES I (1566–1625). King of Scotland and England. Son of Mary, Queen of Scots. Sought to assert the divine right of kings.

JAMES II (1633–1701). King of England, Scotland and Ireland. Son of King Charles I. Favored Roman Catholics and, as a result, was forced to flee to France. English nobles offered the throne to his son-in-law, William of Orange.

JAY, JOHN (1745–1829). First chief justice of the United States from 1789 to 1795. Wrote New York's first constitution. President of the Continental Congress. Served as minister to Spain and England. Strong supporter of the Constitution and one of the authors of *The Federalist*. Appointed chief justice by President Washington but resigned in 1795 when he was elected governor of New York.

JEFFERSON, THOMAS (1743–1826). Third president of the United States, scientist, philosopher, diplomat, and architect. He supported the revolutionary cause and was governor of Virginia. Wrote Declaration of Independence. Supporter of the Constitution but critical of the lack of a bill of rights. First secretary of state in Washington's cabinet. Leader of the Republican Party. Elected vice president in 1796 and was chosen president four years later. Reelected to the presidency in 1804.

JENIFER, DANIEL OF ST. THOMAS (1723–1790). Jenifer was born in 1723 in Maryland. Not much is known about his early years. As an adult, he owned a large estate near Annapolis. He supported the Revolution, serving in the Continental Congress and the Maryland state legislature. Jenifer favored a stronger national government. Although he did not speak often at the Philadelphia Convention, he generally supported the positions of James Madison. He died only three years after the convention.

JOHN, KING OF ENGLAND (1167?–1216). Forced by the nobles to sign the Magna Carta.

JOHNSON, LYNDON B. (1908–1973). Thirty-sixth president of the United States. Served in both the House and the Senate. Elected in 1955 as Senate Majority Leader. Elected vice president in 1960. Succeeded to presidency in 1963 upon the assassination of President Kennedy. Elected president in 1964.

JOHNSON, WILLIAM SAMUEL (1727–1819). Johnson was born in Connecticut. He graduated from Yale and became a lawyer. He held a number of positions in his home state prior to the Revolution, in which he found it difficult to choose sides. He finally decided that his role should be one of peace-maker, which was what he attempted to do during the war. After the war, he was a powerful member of the Continental Congress. He played an important role in the Philadelphia Convention, serving as the chairman of the committee of style, which drafted the final document. He worked for ratification in Connecticut, which he later represented in the Senate. He retired from political office to devote his time to his position as president of Columbia College.

KENNEDY, JOHN F. (1917–1963). Thirty-fifth president of the United States. Elected to the House of Representatives in 1946; six years later, was elected to the Senate. In 1960, Kennedy became the youngest man and first Catholic ever elected president. Assassinated in 1963.

KING, MARTIN LUTHER, JR. (1929–1968). Religious leader and social reformer. Major leader of the civil rights movement in the 1960s, he was an advocate of nonviolence. Formed the Southern Christian Leadership Conference in 1957 and became its president. Won the Nobel Peace Prize in 1964. Assassinated in 1968.

KING, RUFUS (1755–1827). King was born in what is now Maine. He was the eldest son of a wealthy farmer-merchant and graduated from Harvard. He studied the law and entered practice in Massachusetts. An excellent speaker and early opponent of slavery, King served in the Massachusetts legislature and the Continental Congress. One of the youngest delegates to the Philadelphia Convention, King was also one of the best speakers, arguing for a stronger national government. His notes on the events at the convention have been of interest to historians. In 1788, King moved to New York, where he became active in state politics and was chosen as a U.S. senator several times. He also served as a director of the First Bank of the United States and as minister to Great Britain. He ran for vice president twice and president once, but lost all three times.

KNOX, HENRY (1750–1806). Revolutionary military leader. General in the Continental Army and trusted adviser to Washington. Elected secretary of war under the Articles of Confederation and retained by Washington in that position under the new government.

LANGDON, JOHN (1741–1819). Langdon was a native of New Hampshire. He did not receive a great deal of education and began as an apprentice to a merchant. He invested his money in trade and became a wealthy man. Langdon avidly supported the Revolution, leading colonists in a raid on British gunpowder stores, serving in public office, and pledging money to finance various military campaigns. Langdon paid his own way and that of the other New Hampshire delegate to the Philadelphia Convention. He played an important role at the convention, even though he arrived late. He favored a more powerful national government and worked for ratification in New Hampshire. His later service included duty as governor of his home state and U.S. senator.

LANSING, JOHN (1754–1829). Lansing was born in Albany, New York, to a family that had been in America since the 1600s. He practiced law in New York and served in the state legislature and the Continental Congress. He left the Philadelphia Convention in July, along with another New York delegate, because he opposed the creation of an entirely new government. He believed that the Articles of Confederation should simply have been amended. He worked against ratification of the Constitution in New York. Lansing devoted the years after the convention to various public offices in the state of New York.

LIVINGSTON, WILLIAM (1723–1790). Livingston was raised by his grandmother in Albany, New York. He spent one of his teenage years as a missionary among the Mohawk Indians. He graduated from Yale and spent many years in law practice and politics in New York. Tired of law and having lost power in the New York legislature, he moved to New Jersey around 1770. He planned to live in retirement, but instead was caught up in the Revolution. Livingston served in the Continental Congress, in the New Jersey militia, and as governor of the state. At the Philadelphia Convention, he served as chairman of the committee that reached a compromise on slavery (an institution he opposed). He worked for ratification in New Jersey, where his position as governor helped. He served as governor from 1776 until his death in 1790.

LOCKE, JOHN (1632–1704). English philosopher. Wrote *Two Treatises on Government, Letters Concerning Toleration*, and *An Essay Concerning Human Understanding*. Had a great influence on American political thinkers during the Revolutionary period and the early years of the new nation.

MADISON, JAMES (1751–1836). The "Father of the Constitution" was born to a wealthy Virginia family. He was taught at home and in private schools, then graduated from the College of New Jersey. While deciding whether to become a lawyer or minister, Madison became involved in the revolutionary cause, thereby entering state and local politics. His poor health kept him from serving in the military. In 1780, Madison was chosen to serve in the Continental Congress, where he played a major role. He was one of the most influential voices calling for a constitutional convention. He came to the Philadelphia Convention with a plan for the new government, took extensive notes on the proceedings, spoke more than 150 times, and worked tirelessly on various committees. As one of the authors of *The Federalist,* Madison was also a key figure in the battle for ratification. Following the convention, Madison served as a member of the U.S. House of Representatives, helping to frame the Bill of Rights and organize the executive department. Under Jefferson, Madison served as secretary of state. He then succeeded Jefferson as president. In retirement, Madison continued to speak out on public issues.

MARSHALL, JOHN (1755–1835). Chief justice of the United States from 1801 to 1835. Supported ratification of the Constitution and led Federalist Party in Virginia. Member of the House of Representatives. Served 34 years as chief justice, interpreting the Constitution in a manner that reflected his belief in a strong and effective national government.

MARSHALL, THURGOOD (1908–1993). Justice of the Supreme Court, appointed in 1967 by President Johnson. Great-grandson of slaves, he became involved in the civil rights movement. As counsel for the NAACP, he successfully pleaded the case of *Brown v. Board of Education* in 1954. First African American to serve on the U.S. Supreme Court.

MARTIN, ALEXANDER (1740–1807). Martin was born in New Jersey around 1740. He moved to North Carolina after graduating from the College of New Jersey. He served in various local and state offices and was in the military for two years. Martin returned to North Carolina and various state offices. He attended the Philadelphia Convention, but left early and did not sign the document. After the convention, he served as governor, as a U.S. senator, and as a state senator.

MARTIN, LUTHER (1748–1826). Luther Martin was born in New Jersey around 1748. After graduating from the College of New Jersey, he moved to Maryland where he began practicing law. He served as state attorney general and in the Continental Congress. At the Philadelphia Convention, he opposed increasing the power of the federal government. Martin believed in the rights of the states and of the people and wanted each state to have an equal vote in Congress. He also wanted a bill of rights. Although he owned six slaves, Martin opposed slavery, speaking out against it. Because he lost the battles on the issues he thought were important,

Martin left the convention and did not sign the Constitution. He fought against ratification in Maryland. After 27 years in office, Martin resigned as Maryland attorney general in 1805. He served in several other positions, but returned as attorney general in 1818.

MASON, GEORGE (1725–1792). George Mason was born into a wealthy Virginia family. He studied law and managed his large plantation near George Washington's home. Throughout most of his life, Mason preferred private life to public service, although he did serve in the Virginia legislature. At the Philadelphia Convention, Mason spoke often. He argued against giving the president too much power, for a bill of rights, and against slavery (although at his death, he owned 300 slaves). Mason did not sign the Constitution and fought against its ratification. He died shortly after the ratification of the Bill of Rights.

McCLURG, JAMES (1746–1823). McClurg was born in Virginia, the state he later represented at the Philadelphia Convention. He traveled to Scotland to study medicine. After receiving his degree in 1770, he studied in Paris and London. In 1773, he returned to Virginia, where he served as physician general and director of hospitals during the Revolution. He was named a delegate to the Philadelphia Convention when Patrick Henry and Richard Henry Lee refused to attend. He did not sign the Constitution, which he had hoped would include a life term for the president and a federal veto on state laws. His involvement in politics after the convention was minimal as he chose to devote his time to medicine.

McHENRY, JAMES (1723–1816). McHenry was another delegate born in Ireland. He came to America alone in 1771; the next year, he talked his family into coming too. He studied poetry and medicine and did hospital work during the Revolution. In 1781 he left the military to join the Maryland Senate. He also served in the Continental Congress. He was called away from the Philadelphia Convention because of family illness and missed all of June and July's sessions. After the convention, he served in the Maryland legislature and as secretary of war. After retiring in 1800, he spent much of his time writing.

MERCER, JOHN FRANCIS (1750–1821). Mercer was born in Virginia and was educated at the College of William and Mary. He enlisted in the army and served from 1776 to 1779. He studied law under Thomas Jefferson and practiced in Virginia. He served in the Virginia legislature and in the Continental Congress. He moved to Maryland in 1785 when he inherited land. At the Philadelphia Convention, he opposed a strong central government and left before the convention was over. He opposed ratification. He later served in the Maryland legislature, in the U.S. House of Representatives, and as governor of Maryland.

MIFFLIN, THOMAS (1744–1800). Thomas Mifflin was a Pennsylvania Quaker, the son of a rich merchant and politician. He was educated in Philadelphia and entered business upon finishing his education. He was also involved in politics, raising troops and serving in the Continental Army. He was expelled from the Quaker church for doing so. He served in the state legislature and in the Continental Congress. He attended the Philadelphia Convention, but did not speak. He continued in the Pennsylvania legislature and later served ten years as governor.

MONTESQUIEU (1689–1755). French lawyer, author, political philosopher. Wrote the *Spirit of the Laws* (1748) which greatly influenced political thought in Europe and America. Formulated doctrine of separation of powers in government.

MORRIS, GOUVERNEUR (1752–1816). Morris was born in New York to a wealthy family with a history of public service. Early in life, he lost a leg in a carriage accident. He graduated from King's College in New York City and studied law. Many of his family and friends were loyalists, but Morris sided with the patriots. He served in the militia as well as in the New York legislature and the Continental Congress. When he was defeated for Congress in 1779, Morris moved to Philadelphia to practice law. At the Philadelphia Convention, Morris gave more speeches than anyone else. He favored a strong national government ruled by the upper classes. He served on many committees and was the primary author of the actual document. After the convention, Morris spent ten years in Europe. He served briefly in the Senate, but then retired.

MORRIS, ROBERT (1734–1806). Morris was born in England in 1734. He came to America when he was 13. He was educated in Philadelphia and worked there in a shipping-banking firm. As a member of the Continental Congress, he voted against independence, but still worked hard on behalf of the new nation. He served as superintendent of finance under the Articles of Confederation, a very difficult job. At the Philadelphia Convention, Morris said little, although he was known to sympathize with those wanting a stronger central government.

PAINE, THOMAS (1737–1809). Author and political theorist. Born in England, he came to America in November, 1774. In early 1776, he published the pamphlet *Common Sense* which stirred many Americans to the revolutionary cause. During the war, his pamphlet, *The Crisis,* helped support the Revolution and encouraged the soldiers in the Continental Army.

PATERSON, WILLIAM (1745–1806). Born in Ireland, Paterson was brought to the colonies when he was two years old. The family moved often—from Delaware to Connecticut to New Jersey, where they finally settled. Paterson graduated from the College of New Jersey and studied law. He supported the patriots in the Revolutionary War. Paterson served as attorney general of New Jersey from 1776–1783. At the Philadelphia Convention, he argued strongly for the rights of the small states, putting forth the New Jersey Plan in opposition to Madison's Virginia Plan. Although he left the convention in July, he returned to sign the Constitution. Later, Paterson served as a U.S. senator, governor of New Jersey, and a Supreme Court justice.

PIERCE, WILLIAM (1740–1789). It is believed that Pierce was born in Georgia, the state he represented at the Philadelphia Convention, although he often referred to himself as a Virginian. He served in the Revolutionary War, returning to Georgia in 1783 to attend to his personal business. At the Philadelphia Convention, Pierce spoke three times, leaving early. Although he did not sign the document, it is not known whether he actually opposed the Constitution. He is perhaps best known for writing notes on the convention in which he described the personalities of the other delegates.

PINCKNEY, CHARLES (1757–1824). Charles Pinckney was born in South Carolina, the son of a rich lawyer and planter. He trained as a lawyer. He served in the militia during the Revolution, was captured by the British, and remained a prisoner until 1781. He served in the Continental Congress and the South Carolina legislature. At the Philadelphia Convention, Pinckney spoke often. He was a good speaker who contributed to the compromises that made the Constitution possible. After the convention, he held a variety of political offices, including governor and U.S. senator. Although he began his career as a Federalist, he switched to the Republican party and worked to give the vote to all white males. The last public office he held was a seat in the U.S. House of Representatives.

PINCKNEY, CHARLES COTESWORTH (1746–1825). The cousin of the younger Pinckney, Charles Cotesworth was also a native of South Carolina. He was educated in England, where his father was representing South Carolina. In 1769, he returned home to practice law. He served in the military during the Revolution and was held as a prisoner for two years. After the war, he practiced law and served in the South Carolina legislature. Pinckney attended every session of the Philadelphia Convention, arguing for a strong central government. He was an important delegate who contributed to compromises on troublesome issues. He worked for ratification in South Carolina. Pinckney was a Federalist, who ran for vice president once and president twice, losing all three times. He continued to practice law and serve in the South Carolina legislature.

RANDOLPH, EDMUND (1753–1813). Randolph was born into a prominent Virginia family of lawyers. He kept the family tradition, attending the College of William and Mary and then studying law under his father. The Revolution split the family, with the father, mother, and two sisters being loyalists and Edmund and his uncle patriots. Randolph served in the Continental Congress and as governor of Virginia. He gave the first major speech at the Philadelphia Convention, in which he criticized the Articles of Confederation. As the leader of the Virginia delegation to the convention, Randolph presented the Virginia Plan, calling for a stronger national government and proportional representation in Congress. Although the Constitution eventually included many ideas similar to those in the Virginia Plan, Randolph did not sign the document. However, George Washington convinced him to support ratification. Randolph served as attorney general and secretary of state under Washington.

READ, GEORGE (1733–1798). Read was born in Maryland, but his family moved to Delaware soon after his birth. He attended schools in Pennsylvania and studied law in Philadelphia. In 1754, he set up a legal practice in Delaware. He supported "dignified" protests against British actions and voted against independence in 1776, but did sign the Declaration. During the Revolution, Read was busy with state activities. Poor health caused him to retire temporarily in 1779, but he returned to the service of his state in 1782. At the Philadelphia Convention, Read argued for the rights of the small states and for a strong executive. He led the ratification battle in Delaware. Read served in the U.S. Senate for four years, resigning to take the post of chief justice of Delaware, which he held until his death.

REVERE, PAUL (1735–1818). Silversmith and revolutionary patriot. Leader of the Boston Sons of Liberty. Principal express rider for the Boston Committee of Safety, spreading news of revolutionary activities, including his famous ride of April 18, 1775, warning of the forthcoming attack of British troops.

RUTLEDGE, JOHN (1739–1800). Rutledge was born in South Carolina and was educated at home by his father and a tutor. He then studied law in London and returned to South Carolina, where he practiced law and built a fortune. He was politically active in South Carolina in the 1760s and 1770s, being elected to the Continental Congress and to the governorship. When the British seized Charleston, Rutledge had to flee to North Carolina, where he gathered a force to recapture South Carolina. He continued to be politically active through the 1780s. At the Philadelphia Convention, he was an important delegate, speaking often and effectively. He argued strongly for the interests of southern states. Washington appointed Rutledge to the Supreme Court where he served a brief time, returning to South Carolina

to serve on the state supreme court. In 1795, Washington again appointed him to the U.S. Supreme Court, this time as chief justice, but the Senate rejected his nomination.

SHAYS, DANIEL (1747?–1825). Revolutionary soldier and postwar rebel. One of several leaders of the revolt in western Massachusetts against the state government. In 1786, he led armed farmers in a raid on the Springfield arsenal. Fled to Vermont when his band was defeated and later settled in New York.

SHERMAN, ROGER (1721–1793). Born in 1721 in Massachusetts, Sherman spent most of his boyhood helping his father with farming and shoe-making chores. However, he read in whatever spare time he could find. In 1743, he moved to Connecticut, purchasing a store and winning a variety of local political offices. Although Sherman had not formally studied the law, he became a lawyer. His career was distinguished, including service in the state legislature, and work as a judge. Although he gave up the practice of law in 1761, he continued his political career, serving in the Continental Congress. Sherman was one of the members of the committee that drafted the Declaration of Independence and the Articles of Confederation. He attended nearly every session of the Philadelphia Convention and was an important contributor to the Great Compromise. He also worked hard to get Connecticut to ratify the Constitution. Sherman later served as a member of the House of Representatives and the Senate.

SOCRATES (470?–399 BC). Greek philosopher. Used an original question-and-answer method of instruction with his pupils, the most famous of whom was Plato. Drank poison in prison rather than give up his teaching when ordered to do so by authorities.

SPAIGHT, RICHARD DOBBS, SR. (1758–1802). Spaight was born in North Carolina but was sent to Ireland after his parents died when he was eight. He was educated there and in Scotland, returning the North Carolina in 1778. He served in the state militia as well as in the state legislature. He also served in the Continental Congress after the Revolution. At the Philadelphia Convention, he attended every session and spoke on several occasions. He worked to gain ratification in North Carolina. Spaight lost elections for the Senate and for governor, but was elected to the House in 1798.

STRONG, CALEB (1745–1819). Strong was born in Massachusetts. He graduated from Harvard with honors. In his early twenties, he contracted smallpox which damaged his sight. He became a lawyer, serving in various local and state offices in Massachusetts. He declined a seat in the Continental Congress. At the Philadelphia Convention, Strong took part until August, when he left because of an illness in the family. He did not sign the document. He was elected to the U.S. Senate in 1789, resigning in 1795 to return to his law practice.

He served as governor of Massachusetts from 1800–1807 and again from 1812–1816.

THOREAU, HENRY DAVID (1817–1862). Naturalist, philosopher, author. Lived for two years at Walden Pond to demonstrate the simple, self-reliant life. In 1849, he published his essay "On the Duty of Civil Disobedience." Was imprisoned for one day in 1846 for refusing to pay a tax supporting the Mexican War which he opposed.

TRUMAN, HARRY (1884–1972). Thirty-third president of the United States. Elected to the Senate from Missouri in 1934. Chosen as Franklin Roosevelt's running mate in 1944, he succeeded to the presidency upon Roosevelt's death in April 1945, and was reelected in 1948. He was responsible for integrating the Armed Forces.

WARREN, EARL (1891–1974). Chief justice of the United States from 1953 to 1969. Appointed by President Eisenhower. Was attorney general and governor of California. In 1954, he announced the landmark decision in *Brown v. Board of Education.*

WARREN, MERCY OTIS (1728–1814). An author and Anti-Federalist, she knew most of the Revolutionary leaders personally and spent much of her life at the center of events. Her vantage point, combined with her literary talents, made her a well-known historian and poet. She wrote several plays and a three-volume history of the Revolution.

WASHINGTON, GEORGE (1732–1799). George Washington was born in Virginia in 1732. He grew up there on several plantations along the Potomac and Rappahannock Rivers. He was not particularly well educated, but did learn surveying. In 1753, he began his service to the country, which was to continue throughout his life, despite his desire to live a more private existence. Washington's efforts as commander of the Continental Army are well known. After the Treaty of Paris was signed in 1783, Washington returned to his home, Mount Vernon. Although he did not initially want to attend the Philadelphia Convention, his friends convinced him that his presence was necessary. He was elected president of the convention but spoke little. His presence and approval, however, were important. Nearly everyone assumed that Washington would be the first president of the United States, which, of course, he was, serving from 1789–1797.

WILLIAM THE CONQUEROR (1027–1087). First Norman king in England. Introduced the feudal order to the old Anglo-Saxon system of government.

WILLIAMSON, HUGH (1735–1819). Williamson was born in Pennsylvania, the oldest child in a large family. Educated to be a minister, he instead went to Europe to study medicine. At the beginning of the Revolution, he was in Europe where he wrote a pamphlet that urged English support for the American cause. When he returned to America, he settled in North Carolina, where he practiced medicine, serving as surgeon-general for the state's troops. He was an active delegate to the Philadelphia Convention, serving on five committees and debating skillfully. He worked for ratification and served two terms in the U.S. House.

WILSON, JAMES (1741–1798). Wilson was born and educated in Scotland. He arrived in America in 1765, where he taught and studied law. He set up a legal practice in Pennsylvania. He was active in the revolutionary effort, voting for independence and signing the Declaration. After the war, he defended loyalists and their sympathizers. His shift to conservatism angered many people in Pennsylvania, but by the 1780s, Wilson was again elected to the Continental Congress. He was an influential delegate to the Philadelphia Convention, where he spoke even more often than Madison. Wilson led the ratification effort in Pennsylvania. In 1789, he was appointed to the Supreme Court.

WYTHE, GEORGE (1726–1806). Wythe was born on a Virginia plantation. He attended the College of William and Mary and studied law. He entered political life, serving in the Virginia legislature and as mayor of Williamsburg. He signed the Declaration of Independence and worked actively for the Revolution. In 1779, he was named the first professor of law in a U.S. college. Although he was well respected for his knowledge and high ethical standards, he did not contribute greatly to the Philadelphia Convention, leaving early because of other obligations. He did not sign the document.

YATES, ROBERT (1738–1801). Yates was born and educated in New York. He became a lawyer and set up practice in Albany. He spent the greatest amount of time as a justice of the New York Supreme Court, serving eight years as chief justice. Yates left the Philadelphia Convention because he believed it had exceeded its authority. A strong Anti-Federalist, he worked against ratification, writing several essays attacking the document. Yates kept notes of the convention which have been useful to historians.

ZENGER, JOHN PETER (1697–1746). Printer and editor. Served as editor of an anti-government newspaper and, in 1733, was arrested for seditious libel. His defense was handled by Andrew Hamilton who urged jury to consider the truth of Zenger's statements. The jury did so, Zenger was acquitted, and his name became linked with freedom of the press.

Glossary

absolute veto. The inviolable power to cancel or nullify a legislative act.

acquit. To clear a person of a charge by declaring him not guilty.

adversary system. A system of justice in which opposing parties are given full opportunity to present and establish their evidence, and cross-examine the evidence presented by their adversaries before an impartial judge and/or jury.

affirmative action. A plan or program to remedy the effects of past discrimination in employment, education, or other activity and to prevent its recurrence.

aggressive recruitment programs. A form of affirmative action in which extensive efforts are made to notify and solicit applications from underrepresented groups.

agrarian community. A small, tightly-knit community supporting itself through farming.

Alien and Sedition Acts. Four laws passed in 1798 during President John Adams' administration which placed restrictions on aliens and made it a crime for editors, writers, or speakers to criticize the government and its Federalist policies.

Anti-Federalists. The political leaders who were against ratification of the Constitution because they thought it gave too much power to the federal government and did not protect the political rights of the people.

appellate jurisdiction. The legal authority of a court to hear appeals from a lower court.

apportion. The allocation of legislative seats.

Articles of Confederation. The compact made among the thirteen original American states to form the basis of their government; adopted by Congress in 1781 and replaced by the United States Constitution in 1788.

association. A group of people joined together for a common purpose.

autocracy. A government in which the rulers, whether one or many, exercise unlimited power.

bail. Money or other security given to obtain a person's release from custody, which may be forfeited if the person subsequently fails to appear before the court for trial.

balance of power. The division of governmental powers in such a way that no one individual or group can dominate or control the exercise of power by others.

bill of attainder. An act of the legislature that inflicts punishment on an individual or group without a judicial trial.

Black Codes. Regulations passed by Southern state governments during Reconstruction to prohibit African Americans from voting.

Boston Tea Party (1773). In an act of rebellion against British authority, and in particular to protest British taxes on tea imported to the colonies, a band of colonists boarded ships in Boston Harbor and destroyed thousands of dollars' worth of tea by throwing it overboard.

Boston Massacre. On March 5, 1770, a mob of colonists harassed British soldiers guarding the tax collector's office in Boston. The soldiers opened fire, killing five Bostonians, including Crispus Attucks, the first man killed in the American Revolution.

broad construction. The idea that judges should be given great leeway in application of the U.S. Constitution in order to adapt to a changing world.

broad interpretation. The interpretation of the establishment clause of the First Amendment that prevents the government from providing any aid to any religious activity, practice, or institution.

Brown v. Board of Education of Topeka (1954). The Supreme Court case which declared that "separate but equal" educational facilities are inherently unequal and therefore a violation of the equal protection of the laws guaranteed by the Fourteenth Amendment.

burgess. Formerly a member of the British House of Commons (typically a merchant or craftsman) who represented a city or town.

bureaucracy. Governmental departments and agencies, and the nonelected officials who staff them.

capital offense. A crime punishable by death.

capital punishment. The infliction of the death penalty by a judicial system.

capitalism. An economic system in which the means of producing and distributing goods are privately owned and operated for profit in a competitive market.

charter. A written document from a government or ruler which grants certain rights to an individual, a group, an organization, or the people in general.

checks and balances. The distribution and balancing of power among different branches of government so that no one branch is able to dominate the others.

Christendom. The Christian world, or Christians in general, considered as a single society.

city-state. A politically independent community consisting of a city and its surrounding territory.

civic values, principles, skills, and dispositions. The commonly-accepted goals of society and principles of government, and the skills and attitudes of citizens that are necessary to realize those goals and make those principles work.

civic virtue. The dedication of citizens to the common good, even at the cost of their individual interests.

civil disobedience. The refusal to obey a law, usually on the ground that it is morally unjust, or to protest a government policy. Civil disobedience is a form of nonviolent resistance and is aimed at arousing public opinion against the law or policy.

civil rights. Fundamental rights belonging to every member of a society.

Civil Rights Act of 1866. An act of Congress which attempted to protect the rights of African Americans following the Civil War. The act was ineffective because the president refused to enforce it and the Supreme Court refused to hear cases about it.

Civil Rights Act of 1875. An act of Congress which gave the federal government the power to enforce the protections of citizens' rights under the Fourteenth Amendment. The act was not enforced by the president and was declared unconstitutional by the Supreme Court.

Civil Rights Act of 1964. An act of Congress designed to protect the rights of individuals to fair treatment by private persons, groups, organizations, businesses, and government.

Civil War Amendments. The Thirteenth, Fourteenth, and Fifteenth Amendments, passed following the Civil War, which freed the slaves, granted them citizenship, and guaranteed them the rights of citizens.

civility. The respectful treatment of others.

classical republicanism. A theory that holds that the best kind of government is one that promotes the common welfare instead of the interests of one class of citizens. The Roman Republic was thought by the Founders to be one of the best examples of a society living under this theory of government.

clear and present danger. A standard used to justify limitations on speech which will lead directly to harm to others.

commerce clause. The clause in the U.S. Constitution which gives Congress the power "to regulate commerce with foreign nations and among the several States." The clause has been used to regulate organizations which are engaged in interstate relations by prohibiting them from engaging in racial discrimination.

common good. The good of the community as a whole. Also referred to as the common welfare.

common law. The body of unwritten law developed in England from judicial decisions based on custom and earlier judicial decisions, which constitutes the basis of the English legal system and became part of American law.

commonwealth. A self-governing state or nation whose members are expected to help serve the good of all.

compelling state interest. A state interest that takes precedence over individual rights.

confederation. A form of political organization in which the sovereign states combine for certain specified purposes such as defense. The United States was a confederation from 1776 to 1788.

consent. Agreement or acquiescence.

constituents. The people represented by an elected official.

constitution. A set of customs, traditions, rules, and laws that sets forth the way a government is organized and operated.

constitutional government. A government in which the powers of government are limited in practice by a written or unwritten constitution which they must obey.

Constitutional Convention. The meeting held in Philadelphia from May 25 through September 18, 1787, at which the Constitution of the United States was drafted. Also called the "Philadelphia Convention."

contempt of court. Willful disobedience of a judge's command or of an official court order.

content [of expression]. The subject matter or substance of a document, book, speech, or other form of expression.

Continental Congress. The assembly of representatives from the thirteen colonies that first met in 1774 to protest British treatment of the colonies, and that later became the government of the United States.

contract. A binding agreement between two or more persons.

cosmopolitan. Composed of elements from the entire world or from many different parts of the world.

covenant. A binding agreement made by two or more persons or parties.

cruel and unusual punishment. A criminal sanction or penalty that is not in accord with the moral standards of a humane and compassionate society. Such punishments are prohibited by the Eighth Amendment.

custom. An accepted practice or way of behaving that is followed by tradition.

delegate. A person chosen to act for or represent others, as at a convention.

delegated powers. According to the natural rights philosophy, people give or assign certain powers to the government; the powers of government are therefore "delegated powers" in that they come from the people.

democracy. A form of government in which political control is exercised by all the people, either directly or through their elected representatives.

dictatorship. A government controlled by one person or a single group.

diversity. Variation among the members of a community or society.

Dominion of New England. The name applied to a consolidation of colonies and regions of the northeast in 1686. The purpose of the union was to improve the defense and trade of the New England area by centralizing colonial administration into one body.

double jeopardy. The provision in the Fifth Amendment to the U.S. Constitution that one may not be tried twice for the same crime.

***Dred Scott v. Sanford* (1857)**. A Supreme Court case which held that African Americans were not U.S. citizens and that slavery was legal in the western territories.

due process of law. Protection against arbitrary deprivation of life, liberty, or property. The Fifth and Fourteenth Amendments to the U.S. Constitution provide that these rights cannot be taken away without due process of law.

electoral college. The group of presidential electors that casts the official votes for president after a presidential election. Each state has a number equal to the total of its members in the Senate and House of Representatives.

electors. A group of persons selected by each state party to vote for that party's candidates for President and Vice President if the party's candidates win the popular vote in the general election in that state.

electronic city-state. The futurist vision of increased citizen participation in public affairs through a telecommunications-based network, or teledemocracy.

empower. To give power or authority to an individual or group.

English Bill of Rights. An act passed by Parliament in 1689 which limited the power of the monarch. This document established Parliament as the most powerful branch of the English government.

enumerated rights. Those rights and responsibilities of U.S. citizens specifically provided for and listed in the Constitution.

enumerated powers. Those rights and responsibilities of the U.S. government specifically provided for and listed in the Constitution.

enumeration. A specific listing of elements.

equal protection of the law. A requirement of the Fourteenth Amendment to the U.S. Constitution that state laws may not arbitrarily discriminate against persons. One of the key principles of American constitutionalism.

Equal Employment Opportunities Commission (EEOC). A five-member commission created by Title VII of the Civil Rights Act of 1964 to ensure equal opportunity in employment.

equality of condition. Equality in all aspects of life, such as personal possessions, living standards, medical care, and working conditions.

established religion. An official, state-sponsored religion.

establishment clause. The clause in the First Amendment that says the government may not establish an official religion.

ethnicity. Ethnic classification or affiliation.

***ex post facto* law**. A criminal law that makes an act a crime that was not a crime when committed, that increases the penalty for a crime after it was committed, or that changes the rules of evidence to make conviction easier. *Ex post facto* laws are forbidden by Article I of the U.S. Constitution.

exclusionary rule. The rule, established by the Supreme Court, that evidence unconstitutionally gathered by law enforcement officers may not be used against a defendant in a trial.

executive power. The powers of the executive branch of the federal government.

executive departments. Cabinet-level agencies in the federal government.

faction. A group that seeks to promote its own special interests at the expense of the common good.

federal district court. The court of original jurisdiction for most federal cases. This is the only federal court that holds trials in which juries and witnesses are used. Each state has at least one district court.

federal system (federalism). A form of political organization in which governmental power is divided between a central government and territorial subdivisions.

Federalist, The. A series of essays written in 1787–88 and collected in a book by Alexander Hamilton, James Madison, and John Jay, urging the adoption of the U.S. Constitution and supporting the need for a strong national government.

Federalists. Advocates of ratification of the U.S. Constitution and a strong centralized government. Flourished in the 1790s under the leadership of Alexander Hamilton.

felony. A crime, such as murder or rape, considered more serious than a misdemeanor and subject to more stringent punishment.

feudalism. A political system in which land is given by a noble to his vassals in exchange for personal allegiance. Through the Magna Carta and other landmarks, English feudalism provided one of the bases of modern constitutionalism.

First Continental Congress. The body of delegates representing the colonies that first met to protest British rule and that eventually became the government of the United States. The First Continental Congress met in 1774 and drafted a Declaration of Rights.

Four Freedoms, 1941. The four basic rights that Franklin D. Roosevelt declared worthy of fighting a war to preserve: freedom of speech and expression, freedom of worship, freedom from fear, and freedom from want.

free exercise clause. The clause in the First Amendment that states that the government shall make no law prohibiting the free practice of religious beliefs.

Fundamental Orders of Connecticut. Adopted in 1639, this series of laws is the first written constitution in North America.

futurist. A theorist who considers possibilities for the future based on current information and trends.

gag rule. A rule limiting discussion or debate on a particular issue.

general warrant. A legal search warrant that does not describe in detail the places to be searched or the things or persons to be seized.

genocide. The deliberate attempt to destroy a racial, religious, political, or cultural group.

George III. King of England during the American Revolution.

Gitlow v. New York **(1925).** A landmark Supreme Court case that established that the rights of free speech and the press are protected against interference by state government by the due process clause of the Fourteenth Amendment.

Glorious Revolution (1688). English Parliament's successful, bloodless overthrow of James II, establishing Parliament's supremacy and independence from the monarchy.

grandfather clauses. Laws passed by Southern states to prevent African Americans from voting by requiring that a voter's grandfather voted in the past.

Great Awakening. Religious revival in the American colonies of the eighteenth century during which a number of new Protestant churches were established.

Great Compromise (Connecticut Compromise). Adopted at the Philadelphia Convention, this plan provided for equal representation of the states in the Senate and House of Representatives according to population.

Griswold v. Connecticut **(1965).** The Supreme Court case that, in holding that the state regulation of birth control devices was an impermissible invasion of privacy, helped to establish privacy as a constitutionally protected right under the Ninth and Fourteenth Amendments.

guarantee clause. Article IV of the U.S. Constitution provides that the national government shall guarantee to each state a republican form of government. The precise meaning of the guarantee clause has never been determined; the Supreme Court has held this to be a "political question" to be answered by Congress or the President.

guided discretion. The freedom of juries in capital cases to decide whether to impose life sentences or death sentences under standards dictated by the court.

habeas corpus. A court order directing that prisoners be brought to court and to show cause for his or her detention. From the Latin term meaning, "You shall/should have the body."

hierarchical. Organized or classified according to rank, capacity, or authority.

higher law. As used in describing a legal system, refers to the superiority of one set of laws over another. For example, the U.S. Constitution is a higher law than any federal or state law. In the natural rights philosophy, it means that natural law and divine law are superior to laws made by human beings.

human rights. Basic rights and freedoms assumed to belong to all people everywhere.

immunity. In legal terms, exemption from prosecution.

impeachment. Charging a public official with a crime in office for which they can be removed from power.

implied powers. The power of Congress to do all things necessary and proper to carry out the powers delegated to it by Article I of the U.S. Constitution.

inalienable. See unalienable.

incorporation. The process through which the Supreme Court applied the due process clause of the Fourteenth Amendment to extend the protections of the Bill of Rights against state interference.

indentured servants. Voluntary servants who sold their labor for a period of four to seven years in exchange for passage to America. The most important source of labor in the colonies in the seventeenth century and for a large part of the eighteenth century.

independent judiciary. An inviolate judicial branch that serves to protect the U.S. Constitution and prevents the executive and legislative branches from disregarding it.

indictment. A formal charge by a grand jury accusing a person of having committed a crime.

Information Age. The term applied to the era after c. 1970 to describe the availability of large amounts of electronically stored and transmitted information, of increasing importance in business, government and civic matters, and other avenues of modern society.

inquisitorial system. A trial system in which a single person acts as both prosecutor and judge, questioning witnesses, examining evidence, and reaching a verdict.

"Jim Crow" laws. Laws requiring the segregation of the races. In 1896, the Supreme Court upheld such laws under the "separate but equal" doctrine.

Judeo-Christian. Beliefs and practices which have their historical roots in Judaism and Christianity.

judicial restraint. The belief that the Supreme Court should neither overrule the decisions of elected officials nor make public policy.

judicial review. The power of the courts to declare laws and actions of the local, state, or national government invalid if the courts decide they are unconstitutional.

Judiciary Act of 1789. A law passed by the first Congress to establish the federal court system. The act determined the organization and jurisdiction of the courts.

law of nature (natural law). In natural rights philosophy, the law of nature would prevail in the absence of man-made law, and contains universally obligatory standards of justice.

legal remedy. The ability to redress some injury or grievance through the legal system.

legislative power. The power to write and enact laws.

legislative supremacy. A system of government in which the legislative branch has the most power.

libel. Published words or pictures that falsely and maliciously defame a person.

limited government. In natural rights philosophy, a system restricted to protecting natural rights and that does not interfere with other aspects of life.

literacy test. A suffrage qualification used to determine fitness for voting by means of a reading or "understanding" test. The use of literacy tests to discriminate against prospective voters caused Congress to suspend their use in the Voting Rights Act.

lobby. To represent a special interest group in trying to influence legislatures.

Loyalists. Colonists who remained loyal to Great Britain during the American Revolution.

magistrate. A lower-level judicial officer, usually elected in urban areas, who handles traffic violations, minor criminal offenses, and civil suits involving small amounts of money.

Magna Carta. The Great Charter of freedom granted in 1215 by King John of England by demand of his barons. The Magna Carta contained such ideas as trial by a jury of one's peers and the guarantee against loss of life, liberty, or property, except in accordance with law.

majority rule. A principle of democracy which asserts that the greater number of citizens in any political unit should select officials and determine policies.

manorialism. The form of economic life of the Middle Ages, when most people were involved in agriculture and land was divided up into self-contained farms or manors.

Marbury v. Madison **(1803)**. A landmark case in which the Supreme Court, for the first time in American history, struck down an act of Congress as unconstitutional, creating the Court's power of constitutional judicial review.

Massachusetts Body of Liberties (1641). A document that described the rights of citizens and the authority of public officials.

Massachusetts state constitution. Voters in the state ratified the constitution in 1780. It is the oldest written constitution still in effect in the world today

Mayflower Compact. An agreement signed in 1620 by all adult males aboard the ship *Mayflower*, before landing in Plymouth, to form a body politic governed by majority rule.

McCulloch v. Maryland **(1819)**. The Supreme Court decision that upheld the implied powers granted to Congress by the necessary and proper clause of the

Constitution, upheld the supremacy of the national government in carrying out functions assigned to it by the Constitution, and established the doctrine of intergovernmental tax immunity.

melting pot. A term used to describe a society made up of diverse cultures or races which have merged or "melted" into each other.

Middle Ages. A period, lasting from the fifth century to the fourteenth century, during which the political, economic, and military structure was characterized by feudalism. The term "medieval" describes that which occurred during the Middle Ages.

millennium. A span of one thousand years.

Minutemen. Civilian armies of the American Revolution, so called because of their readiness for battle.

misdemeanor. A minor criminal offense.

mixed constitution. The basis of a form of government in which power is divided among different branches.

nation-state. The modern nation as the representative unit of political organization.

National Association for the Advancement of Colored People (NAACP). An interracial group founded in 1909 to advocate the rights of African Americans, primarily through legal and political action.

natural rights. The doctrine of natural rights assumes that human beings had rights in a "state of nature" and create government in order to protect those rights.

naturalized citizen. An individual who gains full citizenship in a country other than that of their birth.

necessary and proper clause. The clause in Article I of the U.S. Constitution that gives Congress the power to make all laws that are "necessary and proper" to carry out the powers expressly delegated to it by the Constitution.

Nineteenth Amendment. An amendment to the U.S. Constitution, adopted in 1920, that prohibits any state from denying the right to vote to any citizen because of gender.

Ninth Amendment. This amendment states, in effect, that the Bill of Rights is only a partial listing of the rights of the people.

nonviolent direct action. Peaceful tactics used as a means of gaining one's civil or political ends.

null and void. Of no legal or binding force; invalid.

ordinance. A municipal statute or regulation.

original jurisdiction. The legal authority of a court to be the first to hear a case.

Palko v. Connecticut **(1937)**. The case in which the Supreme Court ruled that the double jeopardy provision of the Fifth Amendment does not apply to the states through the Fourteenth Amendment. Overruled by *Benton v. Maryland* (1969).

Papacy. The office or authority of the Pope, the spiritual leader of the Roman Catholic church.

Parliament. The British legislature, which consists of two houses: the House of Lords, representing the nobility, and the House of Commons, representing the people.

parliamentary supremacy. The principle that the parliament, or legislative body, has ultimate sovereignty, or control, in a state.

parliamentary government. A system that gives governmental authority to a legislature or parliament which in turn selects the executive from among its own members.

perjury. The deliberate giving of false, misleading, or incomplete testimony under oath.

Petition of Right (1628). A formal acknowledgement that limited the English monarch's power to tax people without the consent of Parliament and which also guaranteed English subjects certain fundamental rights.

plebiscite. An expression of the people's will by direct vote.

Plessy v. Ferguson **(1896)**. A case in which the Supreme Court ruled that "separate but equal" public facilities were permissible under the Constitution.

political action. Any organized attempt to influence the political process, from lobbying legislators to seeking the election (or defeat) of particular candidates.

political parties. Any organization that seeks to achieve political power by electing members to public office so that their political philosophies can be reflected in public policies.

political philosophy. The study of ideas about government and politics.

political rights. All of the implicit (constitutionally guaranteed) and implied (by natural laws) rights of a citizen in a free society.

poll tax. Voters in many Southern states were required to pay taxes before voting. The Supreme Court declared the levying of a poll tax to be unconstitutional in *Harper v. Virginia State Board of Elections* (1966).

popular sovereignty. The natural rights concept that ultimate political authority rests with the people.

positive rights. In the United Nations' Universal Declaration of Rights, rights require governments assume the responsibility of ensuring such things as health care and economic security.

***Powell v. Alabama* (1932)**. A Supreme Court ruling that state courts were required to provide counsel to needy defendants only in capital cases.

precedents. Previous court decisions upon which legal issues are decided.

preferential treatment programs. A form of affirmative action in which underrepresented groups are given preferred treatment in gaining jobs and entrance to colleges and universities. These programs are designed to make up for the effects of past discrimination.

president's cabinet. The secretaries of the departments of the executive branch chosen by the president to serve as his advisors.

prime minister. The highest ranking member of the executive branch of a parliamentary government as in Great Britain and Japan.

primogeniture. The condition of being the first-born child. In law, it refers to the right of the eldest son to inherit all of his parents' estates.

private domain. Areas of human affairs placed off limits to unreasonable government interference.

private morality. The principles of civic virtue as expressed in Judeo-Christian teachings, as well as fundamental ideas about right and wrong that come from religion, ethics, and individual conscience.

privileges and immunities. Special rights and exemptions provided by law. The U.S. Constitution contains two clauses that use the term "privileges and immunities": Article IV, Section 2, and the Fourteenth Amendment.

probable cause. Reasonable grounds for presuming guilt in someone accused of a crime. Required in cases in which a law enforcement officer needs to conduct a search or seizure and cannot, for practical purposes, obtain a search warrant.

procedural due process. Refers to those clauses in the U.S. Constitution that protect individuals from unreasonable and unfair governmental procedures.

proportional representation. The electoral system in which the number of representatives of a state in the House of Representatives is based on the number of people who live in that state.

proprietary colonies. Proprietary colonies were governed by charters issued by the "proprietor," an individual or group to whom the king had made a land grant.

provision. A qualification or clause in a document or agreement.

public forums. Places in the community, such as streets, parks, and computer bulletin boards, where people can express their viewpoints to the public.

public morality. The principles of civic virtue embodied in the Greek and Roman ideals.

Quartering Act of 1765. Also known as the Mutiny Act, the law passed by Parliament that authorized colonial governors to requisition certain buildings for the use, or "quartering," of British troops.

quotas and group entitlements. Benefits provided by government through affirmative action programs to which recipients have a legally enforceable right.

radical. Advocating extreme or revolutionary changes, especially in politics or government.

ratification. Formal approval of the U.S. Constitution by the states.

ratifying conventions. Meetings held in the states to approve the U.S. Constitution.

redress of grievances. The First Amendment protects the right to petition the government to obtain a remedy for a claimed wrong.

Reformation. Sixteenth-century religious movement aimed at reforming the Roman Catholic church and resulting in the establishment of Protestant churches.

***Regents of the University of California v. Bakke* (1978)**. Considered to be the most politically sensitive decision involving race since *Brown v. Board of Education* (1954). The Bakke case held invalid a state medical school's admissions program based on a specific racial quota but upheld the use of race as a factor in admissions decisions.

religious test. A requirement that a person swear to a belief in God or belong to a particular religion in order to qualify for a political office or to vote.

remand. To send a legal case back to a lower court for further proceedings.

remedial programs. A form of affirmative action in which special education programs are provided to help people gain the basic skills they need to succeed in the job market.

removal power. Power to remove officers of government such as the Congress' power to remove the president from office by passing articles of impeachment in the House of Representatives and conviction in the Senate.

Renaissance, The. The great revival of art, literature, and learning in Europe during the fourteenth, fifteenth, and sixteenth centuries, based on classical sources .

representative government. The system of government in which power is held by the people and exercised indirectly through elected representatives.

republic/republicanism. A form of government in which the supreme political power resides in the electorate, and administration is exercised by representatives who are responsible to the people.

resident alien. A foreign-born inhabitant.

retribution. Repayment, such as punishment for crime.

reverse discrimination. The argument that preferential treatment affirmative action programs discriminate against majority groups.

right against self-incrimination. Guaranteed by the Fifth Amendment, the constitutional right to refuse to give testimony that could subject oneself to criminal prosecution.

right to privacy. The right to be free from intrusion into one's private life by government officials.

rights of Englishmen. Basic rights, established over time, that all subjects of the English monarch were understood to have. They included the right not to be kept in prison without a trial and the right to a trial by a jury.

Scottsboro Cases (1932). The Supreme Court cases that established the right of persons accused of capital crimes in state courts to have the right to an attorney.

secession. In U.S. history, the act of a state leaving the Union.

sectionalism. Strong alliance to local interests over those of the whole nation.

secular government. A system of political power not exercised by ecclesiastical bodies or the clergy. Contrasted with theocracy.

Sedition Act of 1798. Endorsed by the Federalist administration of John Adams, the legislation provided penalties for writing, printing, or uttering "false, scandalous, or malicious" statements against the government or Congress.

seditious libel. Written language which seeks to convince others to engage in the overthrow of the government.

segregation. The separation or isolation of a race, class, or ethnic group from the rest of society.

selective incorporation. The selective application of the protections of the federal Bill of Rights to the states. This process is also known as absorption.

"separate but equal" doctrine. The argument, once upheld by the Supreme Court, that separate public facilities were constitutional if the facilities were of equal quality.

separation of powers. The division of powers among different branches of government. In the United States, among a legislative, executive, and judicial branch.

separation of church and state. The concept that religion and government should remain separate. The principle is the basis for the establishment clause of the First Amendment.

Seven Years War. A series of dynastic and colonial wars between England and France. The American phase, fought between 1754 and 1763, is known as the French and Indian War.

Shays' Rebellion. An armed revolt by Massachusetts farmers in 1786-87, seeking relief from debts and possible foreclosures of mortgages. Led by Daniel Shays, the group prevented judges from hearing mortgage foreclosure cases and attempted to capture an arsenal.

sit-in. Nonviolent demonstration in which persons protesting against certain conditions, government policies, or laws, sit down in an appropriate place and refuse to move until their demands are considered or met.

Slaughterhouse Cases (1873). A group of Supreme Court cases in which the Court determined that the privileges and immunities clause of the Fourteenth Amendment applies only to the privileges of the individual by virtue of national citizenship.

social contract. The agreement among all the people in a society to give up part of their freedom to a government in return for the protection of their natural rights by that government.

Sons of Liberty. An organization of radicals created in 1765 in the American colonies to express colonial opposition to the Stamp Act.

sovereignty. The ultimate, supreme power in a state. In the United States, sovereignty rests with the people.

Stamp Act Congress. A meeting in New York in 1765 of twenty-seven delegates from nine colonies, the congress was the first example of united colonial action in the developing struggle against Great Britain. The congress was successful in bringing about a repeal of the Stamp Act.

Stamp Act of 1765. Passed by Parliament in 1765, the law required the payment of a tax through the purchase of stamps for all documents such as newspapers, magazines, and legal and commercial papers of all kinds.

state action. Any official undertaking by government.

state of nature. The basis of natural right philosophy, state of nature is the hypothetical condition of people living together in a society.

strict construction. A narrow interpretation of the U.S. Constitution's provisions, in particular those granting power to government.

student placement laws. Legal tactics employed to impede racial integration of schools through the use of placement tests and other administrative procedures.

substantive due process. Those judicial interpretations of the due process clauses of the Constitution that require that the content of laws be fair and reasonable.

suffrage. The right to vote.

supremacy clause. Article VI, Section 2, of the U.S. Constitution, which states that the Constitution, laws passed by Congress, and treaties of the United States "shall be the supreme law of the land," binding on the states.

Tea Act of 1773. The act by Parliament that conferred upon the East India Company a monopoly importation of tea into the mainland colonies, thus eliminating the profits of the colonial importer and shopkeeper. The act brought about the Boston Tea Party.

telecommunications. The science and technology of sending messages over long distances, especially by electronic means.

teledemocracy. The futurist view of a direct democracy using telecommunications to provide greater opportunities for participation in government.

Tenth Amendment. The last part of the Bill of Rights that holds that the "powers not delegated to the United States by the Constitution, nor prohibited by it to the states, are reserved to the states respectively, or the people." The Tenth Amendment embodies the principle of federalism, which reserves for the states the residue of powers not granted to the federal government or withheld from the states.

three-fifths clause. A clause in the U.S. Constitution, no longer in effect, that provided that each enslaved African should be counted as three-fifths of a person in determining the number of representatives of a state in the House of Representatives and in the collection of direct taxes by Congress.

time, place, and manner regulations. Government regulations which place restrictions on free speech. These regulations, specifying when, where, and in what way speech is allowed, are applied when unrestricted free speech will conflict with the rights of others.

token integration. A show of accommodation to the principle of racial integration by small, merely formal concessions.

totalitarianism. A form of government in which one person or party exercises absolute control over all aspects of life and in which no opposition is allowed.

treason. In the U.S. Constitution, treason is "giving aid and comfort" to the enemy during wartime.

Twenty-fourth Amendment. An amendment to the U.S. Constitution, adopted in 1964, that forbids the levying of a poll tax in primary and general elections for national officials, including the president, vice president, and members of Congress.

Twenty-sixth Amendment. An amendment to the Constitution, adopted in 1971, that lowered the legal voting age to eighteen in the United States. Although eighteen-year-olds had already been accorded the vote in national elections by the Voting Rights Act of 1970, the Twenty-sixth Amendment assured them the vote in all national, state, and local elections.

tyranny. A government in which a single ruler is vested with absolute power.

unalienable (inalienable) rights. Fundamental rights of the people that may not be taken away. This phrase was used in the Virginia Declaration of Rights and the Declaration of Independence.

unconstitutional. Not in agreement with the principles set forth in the constitution of a country, especially the Constitution of the United States.

unenumerated rights. Rights which are not specifically listed in the U.S. Constitution or Bill of Rights, but which have been recognized and protected by the courts.

unguided discretion. The freedom of juries in capital cases to impose life sentences or death sentences without any standards dictated by the court.

unitary government. A centralized form of government in which states or local governments exercise only those powers delegated to them by the central or national government.

United Nations Charter, 1945. A multilateral treaty that serves as the constitution for the United Nations Organization. The Charter was drawn up and signed inSan Francisco on June 26, 1945. It was ratified by fifty-one nations and put into effect on October 24, 1945.

unwritten constitution. The body of political practices developed through custom and tradition.

vassal. In feudal times, a person granted the use of land by a feudal lord, in return for military or other service.

veto. The constitutional power of the president to refuse to sign a bill passed by Congress, thereby preventing it from becoming a law. The president's veto may be overridden by a two-thirds vote of both the Senate and House of Representatives.

Virginia Declaration of Rights. The first state declaration of rights, which served as a model for other state declarations of rights and the Bill of Rights. It was adopted on June 12, 1776.

virtual representation. The theory that citizens are represented by government, even though they do not actually elect any representative.

warrant. An order by a judge authorizing a police officer to make an arrest or search, or to perform some other designated act.

White Citizens Councils. Groups of white people who created private schools, private swimming pools, and other facilities to avoid racial integration in the 1950s and 1960s.

writ of assistance. A document giving a governmental authority the power to search and seize property without restrictions.

writ of mandamus. A court order to a government official to perform a specified act. From the Latin word meaning "we command."

Index

Photo Credits

Page 1: National Portrait Gallery, Library of Congress, National Archives, Library of Congress; 2: AP/Wide World Photos; 3: Library of Congress; 8: National Archives; 11: F.P.G. International; 13: Courtesy Ralph C. Jones; 14: UPI/Bettman News Photo; 16: Library of Congress; 17: Penns Treaty with the Indians by Benjamin West, Courtesy of the Pennsylvania Academy of the Fine Arts; 18: Colonial Williamsburg Foundation; 20: F.P.G. International; 21: UPI/Bettman News Photo; 22: F.P.G. International; 23: Fishmongers Society of London; 26: F.P.G. International; 28: F.P.G. International; 30: Library of Congress; 35: Library of Congress; 36: National Archives, Library of Congress; 38: Library of Congress; 39: Library of Congress; 41: Peabody Museum of Salem; 42: Metropolitan Museum of Art, New York; 43: National Archives; 44: National Archives; 45: National Archives; 46: National Archives; 47: National Archives; 51: Library of Congress, Colonial Williamsburg Society; 55: Independence National Historical Park; 60: Library of Congress; 62: Courtesy of the Art Commission of the City of New York; 62: National Portrait Gallery; 70: National Archives; 71: courtesy of the U.S. Army; 72: U.S. Bureau of Engraving, Library of Congress; 75: National Archives, Library of Congress, National Archives; 76: Library of Congress; 77: Library of Congress; 78: National Archives, Supreme Court Historical Society, Ralph C. Jones; 80: Commission on the Bicentennary of the U.S. House of Representatives; 85: courtesy of the Museum of Fine Arts Boston; 88: National Archives; 89: courtesy of the Art Commission of New York; 91: Office of the Architect of the Capitol; 93: Library of Congress; 96: National Archives; 100: AP/Wide World Photos; 102: Boatmen's National Bank of St. Louis; 103: F.P.G. International; 106: AP/Wide World Photos; 109: Library of Congress; 114: National Archives; 117: American Stock, UPI/Bettman; 119: Missouri Historical Society; 120: Library of Congress; 121: Library of Congress; 123: Cook Collection, Valentine Museum, Richmond, Virginia; 124: Library of Congress; 126: New York Historical Society; 127: F.P.G. International; 134: Library of Congress; 135: UPI/Bettman, AP/Wide World Photo; 136: Library of Congress; 137: AP/Wide World Photos; 138: AP/Wide World Photos; 139: AP/Wide World Photos; 141: AP/Wide World Photos; 142: 143: AP/Wide World Photos; 146: F.P.G. International, Stephen Simpson; 148: AP/Wide World Photos; 150: AP/Wide World Photos; 153: Library of Congress; 154: Culver Pictures; 156: Library of Congress; 158: AP/Wide World Photos; 161: AP/Wide World Photos; 166: Library of Congress, Library of Congress; 167: UPI/Bettman; 170: F.P.G. International, Ron Chapple; 180: Harlee Little; 183: F.P.G. International, Ron Chapple; 186: National Archives; 189: AP/Wide World Photos, F.P.G. International, Ron Chapple, F.P.G. International, Spencer Grant, F.P.G. International, Peter Regan; 191: F.P.G. International, Spencer Grant; 192: AP/Wide World Photos; 193: F.P.G. International; 194: AP/Wide World Photos; 196: AP/Wide World Photos; 1986: AP/Wide World Photos; 199: AP/Wide World Photos, F.P.G. International, Paul Conklin; 200: AP/Wide World Photos; 201: H. Armstrong Roberts; 202: Reuters/Bettman; 204: AP/Wide World Photos; 205: AP/Wide World Photos; 206: AP/Wide World Photos; 207: Rockwell Trust; 210: AP/Wide World Photos, F.P.G. International, Kenneth Garrett; 213: AP/Wide World Photos.